GRRL SCOUTS

STONE GHOST

BY:

JIM MAHFOOD

STORY, ART, COLORS AND LETTERS BY:

BOOK DESIGN BY

CARMEN ACOSTA

PRODUCTION BY

TRICIA RAMOS

LOGO DESIGN BY

ADAM DUMPER

SPECIAL THANKS TO

JUSTIN STEWART

DEDICATED TO

JEFFREY

'BILL SHAG'

SHAGAWAT

GRRL SCOUTS: STONE GHOST. First printing. June 2022. Published by Image Comics, Inc. Office of publication: PO BOX 14457, Portland, OR 97293. Copyright © 2022 Jim Mahfood. All rights reserved. Contains material originally published in single magazine form as GRRL SCOUTS: STONE GHOST #1-5. "Grrl Scouts: Stone Ghost," its logos, and the likenesses of all characters herein are trademarks of Jim Mahfood, unless otherwise noted. "Image" and the Image Comics logos are registered trademarks of Image Comics, Inc. No part of this publication may be reproduced or transmitted, in any form or by any means (except for short excerpts for journalistic or review purposes), without the express written permission of Jim Mahfood, or Image Comics, Inc. All names, characters, events, and locales in this publication are entirely fictional. Any resemblance to actual persons (living or dead), events, or places, without satirical intent, is coincidental. Printed in Canada. For international rights, contact: foreignlicensing@imagecomics.com. ISBN: 978-1-5343-2227-1.

IMAGE COMICS, INC. • **Robert Kirkman**: Chief Operating Officer • **Erik Larsen**: Chief Financial Officer • **Todd McFarlane**: President • **Marc Silvestri**: Chief Executive Officer • **Jim Valentino**: Vice President • **Eric Stephenson**: Publisher / Chief Creative Officer • **Nicole Lapalme**: Controller • **Leanna Caunter**: Accounting Analyst • **Sue Korpela**: Accounting & HR Manager • **Marla Eizik**: Talent Liaison • **Lorelei Bunjes**: Director of Digital Services • **Dirk Wood**: Director of International Sales & Licensing • **Alex Cox**: Director of Direct Market Sales • **Chloe Ramos**: Book Market & Library Sales Manager • **Emilio Bautista**: Digital Sales Coordinator • **Jon Schlaffman**: Specialty Sales Coordinator • **Kat Salazar**: Director of PR & Marketing • **Drew Fitzgerald**: Marketing Content Associate • **Heather Doornink**: Production Director • **Drew Gill**: Art Director • **Hilary DiLoreto**: Print Manager • **Tricia Ramos**: Traffic Manager • **Melissa Gifford**: Content Manager • **Erika Schnatz**: Senior Production Artist • **Ryan Brewer**: Production Artist • **Deanna Phelps**: Production Artist • **IMAGECOMICS.COM**

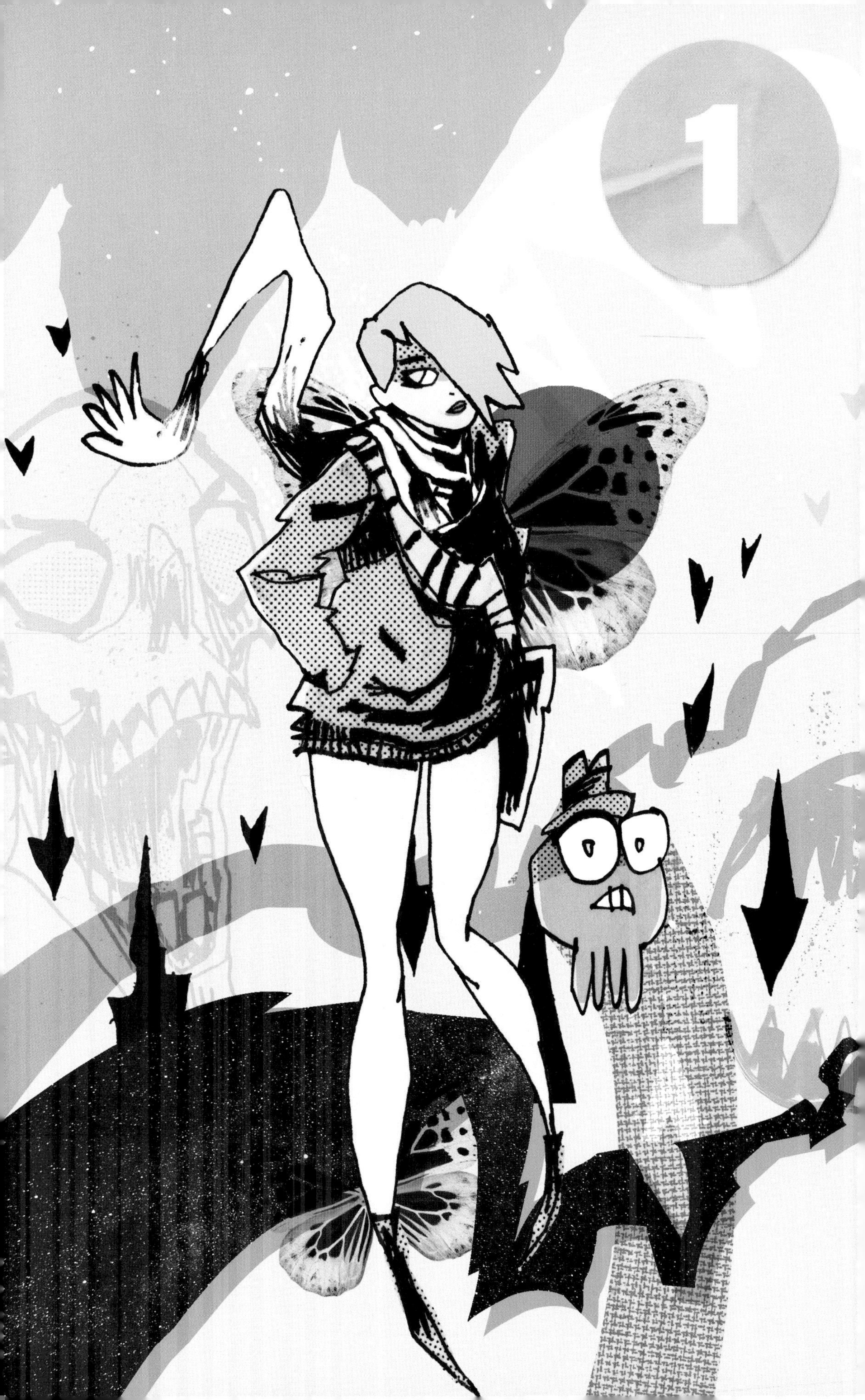
1

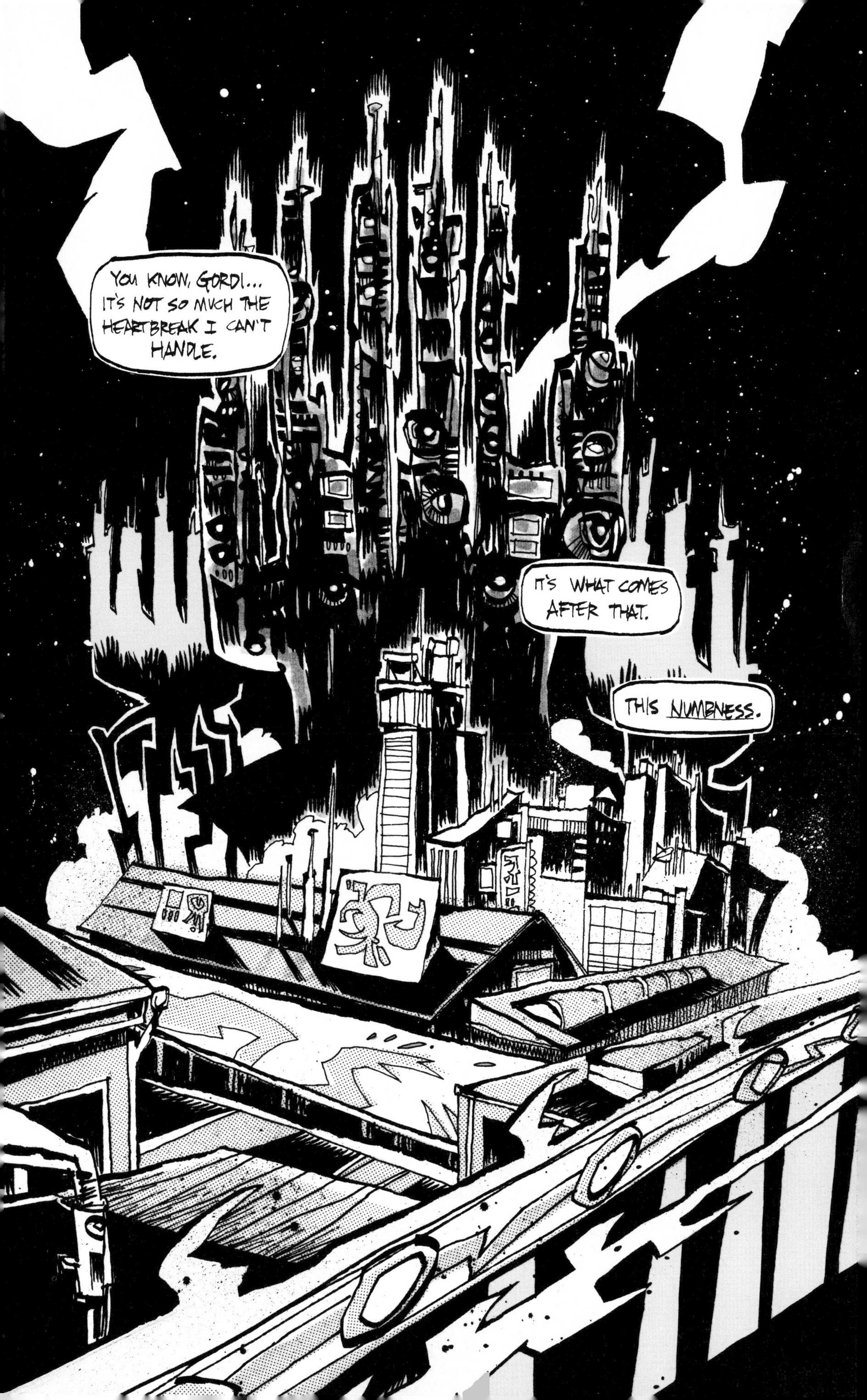
YOU KNOW, GORDI... IT'S NOT SO MUCH THE HEARTBREAK I CAN'T HANDLE.
IT'S WHAT COMES AFTER THAT.
THIS NUMBNESS.

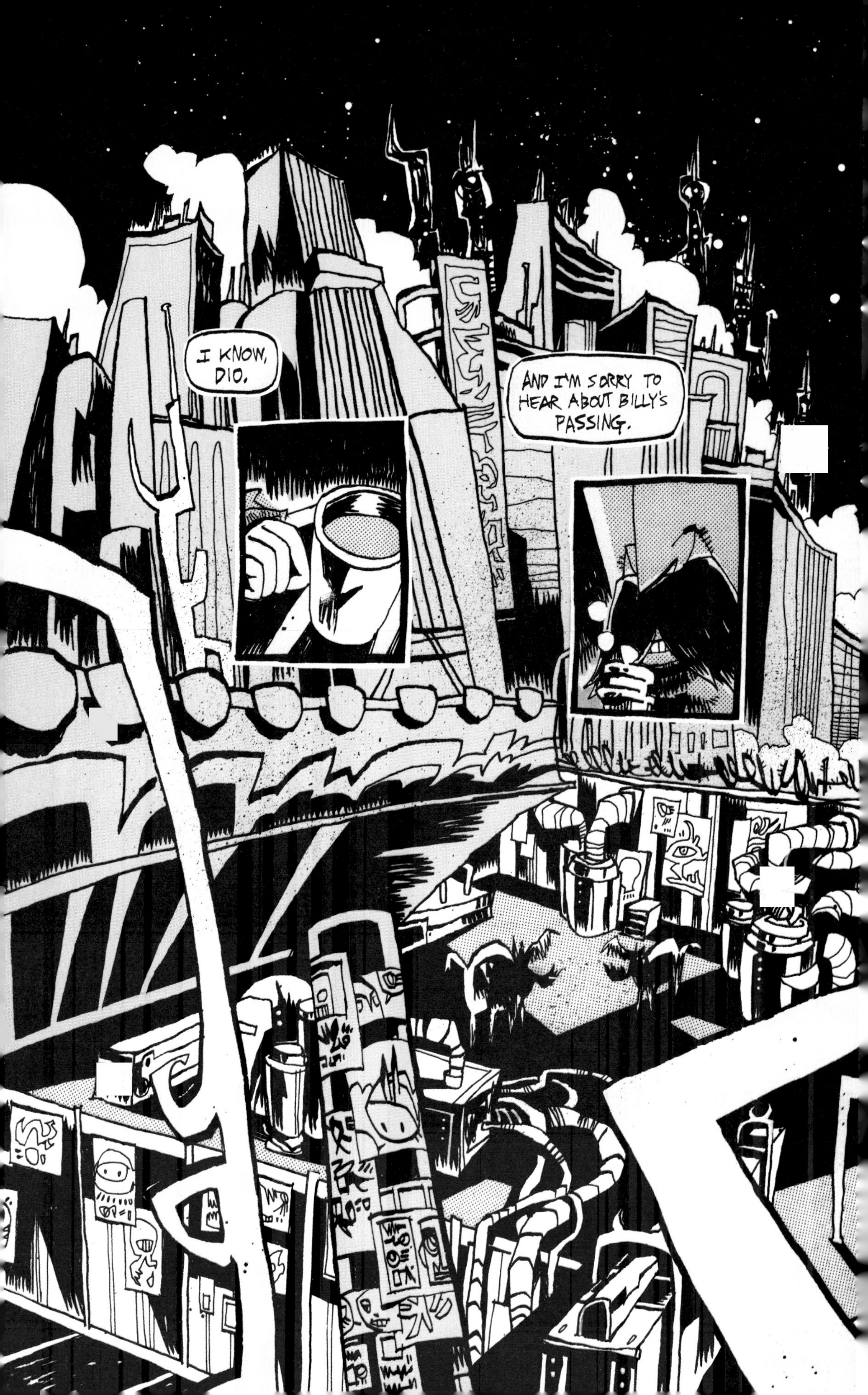
I KNOW, DIO.
AND I'M SORRY TO HEAR ABOUT BILLY'S PASSING.

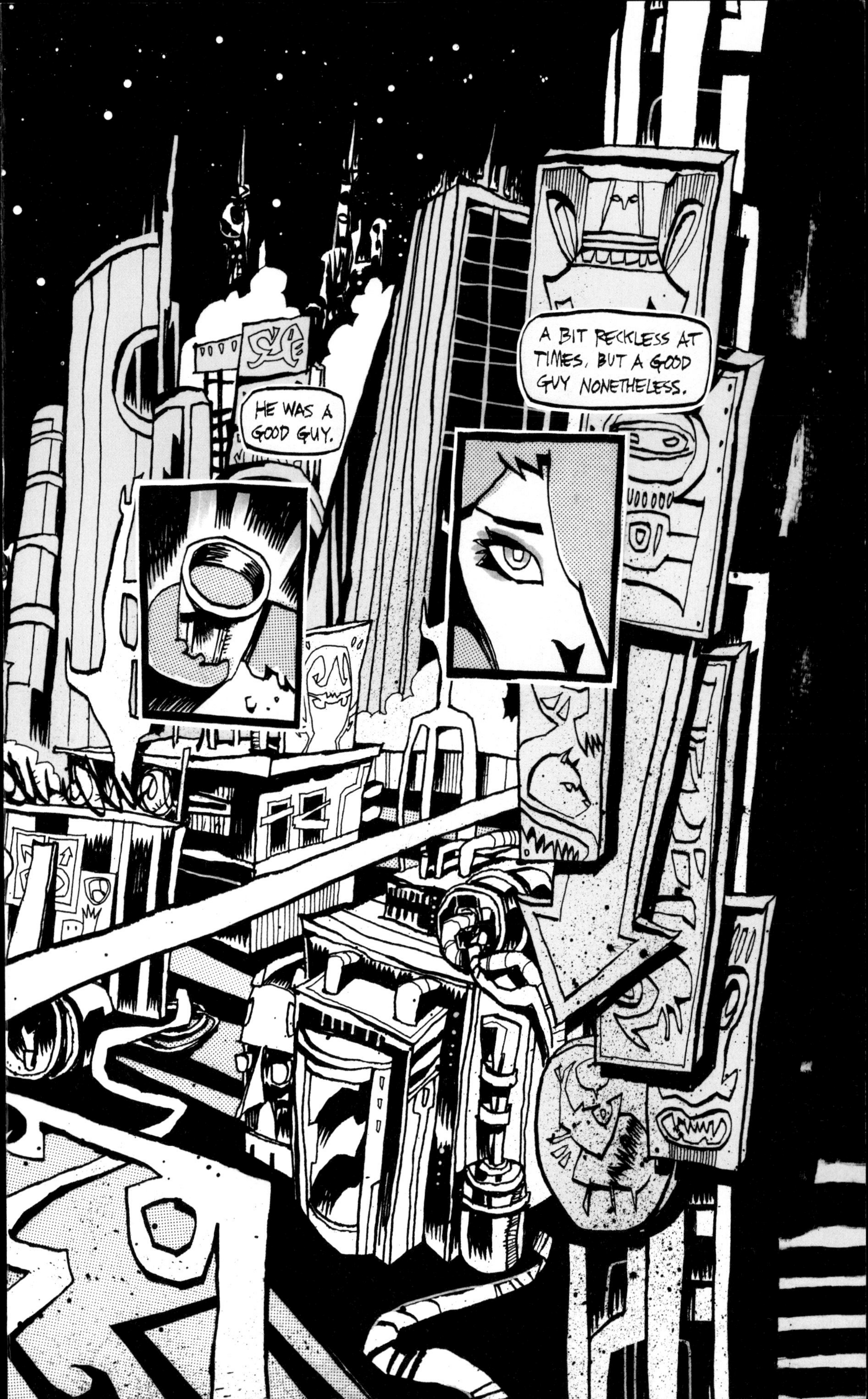
HE WAS A GOOD GUY.
A BIT RECKLESS AT TIMES, BUT A GOOD GUY NONETHELESS.

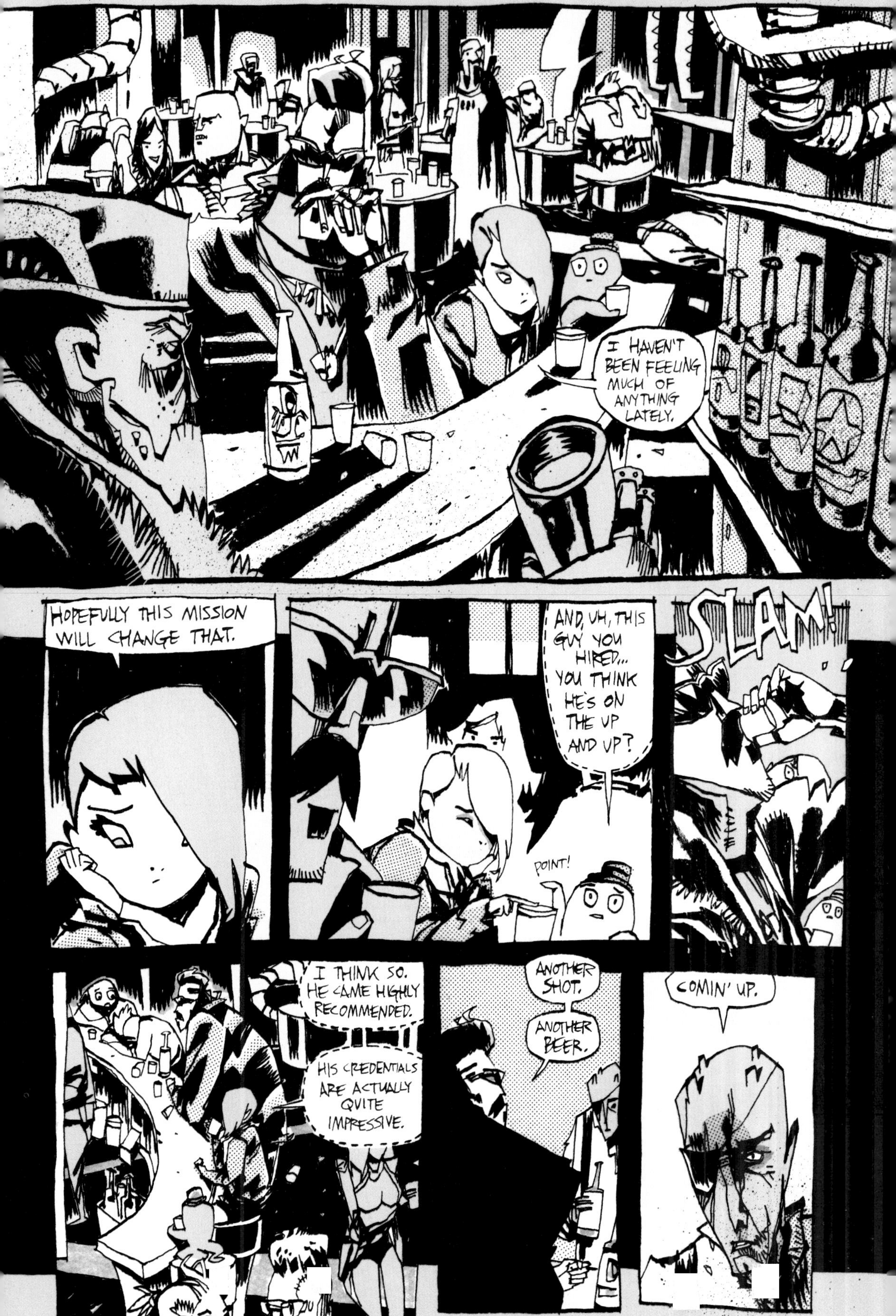
I HAVEN'T BEEN FEELING MUCH OF ANYTHING LATELY.
HOPEFULLY THIS MISSION WILL CHANGE THAT.
AND, UH, THIS GUY YOU HIRED... YOU THINK HE'S ON THE UP AND UP?
POINT!
SLAM!
I THINK SO. HE CAME HIGHLY RECOMMENDED.
HIS CREDENTIALS ARE ACTUALLY QUITE IMPRESSIVE.
ANOTHER SHOT.
ANOTHER BEER.
COMIN' UP.

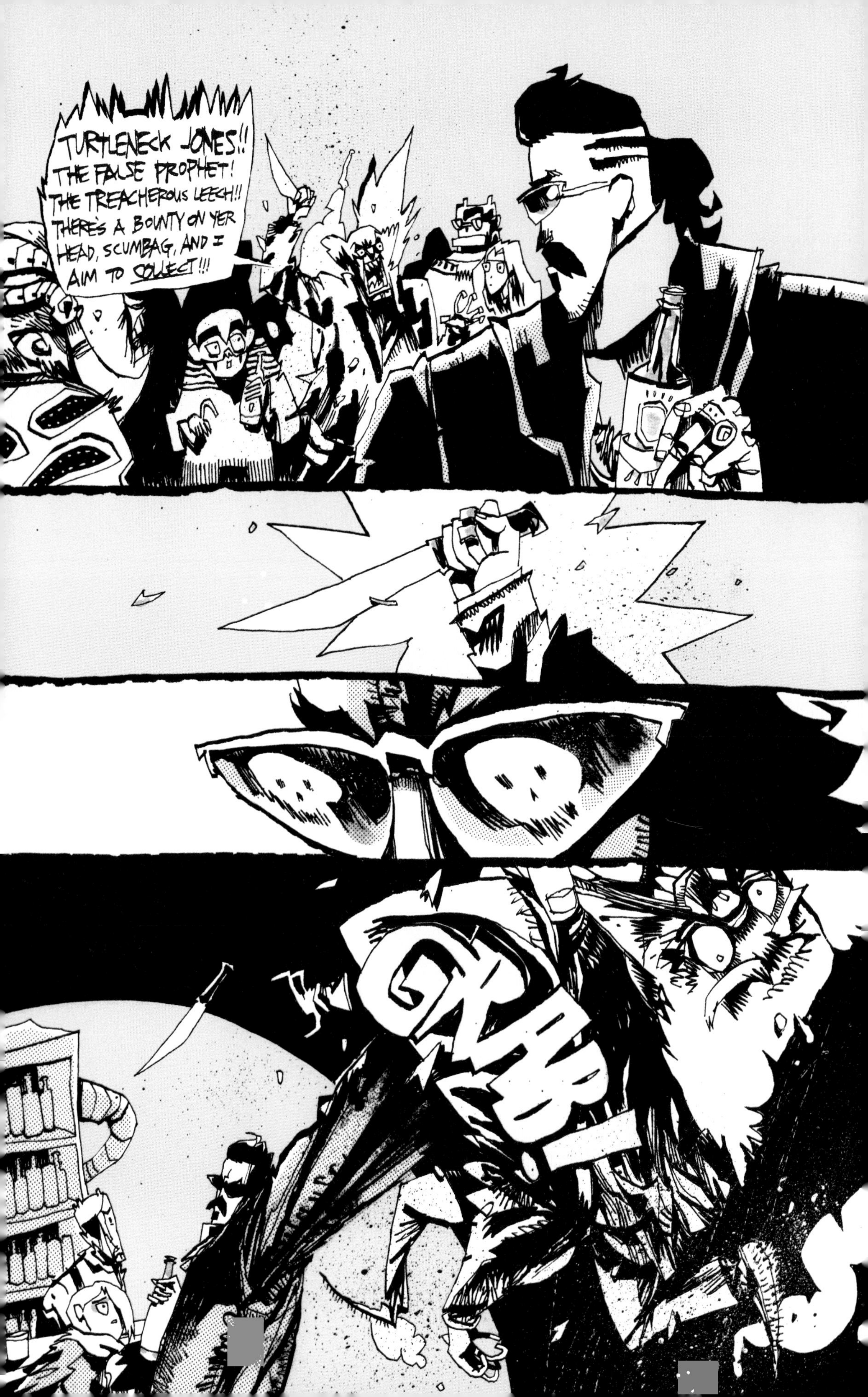
TURTLENECK JONES!! THE FALSE PROPHET! THE TREACHEROUS LEECH!! THERE'S A BOUNTY ON YER HEAD, SCUMBAG, AND I AIM TO COLLECT!!!
GRAB!

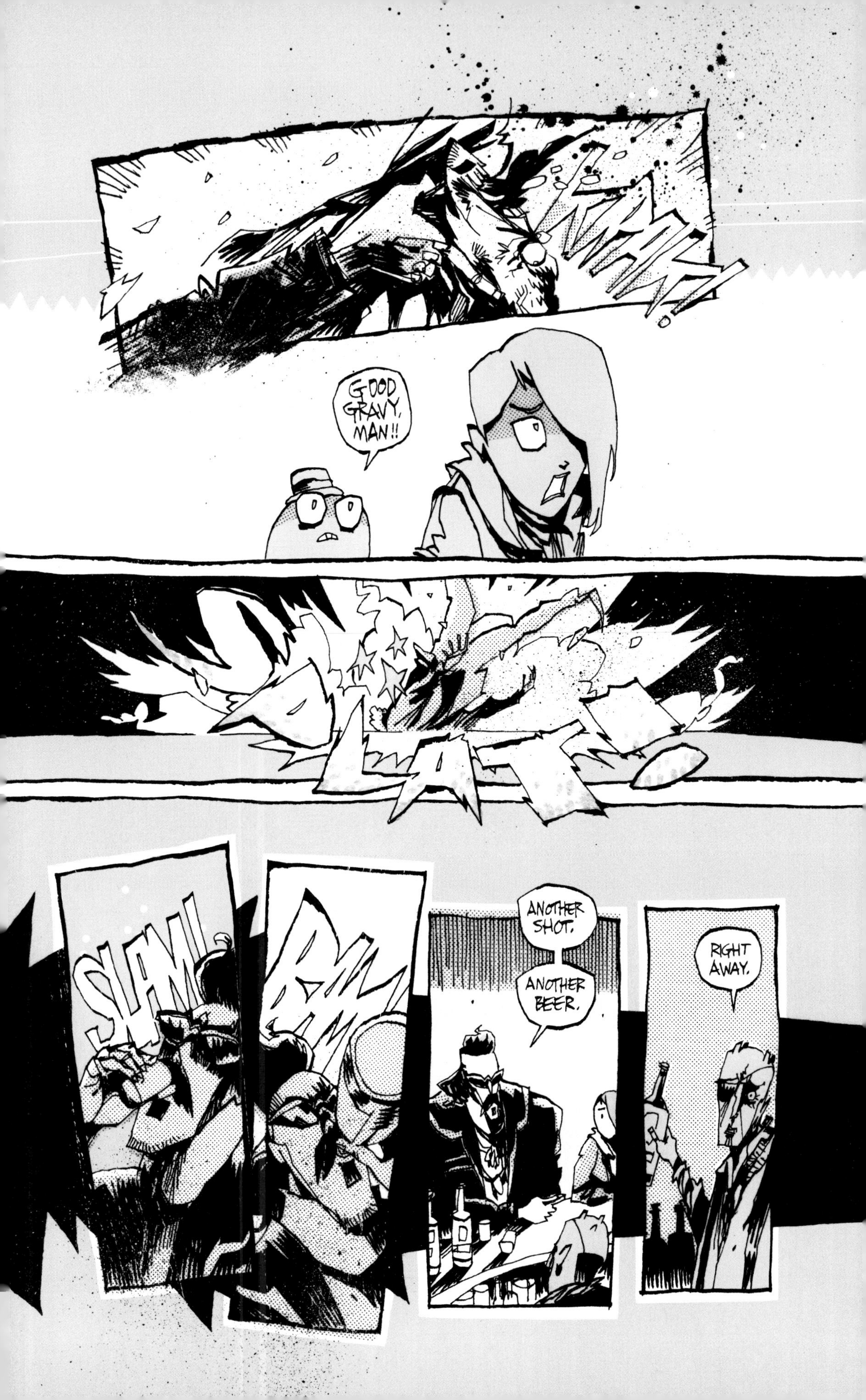
GOOD GRAVY, MAN!!
SLAM!
ANOTHER SHOT.
ANOTHER BEER.
RIGHT AWAY.

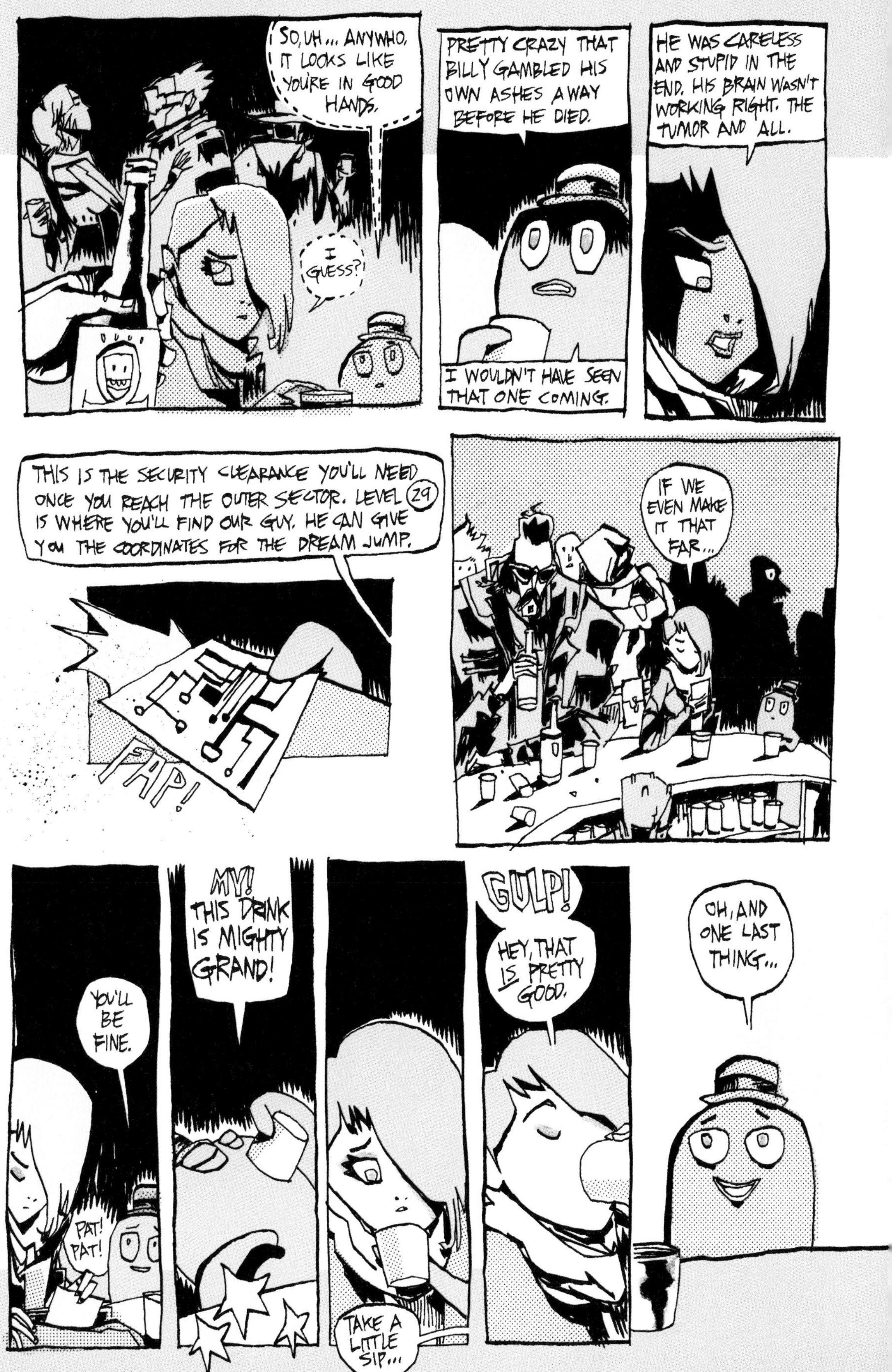
SO, UH... ANYWHO, IT LOOKS LIKE YOU'RE IN GOOD HANDS.
I GUESS?
PRETTY CRAZY THAT BILLY GAMBLED HIS OWN ASHES AWAY BEFORE HE DIED.
I WOULDN'T HAVE SEEN THAT ONE COMING.
HE WAS CARELESS AND STUPID IN THE END. HIS BRAIN WASN'T WORKING RIGHT. THE TUMOR AND ALL.
THIS IS THE SECURITY CLEARANCE YOU'LL NEED ONCE YOU REACH THE OUTER SECTOR. LEVEL 29 IS WHERE YOU'LL FIND OUR GUY. HE CAN GIVE YOU THE COORDINATES FOR THE DREAM JUMP.
FAP!
IF WE EVEN MAKE IT THAT FAR...
YOU'LL BE FINE.
PAT! PAT!
MY! THIS DRINK IS MIGHTY GRAND!
TAKE A LITTLE SIP...
GULP!
HEY, THAT IS PRETTY GOOD.
OH, AND ONE LAST THING...

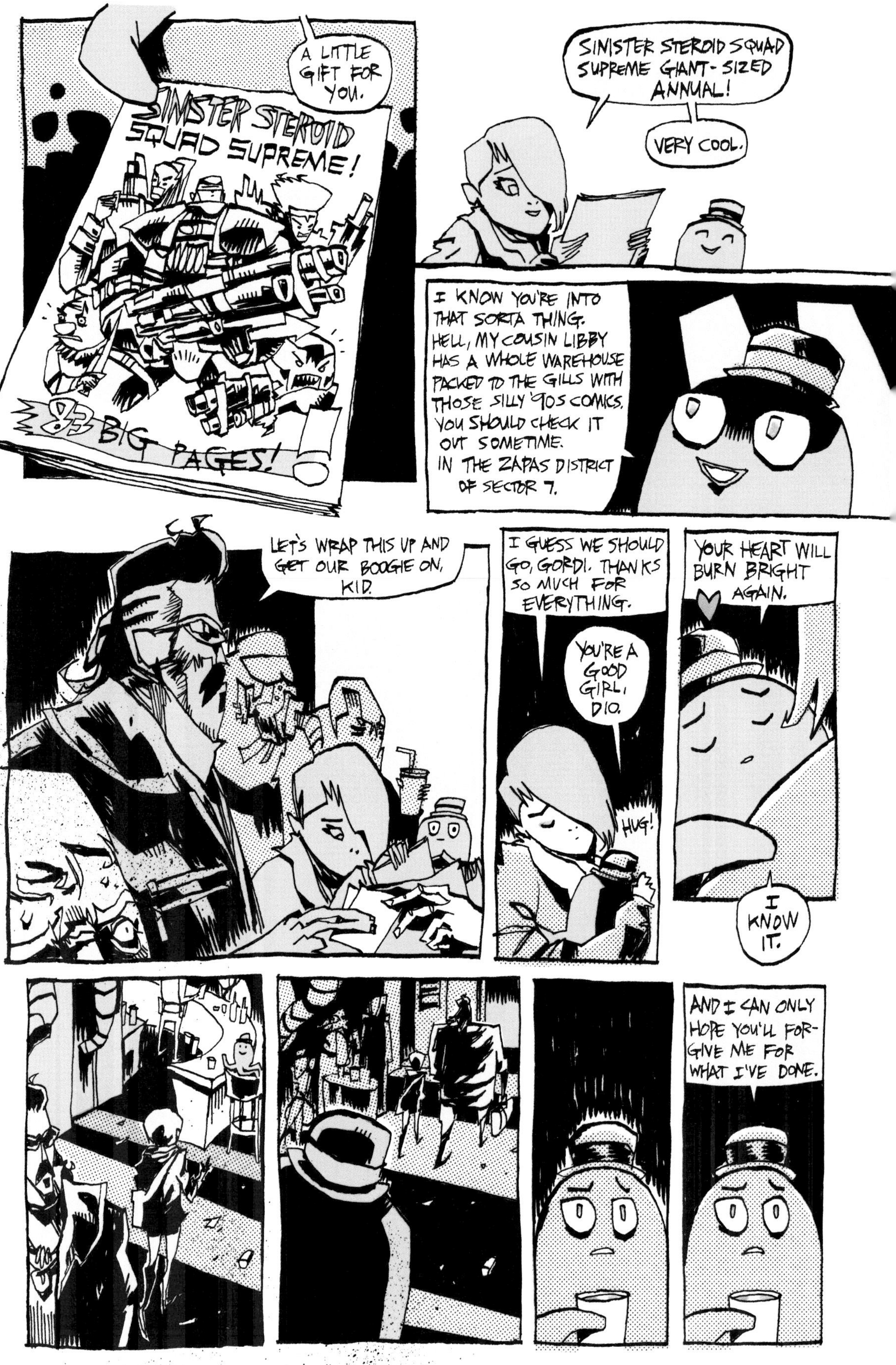
A LITTLE GIFT FOR YOU.
SINISTER STEROID SQUAD SUPREME!
83 BIG PAGES!
SINISTER STEROID SQUAD SUPREME GIANT-SIZED ANNUAL!
VERY COOL.
I KNOW YOU'RE INTO THAT SORTA THING. HELL, MY COUSIN LIBBY HAS A WHOLE WAREHOUSE PACKED TO THE GILLS WITH THOSE SILLY '90S COMICS. YOU SHOULD CHECK IT OUT SOMETIME. IN THE ZAPAS DISTRICT OF SECTOR 7.
LET'S WRAP THIS UP AND GET OUR BOOGIE ON, KID.
I GUESS WE SHOULD GO, GORDI. THANKS SO MUCH FOR EVERYTHING.
YOU'RE A GOOD GIRL, DIO.
HUG!
YOUR HEART WILL BURN BRIGHT AGAIN.
I KNOW IT.
AND I CAN ONLY HOPE YOU'LL FORGIVE ME FOR WHAT I'VE DONE.

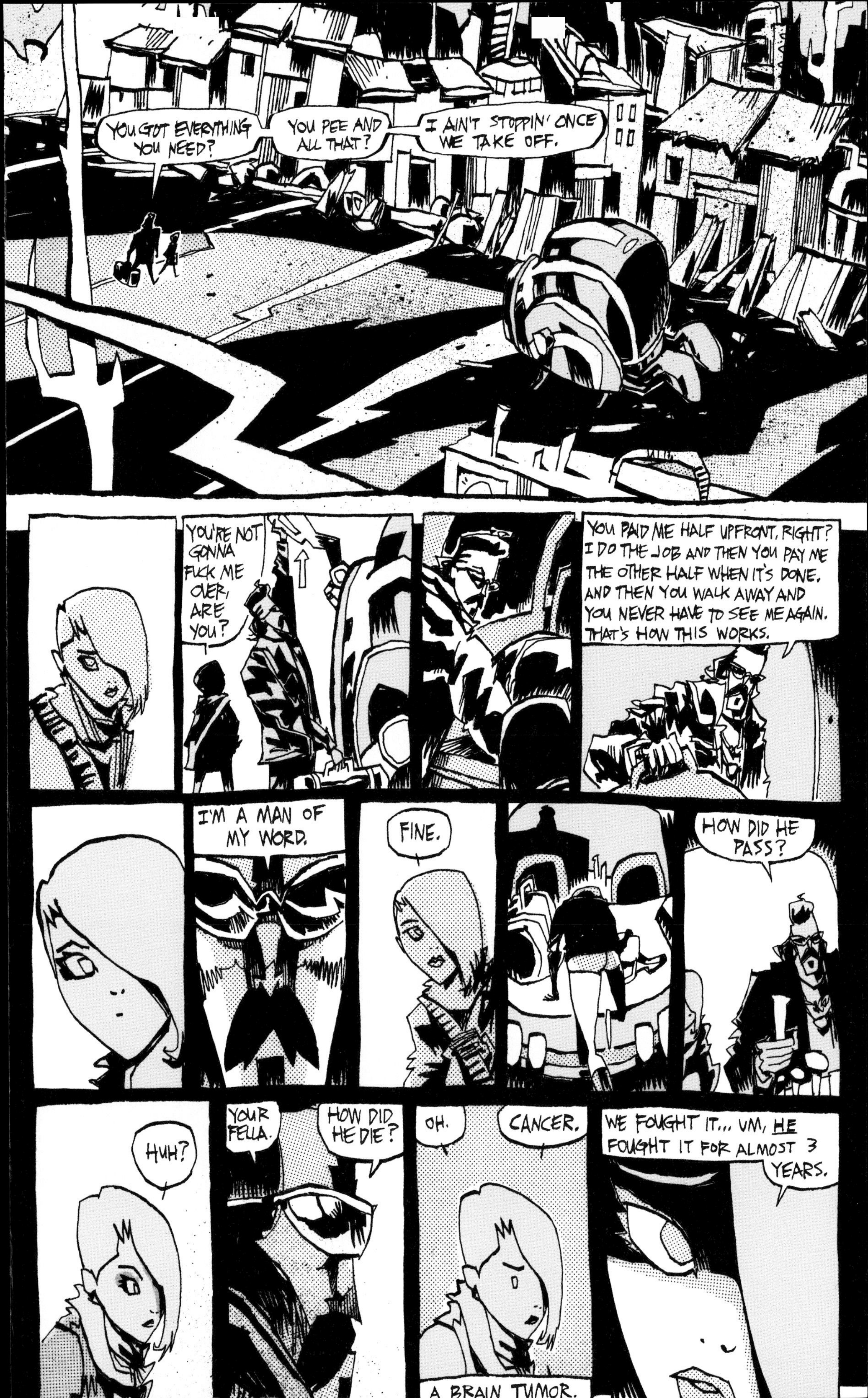
YOU GOT EVERYTHING YOU NEED?
YOU PEE AND ALL THAT?
I AIN'T STOPPIN' ONCE WE TAKE OFF.
YOU'RE NOT GONNA FUCK ME OVER, ARE YOU?
YOU PAID ME HALF UPFRONT, RIGHT? I DO THE JOB AND THEN YOU PAY ME THE OTHER HALF WHEN IT'S DONE. AND THEN YOU WALK AWAY AND YOU NEVER HAVE TO SEE ME AGAIN. THAT'S HOW THIS WORKS.
I'M A MAN OF MY WORD.
FINE.
HOW DID HE PASS?
HUH?
YOUR FELLA.
HOW DID HE DIE?
OH.
CANCER.
A BRAIN TUMOR.
WE FOUGHT IT... UM, HE FOUGHT IT FOR ALMOST 3 YEARS.

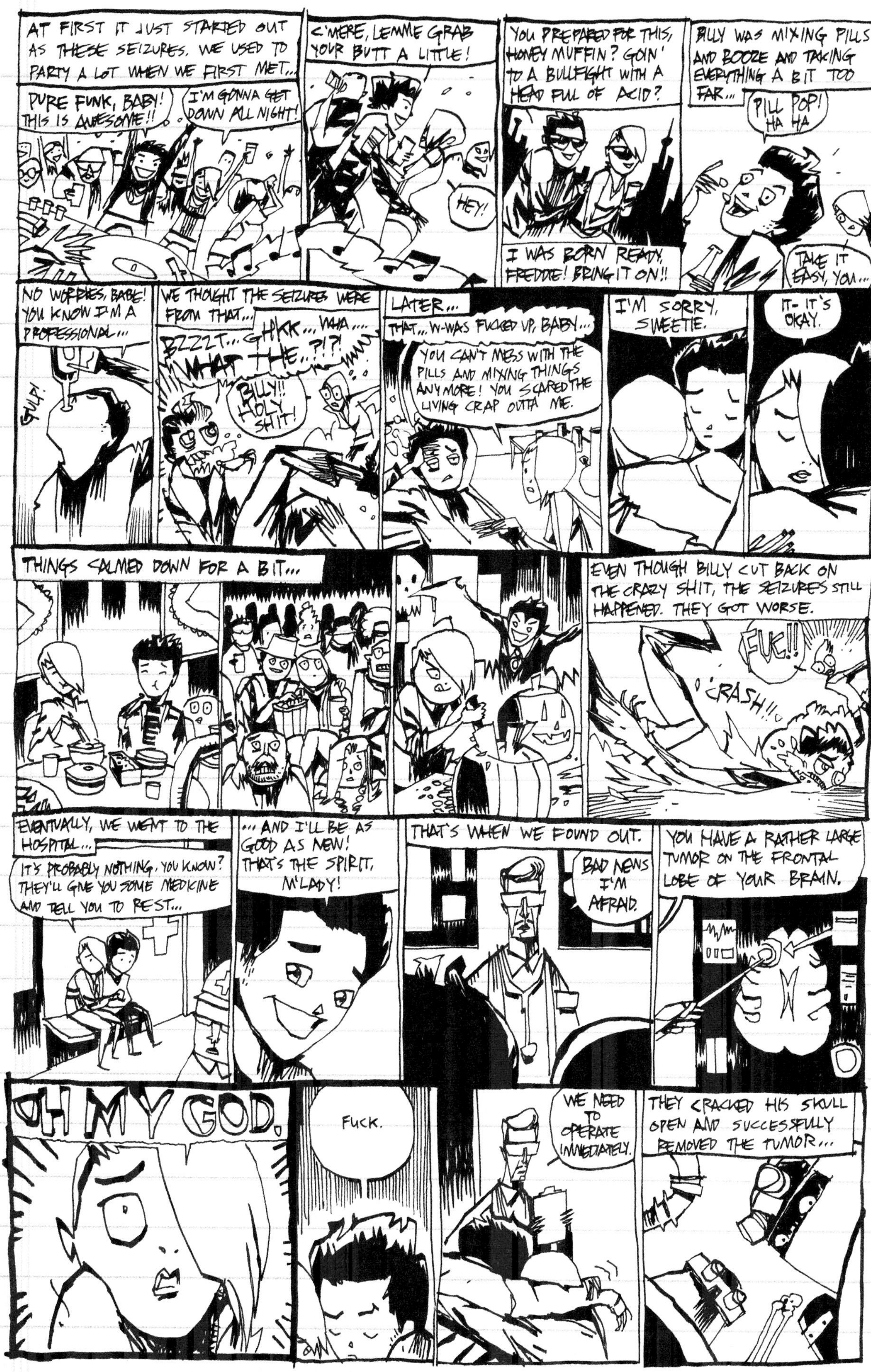
AT FIRST IT JUST STARTED OUT AS THESE SEIZURES. WE USED TO PARTY A LOT WHEN WE FIRST MET...
PURE FUNK, BABY! THIS IS AWESOME!!
I'M GONNA GET DOWN ALL NIGHT!
C'MERE, LEMME GRAB YOUR BUTT A LITTLE!
HEY!
YOU PREPARED FOR THIS, HONEY MUFFIN? GOIN' TO A BULLFIGHT WITH A HEAD FULL OF ACID?
I WAS BORN READY, FREDDIE! BRING IT ON!!
BILLY WAS MIXING PILLS AND BOOZE AND TAKING EVERYTHING A BIT TOO FAR...
PILL POP! HA HA
TAKE IT EASY, YOU...
NO WORRIES, BABE! YOU KNOW I'M A PROFESSIONAL...
GULP!
WE THOUGHT THE SEIZURES WERE FROM THAT...
BZZZT... GHKK... WHA.... WHAT THE...?!?
BILLY!! HOLY SHIT!
LATER...
THAT... W-WAS FUCKED UP, BABY...
YOU CAN'T MESS WITH THE PILLS AND MIXING THINGS ANYMORE! YOU SCARED THE LIVING CRAP OUTTA ME.
I'M SORRY, SWEETIE.
IT- IT'S OKAY.
THINGS CALMED DOWN FOR A BIT...
EVEN THOUGH BILLY CUT BACK ON THE CRAZY SHIT, THE SEIZURES STILL HAPPENED. THEY GOT WORSE.
FUC!!
CRASH!!
EVENTUALLY, WE WENT TO THE HOSPITAL...
IT'S PROBABLY NOTHING, YOU KNOW? THEY'LL GIVE YOU SOME MEDICINE AND TELL YOU TO REST...
...AND I'LL BE AS GOOD AS NEW! THAT'S THE SPIRIT, M'LADY!
THAT'S WHEN WE FOUND OUT.
BAD NEWS I'M AFRAID.
YOU HAVE A RATHER LARGE TUMOR ON THE FRONTAL LOBE OF YOUR BRAIN.
OH MY GOD.
FUCK.
WE NEED TO OPERATE IMMEDIATELY.
THEY CRACKED HIS SKULL OPEN AND SUCCESSFULLY REMOVED THE TUMOR...

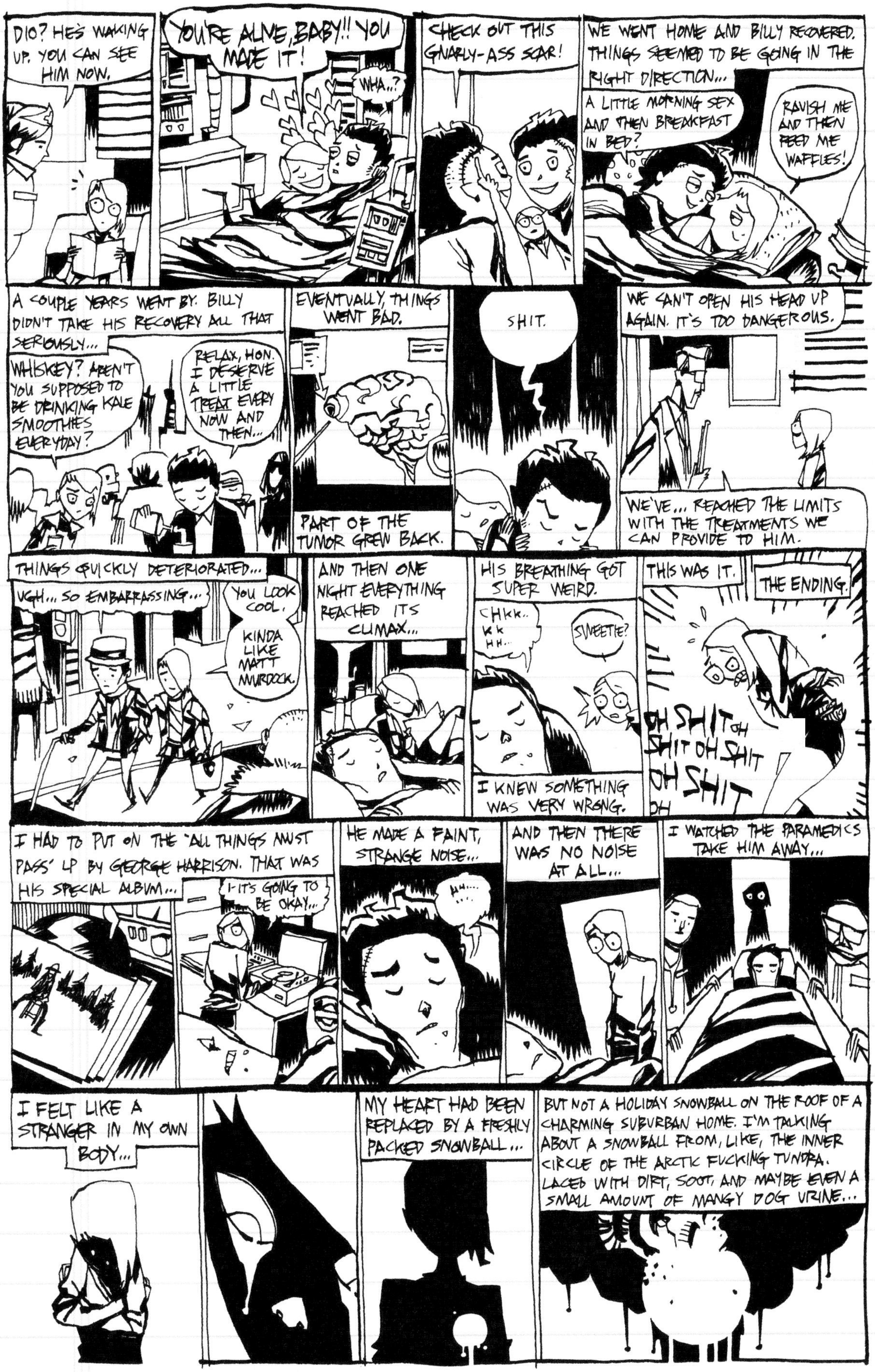
DIO? HE'S WAKING UP. YOU CAN SEE HIM NOW.
YOU'RE ALIVE, BABY!! YOU MADE IT!
WHA..?
CHECK OUT THIS GNARLY-ASS SCAR!
WE WENT HOME AND BILLY RECOVERED. THINGS SEEMED TO BE GOING IN THE RIGHT DIRECTION...
A LITTLE MORNING SEX AND THEN BREAKFAST IN BED?
RAVISH ME AND THEN FEED ME WAFFLES!
A COUPLE YEARS WENT BY. BILLY DIDN'T TAKE HIS RECOVERY ALL THAT SERIOUSLY...
WHISKEY? AREN'T YOU SUPPOSED TO BE DRINKING KALE SMOOTHIES EVERYDAY?
RELAX, HON. I DESERVE A LITTLE TREAT EVERY NOW AND THEN...
EVENTUALLY, THINGS WENT BAD.
PART OF THE TUMOR GREW BACK.
SHIT.
WE CAN'T OPEN HIS HEAD UP AGAIN. IT'S TOO DANGEROUS.
WE'VE... REACHED THE LIMITS WITH THE TREATMENTS WE CAN PROVIDE TO HIM.
THINGS QUICKLY DETERIORATED...
UGH... SO EMBARRASSING...
YOU LOOK COOL.
KINDA LIKE MATT MURDOCK.
AND THEN ONE NIGHT EVERYTHING REACHED ITS CLIMAX...
HIS BREATHING GOT SUPER WEIRD.
CHKK.. KK HH...
SWEETIE?
I KNEW SOMETHING WAS VERY WRONG.
THIS WAS IT.
THE ENDING.
OH SHIT OH SHIT OH SHIT OH SHIT OH
I HAD TO PUT ON THE "ALL THINGS MUST PASS" LP BY GEORGE HARRISON. THAT WAS HIS SPECIAL ALBUM...
I-IT'S GOING TO BE OKAY...
HE MADE A FAINT, STRANGE NOISE...
HH....
AND THEN THERE WAS NO NOISE AT ALL...
I WATCHED THE PARAMEDICS TAKE HIM AWAY...
I FELT LIKE A STRANGER IN MY OWN BODY...
MY HEART HAD BEEN REPLACED BY A FRESHLY PACKED SNOWBALL...
BUT NOT A HOLIDAY SNOWBALL ON THE ROOF OF A CHARMING SUBURBAN HOME. I'M TALKING ABOUT A SNOWBALL FROM, LIKE, THE INNER CIRCLE OF THE ARCTIC FUCKING TUNDRA. LACED WITH DIRT, SOOT, AND MAYBE EVEN A SMALL AMOUNT OF MANGY DOG URINE...

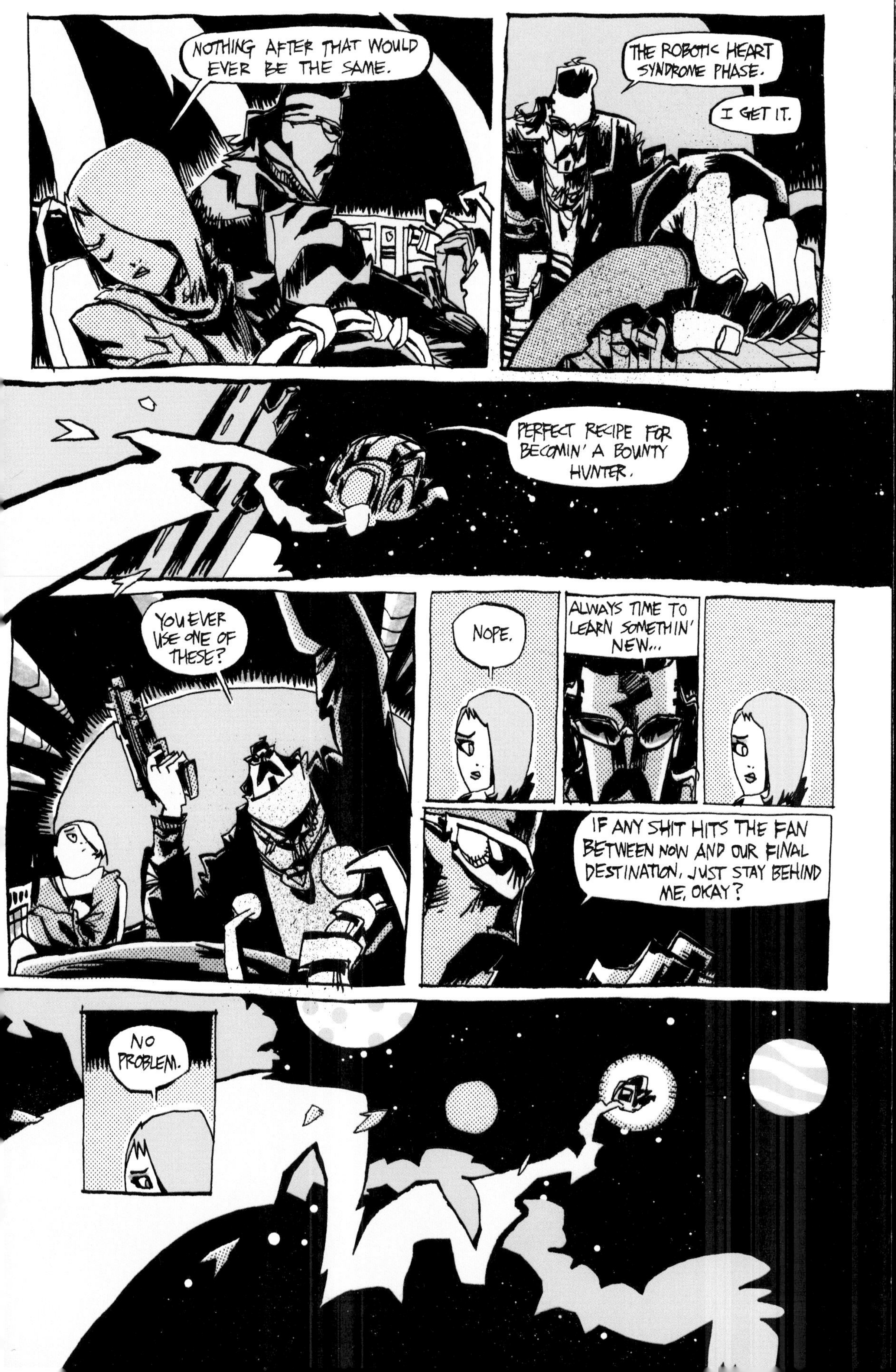
NOTHING AFTER THAT WOULD EVER BE THE SAME.
THE ROBOTIC HEART SYNDROME PHASE.
I GET IT.
PERFECT RECIPE FOR BECOMIN' A BOUNTY HUNTER.
YOU EVER USE ONE OF THESE?
NOPE.
ALWAYS TIME TO LEARN SOMETHIN' NEW...
IF ANY SHIT HITS THE FAN BETWEEN NOW AND OUR FINAL DESTINATION, JUST STAY BEHIND ME, OKAY?
NO PROBLEM.

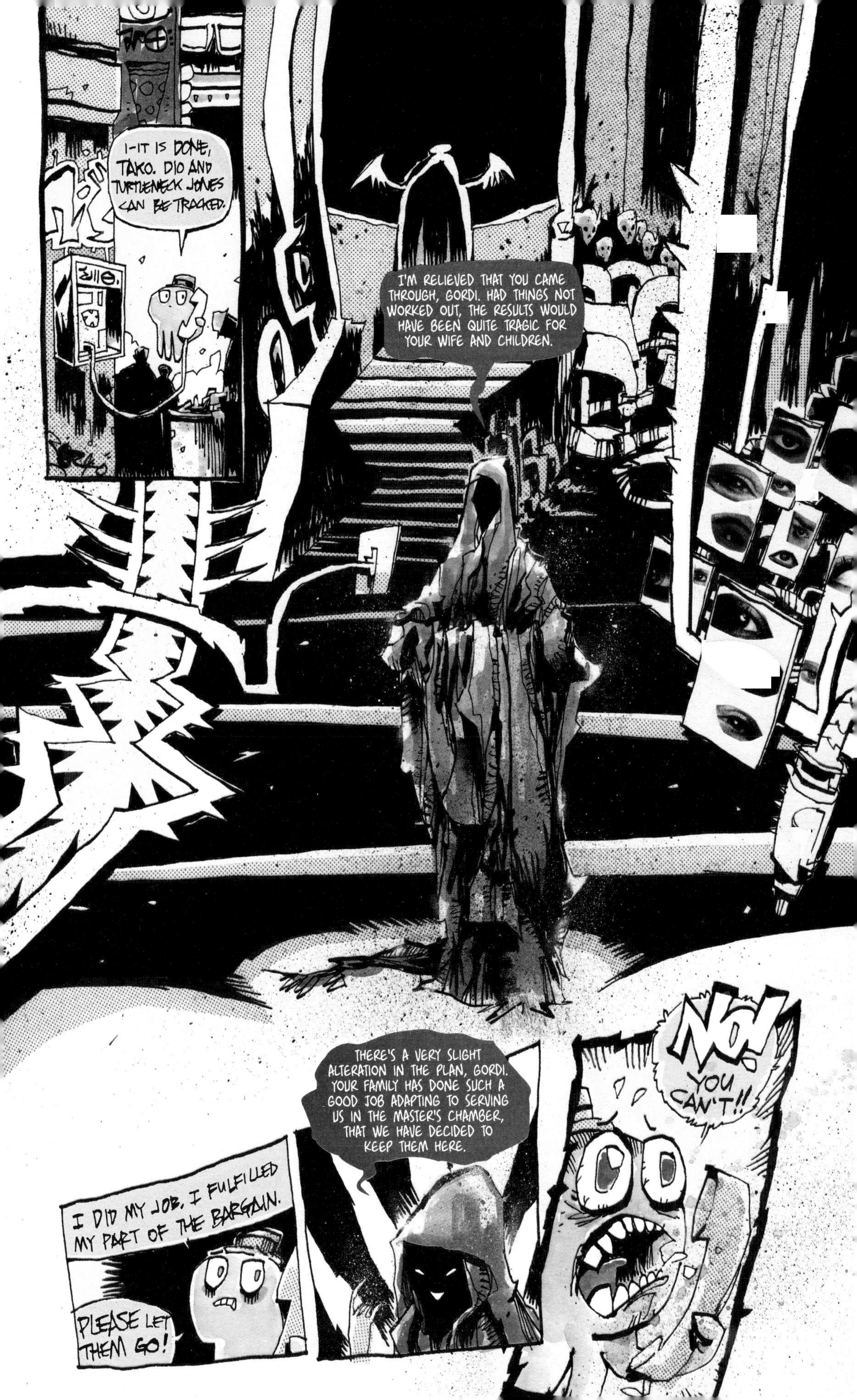
I-IT IS DONE, TAKO. DIO AND TURTLENECK JONES CAN BE TRACKED.
I'M RELIEVED THAT YOU CAME THROUGH, GORDI. HAD THINGS NOT WORKED OUT, THE RESULTS WOULD HAVE BEEN QUITE TRAGIC FOR YOUR WIFE AND CHILDREN.
I DID MY JOB. I FULFILLED MY PART OF THE BARGAIN.
PLEASE LET THEM GO!
THERE'S A VERY SLIGHT ALTERATION IN THE PLAN, GORDI. YOUR FAMILY HAS DONE SUCH A GOOD JOB ADAPTING TO SERVING US IN THE MASTER'S CHAMBER, THAT WE HAVE DECIDED TO KEEP THEM HERE.
NO! YOU CAN'T!!

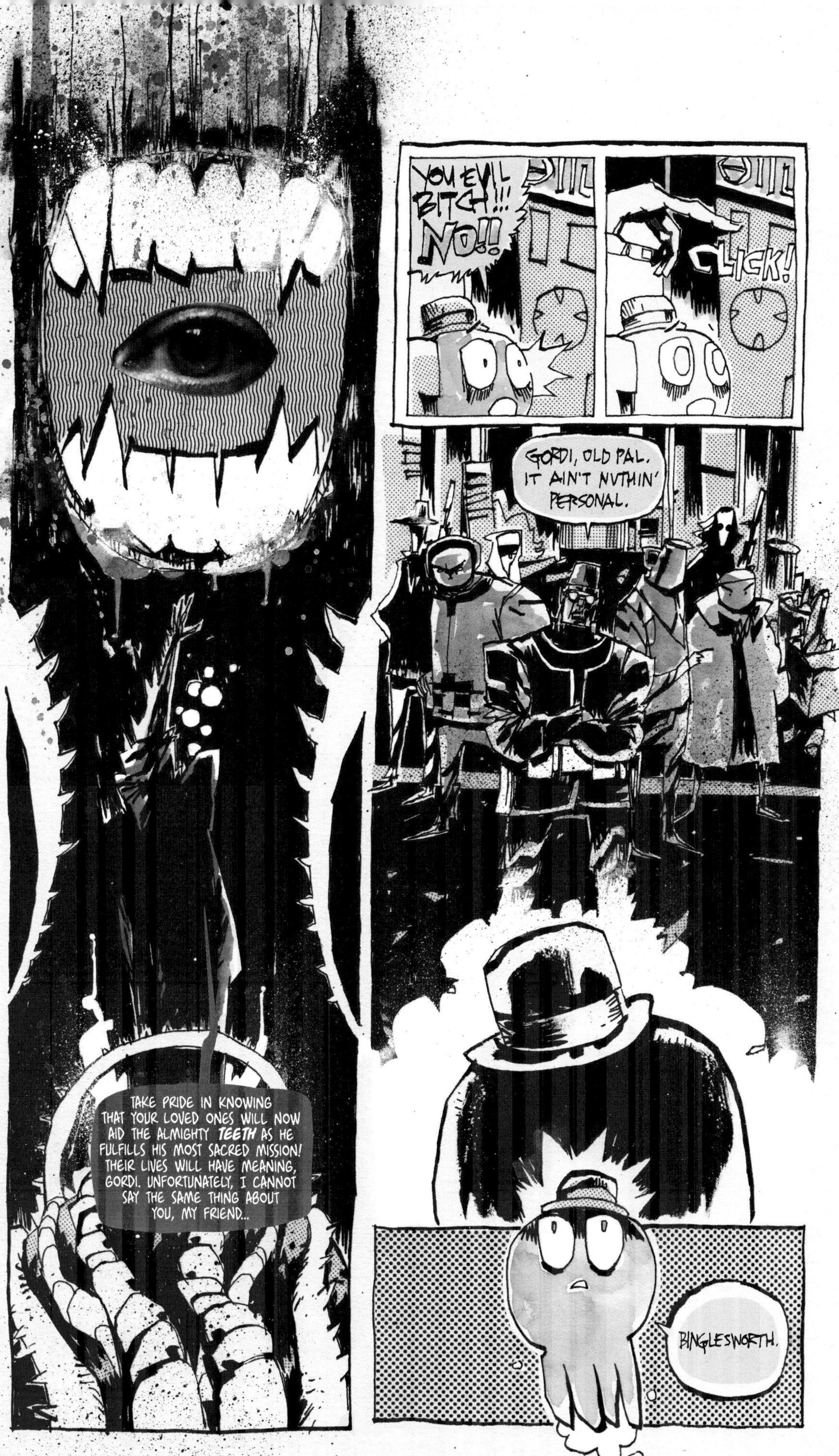
YOU EVIL BITCH!!! NO!!
CLICK!
GORDI, OLD PAL. IT AIN'T NUTHIN' PERSONAL.
TAKE PRIDE IN KNOWING THAT YOUR LOVED ONES WILL NOW AID THE ALMIGHTY TEETH AS HE FULFILLS HIS MOST SACRED MISSION! THEIR LIVES WILL HAVE MEANING, GORDI. UNFORTUNATELY, I CANNOT SAY THE SAME THING ABOUT YOU, MY FRIEND...
BINGLESWORTH.

MY-- MY CHILDREN... SEE THAT THEY'RE TAKEN CARE OF.

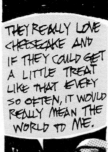

THEY REALLY LOVE CHEESECAKE AND IF THEY COULD GET A LITTLE TREAT LIKE THAT EVERY SO OFTEN, IT WOULD REALLY MEAN THE WORLD TO ME.

WE'VE BEEN MADE AWARE OF THEIR DIETARY PREFERENCES AND WILL DO OUR DAMN BEST.

HELL, CHESTER HERE MAKES ONE OF THE MEANEST CHEESECAKES THIS SIDE OF THE HANCOCK QUADRANT.

THE SECRET IS IN THE GRAHAM CRACKER CRUST! NOT TOO THICK, NOT TOO LIGHT, JUST RIGHT THERE IN THE MIDDLE. A TRUE DELIGHT!

THAT SOUNDS ABOUT RIGHT.

MAKE SURE THAT...

SORRY, GORDI, GOTTA WRAP THINGS UP.

WE GOT A GRRL SCOUT TO TRACK DOWN.

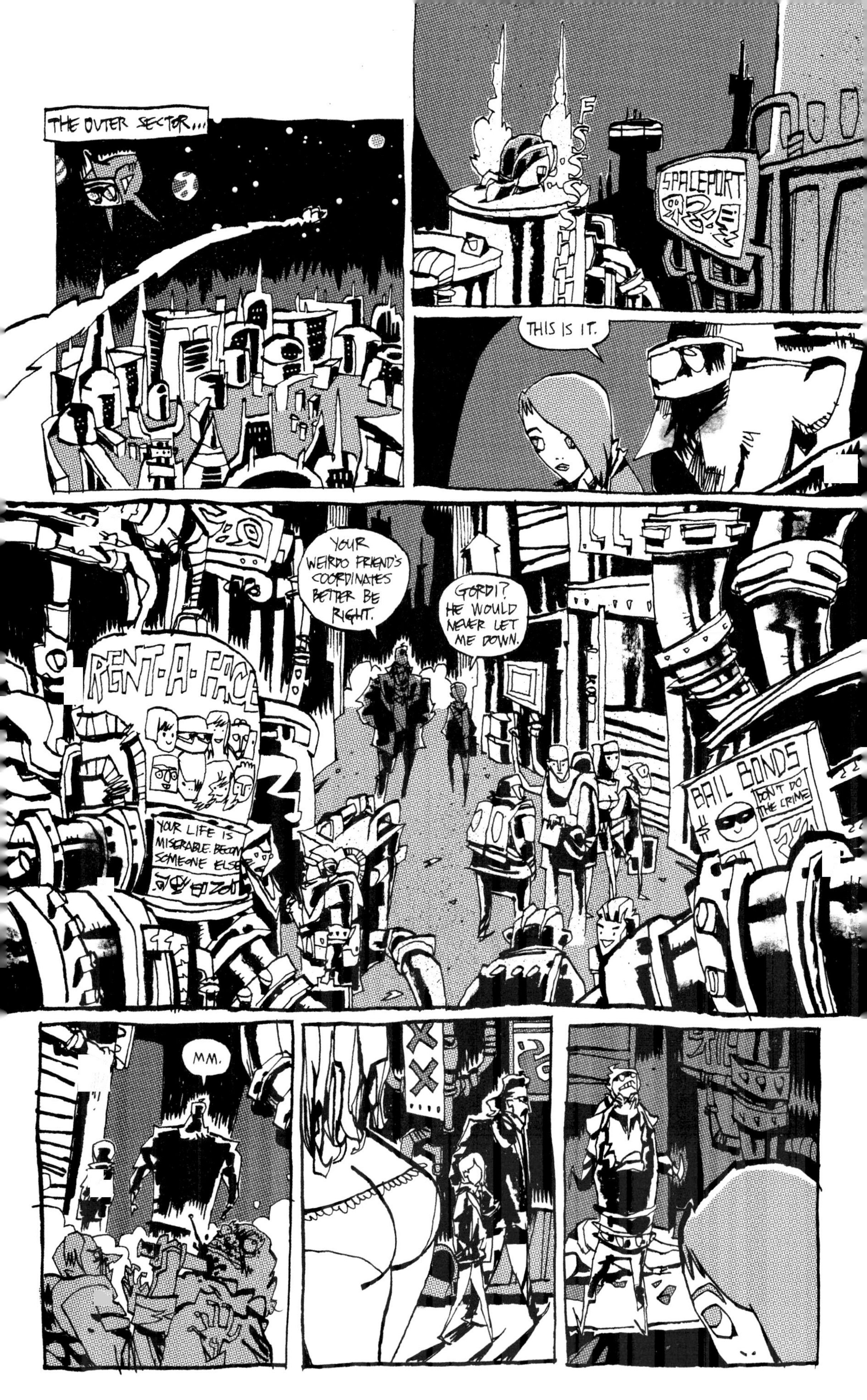
THE OUTER SECTOR...
FSSSHHH
SPACEPORT
THIS IS IT.
YOUR WEIRDO FRIEND'S COORDINATES BETTER BE RIGHT.
GORDI? HE WOULD NEVER LET ME DOWN.
RENT-A-FACE
YOUR LIFE IS MISERABLE. BECOME SOMEONE ELSE
BAIL BONDS
DON'T DO THE CRIME
MM.

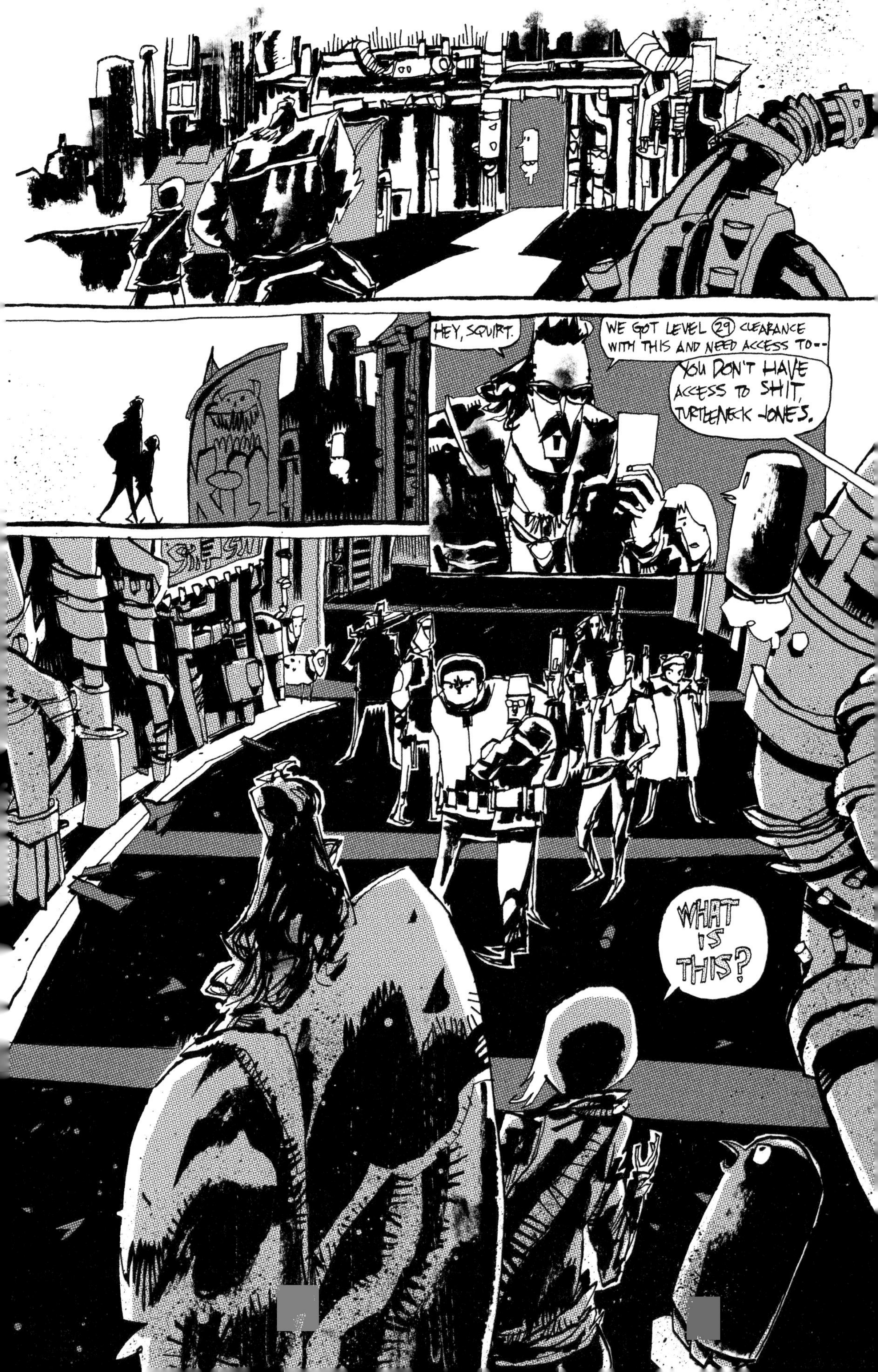
HEY, SQUIRT.
WE GOT LEVEL 29 CLEARANCE WITH THIS AND NEED ACCESS TO--
YOU DON'T HAVE ACCESS TO SHIT, TURTLENECK JONES.
WHAT IS THIS?

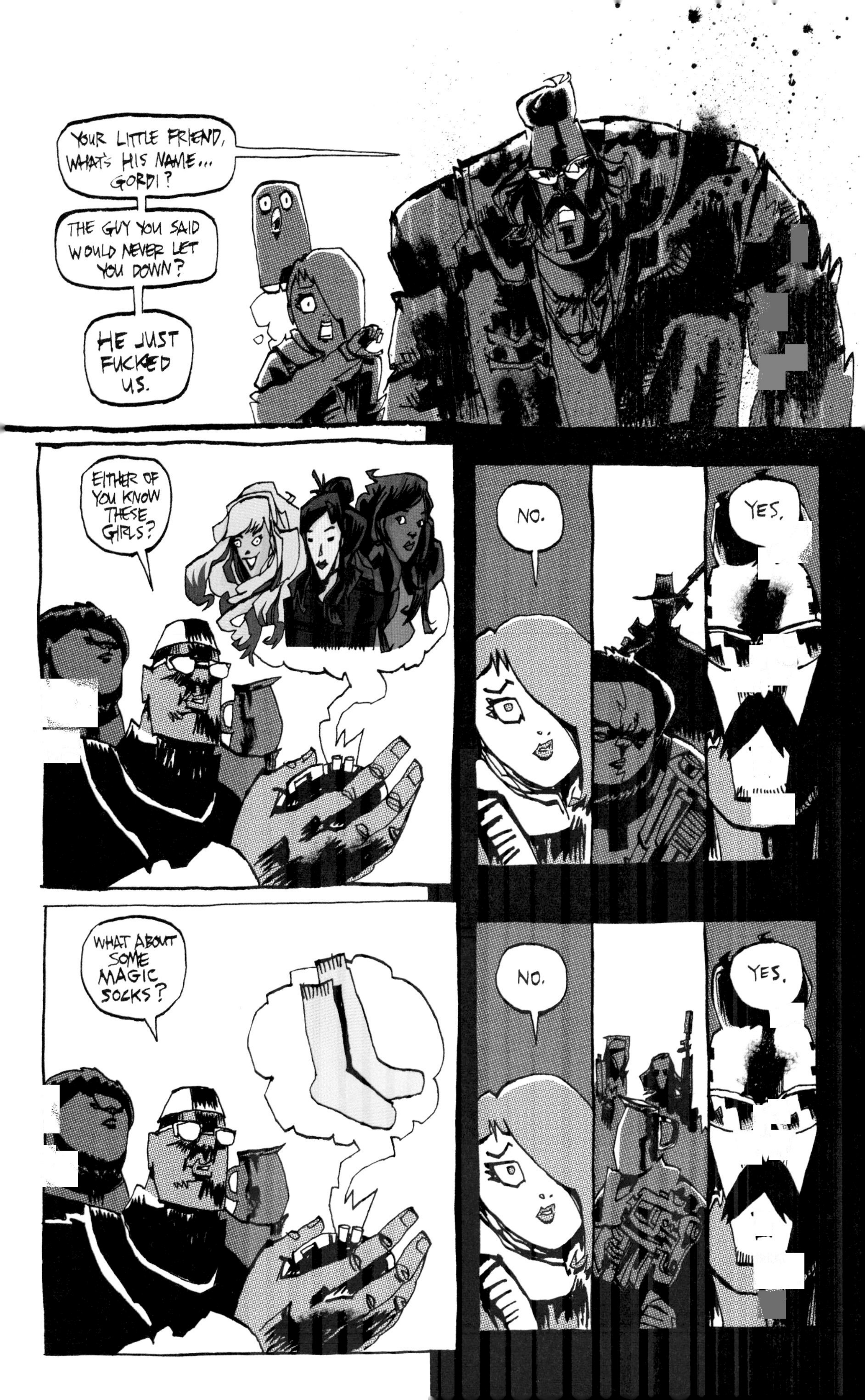
YOUR LITTLE FRIEND, WHAT'S HIS NAME... GORDI?
THE GUY YOU SAID WOULD NEVER LET YOU DOWN?
HE JUST FUCKED US.
EITHER OF YOU KNOW THESE GIRLS?
NO.
YES.
WHAT ABOUT SOME MAGIC SOCKS?
NO.
YES.

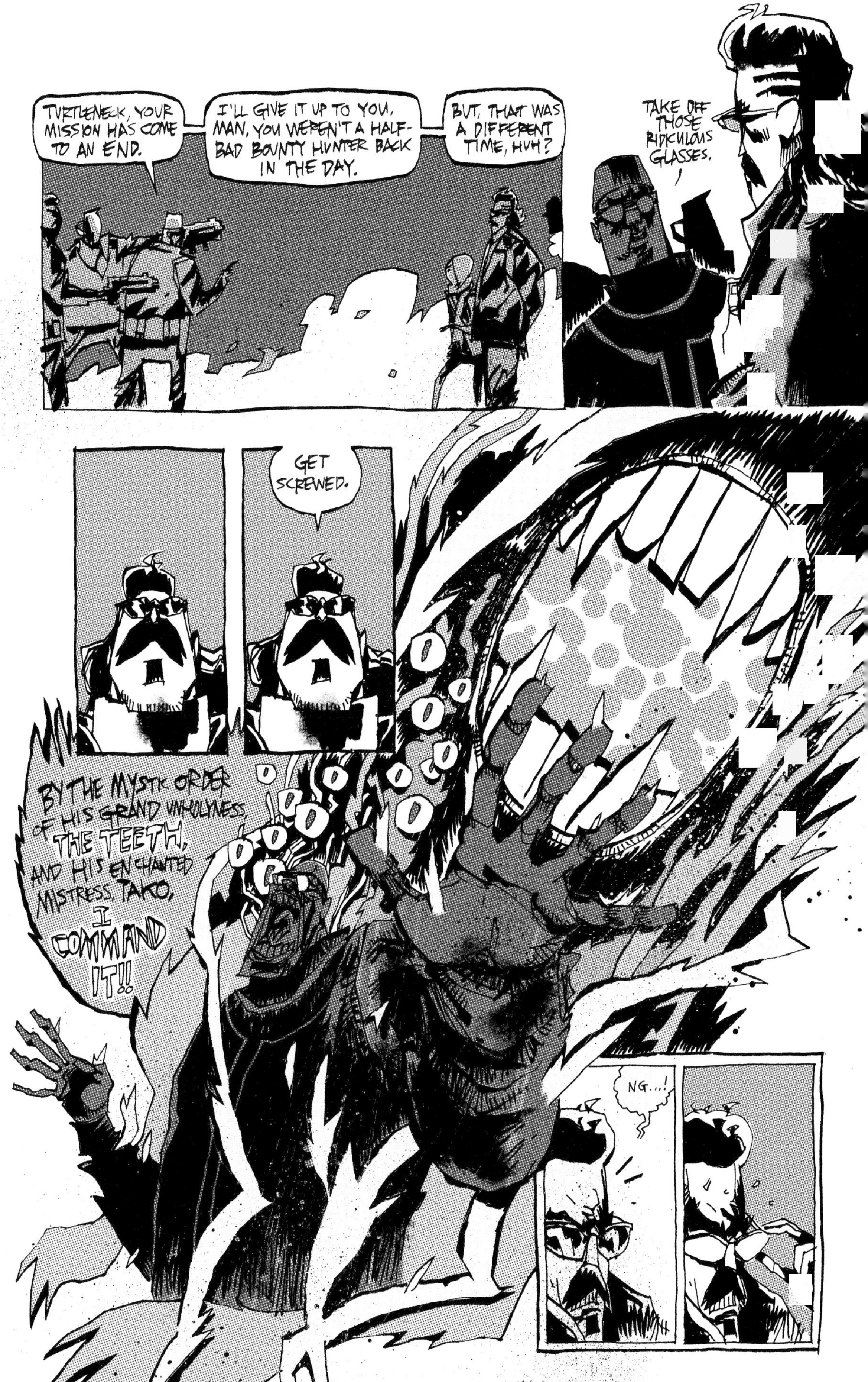
TURTLENECK, YOUR MISSION HAS COME TO AN END.
I'LL GIVE IT UP TO YOU, MAN, YOU WEREN'T A HALF-BAD BOUNTY HUNTER BACK IN THE DAY.
BUT, THAT WAS A DIFFERENT TIME, HUH?
TAKE OFF THOSE RIDICULOUS GLASSES.
GET SCREWED.
BY THE MYSTIC ORDER OF HIS GRAND UNHOLYNESS, THE TEETH, AND HIS ENCHANTED MISTRESS, TAKO, I COMMAND IT!!
NG...!

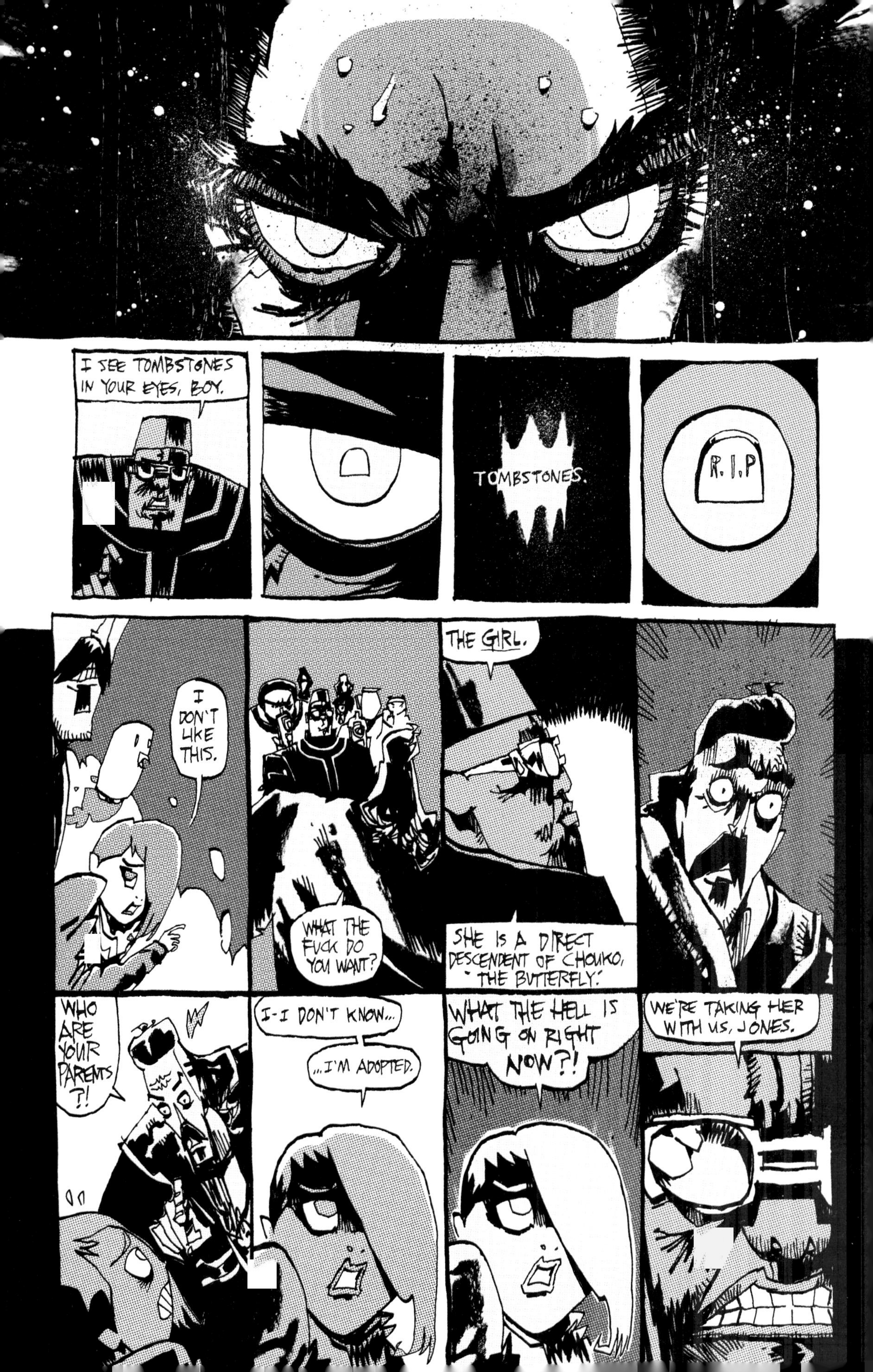
I SEE TOMBSTONES IN YOUR EYES, BOY.
TOMBSTONES.
R.I.P
I DON'T LIKE THIS.
WHAT THE FUCK DO YOU WANT?
THE GIRL.
SHE IS A DIRECT DESCENDENT OF CHOUKO, "THE BUTTERFLY."
WHO ARE YOUR PARENTS?!
I-I DON'T KNOW...
...I'M ADOPTED.
WHAT THE HELL IS GOING ON RIGHT NOW?!
WE'RE TAKING HER WITH US, JONES.

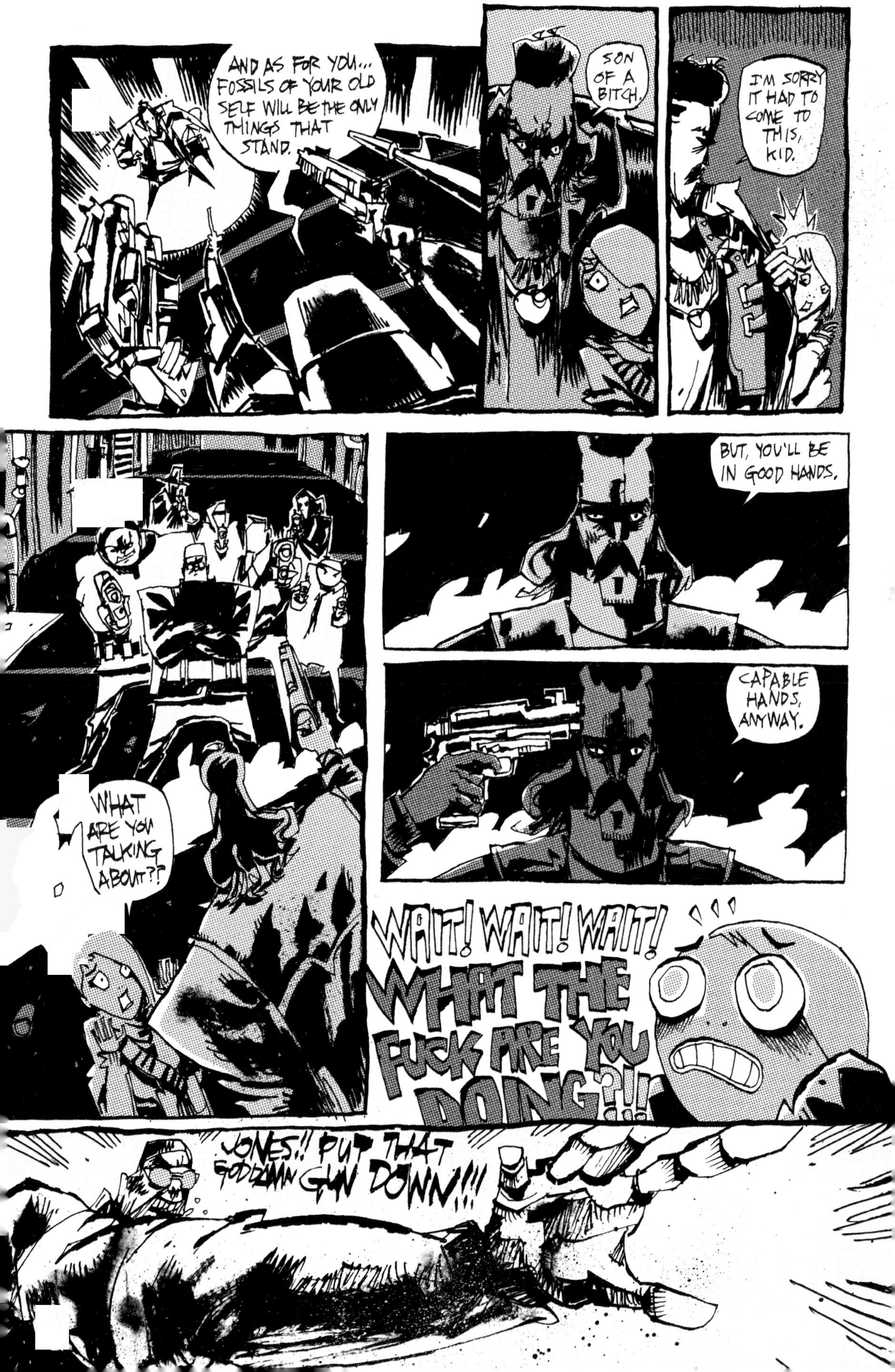
AND AS FOR YOU... FOSSILS OF YOUR OLD SELF WILL BE THE ONLY THINGS THAT STAND.
SON OF A BITCH.
I'M SORRY IT HAD TO COME TO THIS, KID.
WHAT ARE YOU TALKING ABOUT?!
BUT, YOU'LL BE IN GOOD HANDS.
CAPABLE HANDS, ANYWAY.
WAIT! WAIT! WAIT!
WHAT THE FUCK ARE YOU DOING?!!
JONES!! PUT THAT GODDAMN GUN DOWN!!!

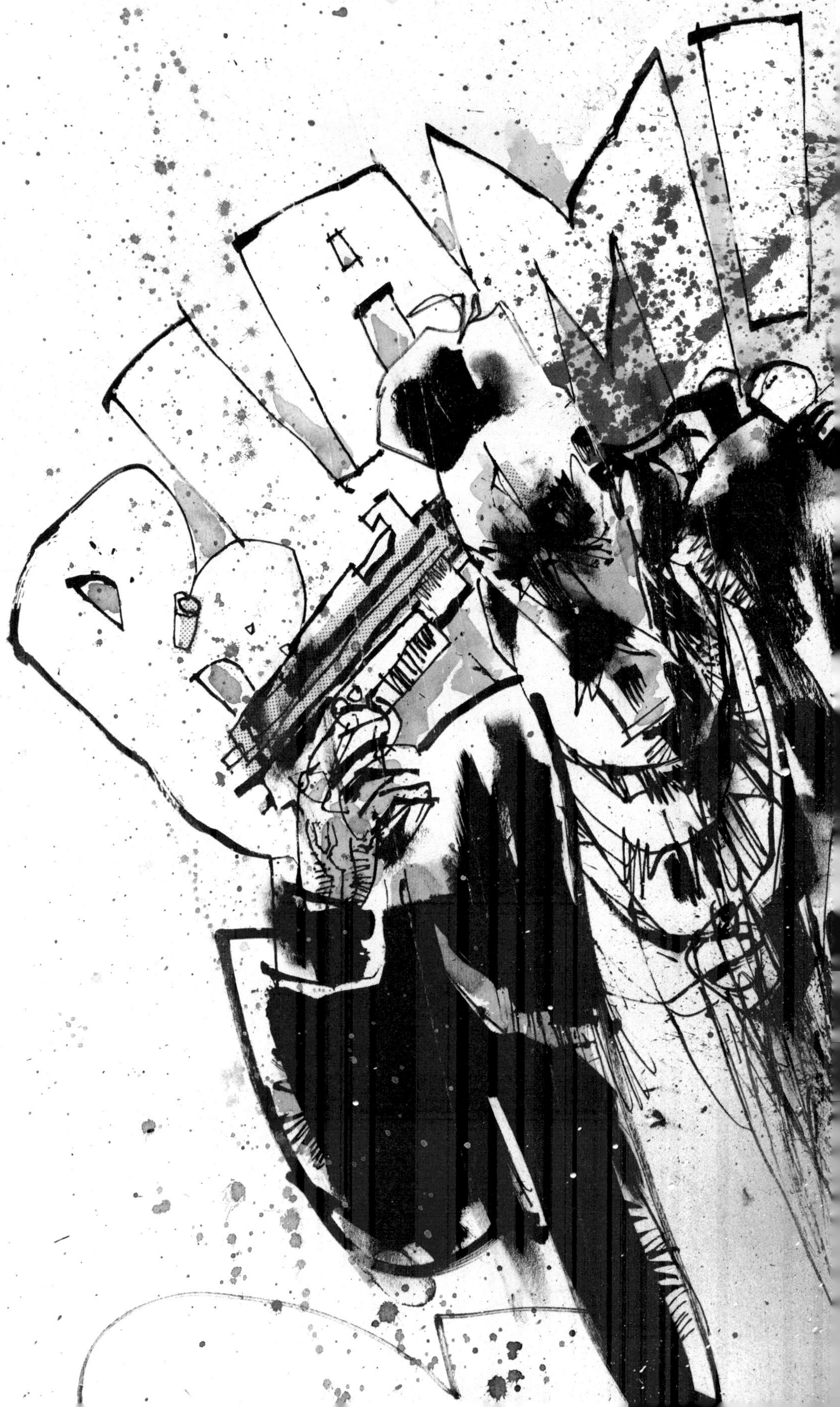

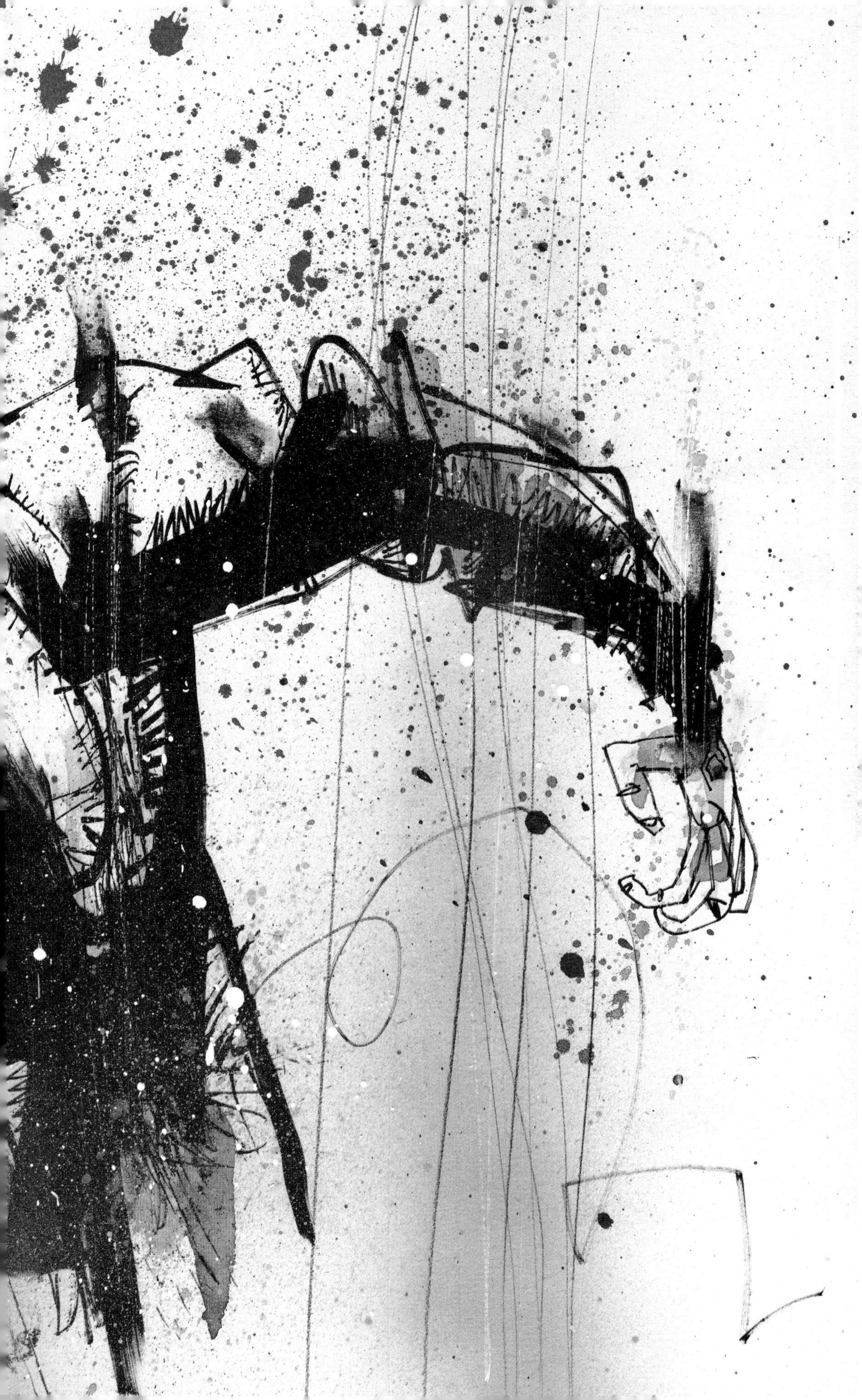

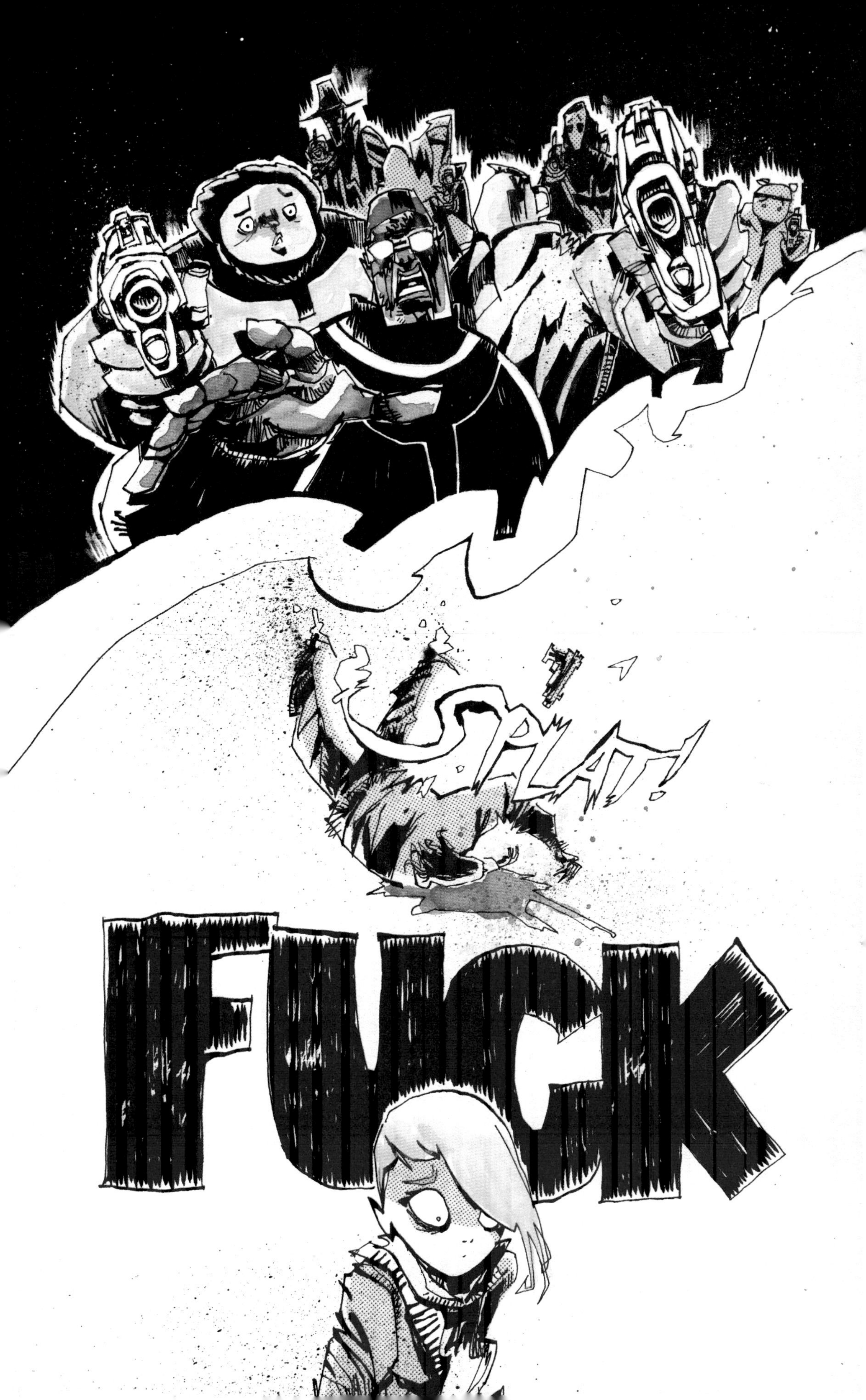
SPLAT!
FUCK

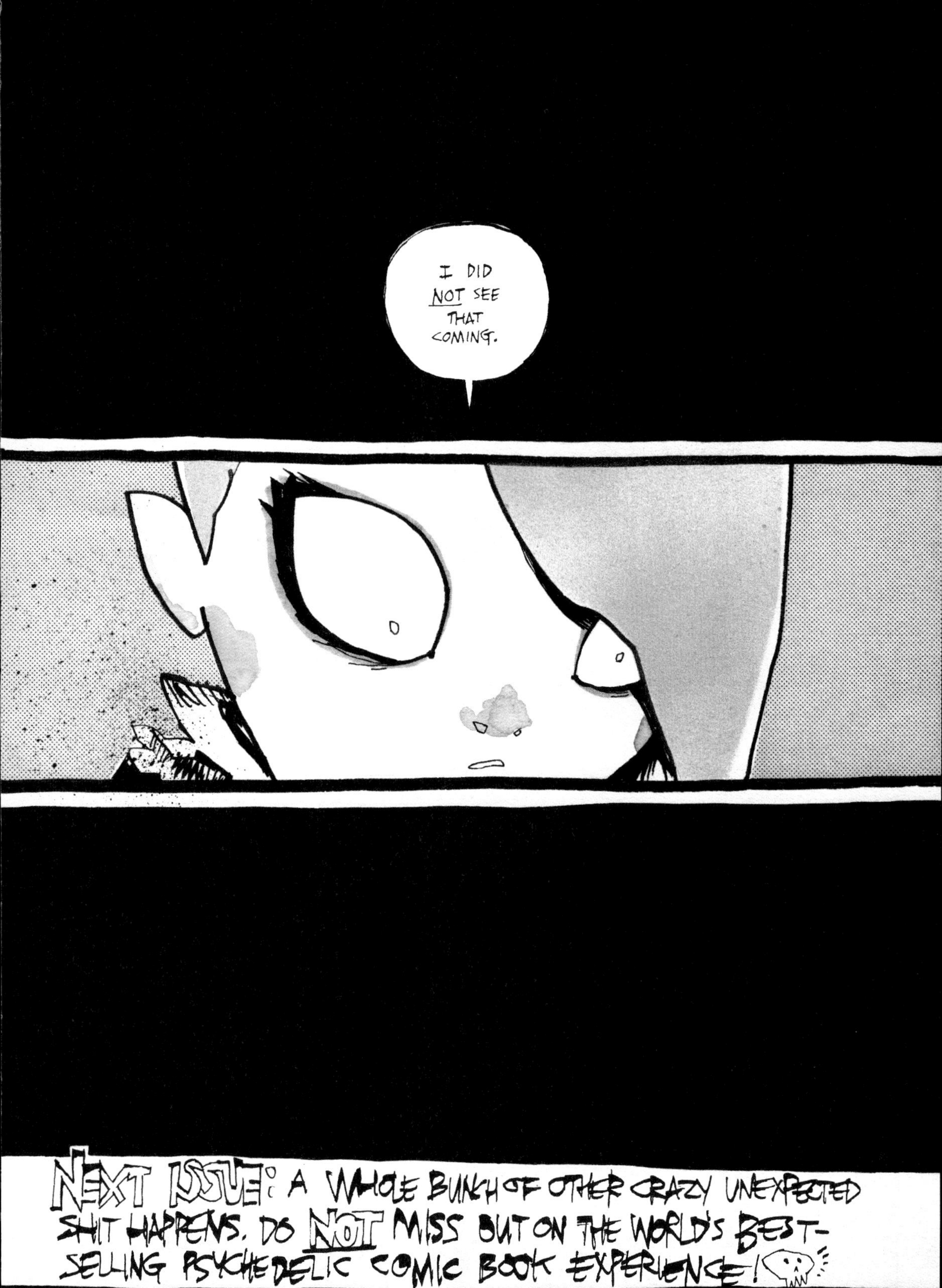
I DID NOT SEE THAT COMING.
NEXT ISSUE: A WHOLE BUNCH OF OTHER CRAZY UNEXPECTED SHIT HAPPENS. DO NOT MISS OUT ON THE WORLD'S BEST-SELLING PSYCHEDELIC COMIC BOOK EXPERIENCE!

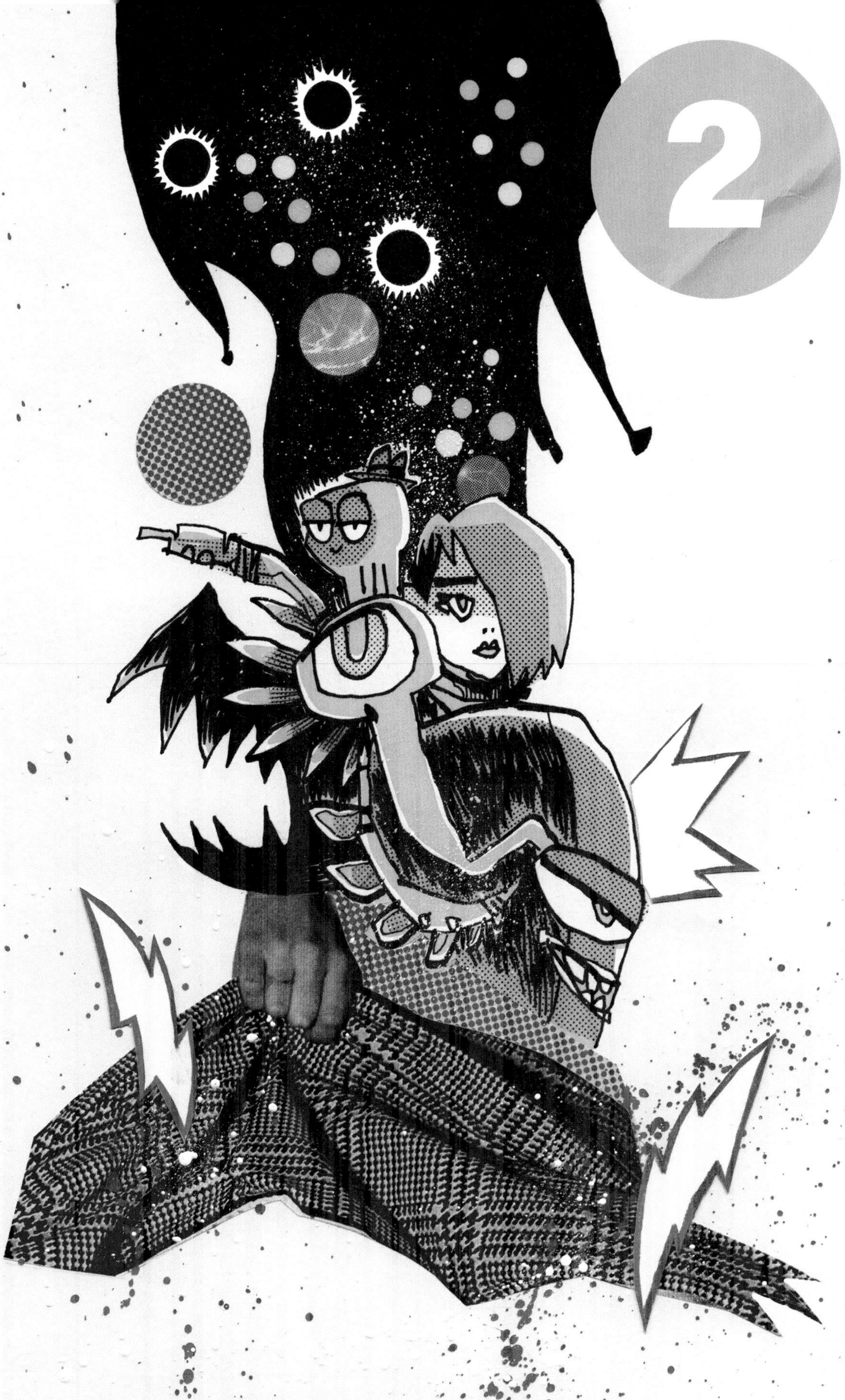
2

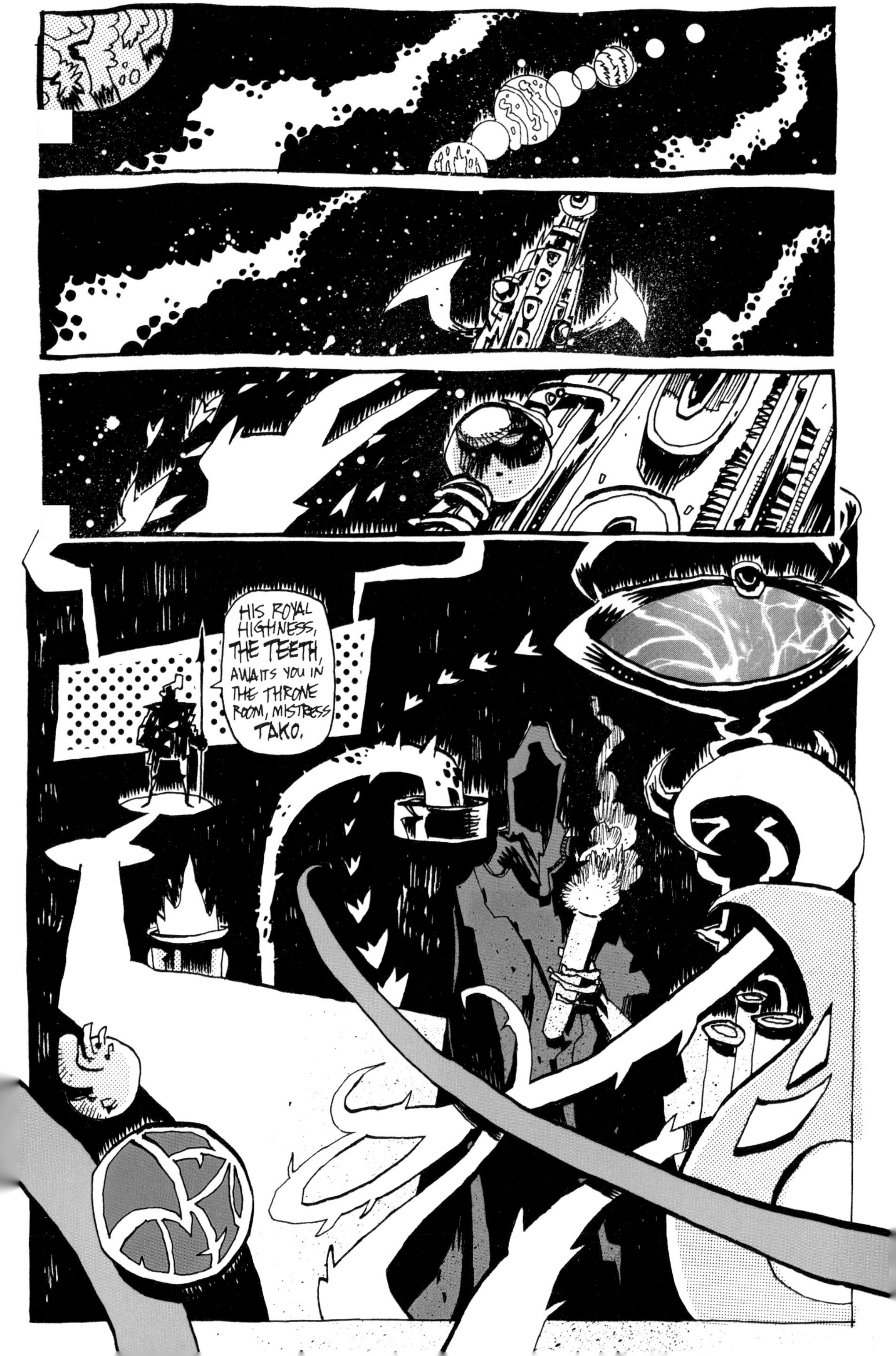
HIS ROYAL HIGHNESS, THE TEETH, AWAITS YOU IN THE THRONE ROOM, MISTRESS TAKO.

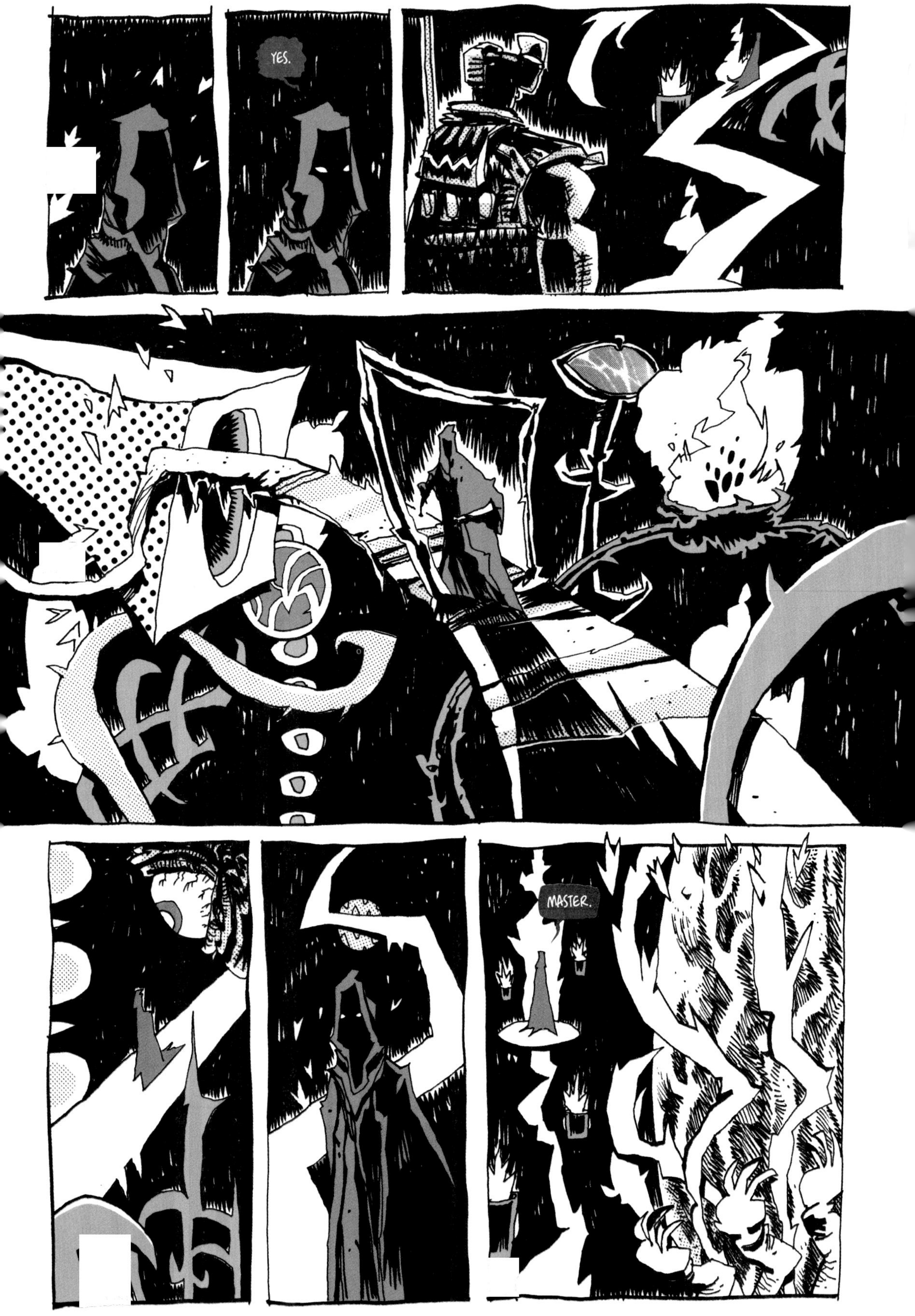
YES.
MASTER.

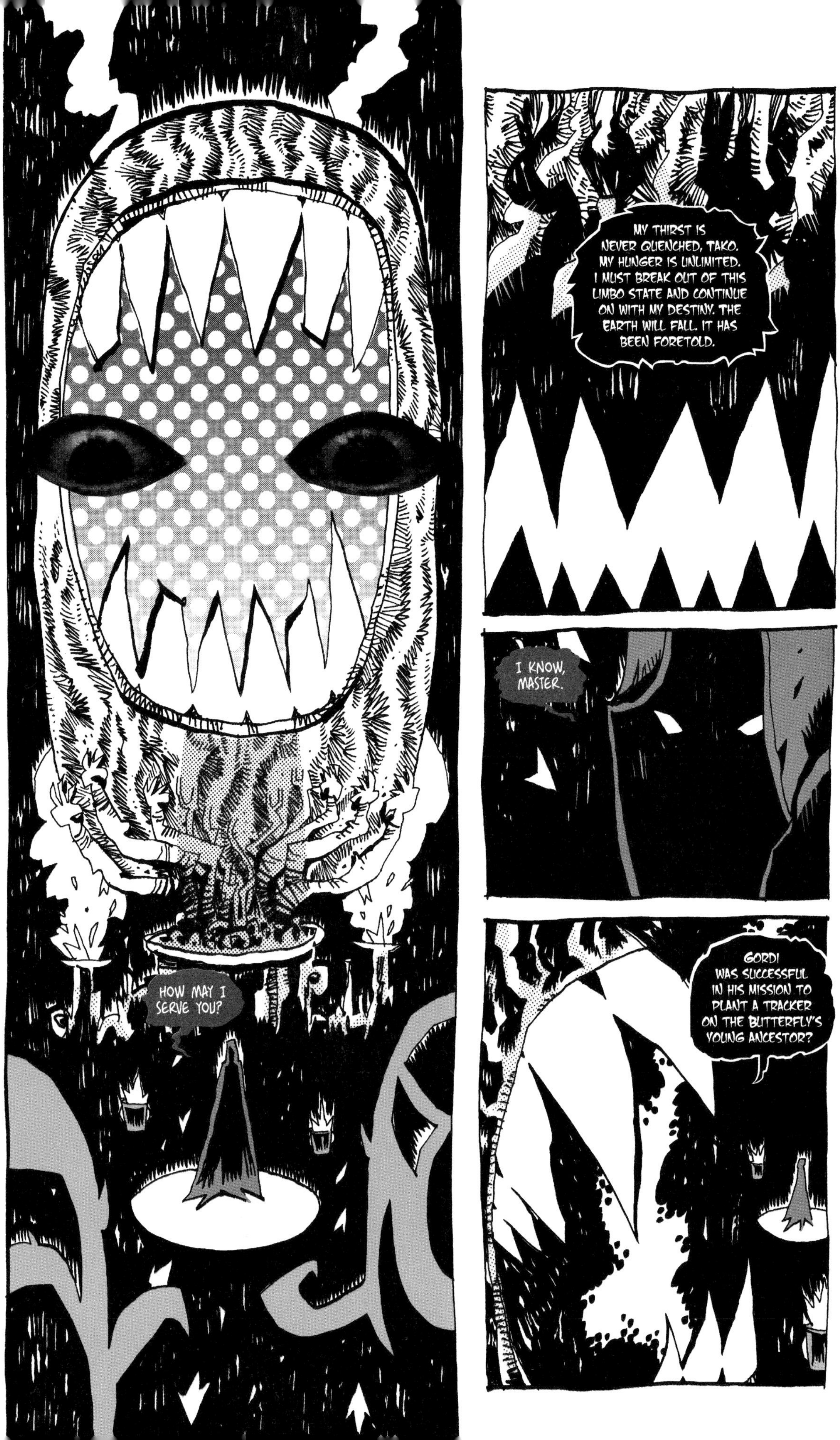
HOW MAY I SERVE YOU?
MY THIRST IS NEVER QUENCHED, TAKO. MY HUNGER IS UNLIMITED. I MUST BREAK OUT OF THIS LIMBO STATE AND CONTINUE ON WITH MY DESTINY. THE EARTH WILL FALL. IT HAS BEEN FORETOLD.
I KNOW, MASTER.
GORDI WAS SUCCESSFUL IN HIS MISSION TO PLANT A TRACKER ON THE BUTTERFLY'S YOUNG ANCESTOR?

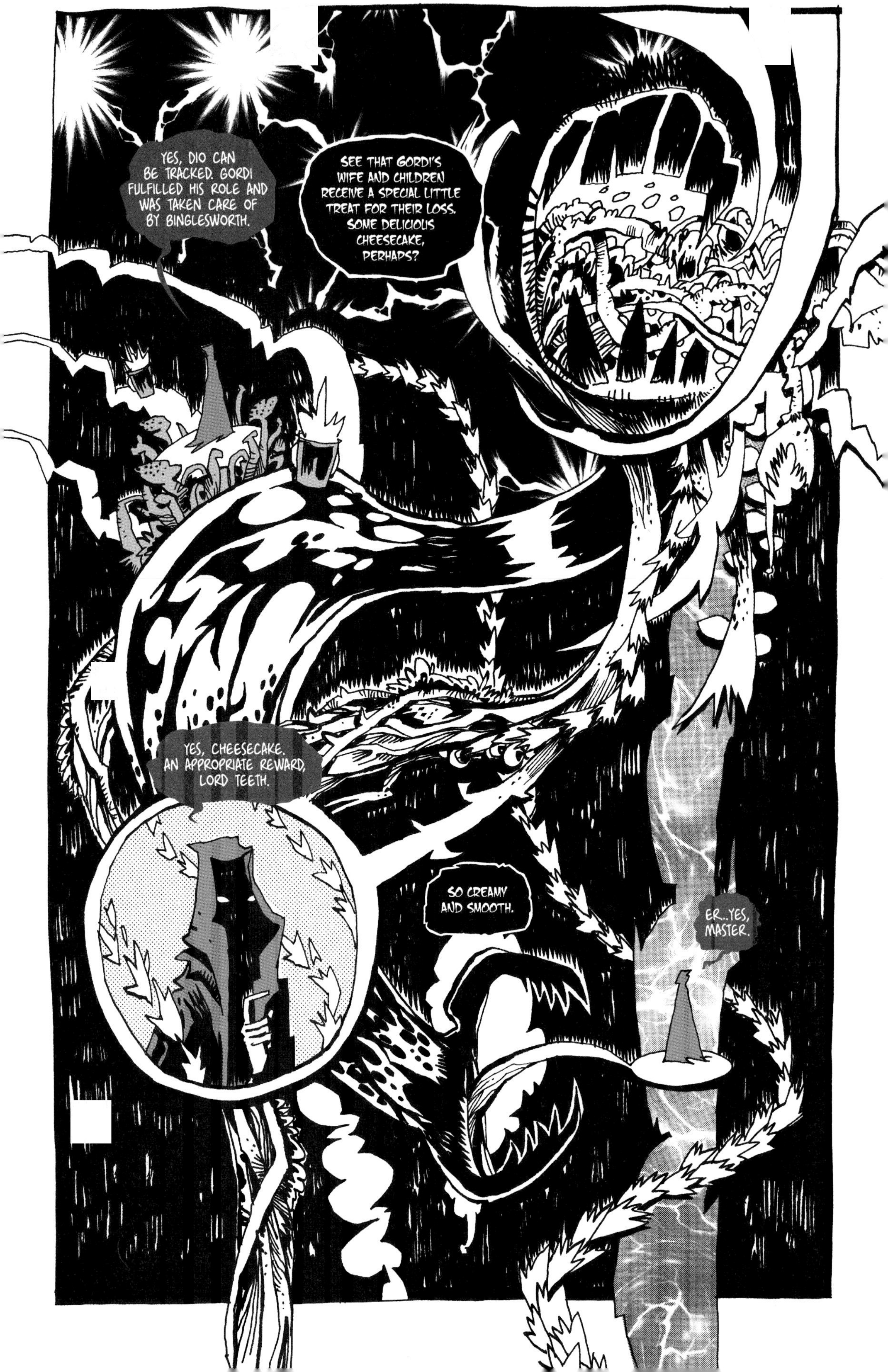
YES, DIO CAN BE TRACKED. GORDI FULFILLED HIS ROLE AND WAS TAKEN CARE OF BY BINGLESWORTH.
SEE THAT GORDI'S WIFE AND CHILDREN RECEIVE A SPECIAL LITTLE TREAT FOR THEIR LOSS. SOME DELICIOUS CHEESECAKE, PERHAPS?
YES, CHEESECAKE. AN APPROPRIATE REWARD, LORD TEETH.
SO CREAMY AND SMOOTH.
ER...YES, MASTER.

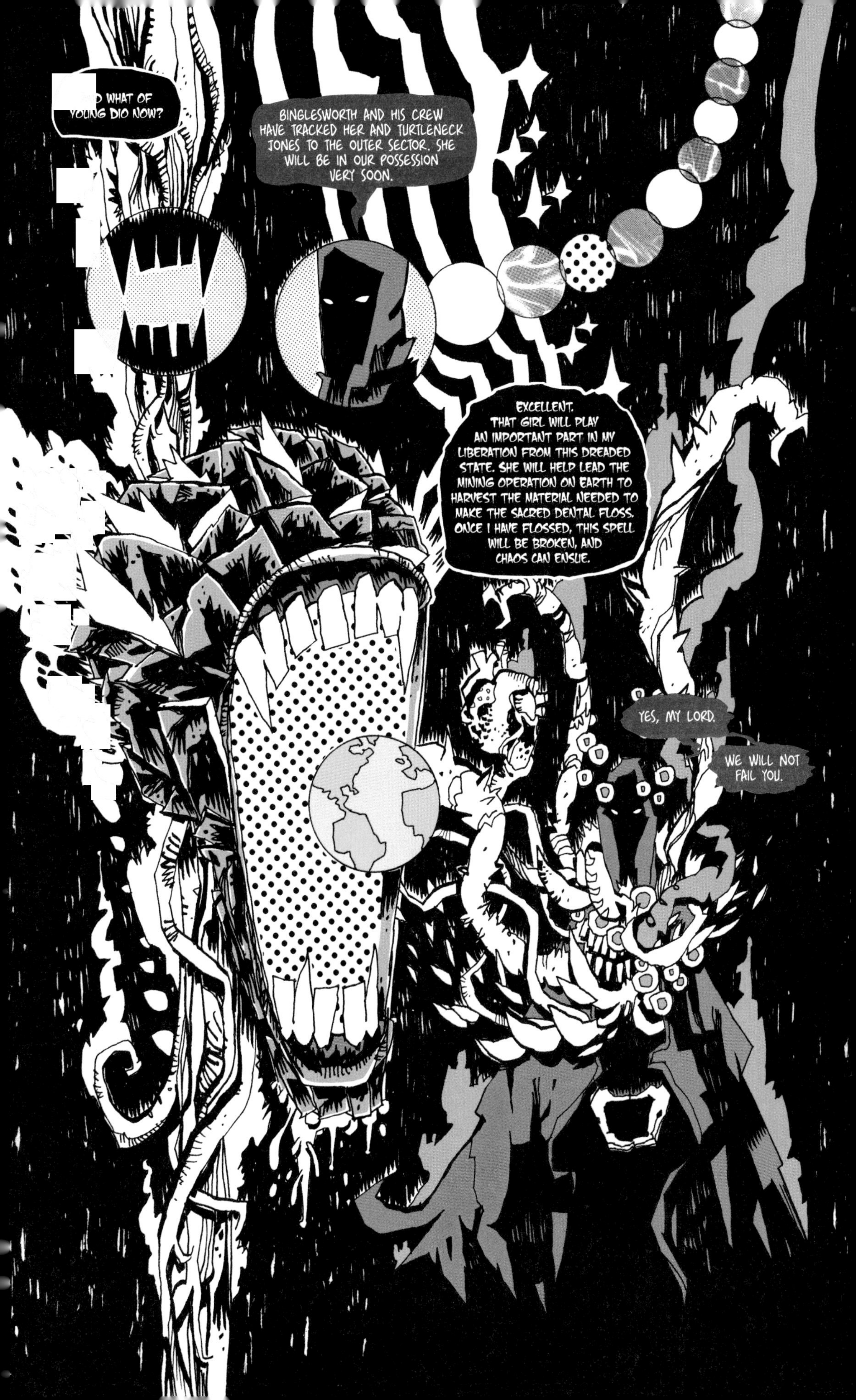

WHAT OF YOUNG DIO NOW?
BINGLESWORTH AND HIS CREW HAVE TRACKED HER AND TURTLENECK JONES TO THE OUTER SECTOR. SHE WILL BE IN OUR POSSESSION VERY SOON.
EXCELLENT. THAT GIRL WILL PLAY AN IMPORTANT PART IN MY LIBERATION FROM THIS DREADED STATE. SHE WILL HELP LEAD THE MINING OPERATION ON EARTH TO HARVEST THE MATERIAL NEEDED TO MAKE THE SACRED DENTAL FLOSS. ONCE I HAVE FLOSSED, THIS SPELL WILL BE BROKEN, AND CHAOS CAN ENSUE.
YES, MY LORD.
WE WILL NOT FAIL YOU.

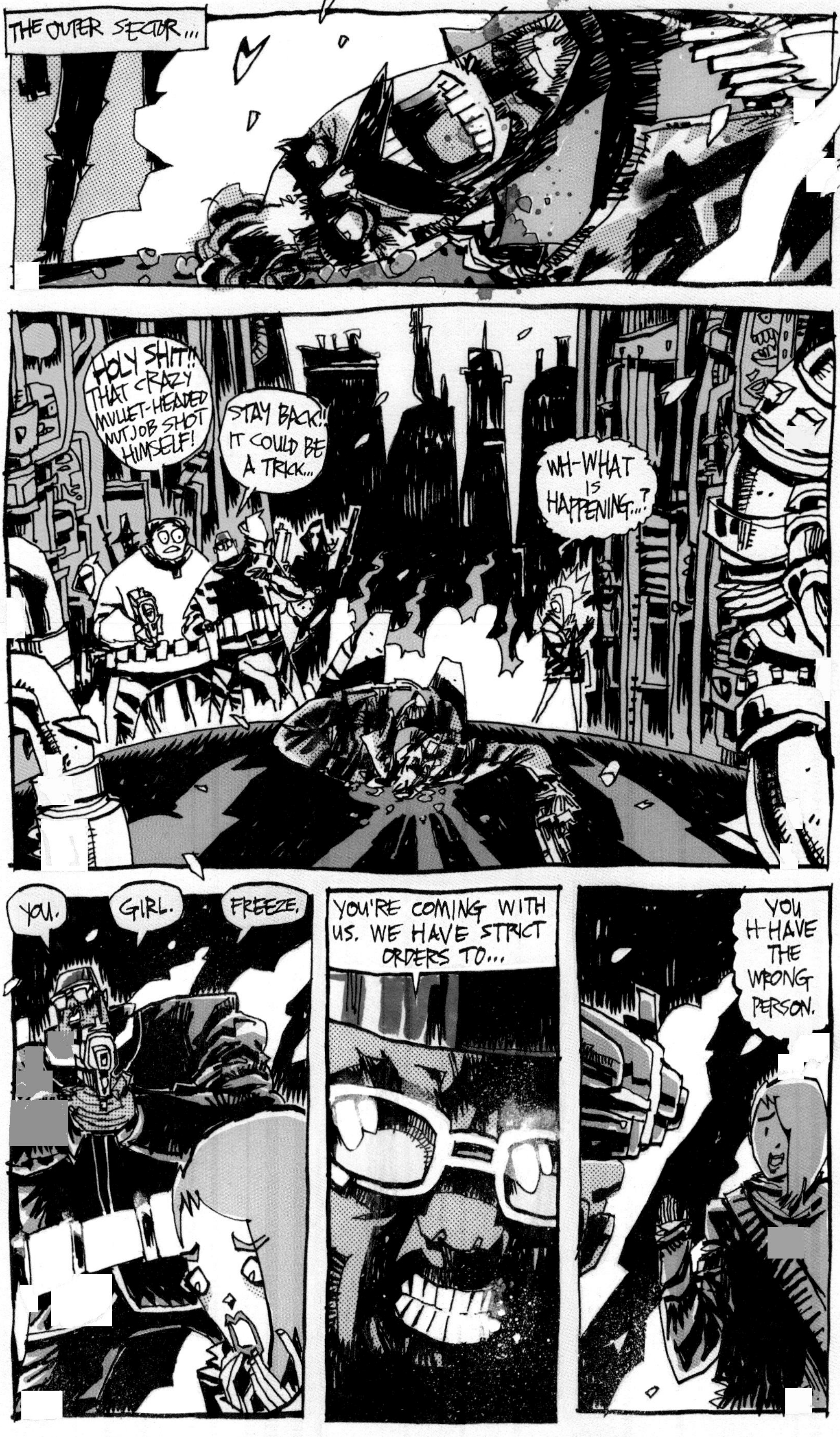
THE OUTER SECTOR...
HOLY SHIT!! THAT CRAZY MULLET-HEADED NUTJOB SHOT HIMSELF!
STAY BACK!! IT COULD BE A TRICK...
WH-WHAT IS HAPPENING...?
YOU.
GIRL.
FREEZE.
YOU'RE COMING WITH US. WE HAVE STRICT ORDERS TO...
YOU H-HAVE THE WRONG PERSON.

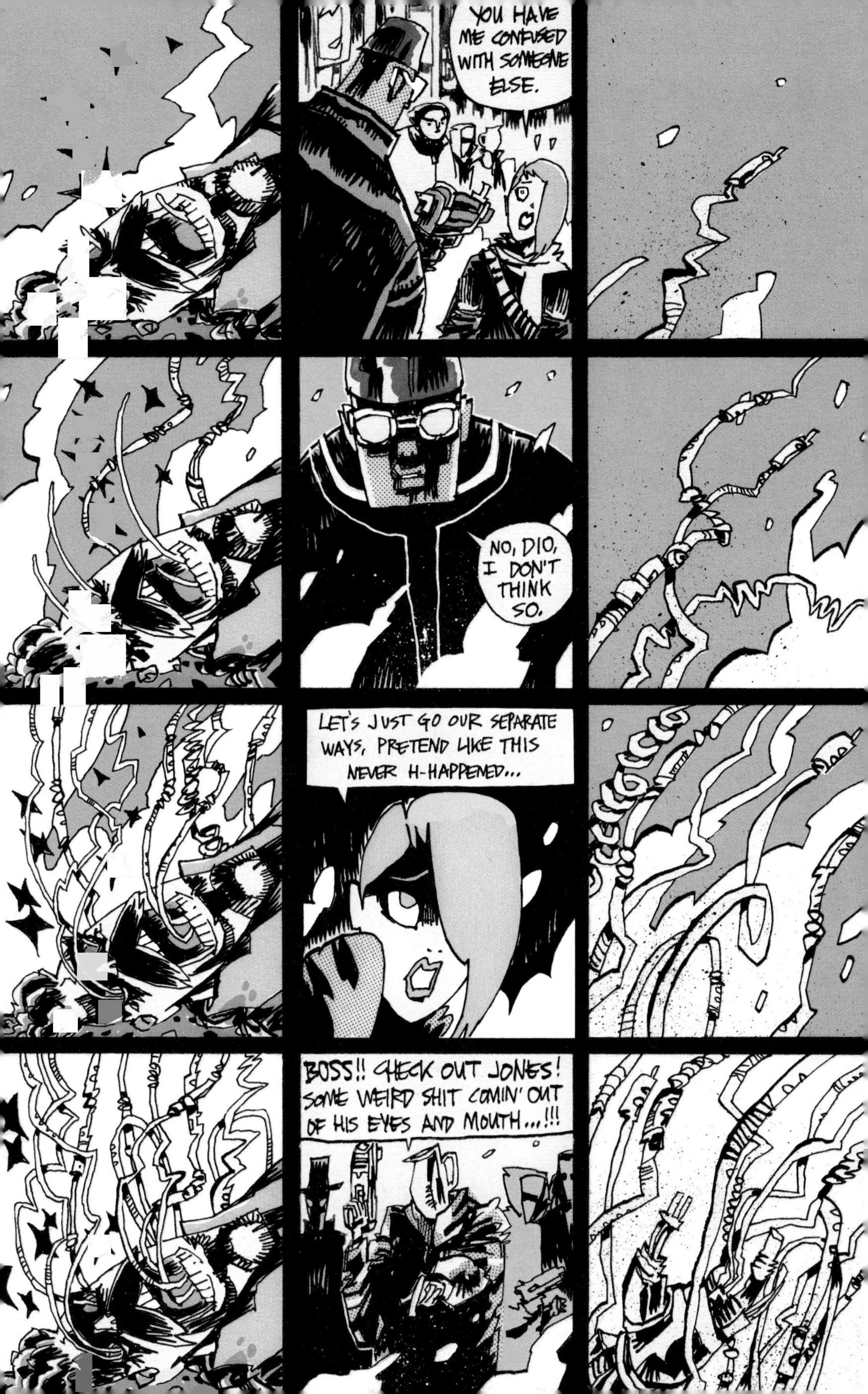
YOU HAVE ME CONFUSED WITH SOMEONE ELSE.
NO, DIO, I DON'T THINK SO.
LET'S JUST GO OUR SEPARATE WAYS, PRETEND LIKE THIS NEVER H-HAPPENED...
BOSS!! CHECK OUT JONES! SOME WEIRD SHIT COMIN' OUT OF HIS EYES AND MOUTH...!!!

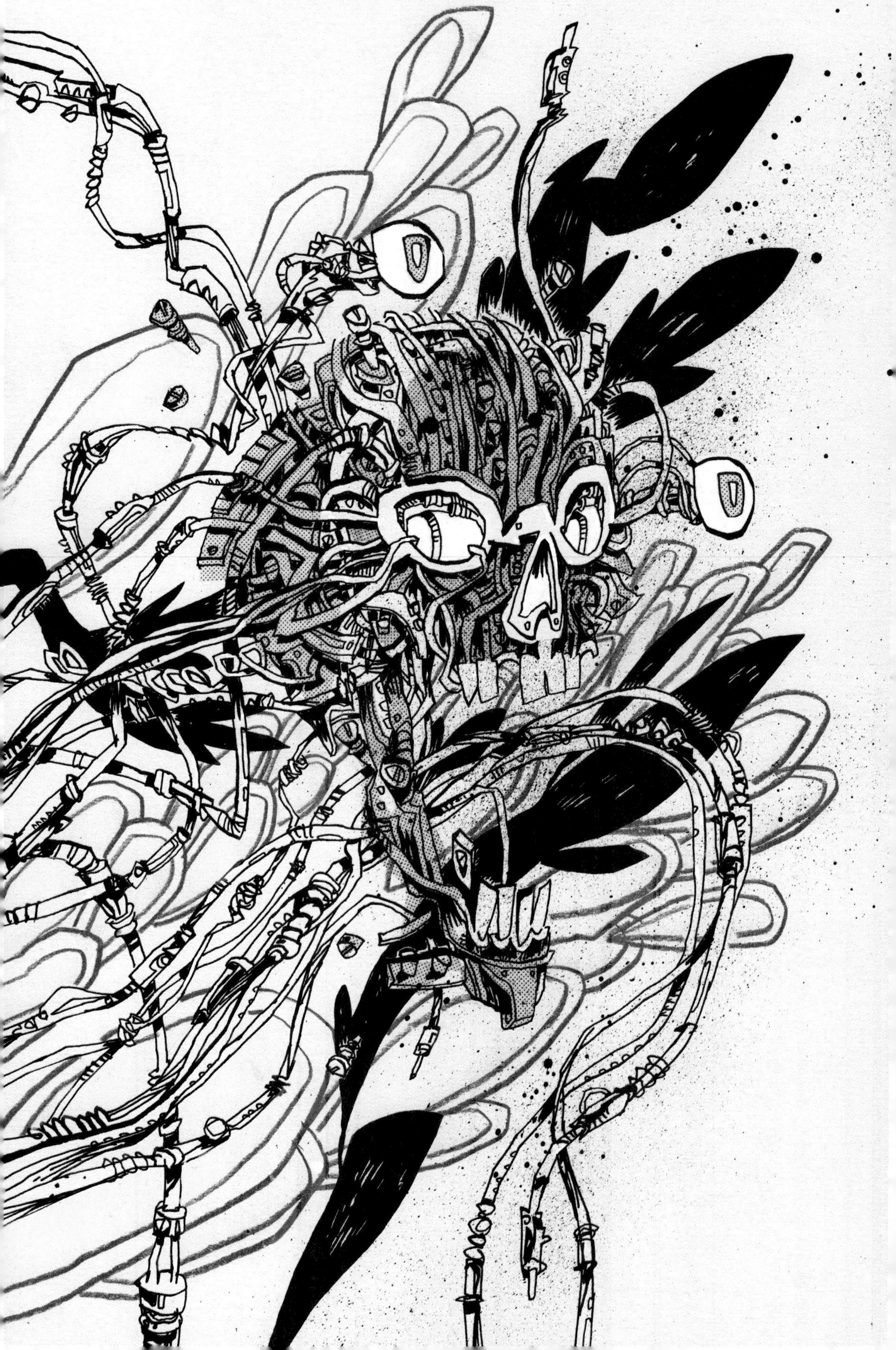

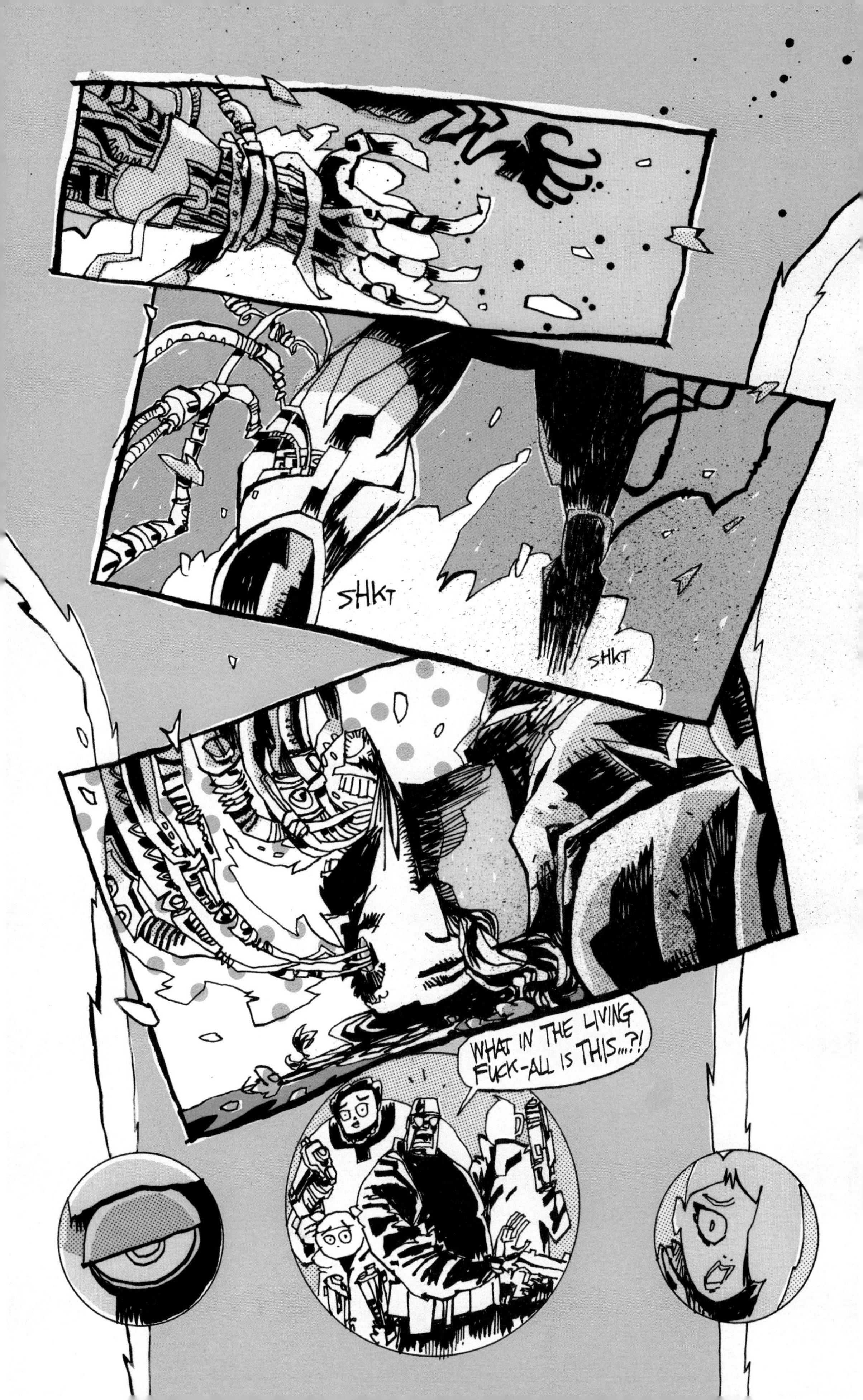
SHKT
SHKT
WHAT IN THE LIVING FUCK-ALL IS THIS...?!

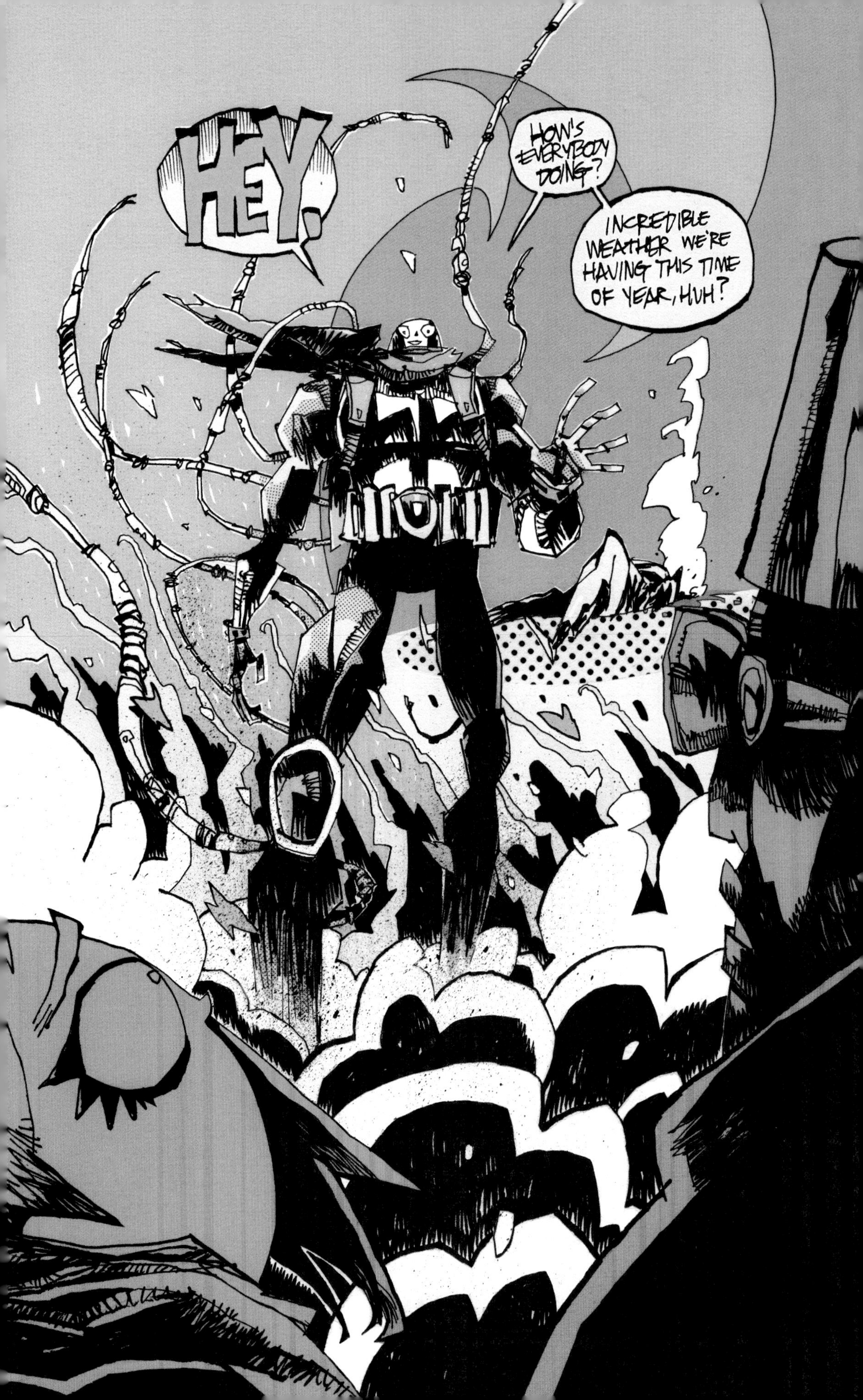
HEY.
HOW'S EVERYBODY DOING?
INCREDIBLE WEATHER WE'RE HAVING THIS TIME OF YEAR, HUH?

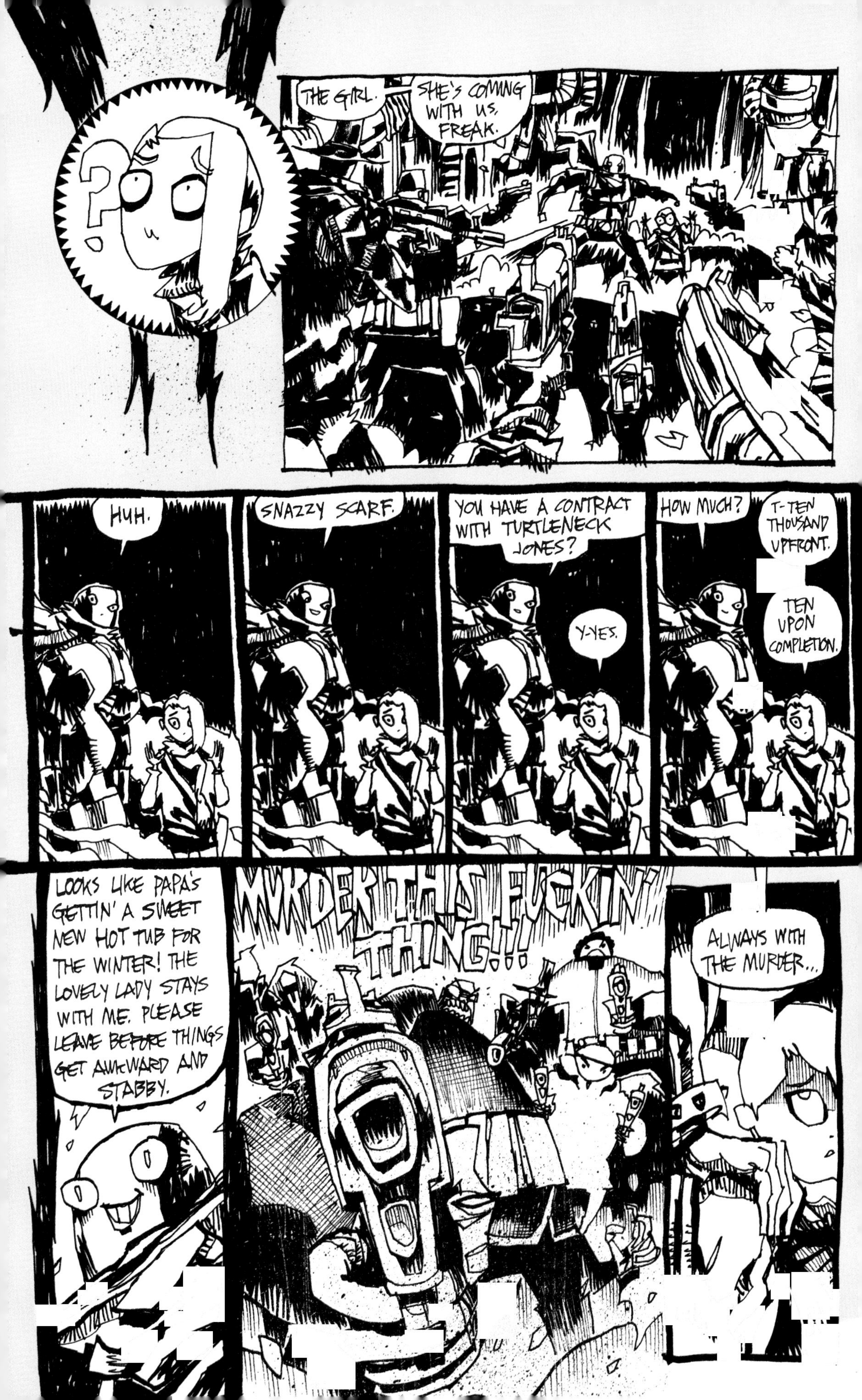
THE GIRL.
SHE'S COMING WITH US, FREAK.
HUH.
SNAZZY SCARF.
YOU HAVE A CONTRACT WITH TURTLENECK JONES?
Y-YES.
HOW MUCH?
T-TEN THOUSAND UPFRONT.
TEN UPON COMPLETION.
LOOKS LIKE PAPA'S GETTIN' A SWEET NEW HOT TUB FOR THE WINTER! THE LOVELY LADY STAYS WITH ME. PLEASE LEAVE BEFORE THINGS GET AWKWARD AND STABBY.
MURDER THIS FUCKIN' THING!!!
ALWAYS WITH THE MURDER...

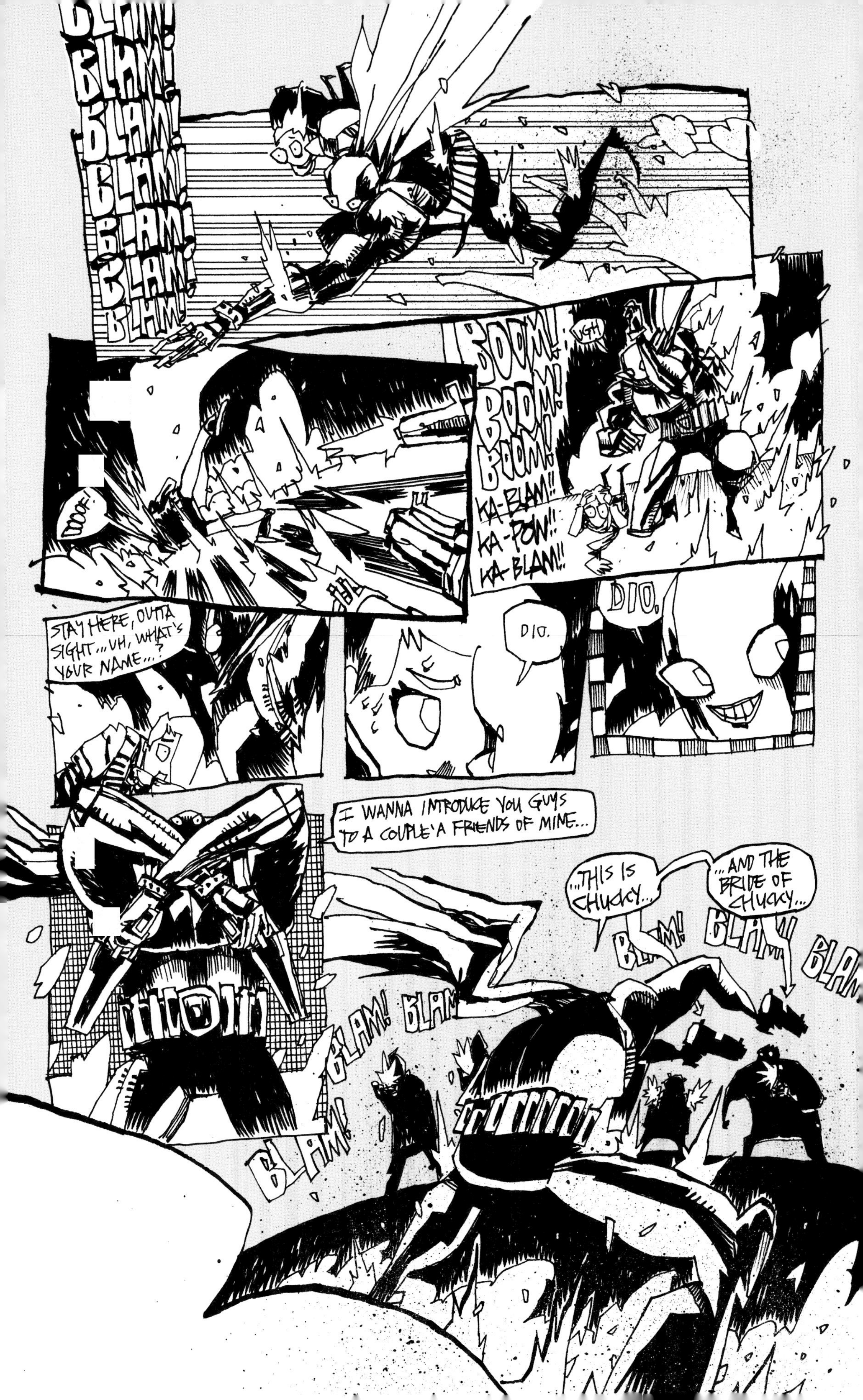
BLAM!
BLAM!
BLAM!
BLAM!
BLAM!
BLAM!
BLAM!
OOOF!
BOOM!
BOOM!
BOOM!
UGH
KA-BLAM!!
KA-POW!!
KA-BLAM!!
STAY HERE, OUTTA SIGHT... UH, WHAT'S YOUR NAME...?
DIO.
DIO.
I WANNA INTRODUCE YOU GUYS TO A COUPLE'A FRIENDS OF MINE...
...THIS IS CHUCKY...
...AND THE BRIDE OF CHUCKY...
BLAM! BLAM!
BLAM!

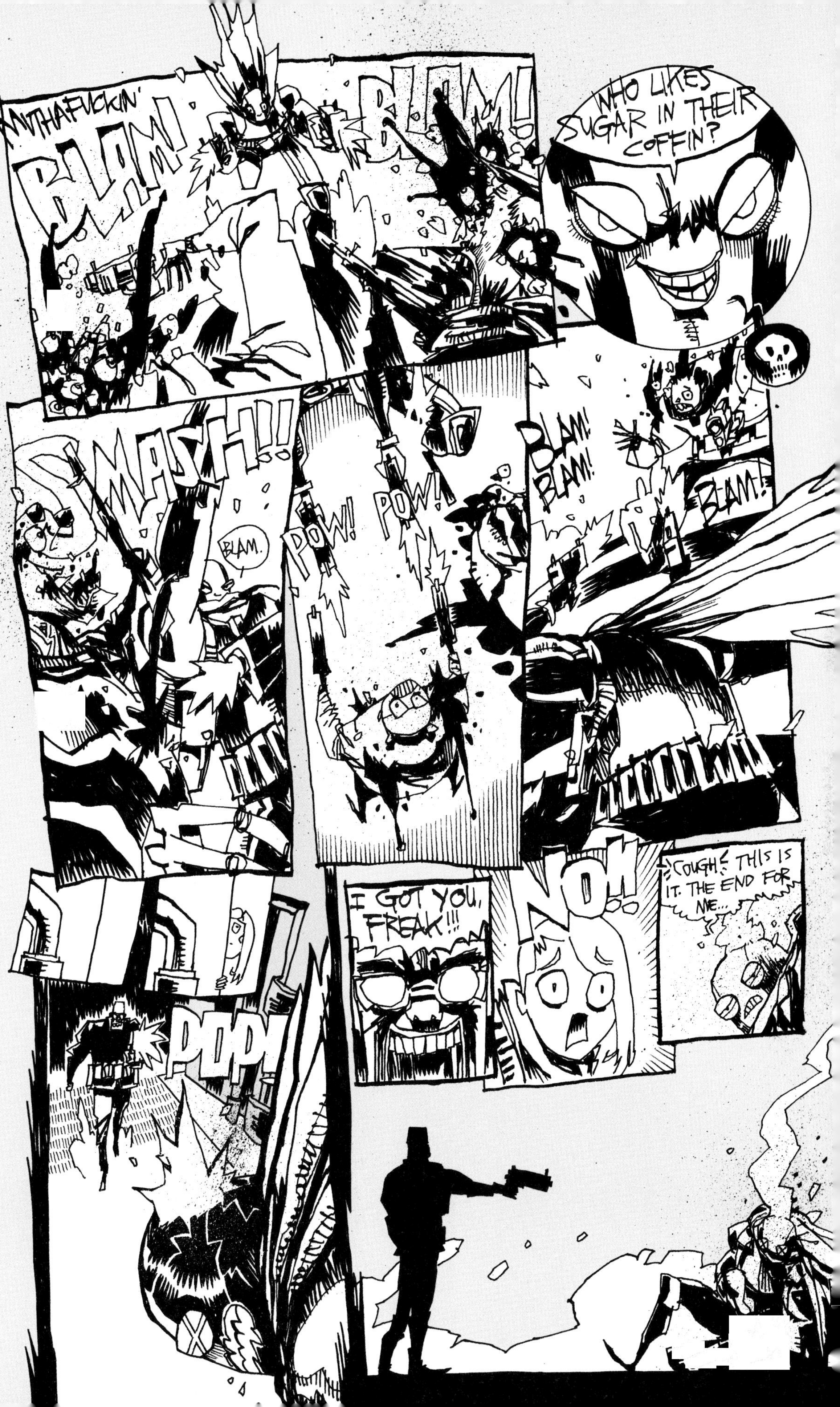

MUTHAFUCKIN'
BLAM!
BLAM!
WHO LIKES SUGAR IN THEIR COFFIN?
SMASH!!
BLAM.
POW! POW!
BLAM! BLAM!
BLAM!
I GOT YOU, FREAK!!!
NO!!
COUGH! THIS IS IT. THE END FOR ME...
POP!

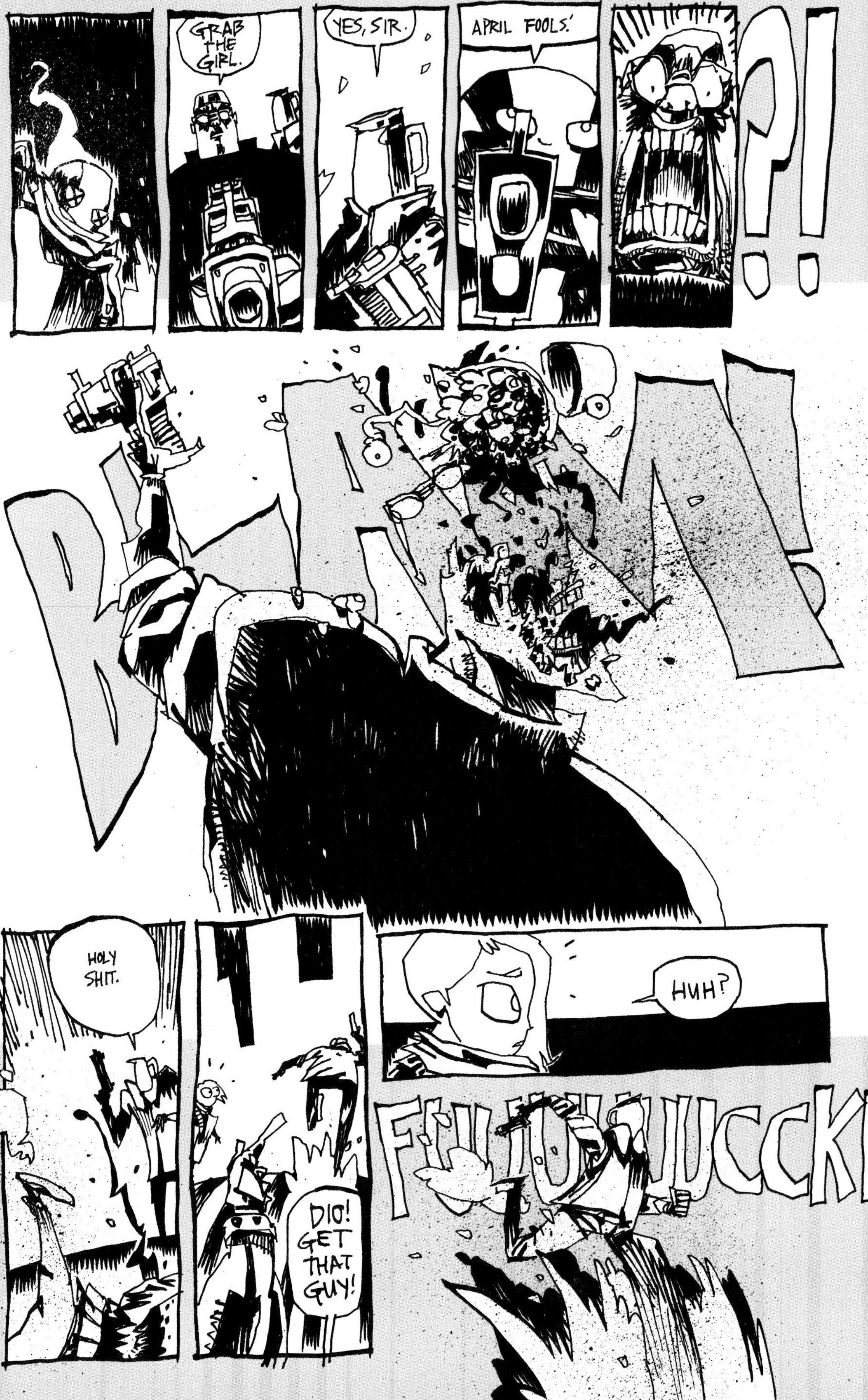
GRAB THE GIRL.
YES, SIR.
APRIL FOOLS!
?!
BLAM!
HOLY SHIT.
DIO! GET THAT GUY!
HUH?

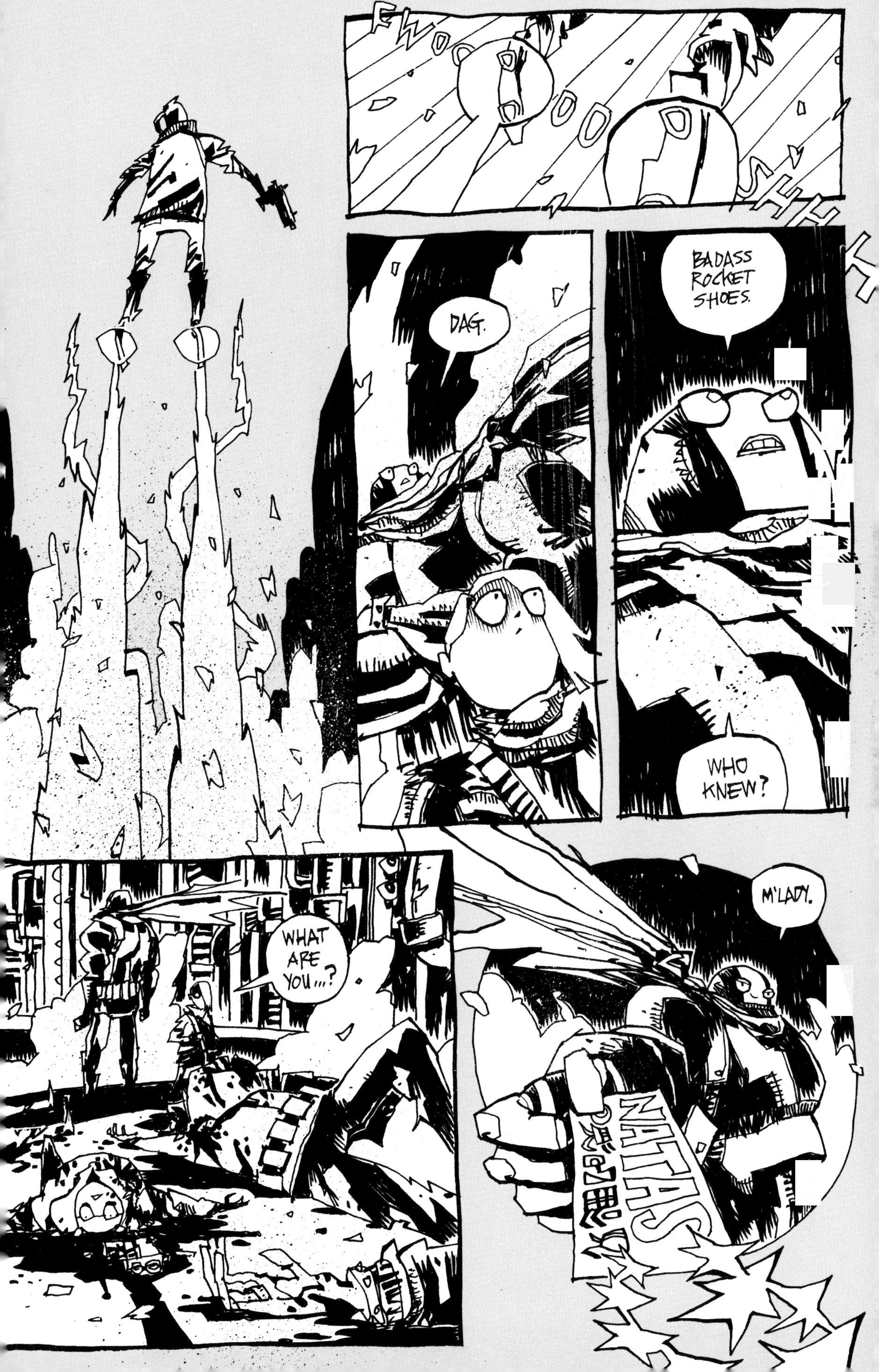
FWOOOOOOSHHK
DAG.
BADASS ROCKET SHOES.
WHO KNEW?
WHAT ARE YOU...?
M'LADY.
NATAS

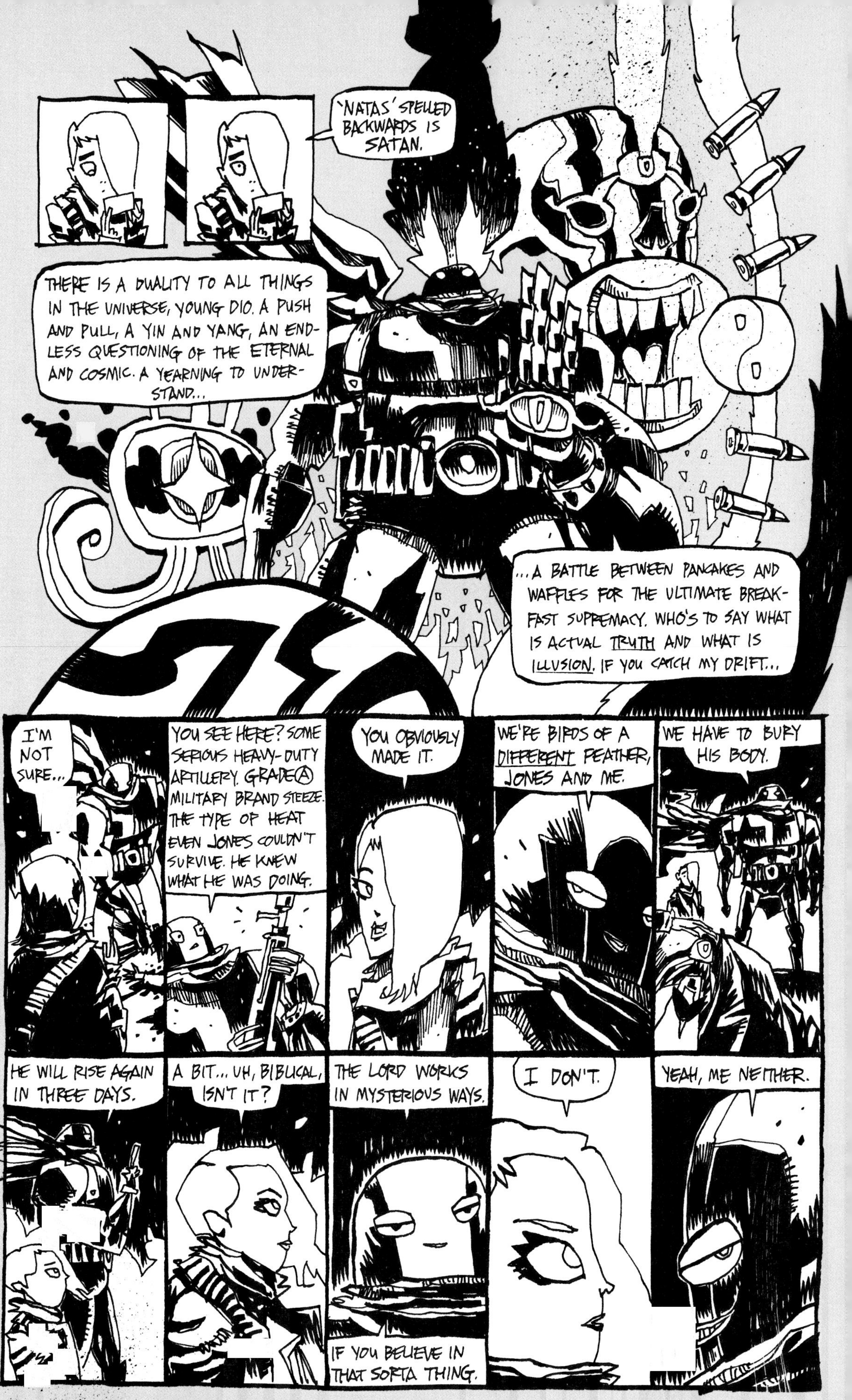

`NATAS' SPELLED BACKWARDS IS SATAN.
THERE IS A DUALITY TO ALL THINGS IN THE UNIVERSE, YOUNG DIO. A PUSH AND PULL, A YIN AND YANG, AN ENDLESS QUESTIONING OF THE ETERNAL AND COSMIC. A YEARNING TO UNDERSTAND...
...A BATTLE BETWEEN PANCAKES AND WAFFLES FOR THE ULTIMATE BREAKFAST SUPREMACY. WHO'S TO SAY WHAT IS ACTUAL TRUTH AND WHAT IS ILLUSION. IF YOU CATCH MY DRIFT...
I'M NOT SURE...
YOU SEE HERE? SOME SERIOUS HEAVY-DUTY ARTILLERY. GRADE Ⓐ MILITARY BRAND STEEZE. THE TYPE OF HEAT EVEN JONES COULDN'T SURVIVE. HE KNEW WHAT HE WAS DOING.
YOU OBVIOUSLY MADE IT.
WE'RE BIRDS OF A DIFFERENT FEATHER, JONES AND ME.
WE HAVE TO BURY HIS BODY.
HE WILL RISE AGAIN IN THREE DAYS.
A BIT... UH, BIBLICAL, ISN'T IT?
THE LORD WORKS IN MYSTERIOUS WAYS.
IF YOU BELIEVE IN THAT SORTA THING.
I DON'T.
YEAH, ME NEITHER.

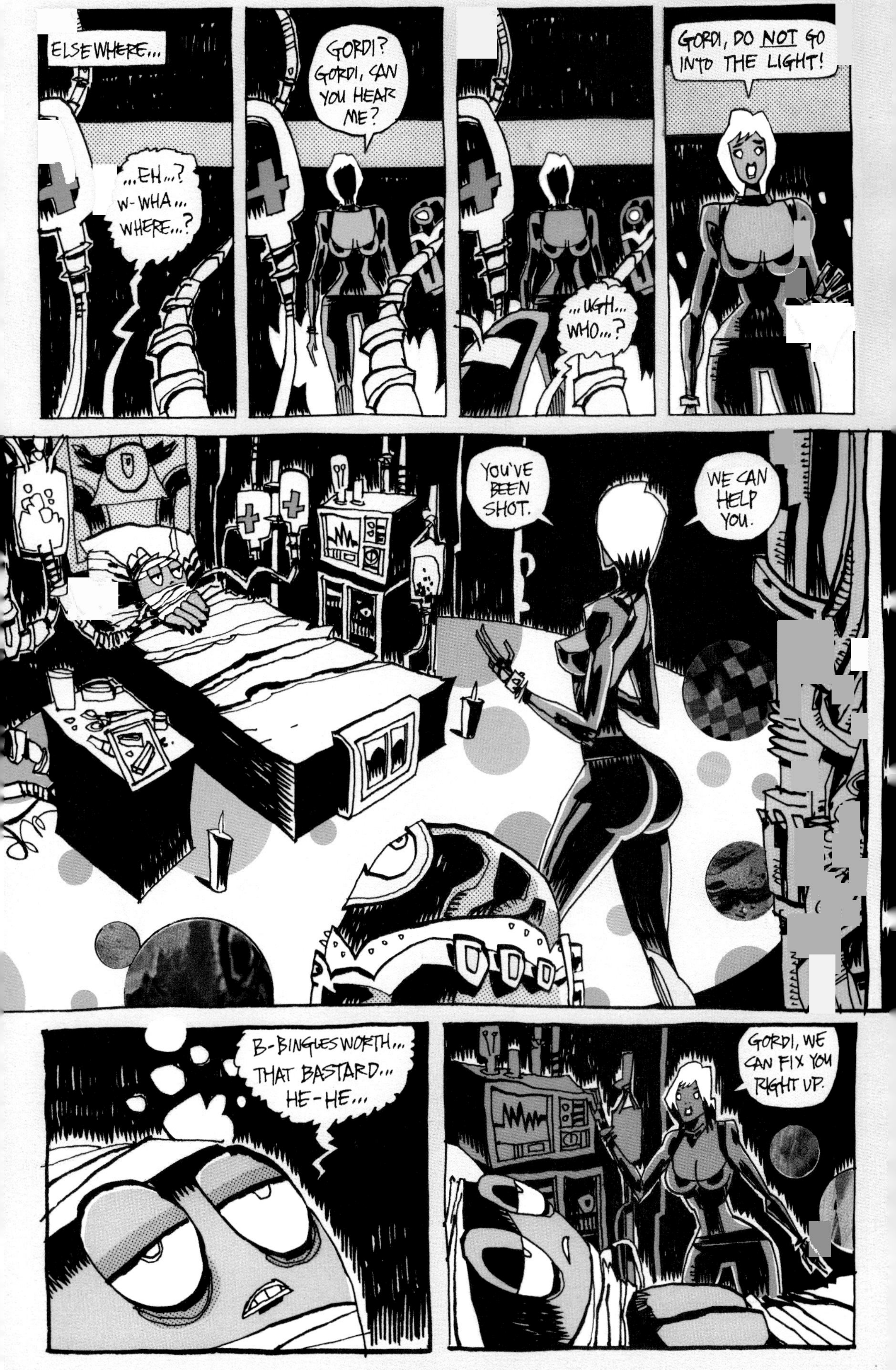
ELSEWHERE...
...EH...? W-WHA... WHERE...?
GORDI? GORDI, CAN YOU HEAR ME?
...UGH... WHO...?
GORDI, DO NOT GO INTO THE LIGHT!
YOU'VE BEEN SHOT.
WE CAN HELP YOU.
B-BINGLESWORTH... THAT BASTARD... HE-HE...
GORDI, WE CAN FIX YOU RIGHT UP.

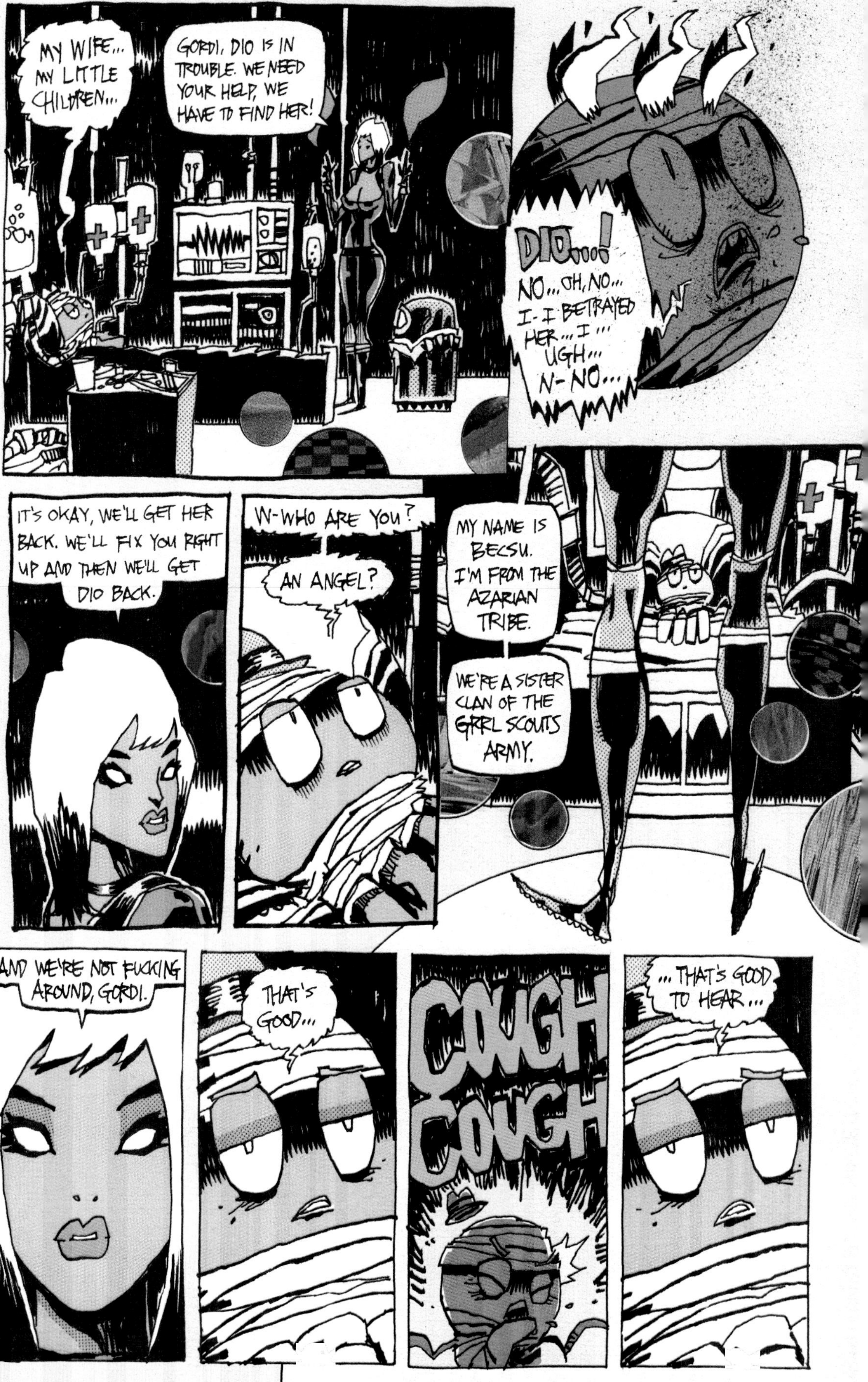
MY WIFE... MY LITTLE CHILDREN...
GORDI, DIO IS IN TROUBLE. WE NEED YOUR HELP, WE HAVE TO FIND HER!
DIO...!
NO... OH, NO... I-I BETRAYED HER... I... UGH... N-NO...
IT'S OKAY, WE'LL GET HER BACK. WE'LL FIX YOU RIGHT UP AND THEN WE'LL GET DIO BACK.
W-WHO ARE YOU?
AN ANGEL?
MY NAME IS BECSU. I'M FROM THE AZARIAN TRIBE.
WE'RE A SISTER CLAN OF THE GRRL SCOUTS ARMY.
AND WE'RE NOT FUCKING AROUND, GORDI.
THAT'S GOOD...
COUGH
COUGH
...THAT'S GOOD TO HEAR...

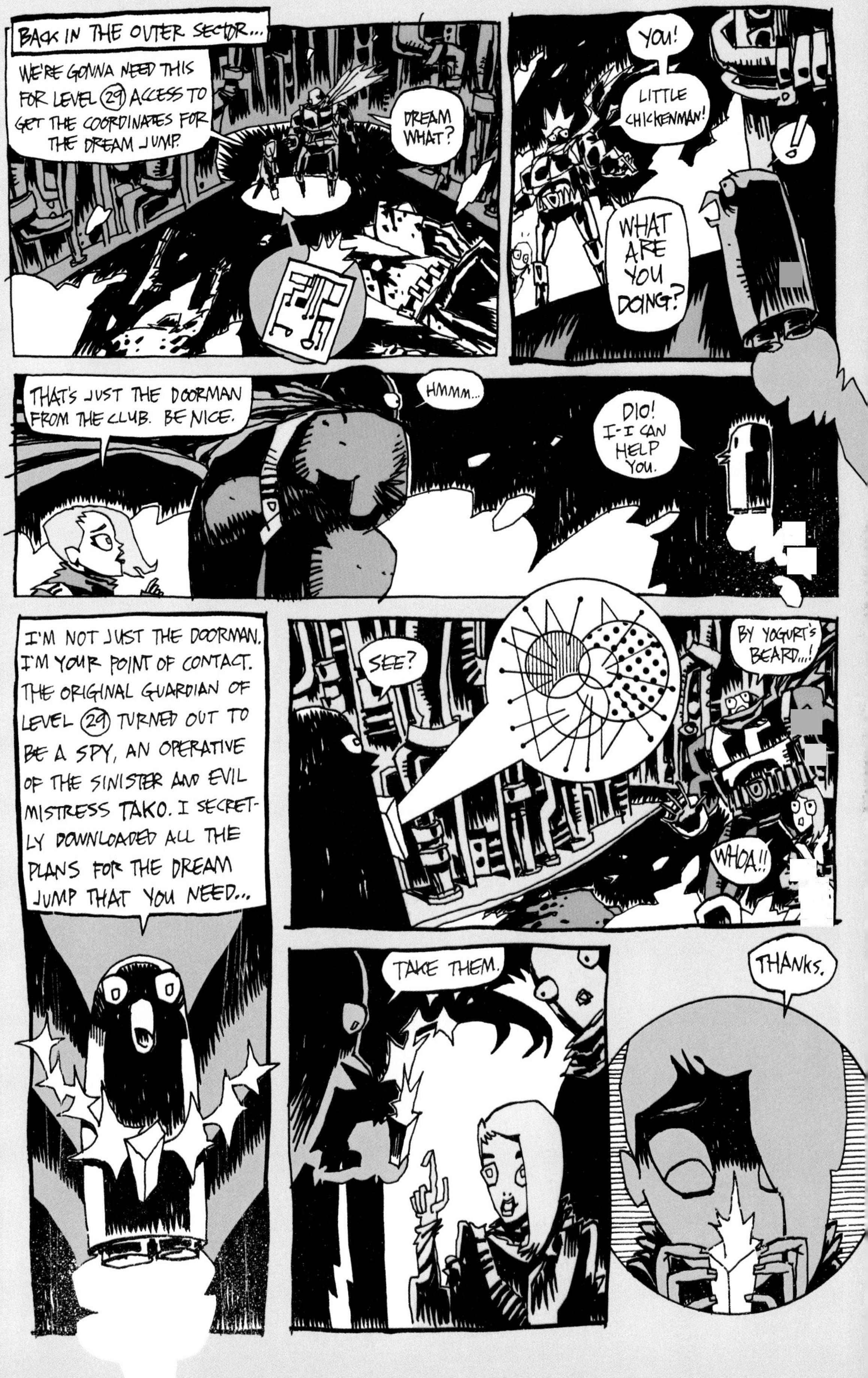
BACK IN THE OUTER SECTOR...
WE'RE GONNA NEED THIS FOR LEVEL 29 ACCESS TO GET THE COORDINATES FOR THE DREAM JUMP.
DREAM WHAT?
YOU!
LITTLE CHICKENMAN!
!
WHAT ARE YOU DOING?
THAT'S JUST THE DOORMAN FROM THE CLUB. BE NICE.
HMMM...
DIO! I-I CAN HELP YOU.
I'M NOT JUST THE DOORMAN. I'M YOUR POINT OF CONTACT. THE ORIGINAL GUARDIAN OF LEVEL 29 TURNED OUT TO BE A SPY, AN OPERATIVE OF THE SINISTER AND EVIL MISTRESS TAKO. I SECRETLY DOWNLOADED ALL THE PLANS FOR THE DREAM JUMP THAT YOU NEED...
SEE?
BY YOGURT'S BEARD...!
WHOA!!
TAKE THEM.
THANKS.

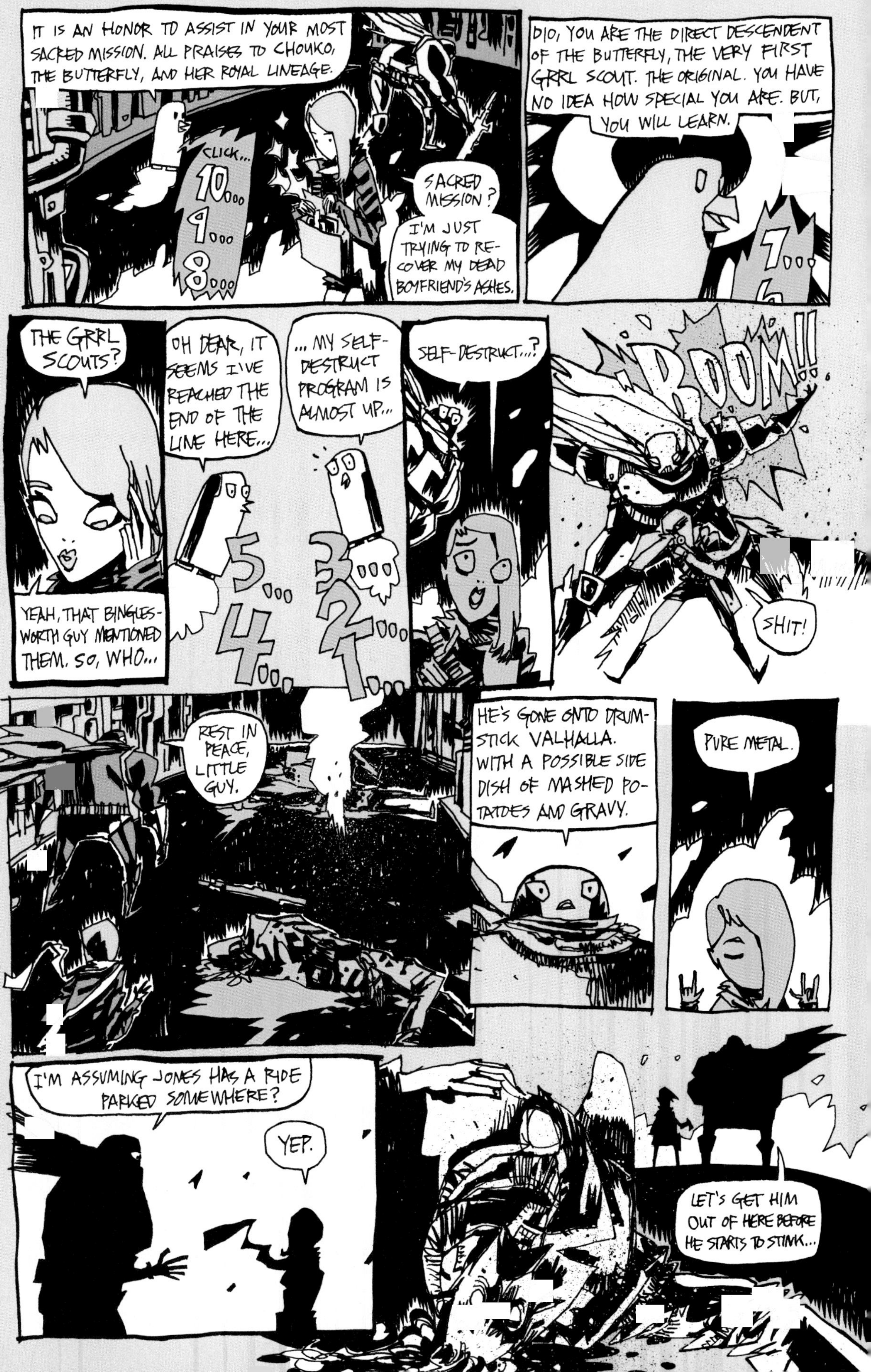
IT IS AN HONOR TO ASSIST IN YOUR MOST SACRED MISSION. ALL PRAISES TO CHOUKO, THE BUTTERFLY, AND HER ROYAL LINEAGE.
CLICK...
10...
9...
8...
SACRED MISSION?
I'M JUST TRYING TO RE-COVER MY DEAD BOYFRIEND'S ASHES.
DIO, YOU ARE THE DIRECT DESCENDENT OF THE BUTTERFLY, THE VERY FIRST GRRL SCOUT. THE ORIGINAL. YOU HAVE NO IDEA HOW SPECIAL YOU ARE. BUT, YOU WILL LEARN.
7...
THE GRRL SCOUTS?
YEAH, THAT BINGLES-WORTH GUY MENTIONED THEM. SO, WHO...
OH DEAR, IT SEEMS I'VE REACHED THE END OF THE LINE HERE...
5...
4...
...MY SELF-DESTRUCT PROGRAM IS ALMOST UP...
3...
2...
1...
SELF-DESTRUCT...?
BOOM!!
SHIT!
REST IN PEACE, LITTLE GUY.
HE'S GONE ONTO DRUM-STICK VALHALLA. WITH A POSSIBLE SIDE DISH OF MASHED PO-TATOES AND GRAVY.
PURE METAL.
I'M ASSUMING JONES HAS A RIDE PARKED SOMEWHERE?
YEP.
LET'S GET HIM OUT OF HERE BEFORE HE STARTS TO STINK...

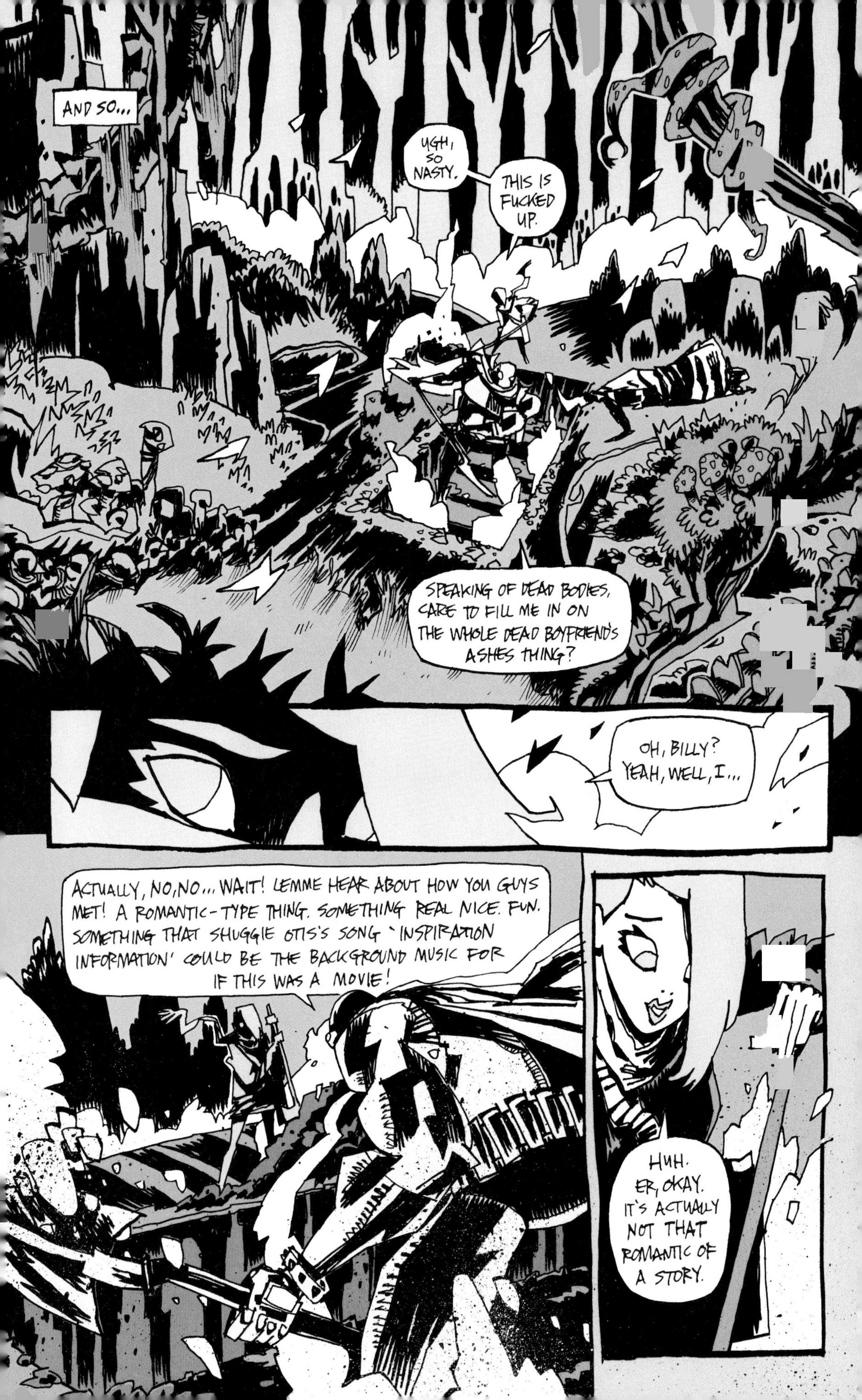
AND SO...
UGH, SO NASTY.
THIS IS FUCKED UP.
SPEAKING OF DEAD BODIES, CARE TO FILL ME IN ON THE WHOLE DEAD BOYFRIEND'S ASHES THING?
OH, BILLY? YEAH, WELL, I...
ACTUALLY, NO, NO... WAIT! LEMME HEAR ABOUT HOW YOU GUYS MET! A ROMANTIC-TYPE THING. SOMETHING REAL NICE. FUN. SOMETHING THAT SHUGGIE OTIS'S SONG 'INSPIRATION INFORMATION' COULD BE THE BACKGROUND MUSIC FOR IF THIS WAS A MOVIE!
HUH. ER, OKAY. IT'S ACTUALLY NOT THAT ROMANTIC OF A STORY.

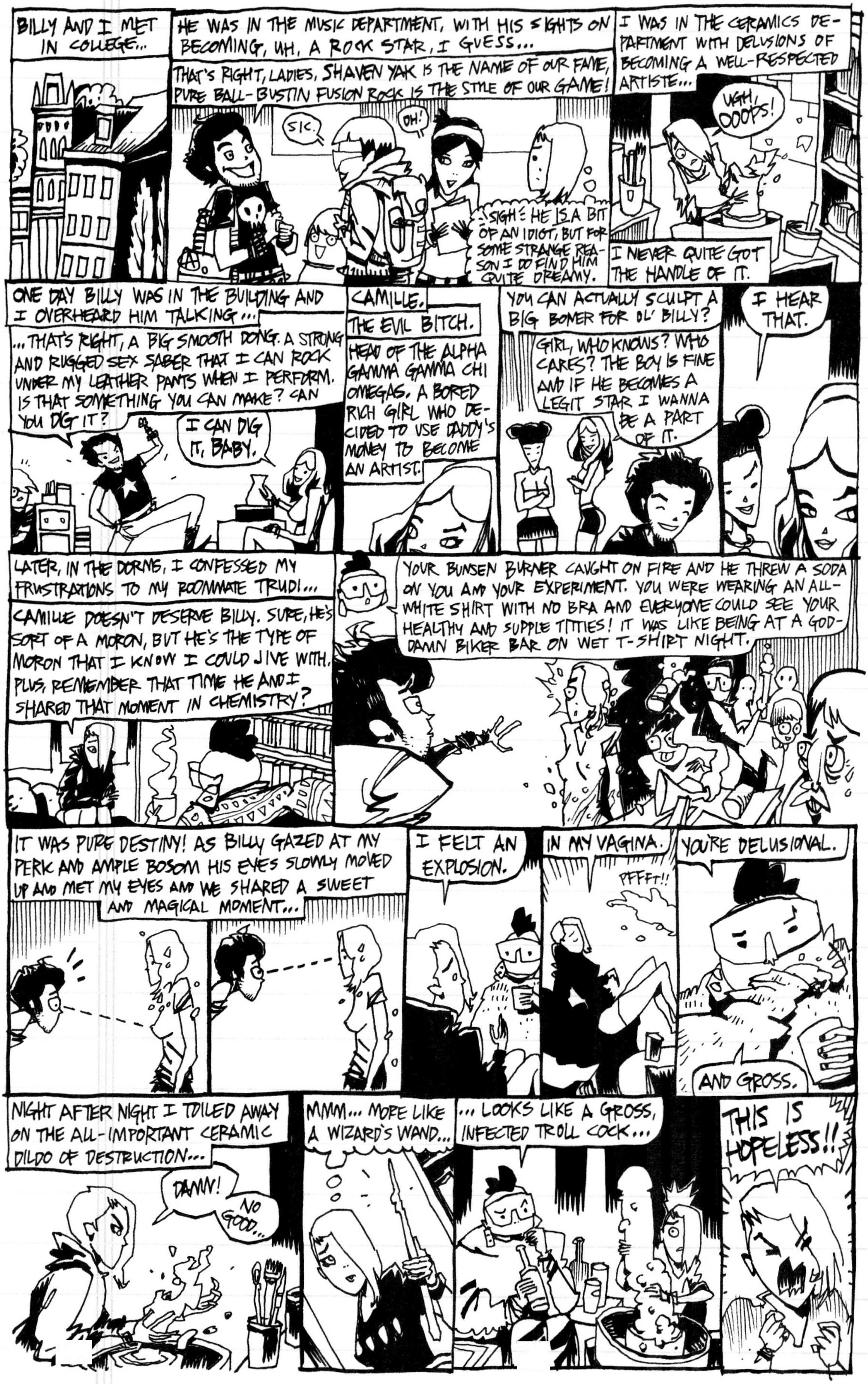
BILLY AND I MET IN COLLEGE...
HE WAS IN THE MUSIC DEPARTMENT, WITH HIS SIGHTS ON BECOMING, UH, A ROCK STAR, I GUESS...
THAT'S RIGHT, LADIES, SHAVEN YAK IS THE NAME OF OUR FAME, PURE BALL-BUSTIN FUSION ROCK IS THE STYLE OF OUR GAME!
SIC.
OH!
:SIGH: HE IS A BIT OF AN IDIOT, BUT FOR SOME STRANGE REASON I DO FIND HIM QUITE DREAMY.
I WAS IN THE CERAMICS DEPARTMENT WITH DELUSIONS OF BECOMING A WELL-RESPECTED ARTISTE...
UGH! OOOPS!
I NEVER QUITE GOT THE HANDLE OF IT.
ONE DAY BILLY WAS IN THE BUILDING AND I OVERHEARD HIM TALKING...
...THAT'S RIGHT, A BIG SMOOTH DONG. A STRONG AND RUGGED SEX SABER THAT I CAN ROCK UNDER MY LEATHER PANTS WHEN I PERFORM. IS THAT SOMETHING YOU CAN MAKE? CAN YOU DIG IT?
I CAN DIG IT, BABY.
CAMILLE.
THE EVIL BITCH.
HEAD OF THE ALPHA GAMMA GAMMA CHI OMEGAS. A BORED RICH GIRL WHO DECIDED TO USE DADDY'S MONEY TO BECOME AN ARTIST.
YOU CAN ACTUALLY SCULPT A BIG BONER FOR OL' BILLY?
GIRL, WHO KNOWS? WHO CARES? THE BOY IS FINE AND IF HE BECOMES A LEGIT STAR I WANNA BE A PART OF IT.
I HEAR THAT.
LATER, IN THE DORMS, I CONFESSED MY FRUSTRATIONS TO MY ROOMMATE TRUDI...
CAMILLE DOESN'T DESERVE BILLY. SURE, HE'S SORT OF A MORON, BUT HE'S THE TYPE OF MORON THAT I KNOW I COULD JIVE WITH. PLUS, REMEMBER THAT TIME HE AND I SHARED THAT MOMENT IN CHEMISTRY?
YOUR BUNSEN BURNER CAUGHT ON FIRE AND HE THREW A SODA ON YOU AND YOUR EXPERIMENT. YOU WERE WEARING AN ALL-WHITE SHIRT WITH NO BRA AND EVERYONE COULD SEE YOUR HEALTHY AND SUPPLE TITTIES! IT WAS LIKE BEING AT A GOD-DAMN BIKER BAR ON WET T-SHIRT NIGHT.
IT WAS PURE DESTINY! AS BILLY GAZED AT MY PERK AND AMPLE BOSOM HIS EYES SLOWLY MOVED UP AND MET MY EYES AND WE SHARED A SWEET AND MAGICAL MOMENT...
I FELT AN EXPLOSION.
IN MY VAGINA.
PFFFT!!
YOU'RE DELUSIONAL.
AND GROSS.
NIGHT AFTER NIGHT I TOILED AWAY ON THE ALL-IMPORTANT CERAMIC DILDO OF DESTRUCTION...
DAMN!
NO GOOD...
MMM... MORE LIKE A WIZARD'S WAND...
...LOOKS LIKE A GROSS, INFECTED TROLL COCK...
THIS IS HOPELESS!!

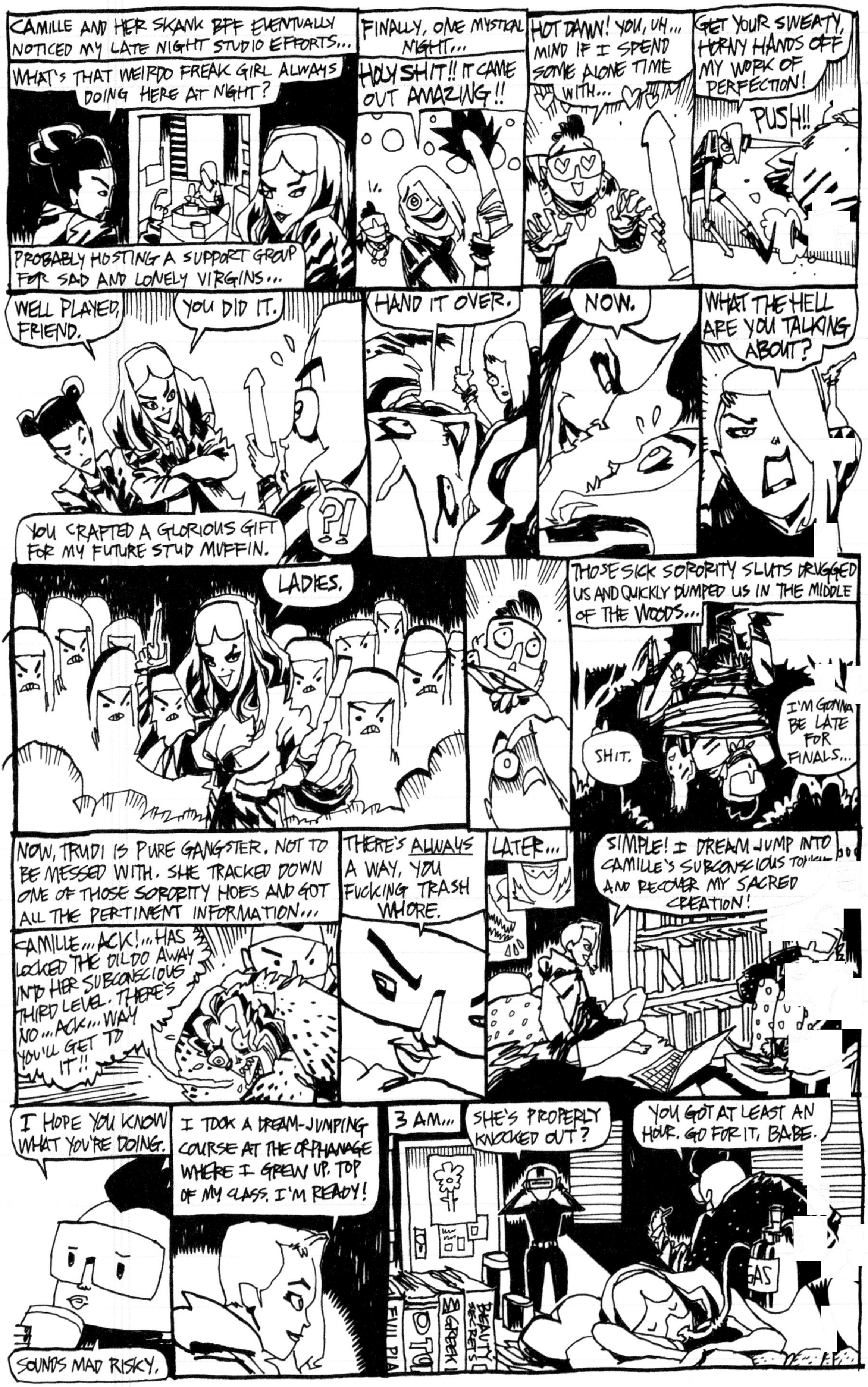

CAMILLE AND HER SKANK BFF EVENTUALLY NOTICED MY LATE NIGHT STUDIO EFFORTS...
WHAT'S THAT WEIRDO FREAK GIRL ALWAYS DOING HERE AT NIGHT?
PROBABLY HOSTING A SUPPORT GROUP FOR SAD AND LONELY VIRGINS...
FINALLY, ONE MYSTICAL NIGHT...
HOLY SHIT!! IT CAME OUT AMAZING!!
HOT DAMN! YOU, UH... MIND IF I SPEND SOME ALONE TIME WITH...
GET YOUR SWEATY, HORNY HANDS OFF MY WORK OF PERFECTION!
PUSH!!
WELL PLAYED, FRIEND.
YOU DID IT.
YOU CRAFTED A GLORIOUS GIFT FOR MY FUTURE STUD MUFFIN.
?!
HAND IT OVER.
NOW.
WHAT THE HELL ARE YOU TALKING ABOUT?
LADIES.
THOSE SICK SORORITY SLUTS DRUGGED US AND QUICKLY DUMPED US IN THE MIDDLE OF THE WOODS...
SHIT.
I'M GONNA BE LATE FOR FINALS...
NOW, TRUDI IS PURE GANGSTER. NOT TO BE MESSED WITH. SHE TRACKED DOWN ONE OF THOSE SORORITY HOES AND GOT ALL THE PERTINENT INFORMATION...
CAMILLE... ACK!... HAS LOCKED THE DILDO AWAY INTO HER SUBCONSCIOUS THIRD LEVEL. THERE'S NO... ACK... WAY YOU'LL GET TO IT!!
THERE'S ALWAYS A WAY, YOU FUCKING TRASH WHORE.
LATER...
SIMPLE! I DREAM JUMP INTO CAMILLE'S SUBCONSCIOUS TON
AND RECOVER MY SACRED CREATION!
I HOPE YOU KNOW WHAT YOU'RE DOING.
SOUNDS MAD RISKY.
I TOOK A DREAM-JUMPING COURSE AT THE ORPHANAGE WHERE I GREW UP. TOP OF MY CLASS. I'M READY!
3 AM...
SHE'S PROPERLY KNOCKED OUT?
YOU GOT AT LEAST AN HOUR. GO FOR IT, BABE.
GAS
GREEK
BEAUTY SECRETS

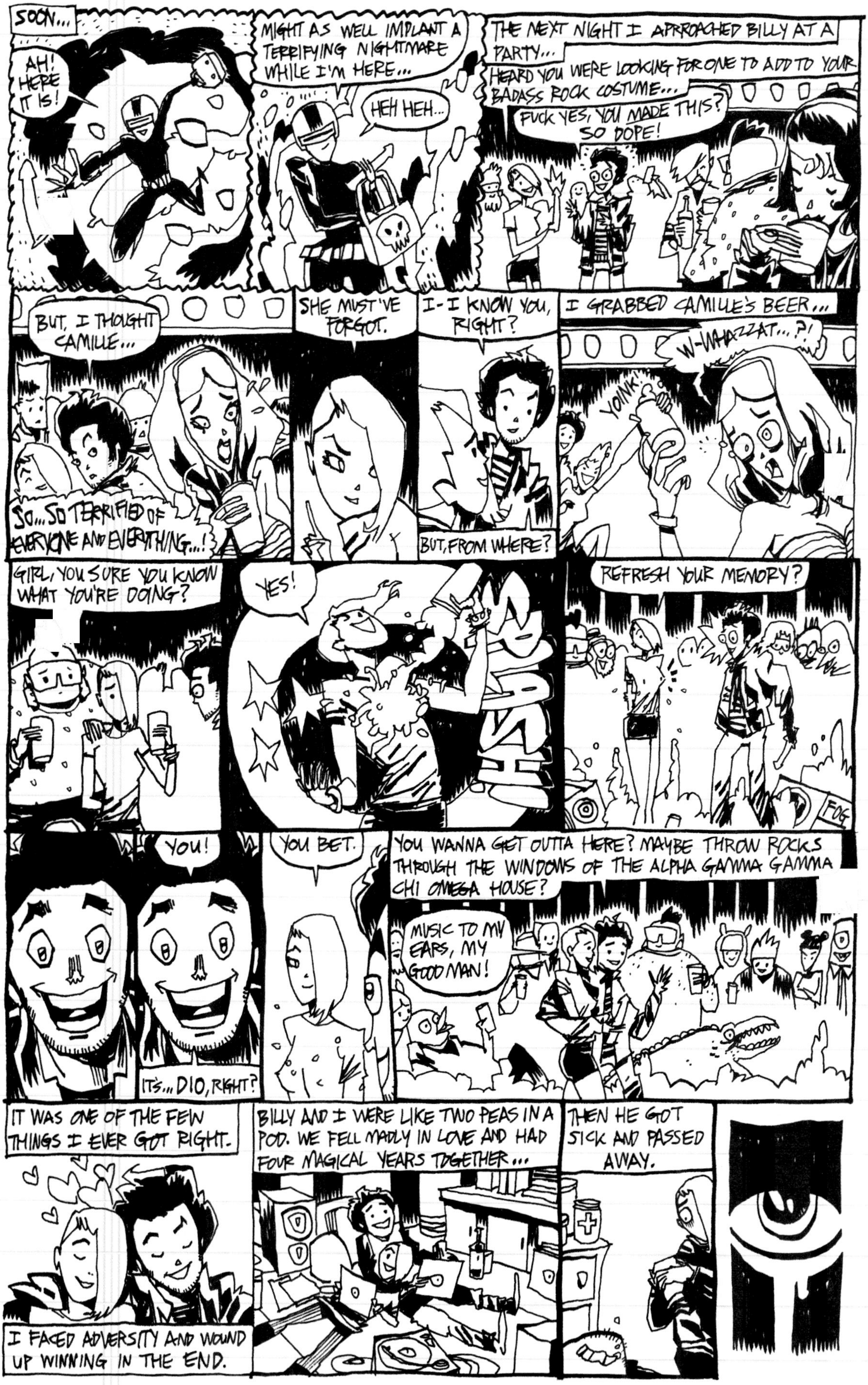
SOON...
AH! HERE IT IS!
MIGHT AS WELL IMPLANT A TERRIFYING NIGHTMARE WHILE I'M HERE...
HEH HEH...
THE NEXT NIGHT I APPROACHED BILLY AT A PARTY...
HEARD YOU WERE LOOKING FOR ONE TO ADD TO YOUR BADASS ROCK COSTUME...
FUCK YES, YOU MADE THIS? SO DOPE!
BUT, I THOUGHT CAMILLE...
SO... SO TERRIFIED OF EVERYONE AND EVERYTHING...!
SHE MUST'VE FORGOT.
I-I KNOW YOU, RIGHT?
BUT, FROM WHERE?
I GRABBED CAMILLE'S BEER...
W-WHAZZAT...?!
YOINK!
GIRL, YOU SURE YOU KNOW WHAT YOU'RE DOING?
YES!
REFRESH YOUR MEMORY?
FOG
YOU!
IT'S... DIO, RIGHT?
YOU BET.
YOU WANNA GET OUTTA HERE? MAYBE THROW ROCKS THROUGH THE WINDOWS OF THE ALPHA GAMMA GAMMA CHI OMEGA HOUSE?
MUSIC TO MY EARS, MY GOOD MAN!
IT WAS ONE OF THE FEW THINGS I EVER GOT RIGHT.
I FACED ADVERSITY AND WOUND UP WINNING IN THE END.
BILLY AND I WERE LIKE TWO PEAS IN A POD. WE FELL MADLY IN LOVE AND HAD FOUR MAGICAL YEARS TOGETHER...
THEN HE GOT SICK AND PASSED AWAY.

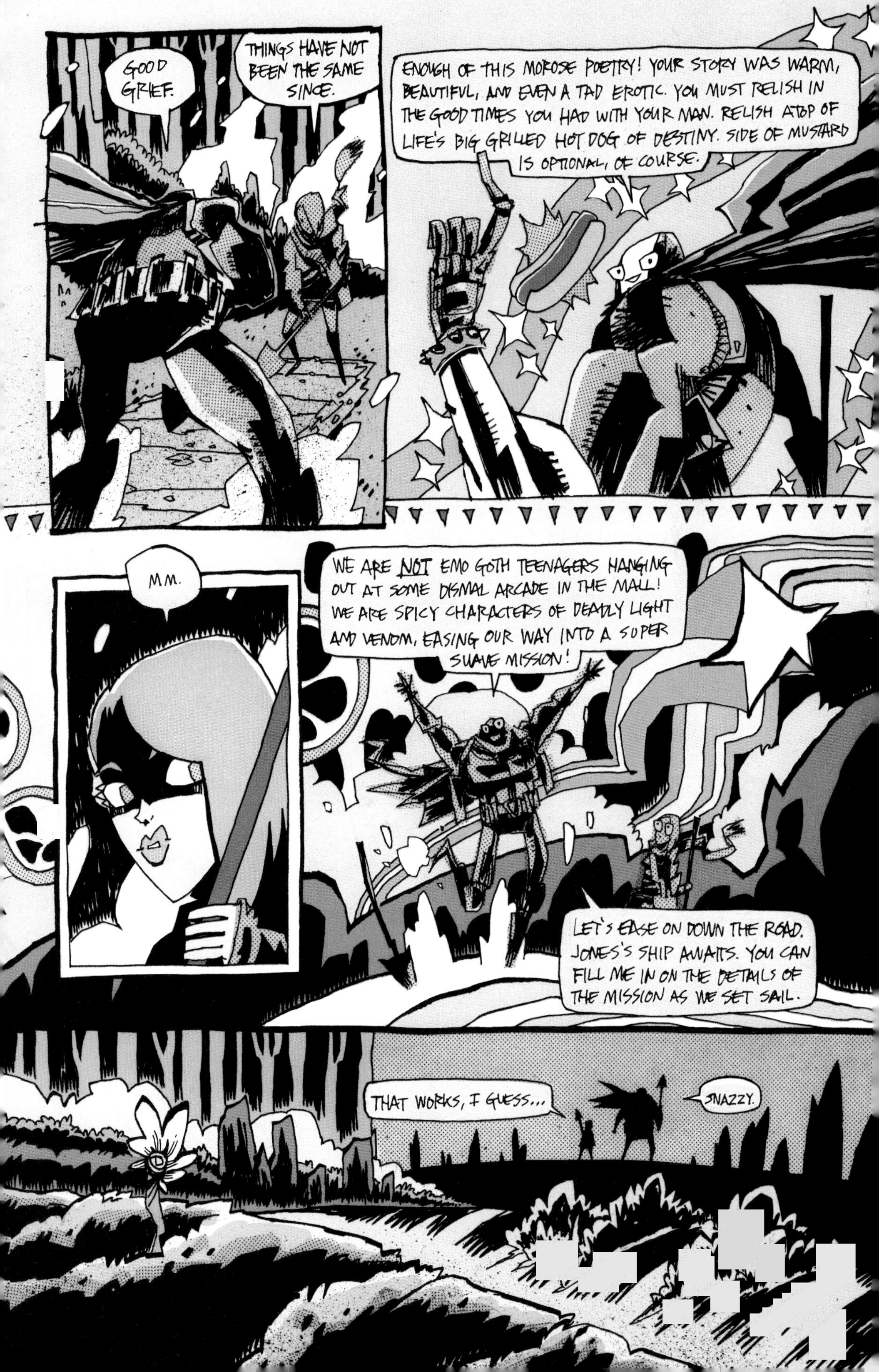
GOOD GRIEF.
THINGS HAVE NOT BEEN THE SAME SINCE.
ENOUGH OF THIS MOROSE POETRY! YOUR STORY WAS WARM, BEAUTIFUL, AND EVEN A TAD EROTIC. YOU MUST RELISH IN THE GOOD TIMES YOU HAD WITH YOUR MAN. RELISH ATOP OF LIFE'S BIG GRILLED HOT DOG OF DESTINY. SIDE OF MUSTARD IS OPTIONAL, OF COURSE.
MM.
WE ARE NOT EMO GOTH TEENAGERS HANGING OUT AT SOME DISMAL ARCADE IN THE MALL! WE ARE SPICY CHARACTERS OF DEADLY LIGHT AND VENOM, EASING OUR WAY INTO A SUPER SUAVE MISSION!
LET'S EASE ON DOWN THE ROAD. JONES'S SHIP AWAITS. YOU CAN FILL ME IN ON THE DETAILS OF THE MISSION AS WE SET SAIL.
THAT WORKS, I GUESS...
SNAZZY.

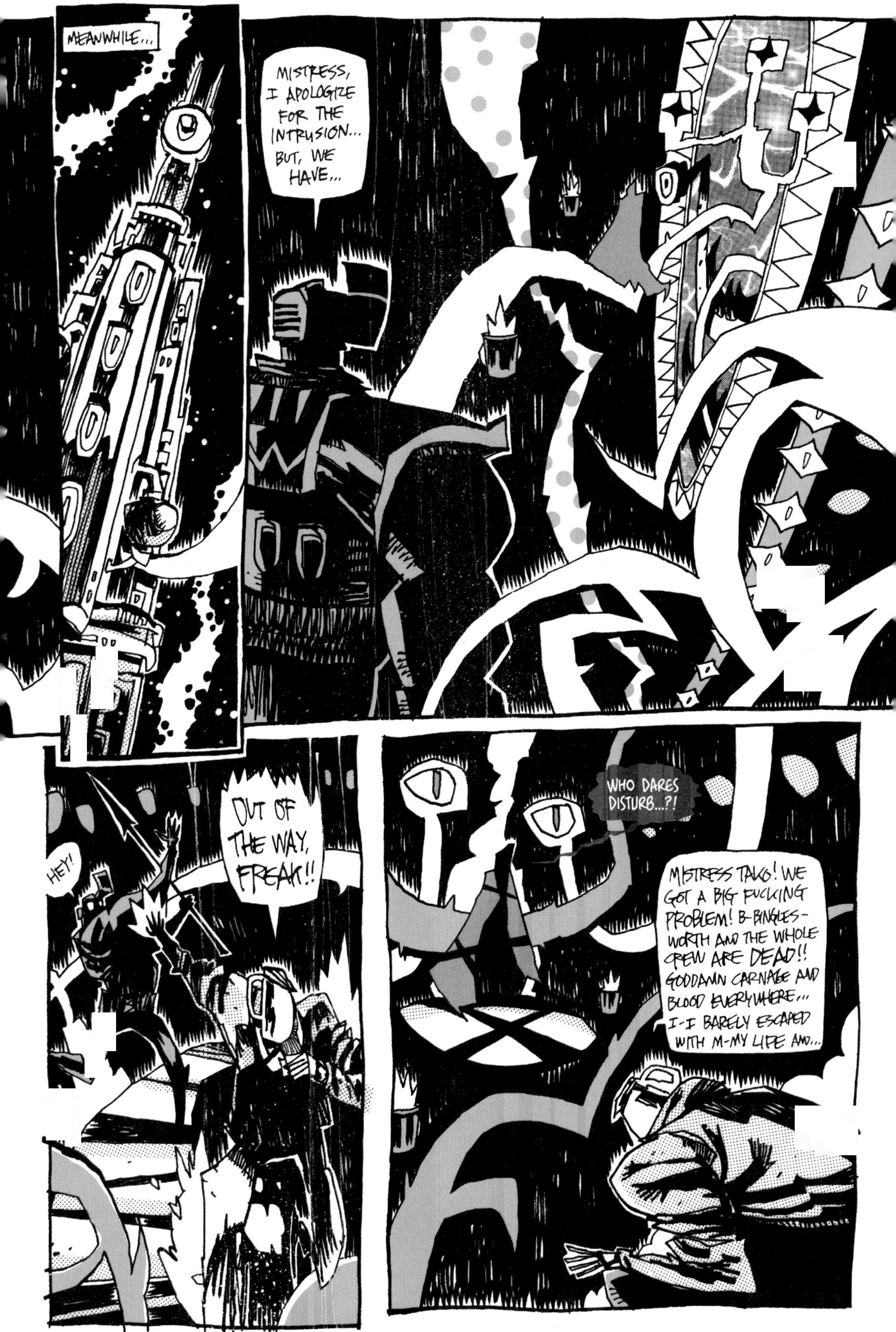
MEANWHILE...
MISTRESS, I APOLOGIZE FOR THE INTRUSION... BUT, WE HAVE...
HEY!
OUT OF THE WAY, FREAK!!
WHO DARES DISTURB...?!
MISTRESS TAKO! WE GOT A BIG FUCKING PROBLEM! B-BINGLESWORTH AND THE WHOLE CREW ARE DEAD!! GODDAMN CARNAGE AND BLOOD EVERYWHERE... I-I BARELY ESCAPED WITH M-MY LIFE AND...

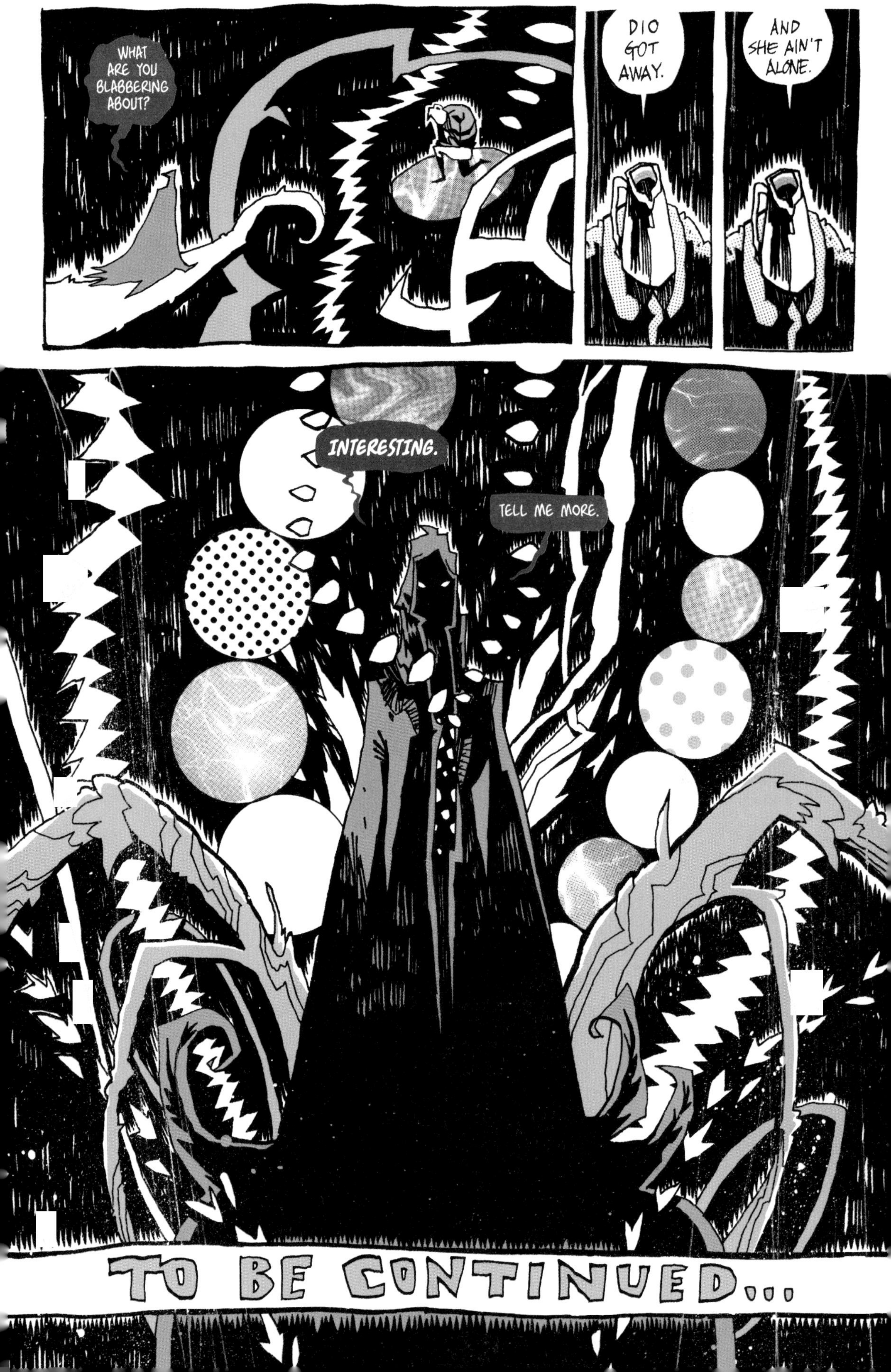
WHAT ARE YOU BLABBERING ABOUT?
DIO GOT AWAY.
AND SHE AIN'T ALONE.
INTERESTING.
TELL ME MORE.
TO BE CONTINUED...

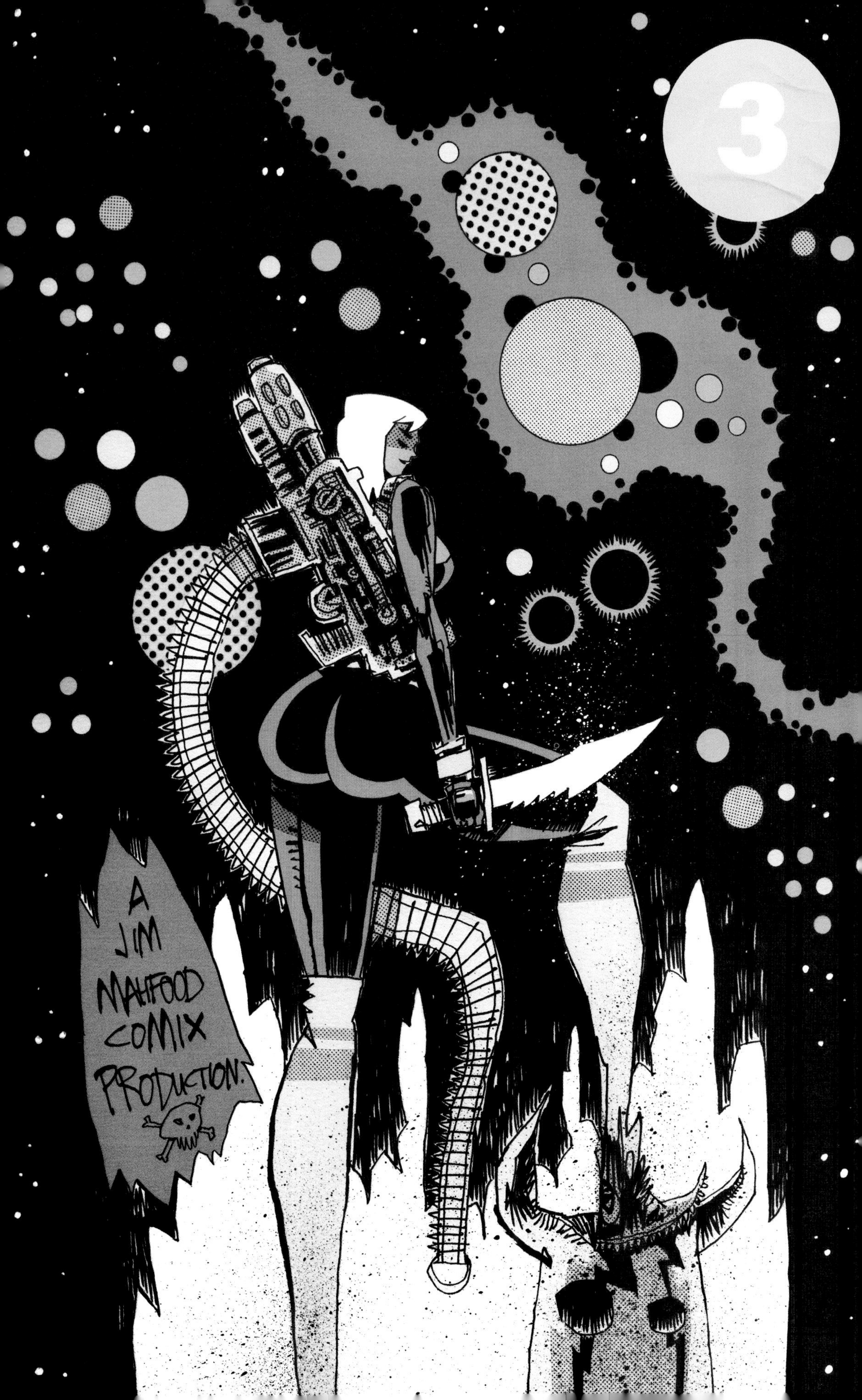
3
A JIM MAHFOOD COMIX PRODUCTION.

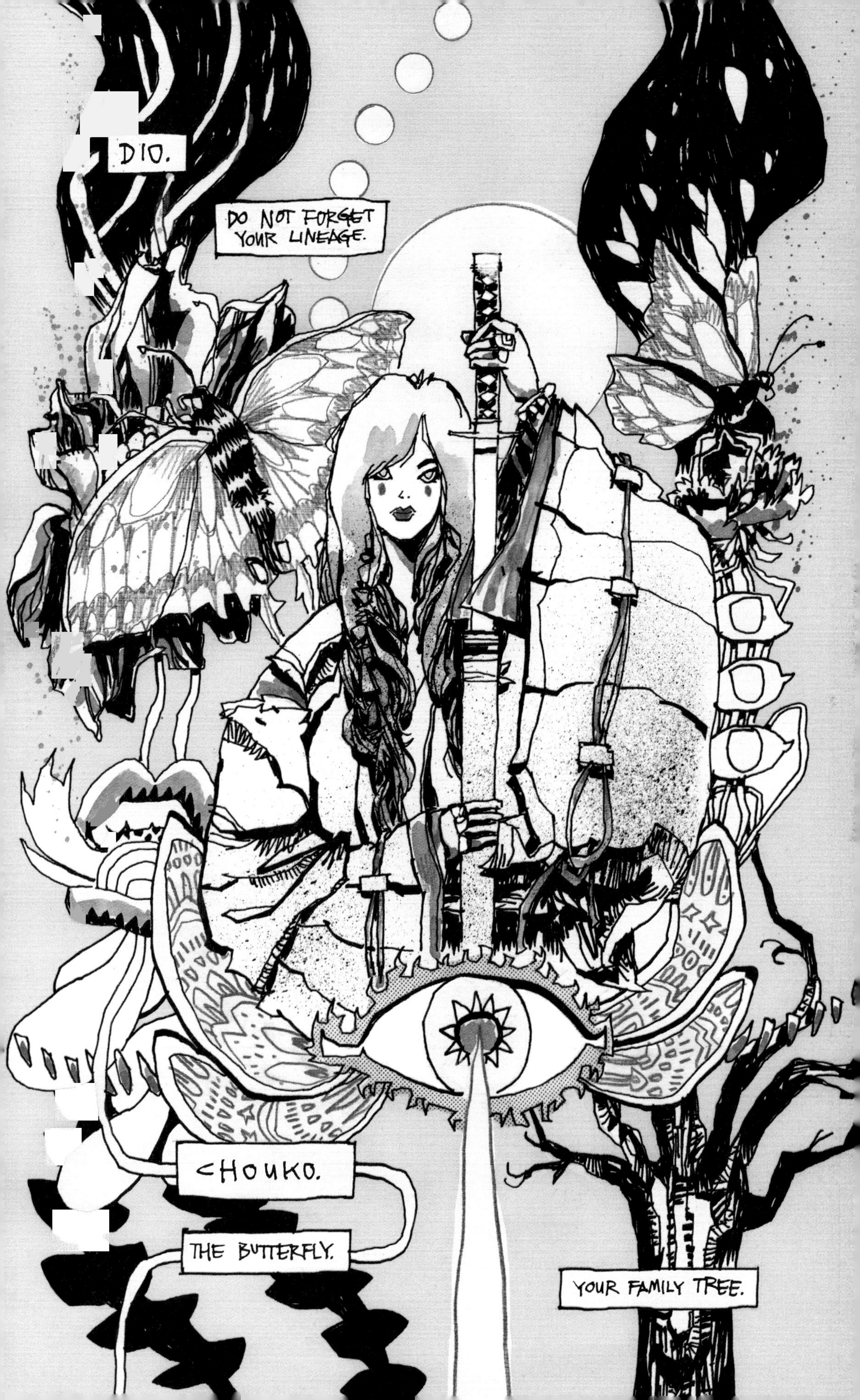
DIO.
DO NOT FORGET YOUR LINEAGE.
CHOUKO.
THE BUTTERFLY.
YOUR FAMILY TREE.

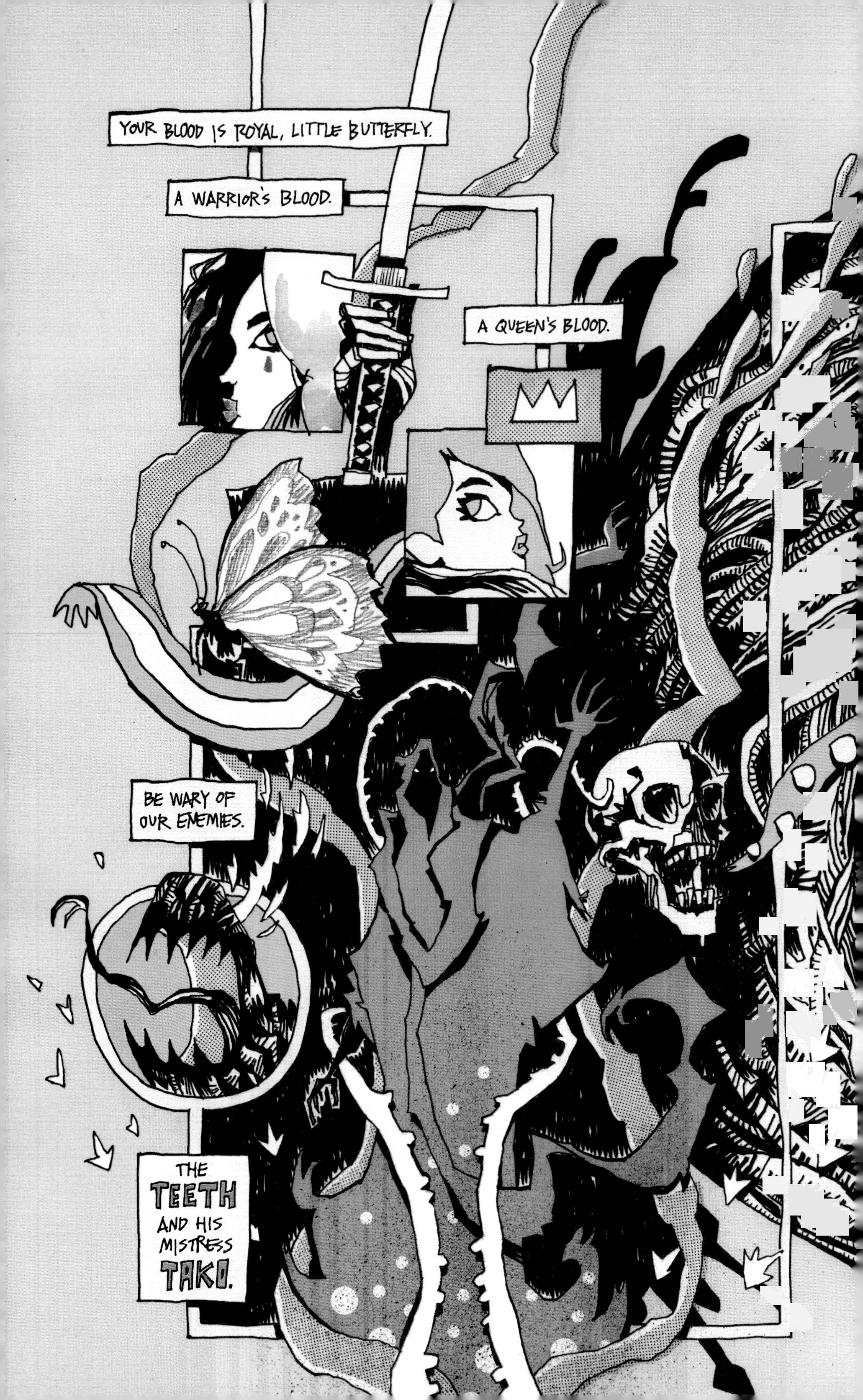
YOUR BLOOD IS ROYAL, LITTLE BUTTERFLY.
A WARRIOR'S BLOOD.
A QUEEN'S BLOOD.
BE WARY OF OUR ENEMIES.
THE TEETH AND HIS MISTRESS TAKO.

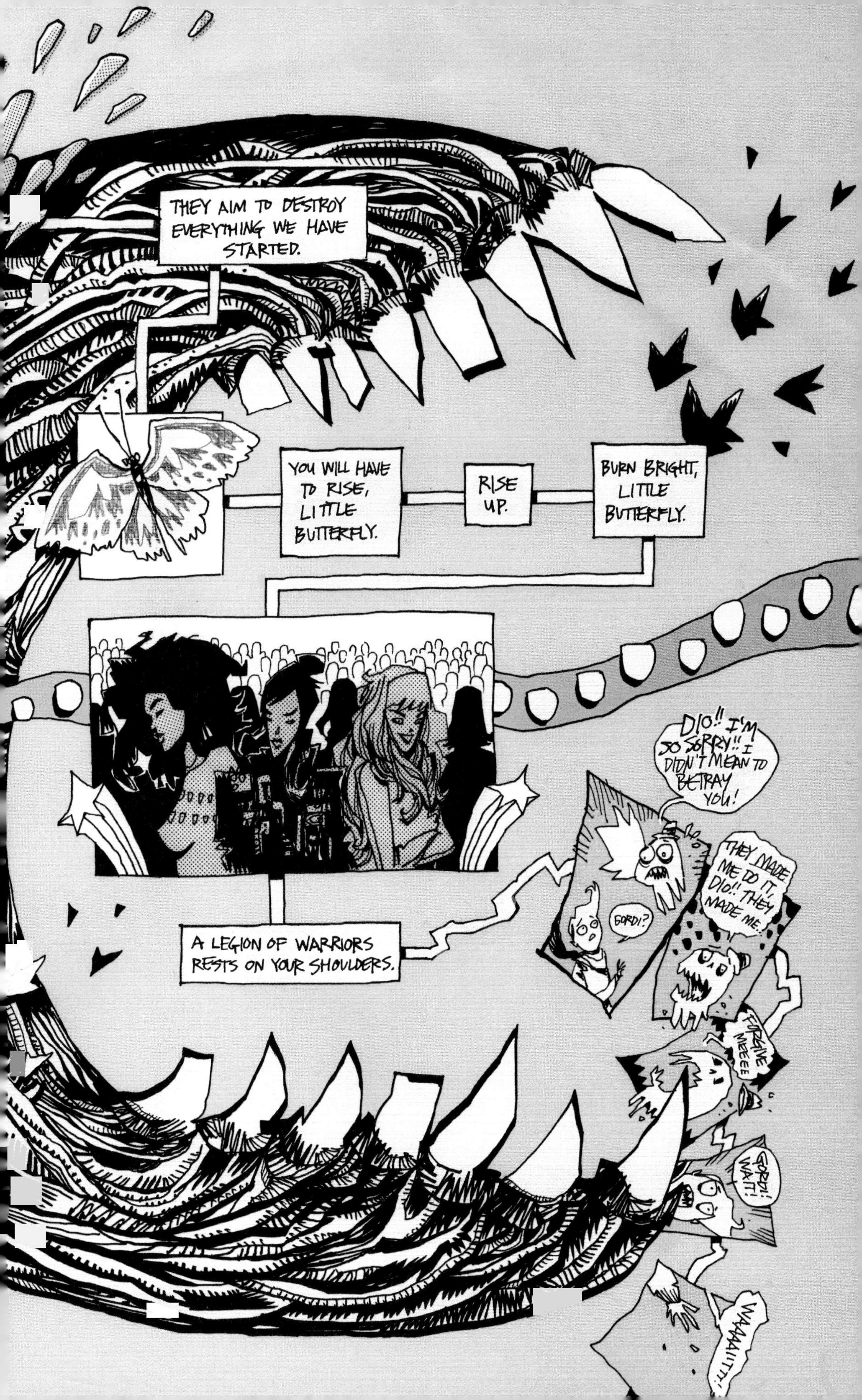

THEY AIM TO DESTROY EVERYTHING WE HAVE STARTED.
YOU WILL HAVE TO RISE, LITTLE BUTTERFLY.
RISE UP.
BURN BRIGHT, LITTLE BUTTERFLY.
A LEGION OF WARRIORS RESTS ON YOUR SHOULDERS.
DIO!! I'M SO SORRY!! I DIDN'T MEAN TO BETRAY YOU!
GORDI?
THEY MADE ME DO IT, DIO!! THEY MADE ME.
FORGIVE MEEEE
GORDI! WAIT!
WAAAAAIIITTT!

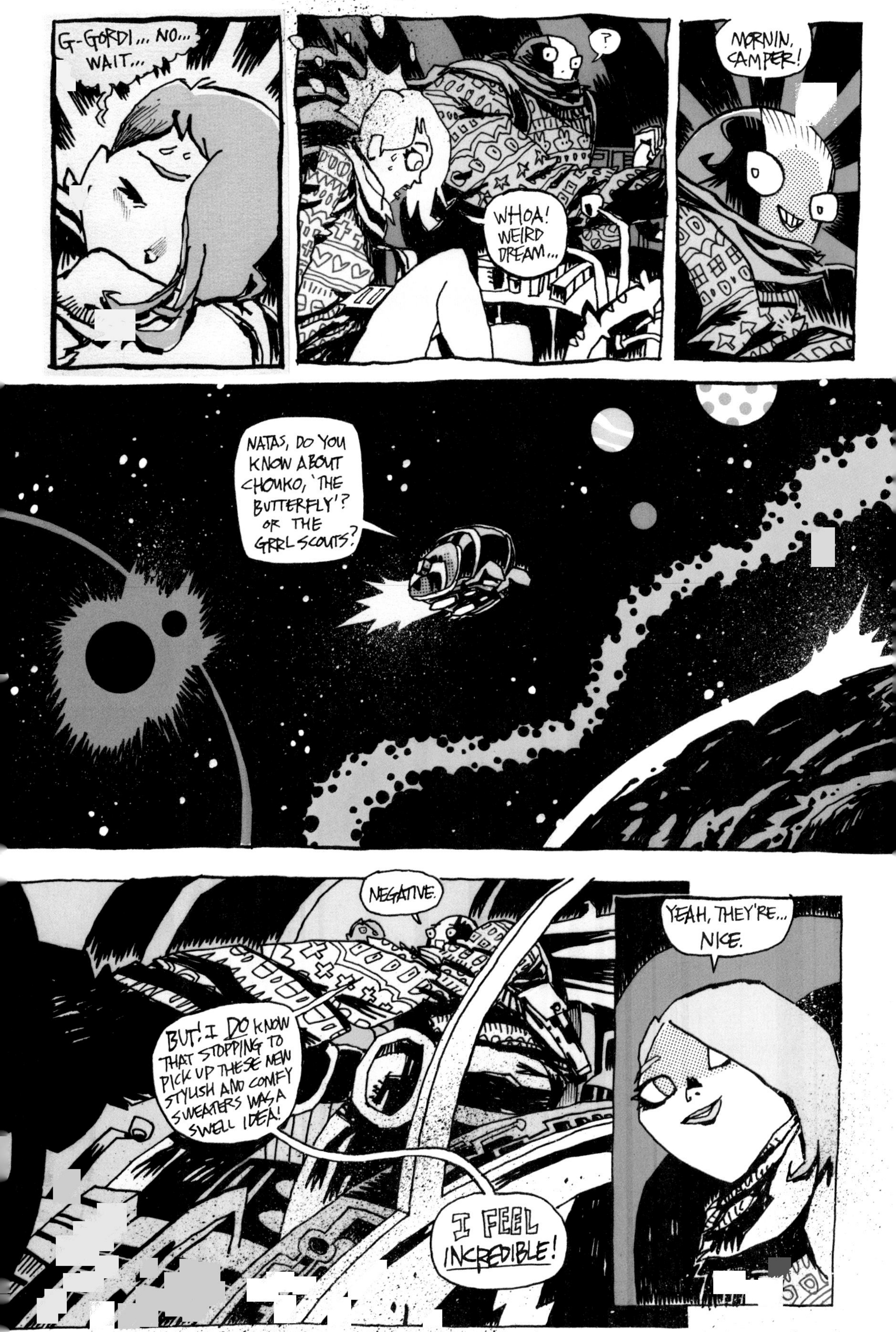
G-GORDI... NO... WAIT...
?
WHOA! WEIRD DREAM...
MORNIN, CAMPER!
NATAS, DO YOU KNOW ABOUT CHOUKO, 'THE BUTTERFLY'? OR THE GRRL SCOUTS?
NEGATIVE.
BUT! I DO KNOW THAT STOPPING TO PICK UP THESE NEW STYLISH AND COMFY SWEATERS WAS A SWELL IDEA!
I FEEL INCREDIBLE!
YEAH, THEY'RE... NICE.

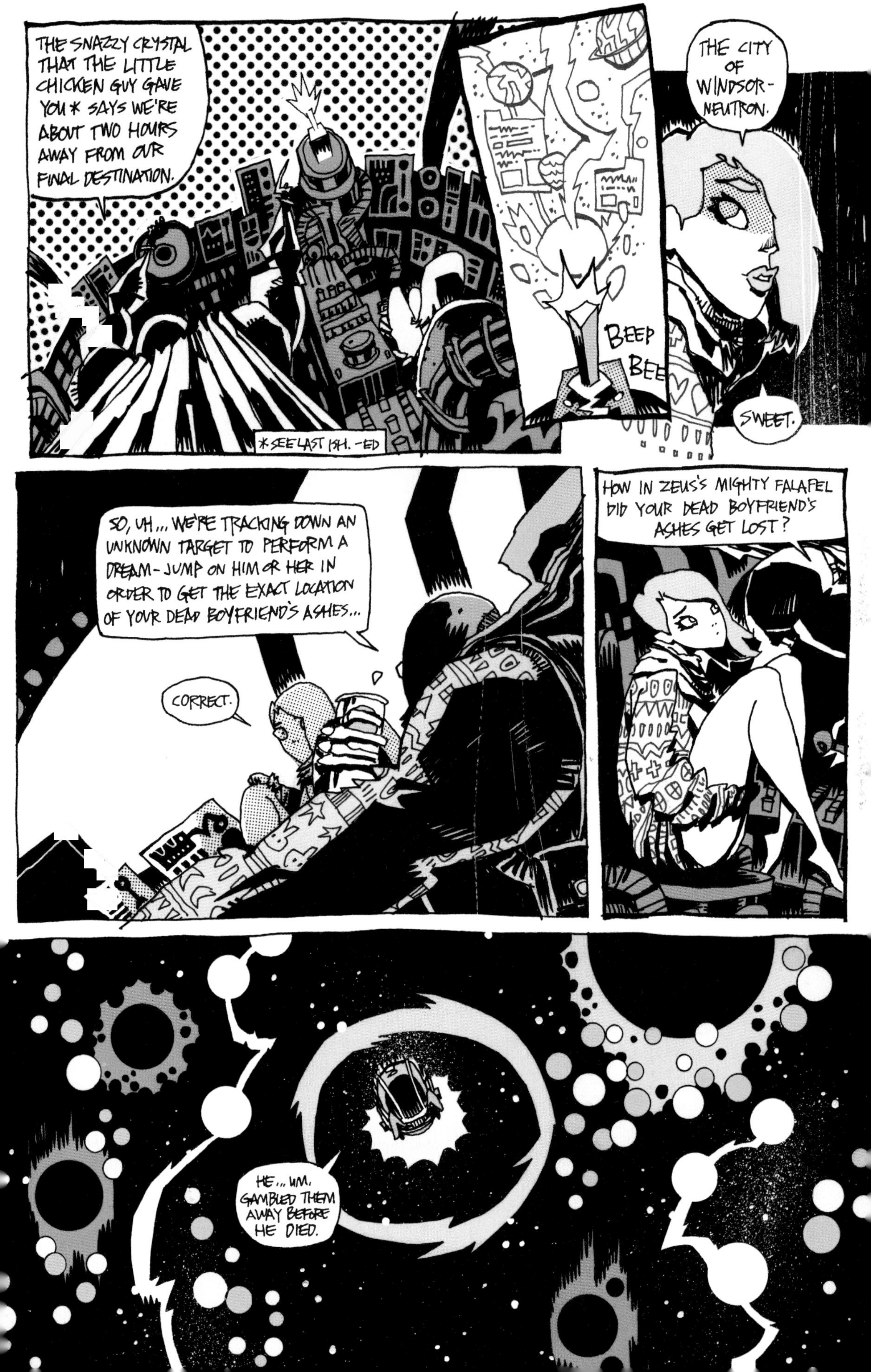
THE SNAZZY CRYSTAL THAT THE LITTLE CHICKEN GUY GAVE YOU* SAYS WE'RE ABOUT TWO HOURS AWAY FROM OUR FINAL DESTINATION.
*SEE LAST ISH. -ED
BEEP
BEE
THE CITY OF WINDSOR-NEUTRON.
SWEET.
SO, UH... WE'RE TRACKING DOWN AN UNKNOWN TARGET TO PERFORM A DREAM-JUMP ON HIM OR HER IN ORDER TO GET THE EXACT LOCATION OF YOUR DEAD BOYFRIEND'S ASHES...
CORRECT.
HOW IN ZEUS'S MIGHTY FALAFEL DID YOUR DEAD BOYFRIEND'S ASHES GET LOST?
HE... UM, GAMBLED THEM AWAY BEFORE HE DIED.

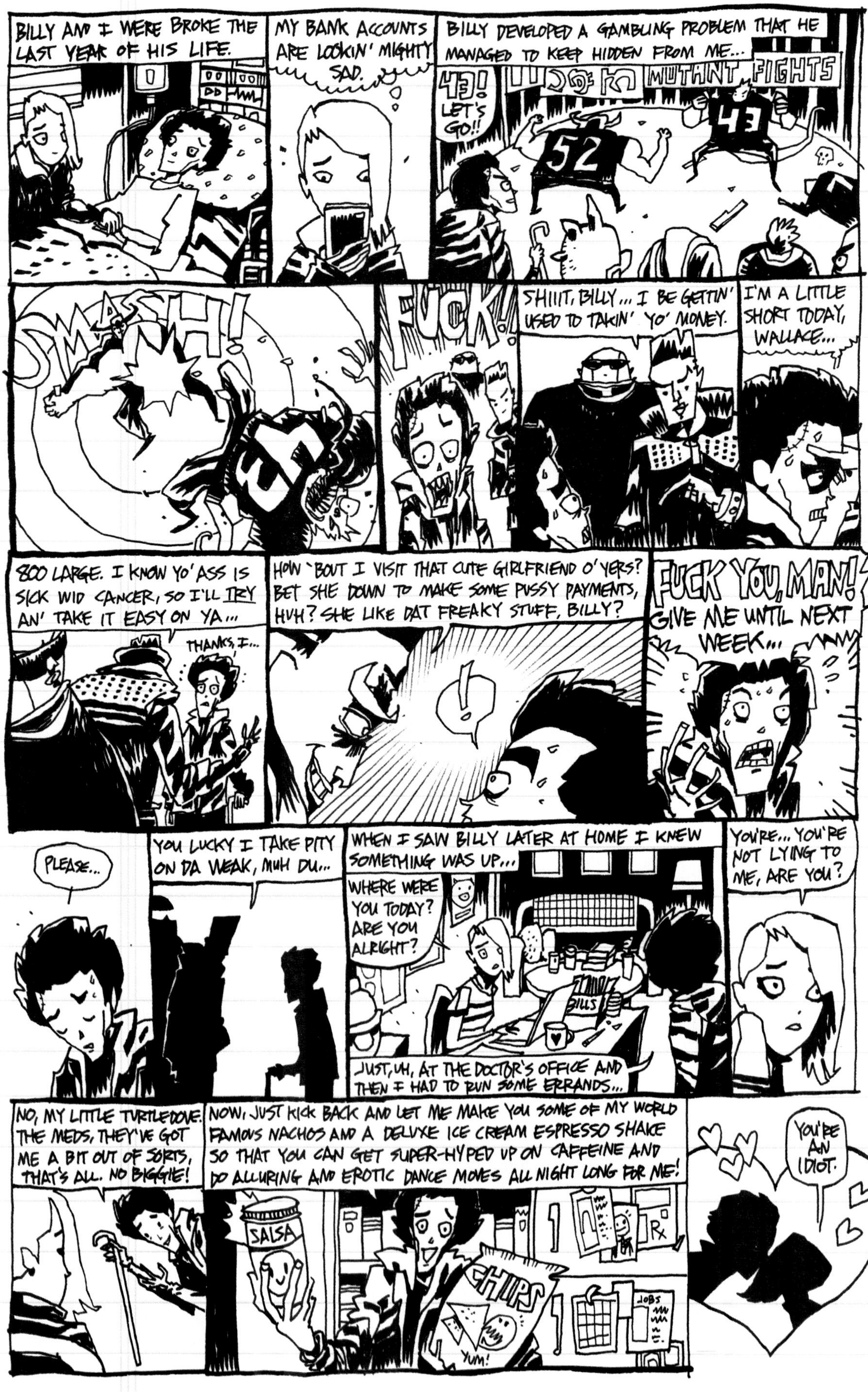
BILLY AND I WERE BROKE THE LAST YEAR OF HIS LIFE.
MY BANK ACCOUNTS ARE LOOKIN' MIGHTY SAD.
BILLY DEVELOPED A GAMBLING PROBLEM THAT HE MANAGED TO KEEP HIDDEN FROM ME...
MUTANT FIGHTS
43! LET'S GO!!
52
43
SMASH!
FUCK!!
SHIIIT, BILLY... I BE GETTIN' USED TO TAKIN' YO' MONEY.
I'M A LITTLE SHORT TODAY, WALLACE...
800 LARGE. I KNOW YO' ASS IS SICK WID CANCER, SO I'LL TRY AN' TAKE IT EASY ON YA...
THANKS, I...
HOW 'BOUT I VISIT THAT CUTE GIRLFRIEND O' YERS? BET SHE DOWN TO MAKE SOME PUSSY PAYMENTS, HUH? SHE LIKE DAT FREAKY STUFF, BILLY?
!
FUCK YOU, MAN! GIVE ME UNTIL NEXT WEEK...
PLEASE...
YOU LUCKY I TAKE PITY ON DA WEAK, MUH DU...
WHEN I SAW BILLY LATER AT HOME I KNEW SOMETHING WAS UP...
WHERE WERE YOU TODAY? ARE YOU ALRIGHT?
BILLS
JUST, UH, AT THE DOCTOR'S OFFICE AND THEN I HAD TO RUN SOME ERRANDS...
YOU'RE... YOU'RE NOT LYING TO ME, ARE YOU?
NO, MY LITTLE TURTLEDOVE. THE MEDS, THEY'VE GOT ME A BIT OUT OF SORTS, THAT'S ALL. NO BIGGIE!
NOW, JUST KICK BACK AND LET ME MAKE YOU SOME OF MY WORLD FAMOUS NACHOS AND A DELUXE ICE CREAM ESPRESSO SHAKE SO THAT YOU CAN GET SUPER-HYPED UP ON CAFFEINE AND DO ALLURING AND EROTIC DANCE MOVES ALL NIGHT LONG FOR ME!
SALSA
CHIPS
YUM!
JOBS
Rx
YOU'RE AN IDIOT.

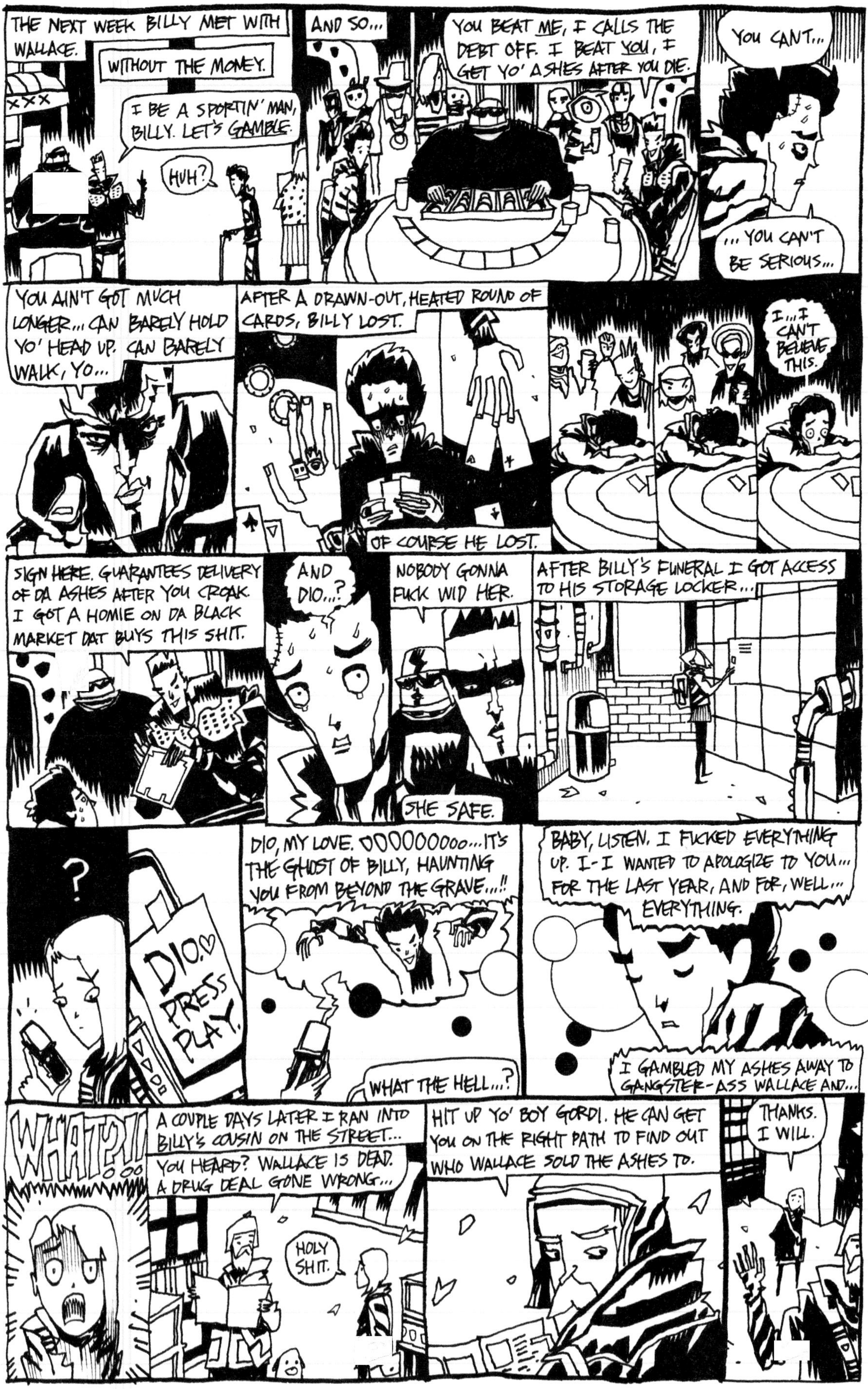
THE NEXT WEEK BILLY MET WITH WALLACE.
WITHOUT THE MONEY.
I BE A SPORTIN' MAN, BILLY. LET'S GAMBLE.
HUH?
AND SO...
YOU BEAT ME, I CALLS THE DEBT OFF. I BEAT YOU, I GET YO' ASHES AFTER YOU DIE.
YOU CAN'T...
...YOU CAN'T BE SERIOUS...
YOU AIN'T GOT MUCH LONGER... CAN BARELY HOLD YO' HEAD UP. CAN BARELY WALK, YO...
AFTER A DRAWN-OUT, HEATED ROUND OF CARDS, BILLY LOST.
OF COURSE HE LOST.
I...I CAN'T BELIEVE THIS.
SIGN HERE. GUARANTEES DELIVERY OF DA ASHES AFTER YOU CROAK. I GOT A HOMIE ON DA BLACK MARKET DAT BUYS THIS SHIT.
AND DIO...?
NOBODY GONNA FUCK WID HER.
SHE SAFE.
AFTER BILLY'S FUNERAL I GOT ACCESS TO HIS STORAGE LOCKER...
?
DIO ♡ PRESS PLAY.
DIO, MY LOVE. OOOOOOOoo...IT'S THE GHOST OF BILLY, HAUNTING YOU FROM BEYOND THE GRAVE...!!
WHAT THE HELL...?
BABY, LISTEN. I FUCKED EVERYTHING UP. I-I WANTED TO APOLOGIZE TO YOU... FOR THE LAST YEAR, AND FOR, WELL... EVERYTHING.
I GAMBLED MY ASHES AWAY TO GANGSTER-ASS WALLACE AND...
WHAT?!!
A COUPLE DAYS LATER I RAN INTO BILLY'S COUSIN ON THE STREET...
YOU HEARD? WALLACE IS DEAD. A DRUG DEAL GONE WRONG...
HOLY SHIT.
HIT UP YO' BOY GORDI. HE CAN GET YOU ON THE RIGHT PATH TO FIND OUT WHO WALLACE SOLD THE ASHES TO.
THANKS. I WILL.

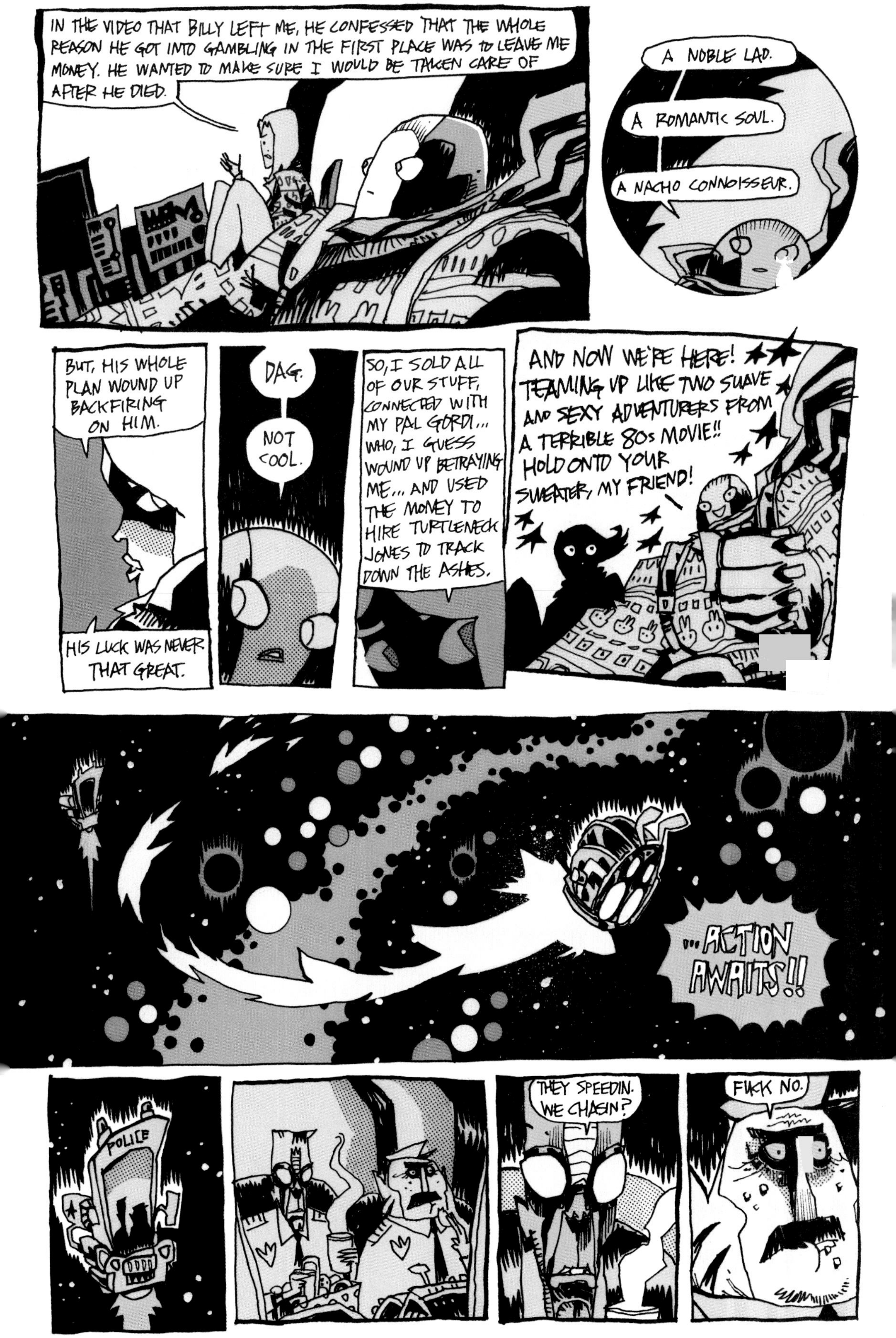
IN THE VIDEO THAT BILLY LEFT ME, HE CONFESSED THAT THE WHOLE REASON HE GOT INTO GAMBLING IN THE FIRST PLACE WAS TO LEAVE ME MONEY. HE WANTED TO MAKE SURE I WOULD BE TAKEN CARE OF AFTER HE DIED.
A NOBLE LAD.
A ROMANTIC SOUL.
A NACHO CONNOISSEUR.
BUT, HIS WHOLE PLAN WOUND UP BACKFIRING ON HIM.
HIS LUCK WAS NEVER THAT GREAT.
DAG.
NOT COOL.
SO, I SOLD ALL OF OUR STUFF, CONNECTED WITH MY PAL GORDI... WHO, I GUESS WOUND UP BETRAYING ME... AND USED THE MONEY TO HIRE TURTLENECK JONES TO TRACK DOWN THE ASHES.
AND NOW WE'RE HERE! TEAMING UP LIKE TWO SUAVE AND SEXY ADVENTURERS FROM A TERRIBLE 80s MOVIE!! HOLD ONTO YOUR SWEATER, MY FRIEND!
...ACTION AWAITS!!
POLICE
THEY SPEEDIN. WE CHASIN?
FUCK NO.

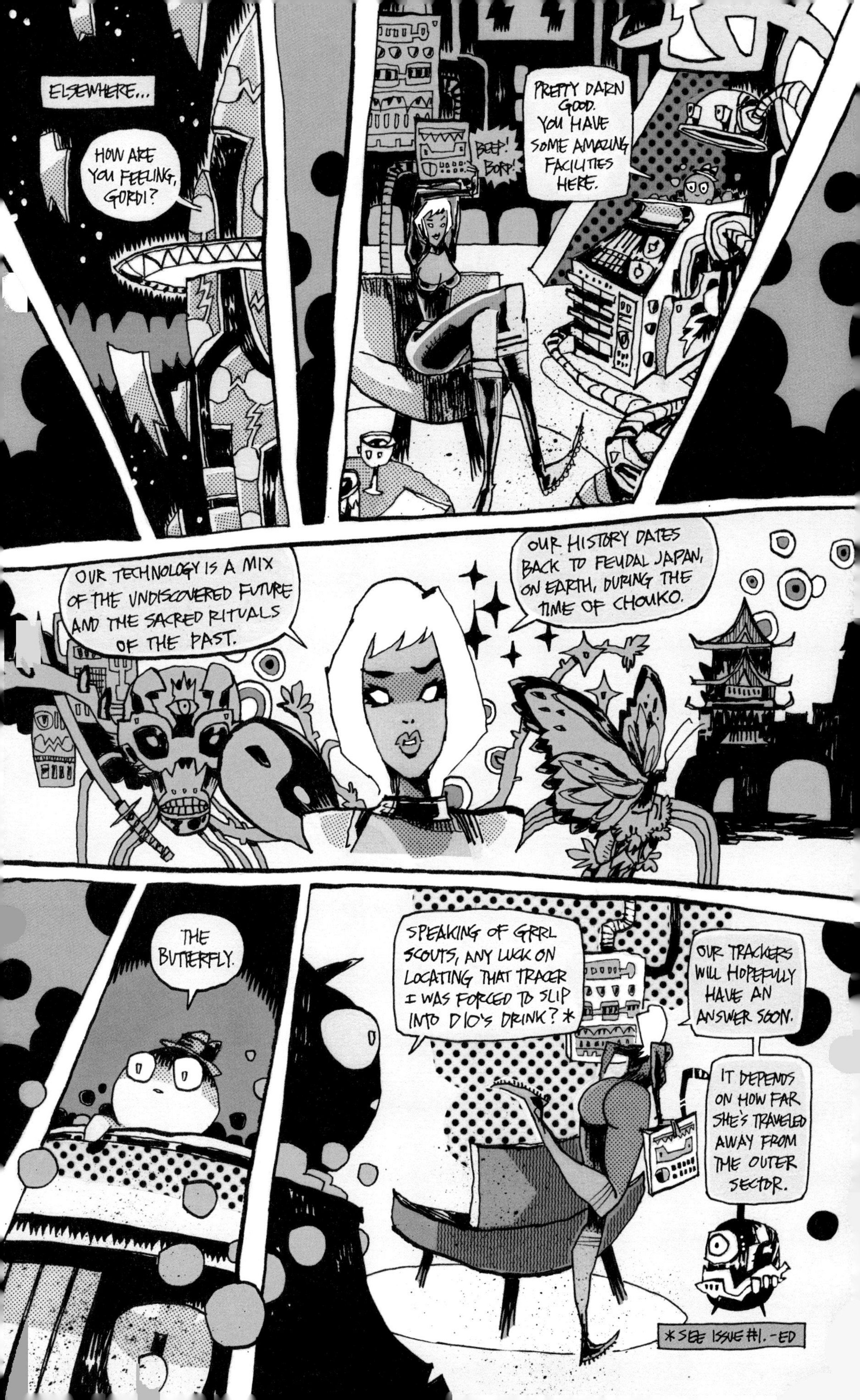
ELSEWHERE...
HOW ARE YOU FEELING, GORDI?
BEEP! BORP!
PRETTY DARN GOOD. YOU HAVE SOME AMAZING FACILITIES HERE.
OUR TECHNOLOGY IS A MIX OF THE UNDISCOVERED FUTURE AND THE SACRED RITUALS OF THE PAST.
OUR HISTORY DATES BACK TO FEUDAL JAPAN, ON EARTH, DURING THE TIME OF CHOUKO.
THE BUTTERFLY.
SPEAKING OF GRRL SCOUTS, ANY LUCK ON LOCATING THAT TRACER I WAS FORCED TO SLIP INTO DIO'S DRINK? *
OUR TRACKERS WILL HOPEFULLY HAVE AN ANSWER SOON.
IT DEPENDS ON HOW FAR SHE'S TRAVELED AWAY FROM THE OUTER SECTOR.
* SEE ISSUE #1. -ED

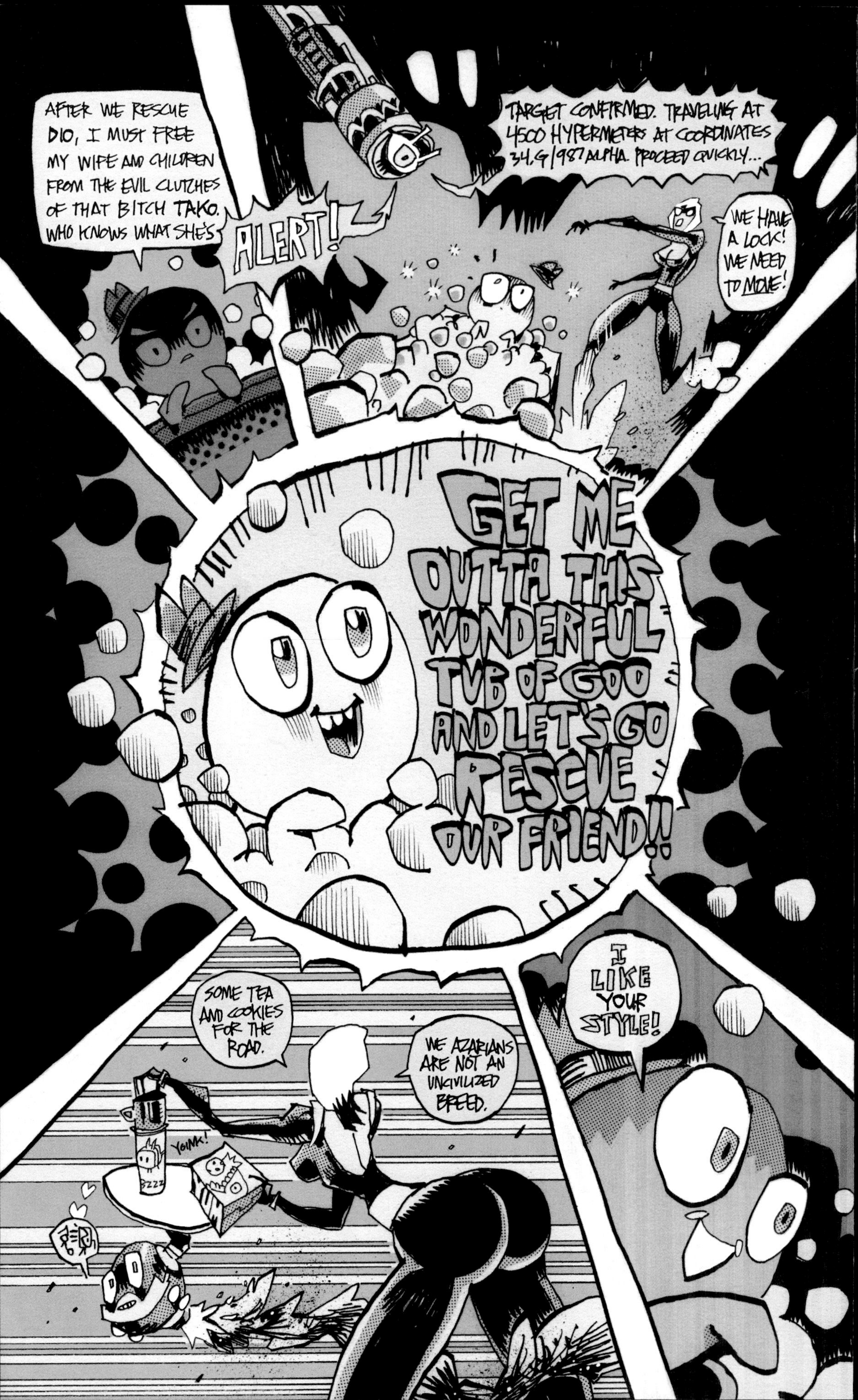
AFTER WE RESCUE DIO, I MUST FREE MY WIFE AND CHILDREN FROM THE EVIL CLUTCHES OF THAT BITCH TAKO. WHO KNOWS WHAT SHE'S
ALERT!
TARGET CONFIRMED. TRAVELING AT 4500 HYPERMETERS AT COORDINATES 34,G/987 ALPHA. PROCEED QUICKLY...
WE HAVE A LOCK! WE NEED TO MOVE!
GET ME OUTTA THIS WONDERFUL TUB OF GOO AND LET'S GO RESCUE OUR FRIEND!!
SOME TEA AND COOKIES FOR THE ROAD.
WE AZARIANS ARE NOT AN UNCIVILIZED BREED.
I LIKE YOUR STYLE!
YOINK!
ZZZZ

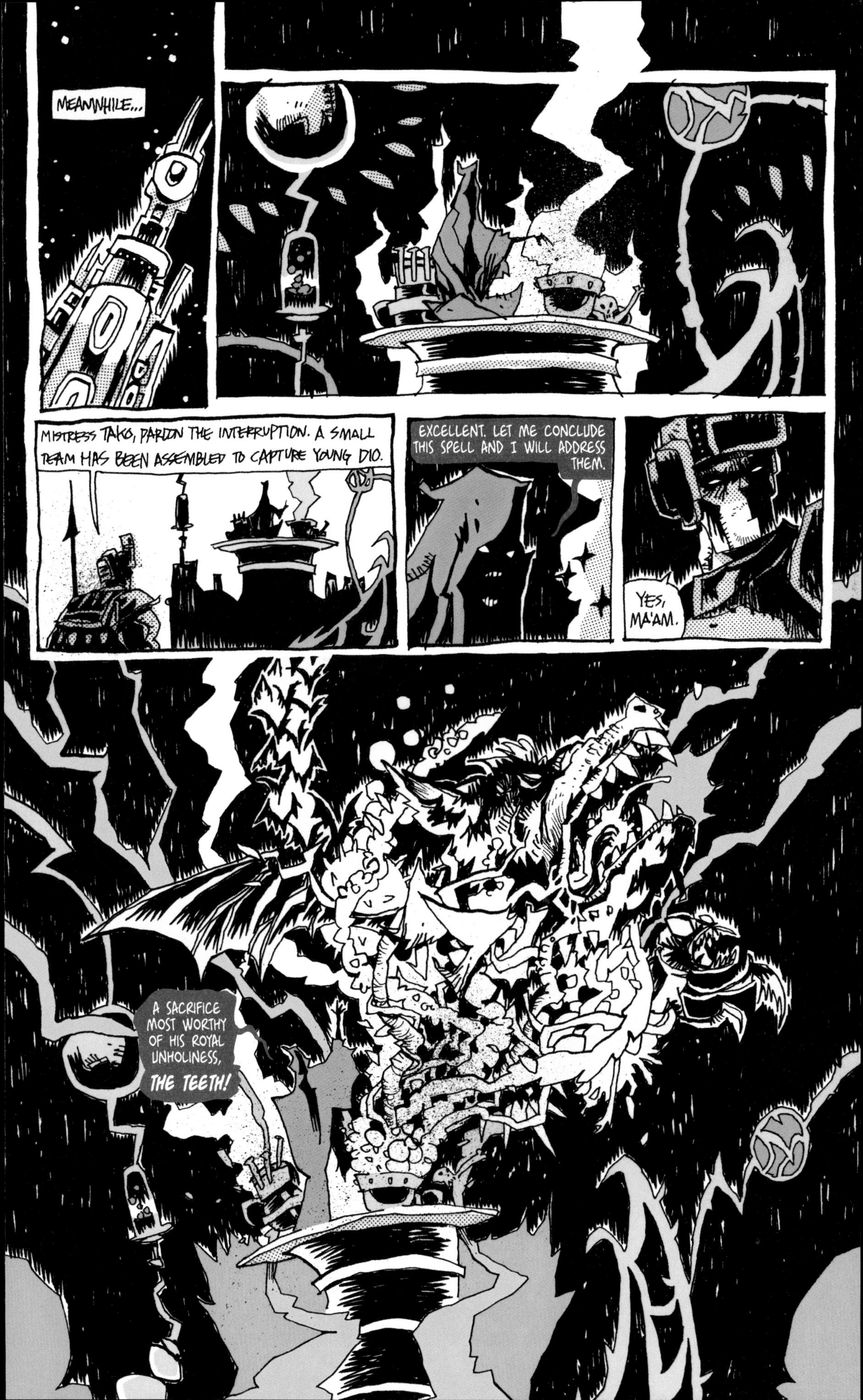
MEANWHILE...
MISTRESS TAKO, PARDON THE INTERRUPTION. A SMALL TEAM HAS BEEN ASSEMBLED TO CAPTURE YOUNG DIO.
EXCELLENT. LET ME CONCLUDE THIS SPELL AND I WILL ADDRESS THEM.
YES, MA'AM.
A SACRIFICE MOST WORTHY OF HIS ROYAL UNHOLINESS, THE TEETH!

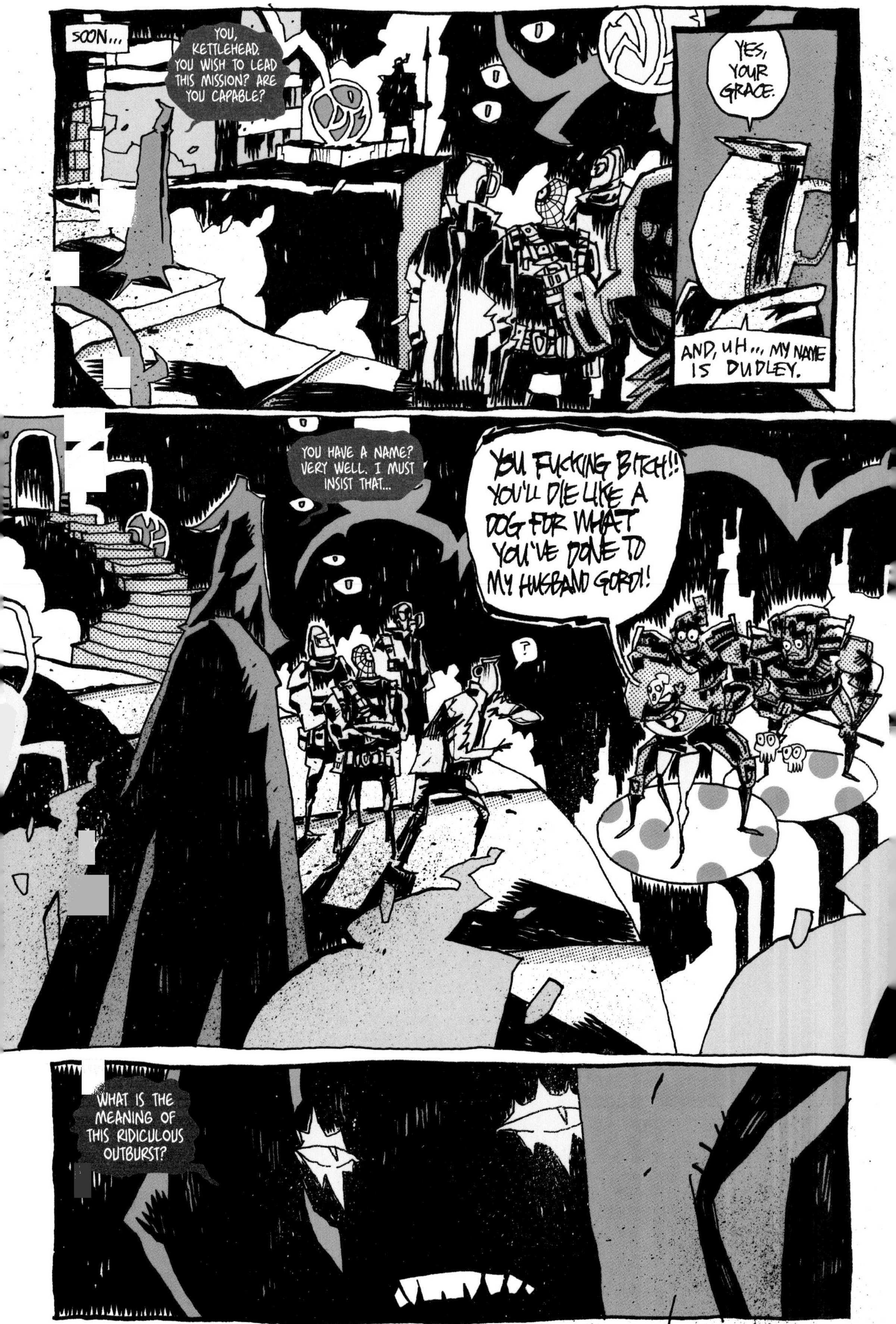
SOON...
YOU, KETTLEHEAD. YOU WISH TO LEAD THIS MISSION? ARE YOU CAPABLE?
YES, YOUR GRACE.
AND, UH... MY NAME IS DUDLEY.
YOU HAVE A NAME? VERY WELL. I MUST INSIST THAT...
YOU FUCKING BITCH!! YOU'LL DIE LIKE A DOG FOR WHAT YOU'VE DONE TO MY HUSBAND GORDI!
?
WHAT IS THE MEANING OF THIS RIDICULOUS OUTBURST?

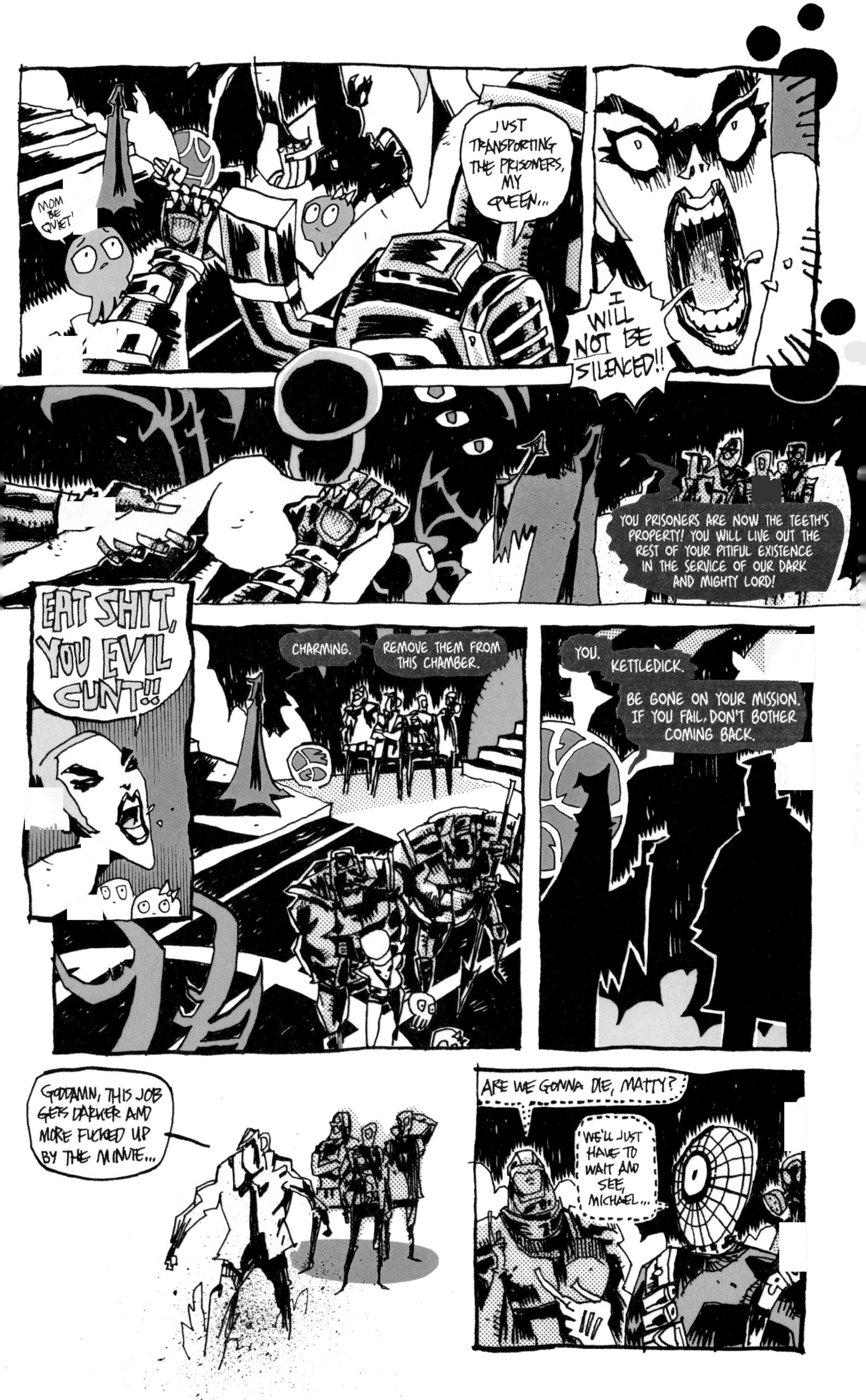
MOM BE QUIET!
JUST TRANSPORTING THE PRISONERS, MY QUEEN...
I WILL NOT BE SILENCED!!
YOU PRISONERS ARE NOW THE TEETH'S PROPERTY! YOU WILL LIVE OUT THE REST OF YOUR PITIFUL EXISTENCE IN THE SERVICE OF OUR DARK AND MIGHTY LORD!
EAT SHIT, YOU EVIL CUNT!!
CHARMING.
REMOVE THEM FROM THIS CHAMBER.
YOU.
KETTLEDICK.
BE GONE ON YOUR MISSION. IF YOU FAIL, DON'T BOTHER COMING BACK.
GODDAMN, THIS JOB GETS DARKER AND MORE FUCKED UP BY THE MINUTE...
ARE WE GONNA DIE, MATTY?
WE'LL JUST HAVE TO WAIT AND SEE, MICHAEL...

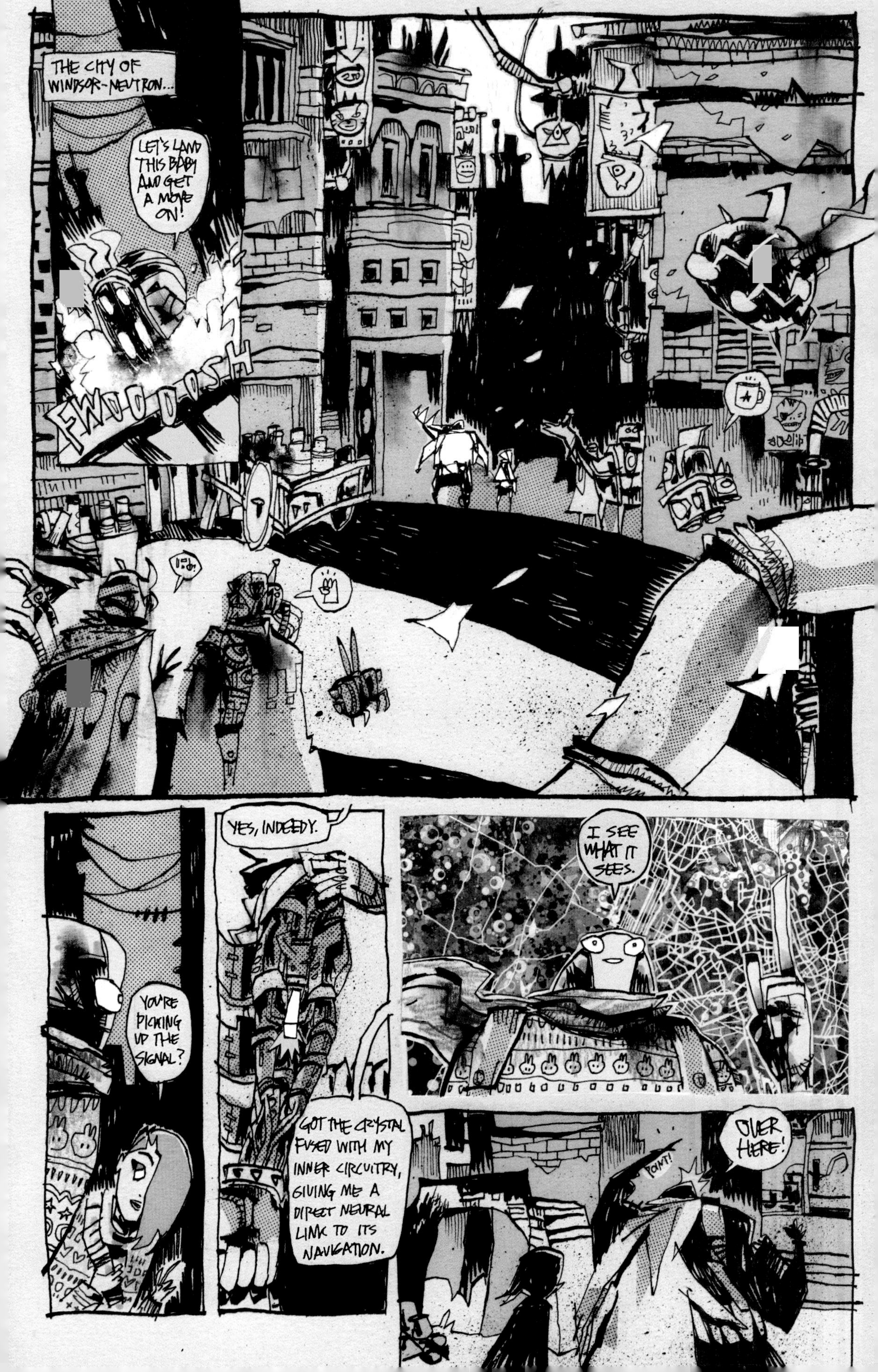
THE CITY OF WINDSOR-NEUTRON...
LET'S LAND THIS BABY AND GET A MOVE ON!
FWOOOOSH
YOU'RE PICKING UP THE SIGNAL?
YES, INDEEDY.
GOT THE CRYSTAL FUSED WITH MY INNER CIRCUITRY, GIVING ME A DIRECT NEURAL LINK TO ITS NAVIGATION.
I SEE WHAT IT SEES.
POINT!
OVER HERE!

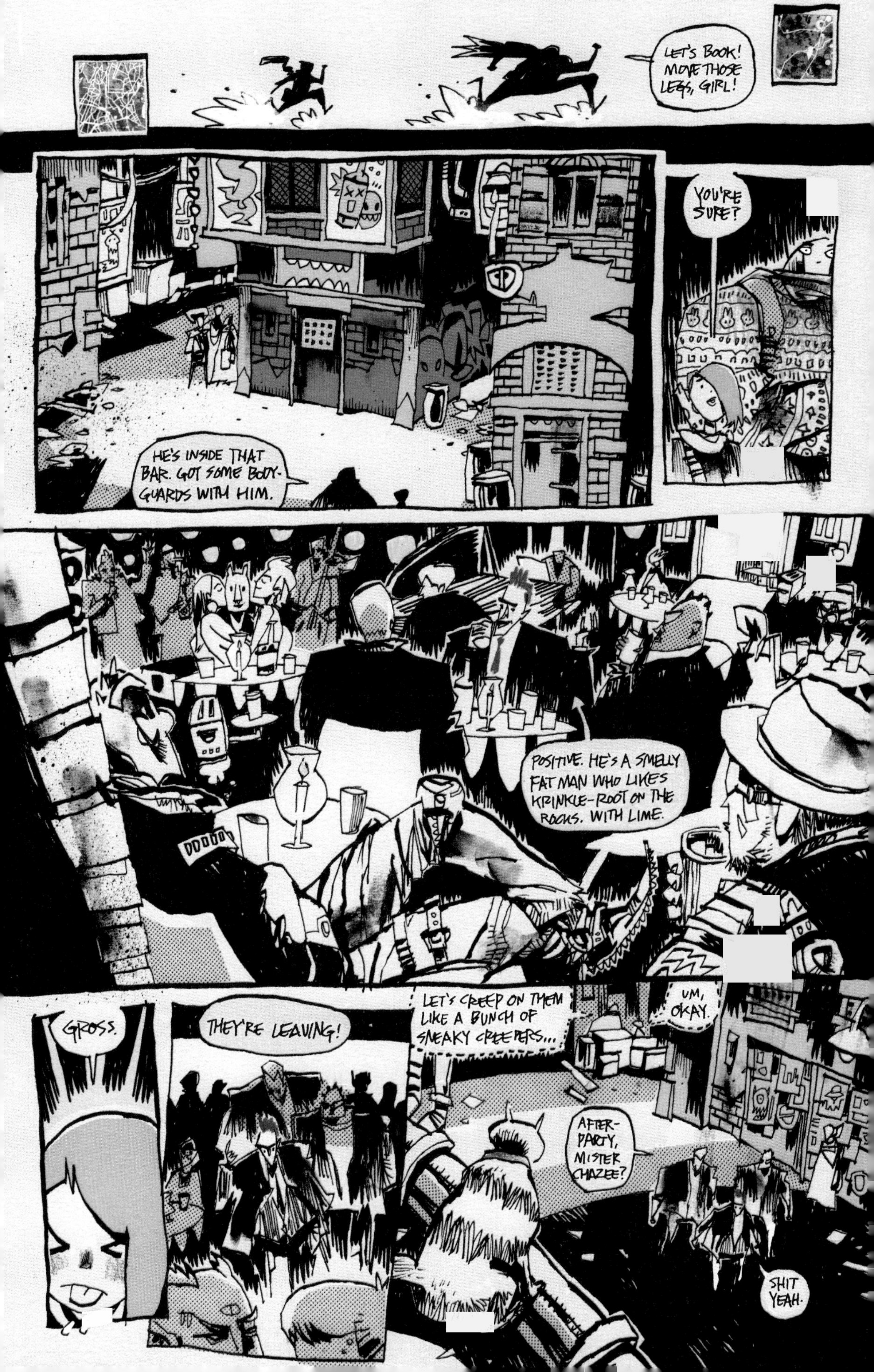
LET'S BOOK! MOVE THOSE LEGS, GIRL!
HE'S INSIDE THAT BAR. GOT SOME BODY-GUARDS WITH HIM.
YOU'RE SURE?
POSITIVE. HE'S A SMELLY FAT MAN WHO LIKES KRINKLE-ROOT ON THE ROCKS. WITH LIME.
GROSS.
THEY'RE LEAVING!
LET'S CREEP ON THEM LIKE A BUNCH OF SNEAKY CREEPERS...
UM, OKAY.
AFTER-PARTY, MISTER CHAZEE?
SHIT YEAH.

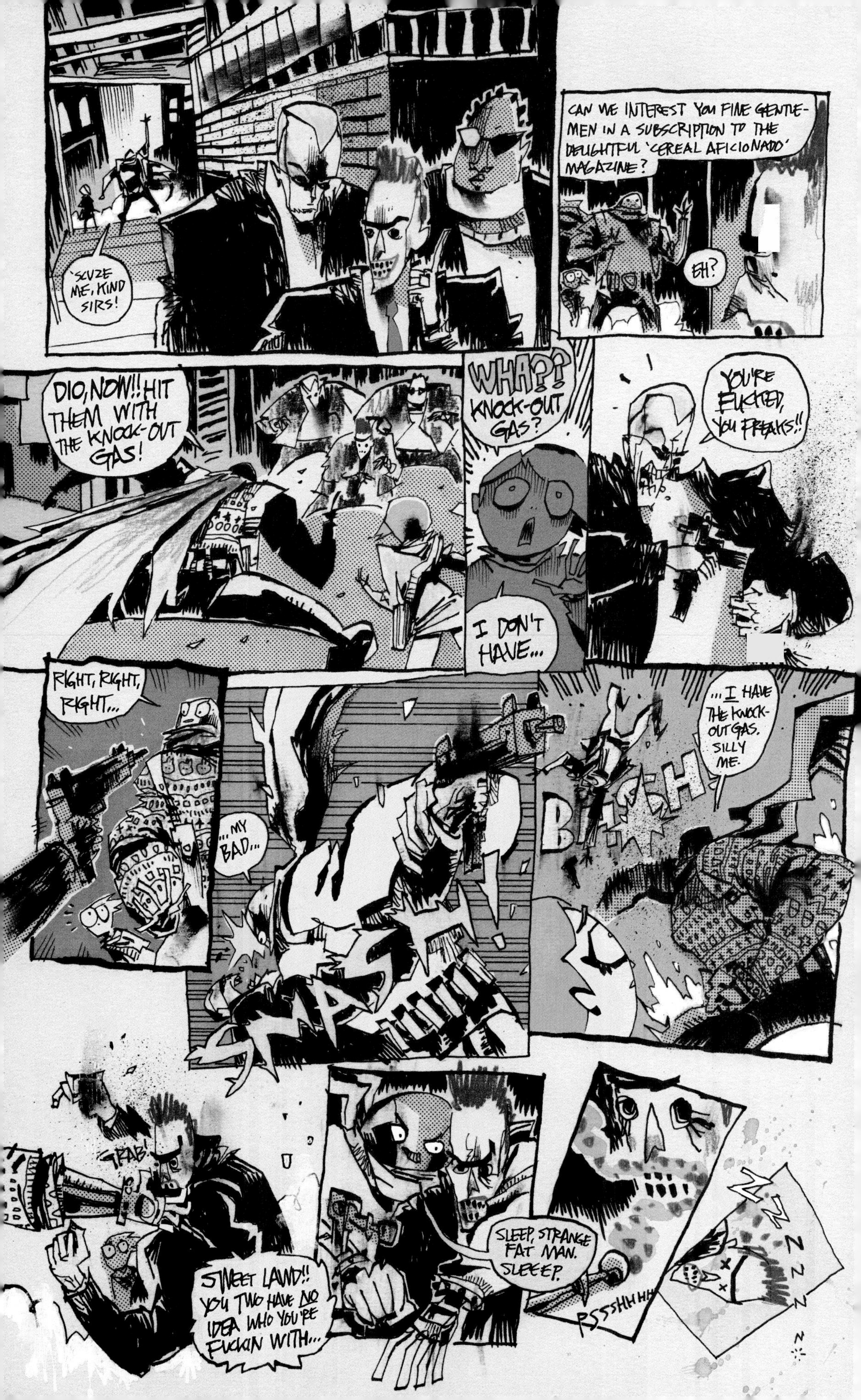
'SCUZE ME, KIND SIRS!
CAN WE INTEREST YOU FINE GENTLE-MEN IN A SUBSCRIPTION TO THE DELIGHTFUL 'CEREAL AFICIONADO' MAGAZINE?
EH?
DIO, NOW!! HIT THEM WITH THE KNOCK-OUT GAS!
WHA?! KNOCK-OUT GAS?
I DON'T HAVE...
YOU'RE FUCKED, YOU FREAKS!!
RIGHT, RIGHT, RIGHT...
...MY BAD...
...I HAVE THE KNOCK-OUT GAS. SILLY ME.
BASH
GRAB!
SWEET LAND!! YOU TWO HAVE NO IDEA WHO YOU'RE FUCKIN WITH...
SLEEP, STRANGE FAT MAN. SLEEEP.
PSSSHHHH
Z Z N N N N

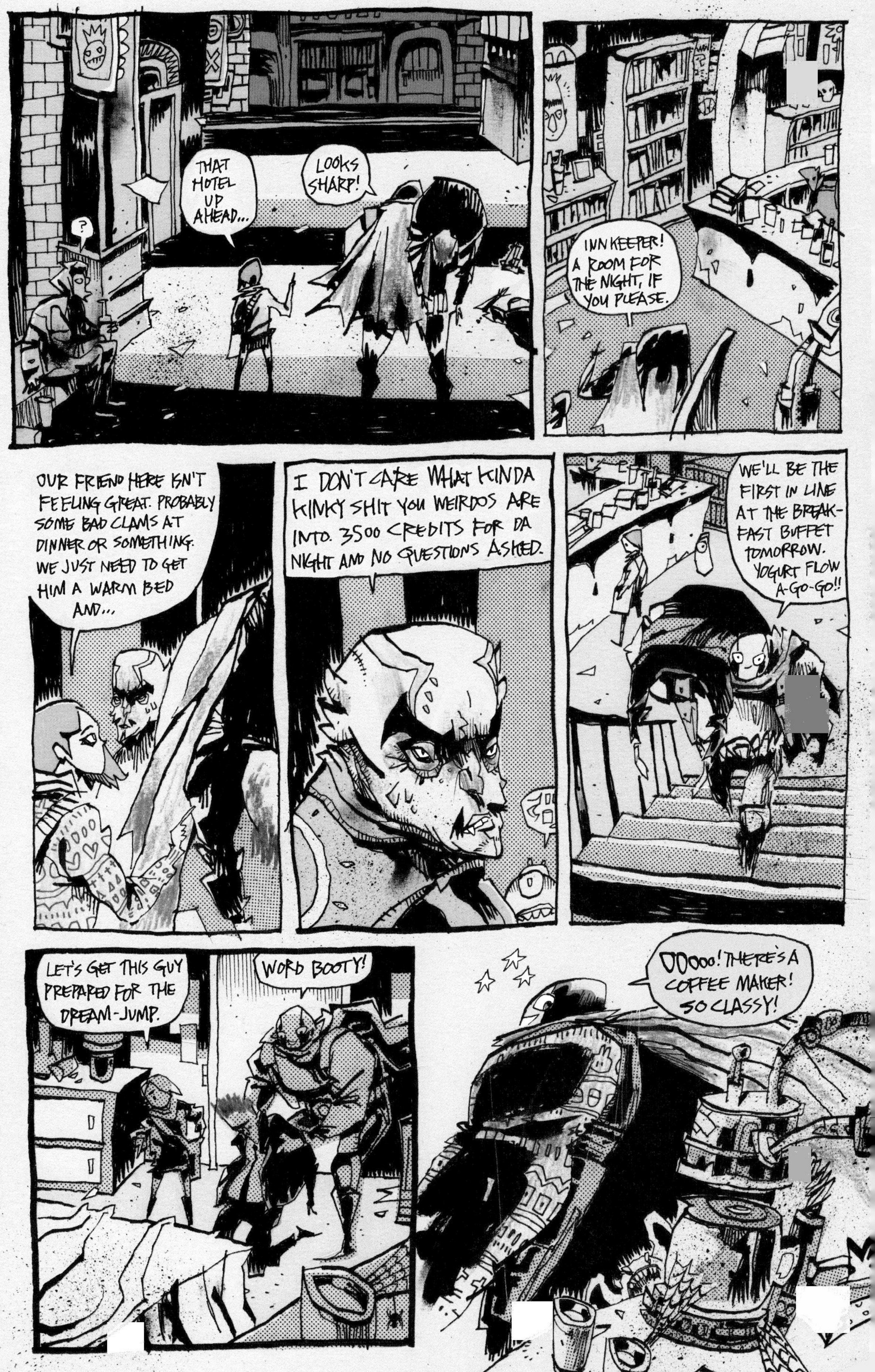
?
THAT HOTEL UP AHEAD...
LOOKS SHARP!
INNKEEPER! A ROOM FOR THE NIGHT, IF YOU PLEASE.
OUR FRIEND HERE ISN'T FEELING GREAT. PROBABLY SOME BAD CLAMS AT DINNER OR SOMETHING. WE JUST NEED TO GET HIM A WARM BED AND...
I DON'T CARE WHAT KINDA KINKY SHIT YOU WEIRDOS ARE INTO. 3500 CREDITS FOR DA NIGHT AND NO QUESTIONS ASKED.
WE'LL BE THE FIRST IN LINE AT THE BREAK-FAST BUFFET TOMORROW. YOGURT FLOW A-GO-GO!!
LET'S GET THIS GUY PREPARED FOR THE DREAM-JUMP.
WORD BOOTY!
OOOOO! THERE'S A COFFEE MAKER! SO CLASSY!

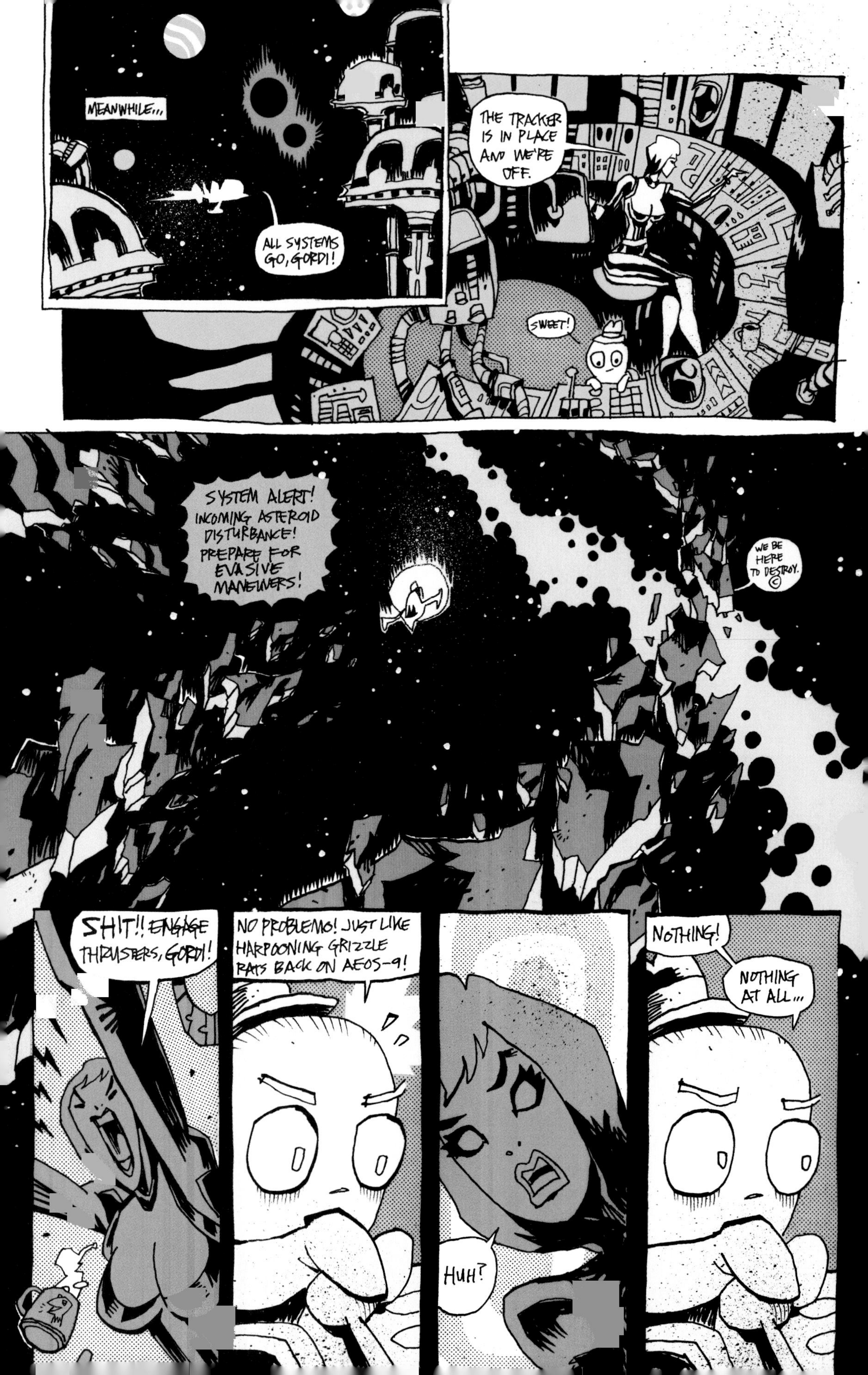
MEANWHILE...
ALL SYSTEMS GO, GORDI!
THE TRACKER IS IN PLACE AND WE'RE OFF.
SWEET!
SYSTEM ALERT! INCOMING ASTEROID DISTURBANCE! PREPARE FOR EVASIVE MANEUVERS!
WE BE HERE TO DESTROY. ©
SHIT!! ENGAGE THRUSTERS, GORDI!
NO PROBLEMO! JUST LIKE HARPOONING GRIZZLE RATS BACK ON AEOS-9!
HUH?
NOTHING!
NOTHING AT ALL...

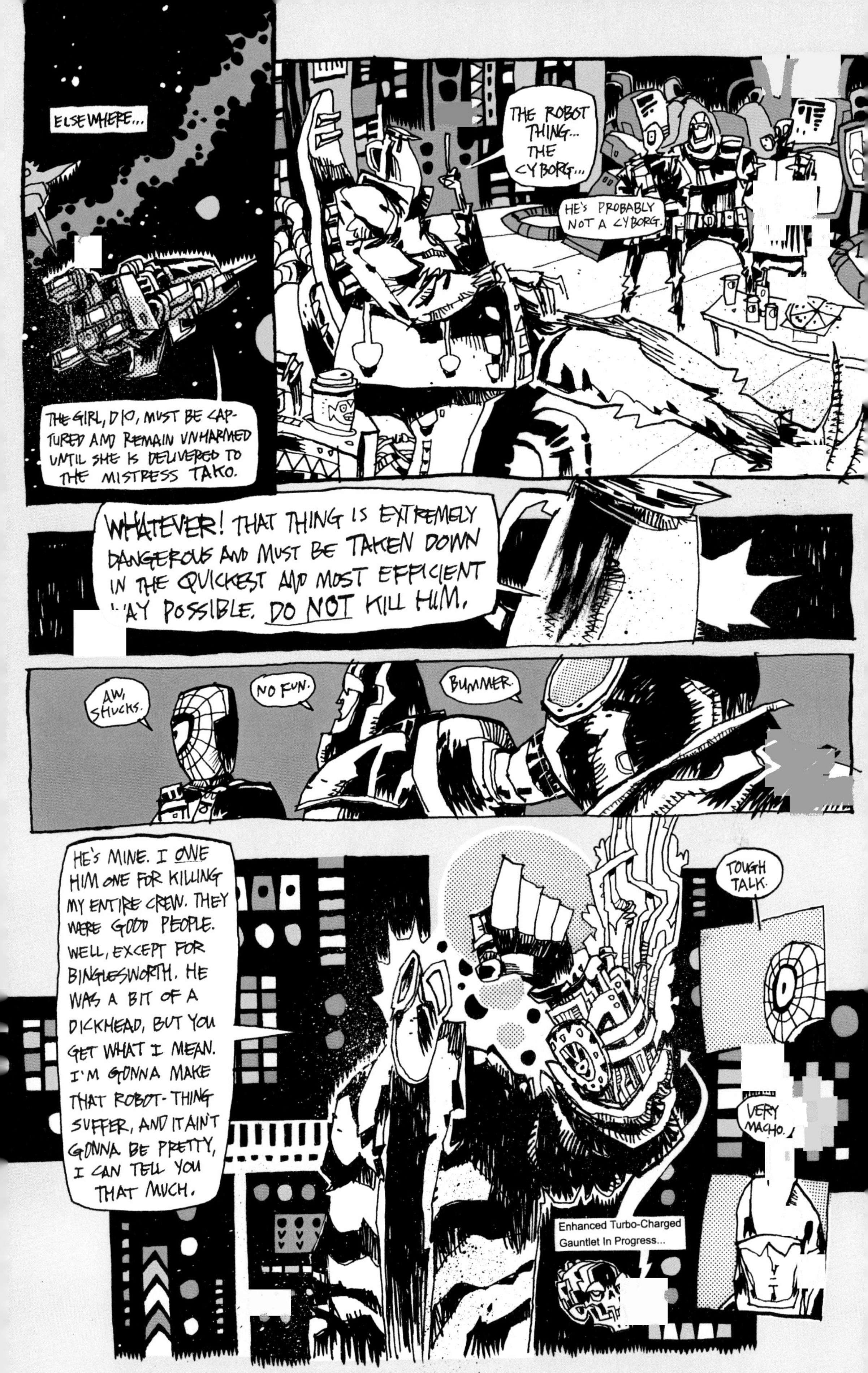
ELSEWHERE...
THE GIRL, DIO, MUST BE CAPTURED AND REMAIN UNHARMED UNTIL SHE IS DELIVERED TO THE MISTRESS TAKO.
THE ROBOT THING... THE CYBORG...
HE'S PROBABLY NOT A CYBORG.
WHATEVER! THAT THING IS EXTREMELY DANGEROUS AND MUST BE TAKEN DOWN IN THE QUICKEST AND MOST EFFICIENT WAY POSSIBLE. DO NOT KILL HIM.
AW, SHUCKS.
NO FUN.
BUMMER.
HE'S MINE. I OWE HIM ONE FOR KILLING MY ENTIRE CREW. THEY WERE GOOD PEOPLE. WELL, EXCEPT FOR BINGLESWORTH. HE WAS A BIT OF A DICKHEAD, BUT YOU GET WHAT I MEAN. I'M GONNA MAKE THAT ROBOT-THING SUFFER, AND IT AIN'T GONNA BE PRETTY, I CAN TELL YOU THAT MUCH.
TOUGH TALK.
VERY MACHO.
Enhanced Turbo-Charged Gauntlet In Progress...

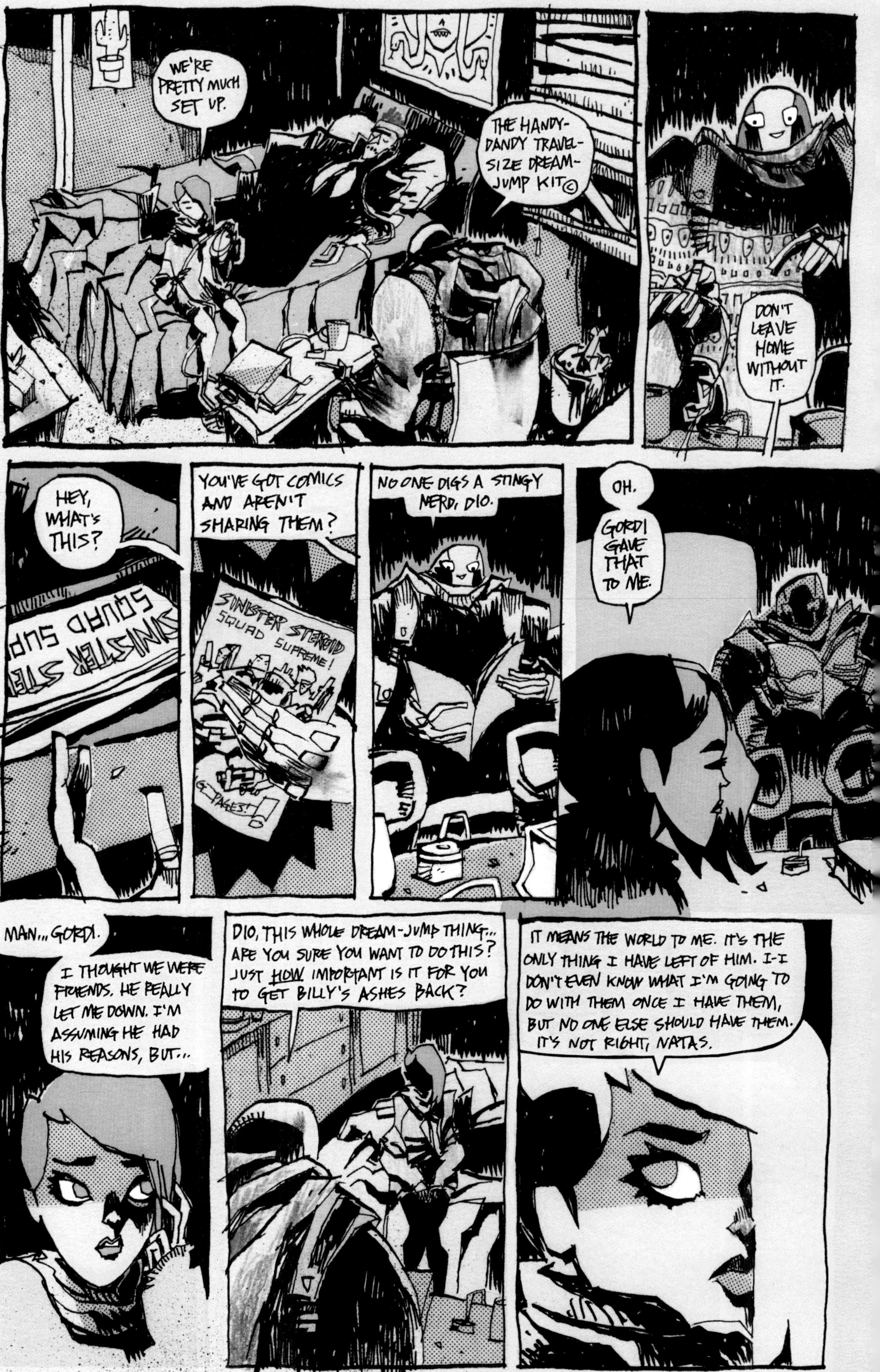
WE'RE PRETTY MUCH SET UP.
THE HANDY-DANDY TRAVEL-SIZE DREAM-JUMP KIT©
DON'T LEAVE HOME WITHOUT IT.
HEY, WHAT'S THIS?
SINISTER STE SQUAD SUP
YOU'VE GOT COMICS AND AREN'T SHARING THEM?
SINISTER STEROID SQUAD SUPREME!
NO ONE DIGS A STINGY NERD, DIO.
OH.
GORDI GAVE THAT TO ME.
MAN... GORDI.
I THOUGHT WE WERE FRIENDS. HE REALLY LET ME DOWN. I'M ASSUMING HE HAD HIS REASONS, BUT...
DIO, THIS WHOLE DREAM-JUMP THING... ARE YOU SURE YOU WANT TO DO THIS? JUST HOW IMPORTANT IS IT FOR YOU TO GET BILLY'S ASHES BACK?
IT MEANS THE WORLD TO ME. IT'S THE ONLY THING I HAVE LEFT OF HIM. I-I DON'T EVEN KNOW WHAT I'M GOING TO DO WITH THEM ONCE I HAVE THEM, BUT NO ONE ELSE SHOULD HAVE THEM. IT'S NOT RIGHT, NATAS.

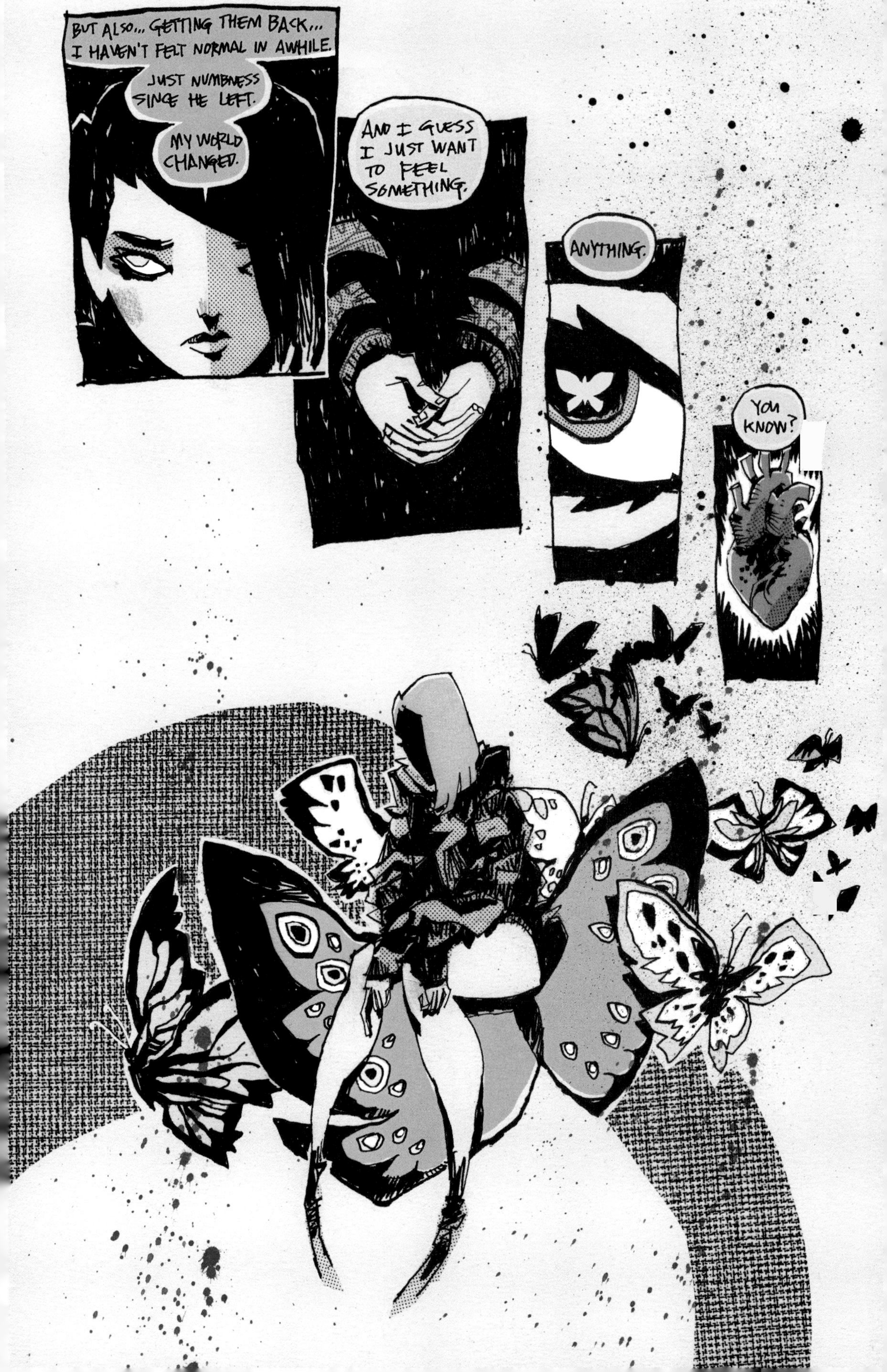
BUT ALSO... GETTING THEM BACK... I HAVEN'T FELT NORMAL IN AWHILE.
JUST NUMBNESS SINCE HE LEFT.
MY WORLD CHANGED.
AND I GUESS I JUST WANT TO FEEL SOMETHING.
ANYTHING.
YOU KNOW?

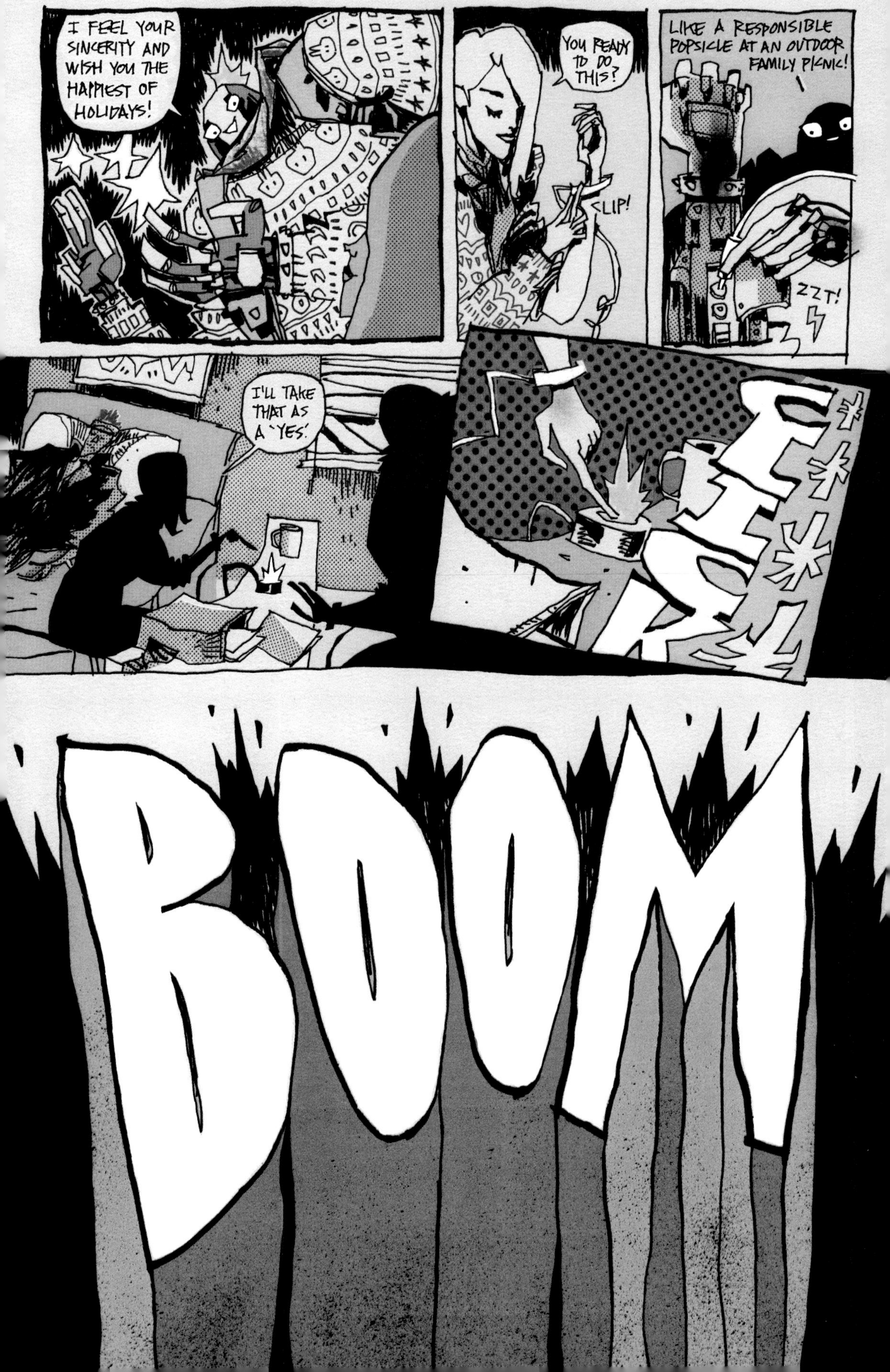
I FEEL YOUR SINCERITY AND WISH YOU THE HAPPIEST OF HOLIDAYS!
YOU READY TO DO THIS?
SLIP!
LIKE A RESPONSIBLE POPSICLE AT AN OUTDOOR FAMILY PICNIC!
ZZT!
I'LL TAKE THAT AS A 'YES'.
CLICK
BOOM

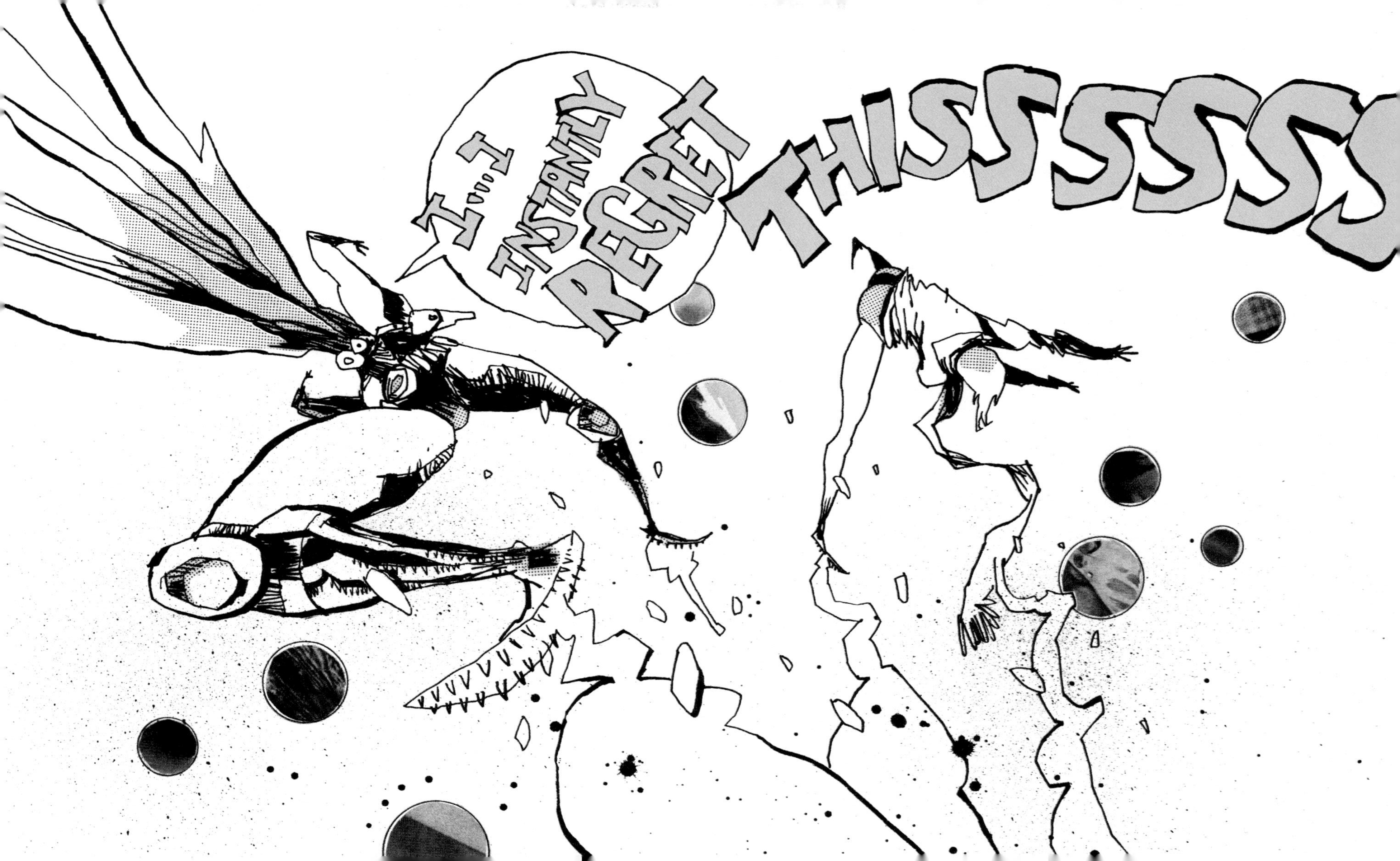
I...I INSTANTLY REGRET
THISSSSSS

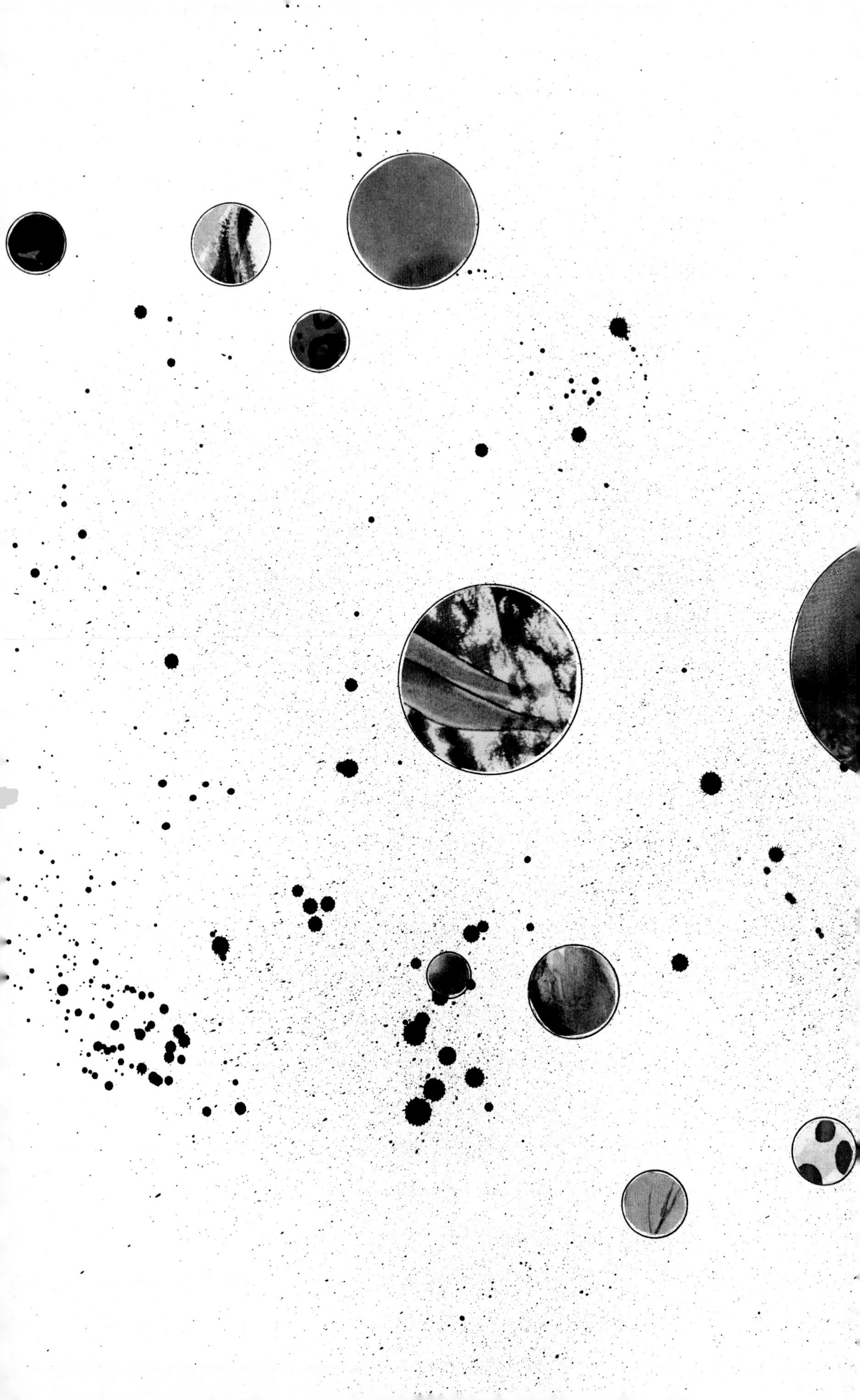

TO BE CONTINUED....

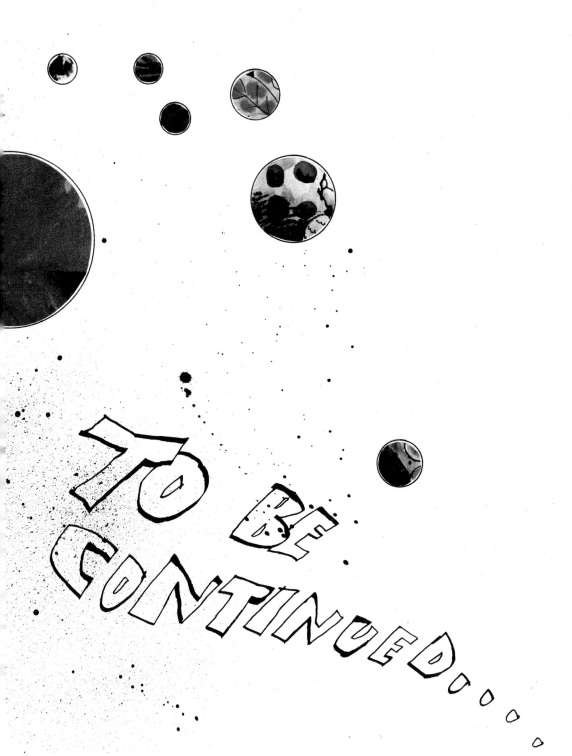

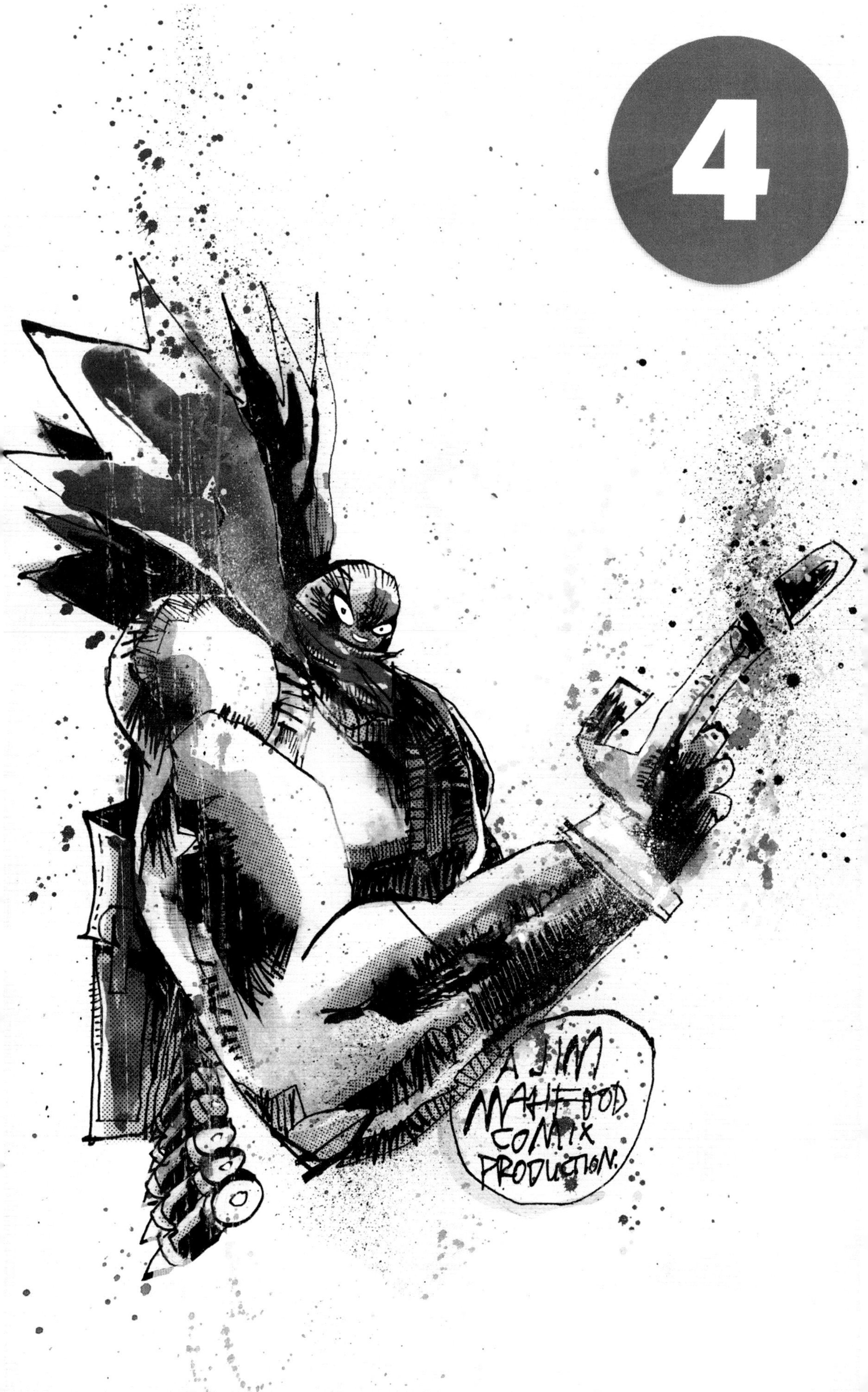
4
A JIM MAHFOOD COMIX PRODUCTION.

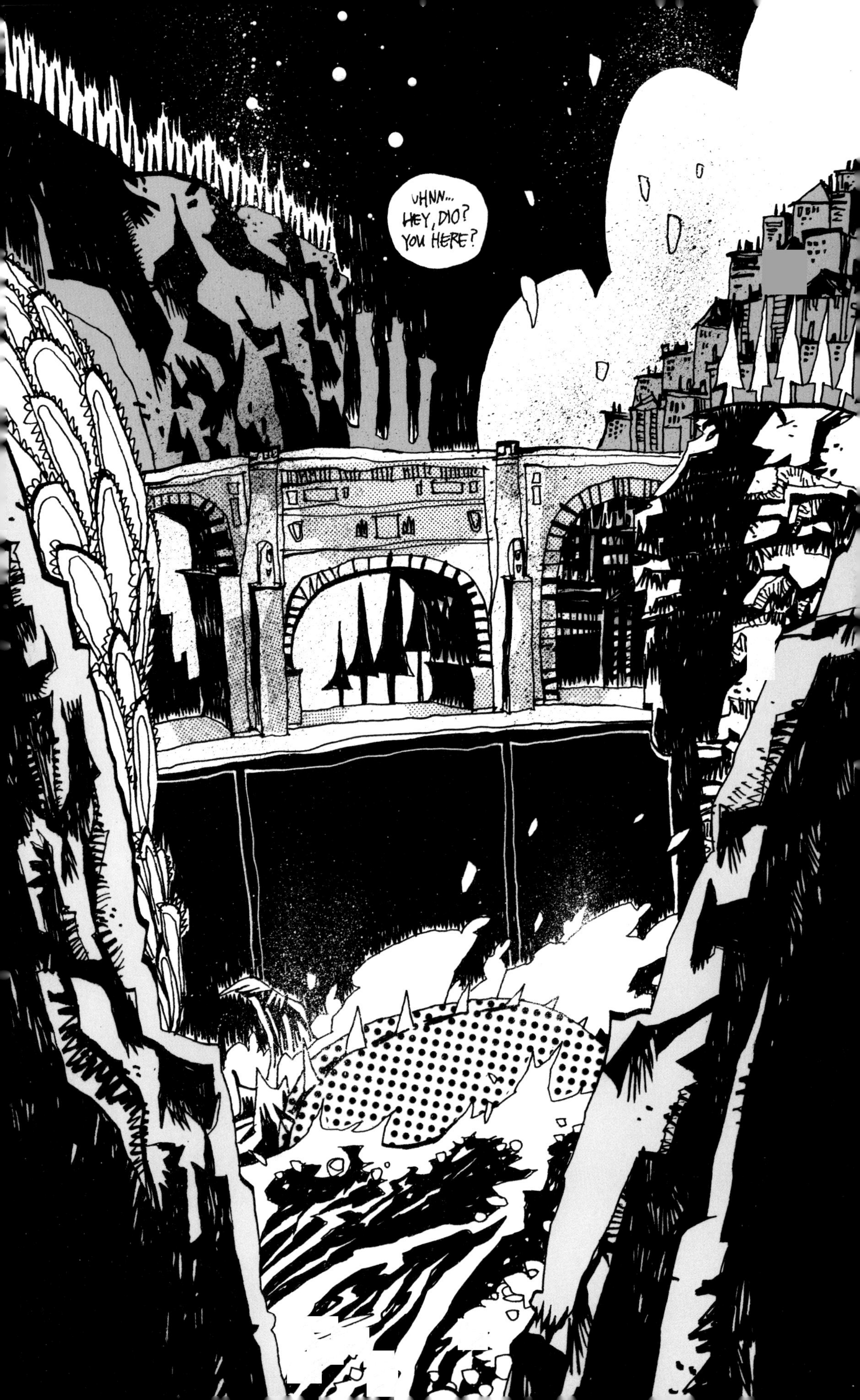
UHNN... HEY, DIO? YOU HERE?

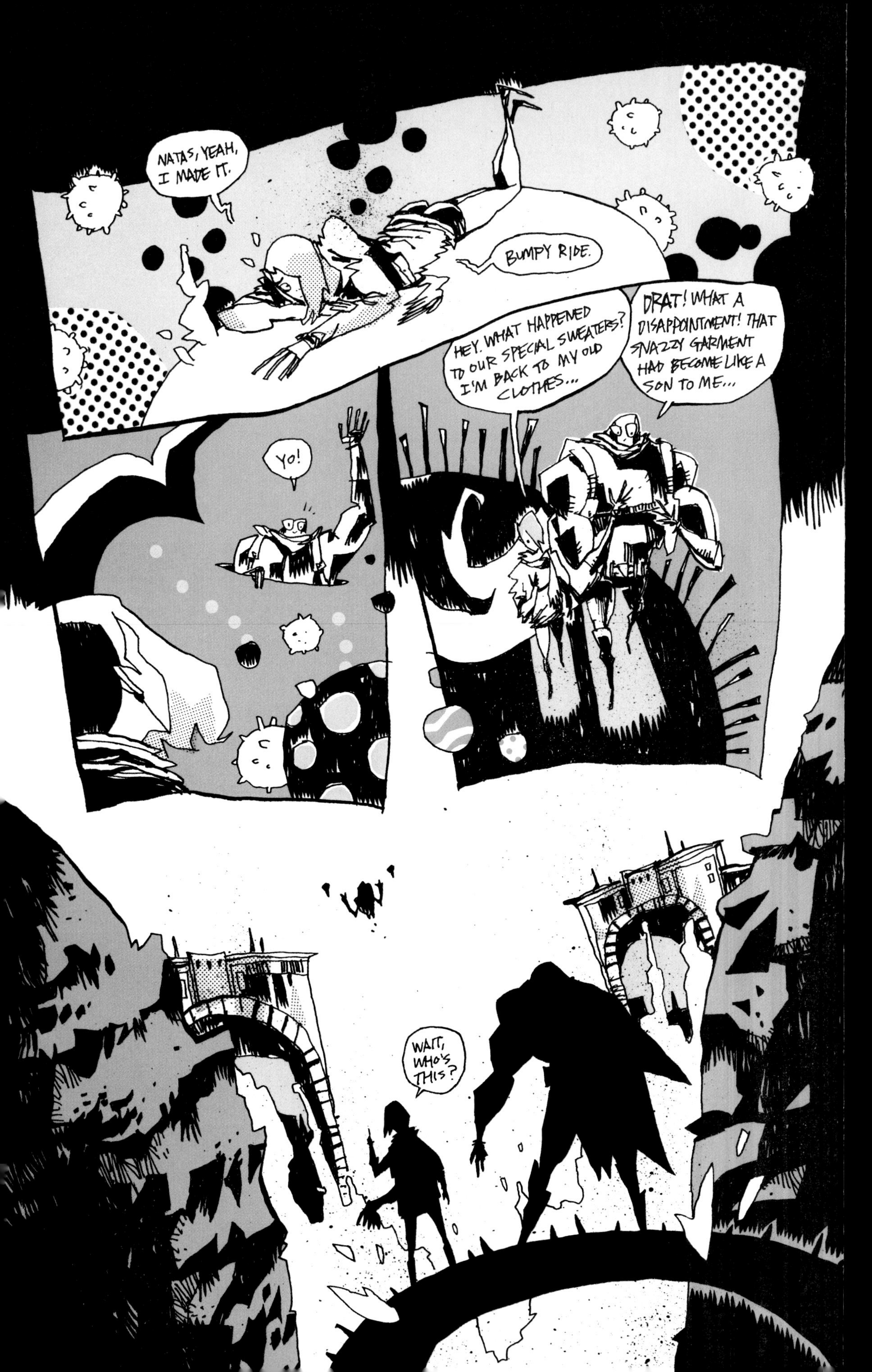
NATAS, YEAH, I MADE IT.
BUMPY RIDE.
YO!
HEY. WHAT HAPPENED TO OUR SPECIAL SWEATERS? I'M BACK TO MY OLD CLOTHES...
DRAT! WHAT A DISAPPOINTMENT! THAT SNAZZY GARMENT HAD BECOME LIKE A SON TO ME...
WAIT, WHO'S THIS?

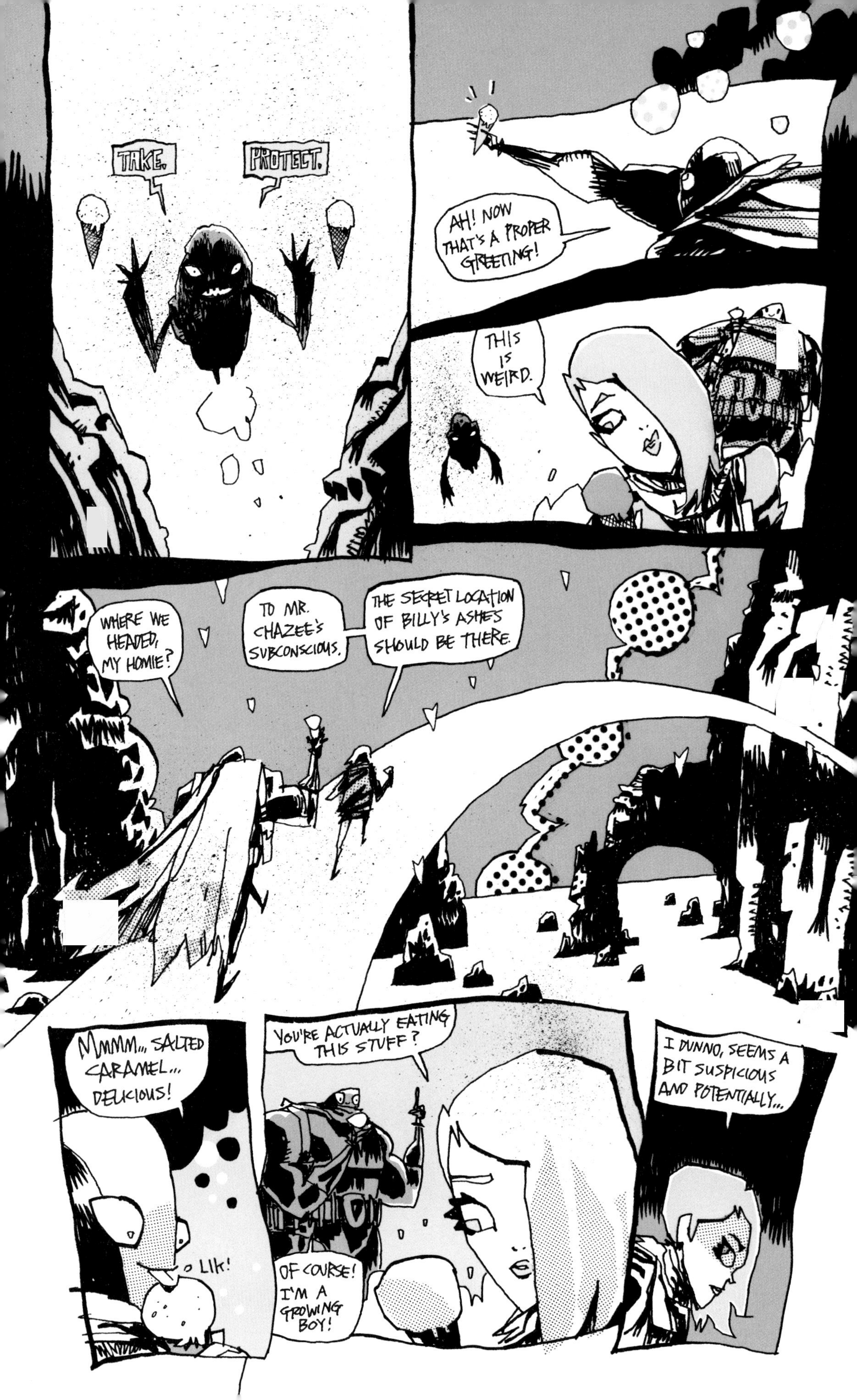
TAKE.
PROTECT.
AH! NOW THAT'S A PROPER GREETING!
THIS IS WEIRD.
WHERE WE HEADED, MY HOMIE?
TO MR. CHAZEE'S SUBCONSCIOUS.
THE SECRET LOCATION OF BILLY'S ASHES SHOULD BE THERE.
MMMM... SALTED CARAMEL... DELICIOUS!
LIK!
YOU'RE ACTUALLY EATING THIS STUFF?
OF COURSE! I'M A GROWING BOY!
I DUNNO, SEEMS A BIT SUSPICIOUS AND POTENTIALLY...

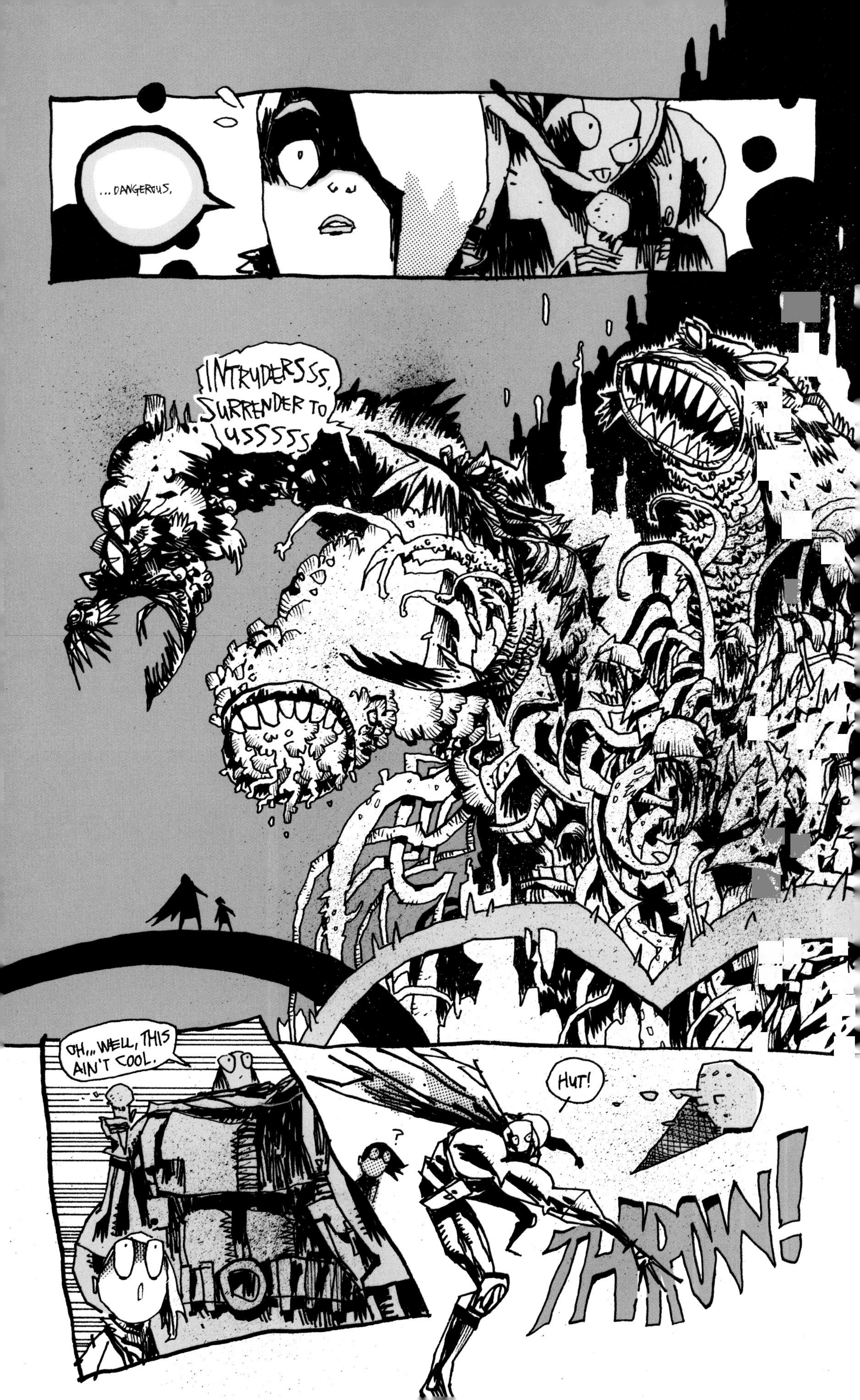
...DANGEROUS.
INTRUDERSSS. SURRENDER TO USSSSS
OH... WELL, THIS AIN'T COOL.
HUT!
?
THROW!

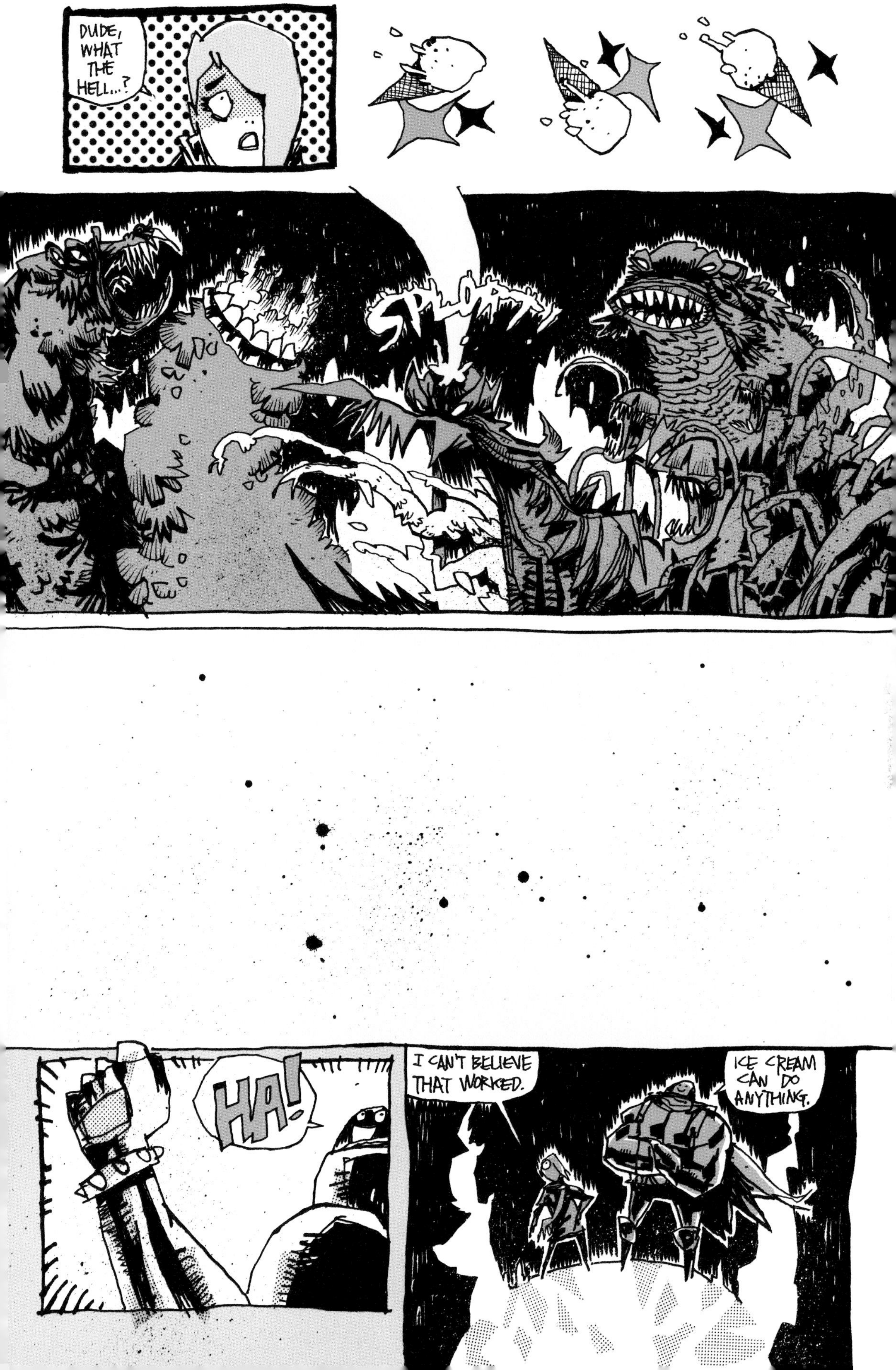
DUDE, WHAT THE HELL...?
SPLORT!
HA!
I CAN'T BELIEVE THAT WORKED.
ICE CREAM CAN DO ANYTHING.

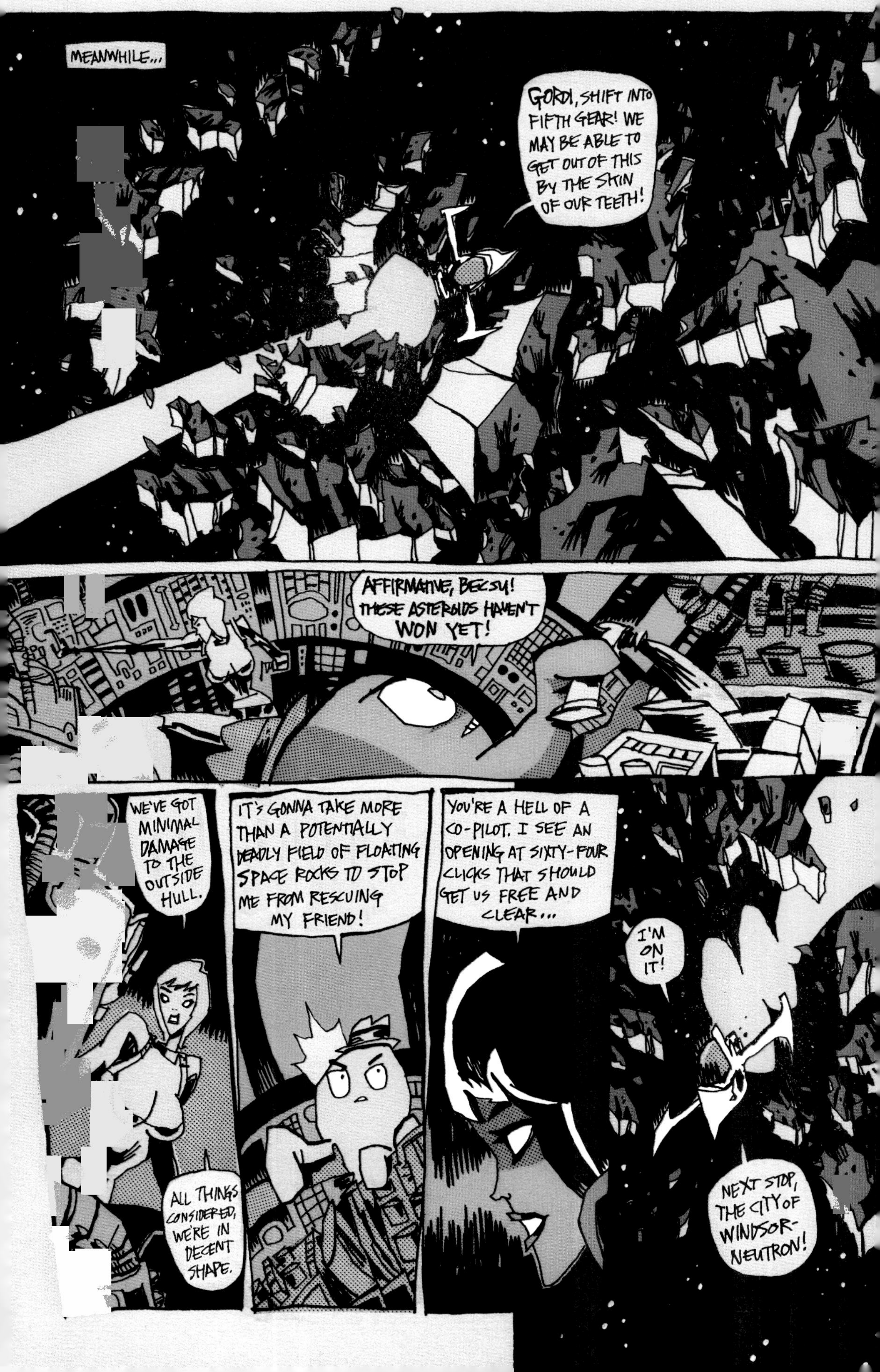
MEANWHILE...
GORDI, SHIFT INTO FIFTH GEAR! WE MAY BE ABLE TO GET OUT OF THIS BY THE SKIN OF OUR TEETH!
AFFIRMATIVE, BECSY! THESE ASTEROIDS HAVEN'T WON YET!
WE'VE GOT MINIMAL DAMAGE TO THE OUTSIDE HULL.
ALL THINGS CONSIDERED, WE'RE IN DECENT SHAPE.
IT'S GONNA TAKE MORE THAN A POTENTIALLY DEADLY FIELD OF FLOATING SPACE ROCKS TO STOP ME FROM RESCUING MY FRIEND!
YOU'RE A HELL OF A CO-PILOT. I SEE AN OPENING AT SIXTY-FOUR CLICKS THAT SHOULD GET US FREE AND CLEAR...
I'M ON IT!
NEXT STOP, THE CITY OF WINDSOR-NEUTRON!

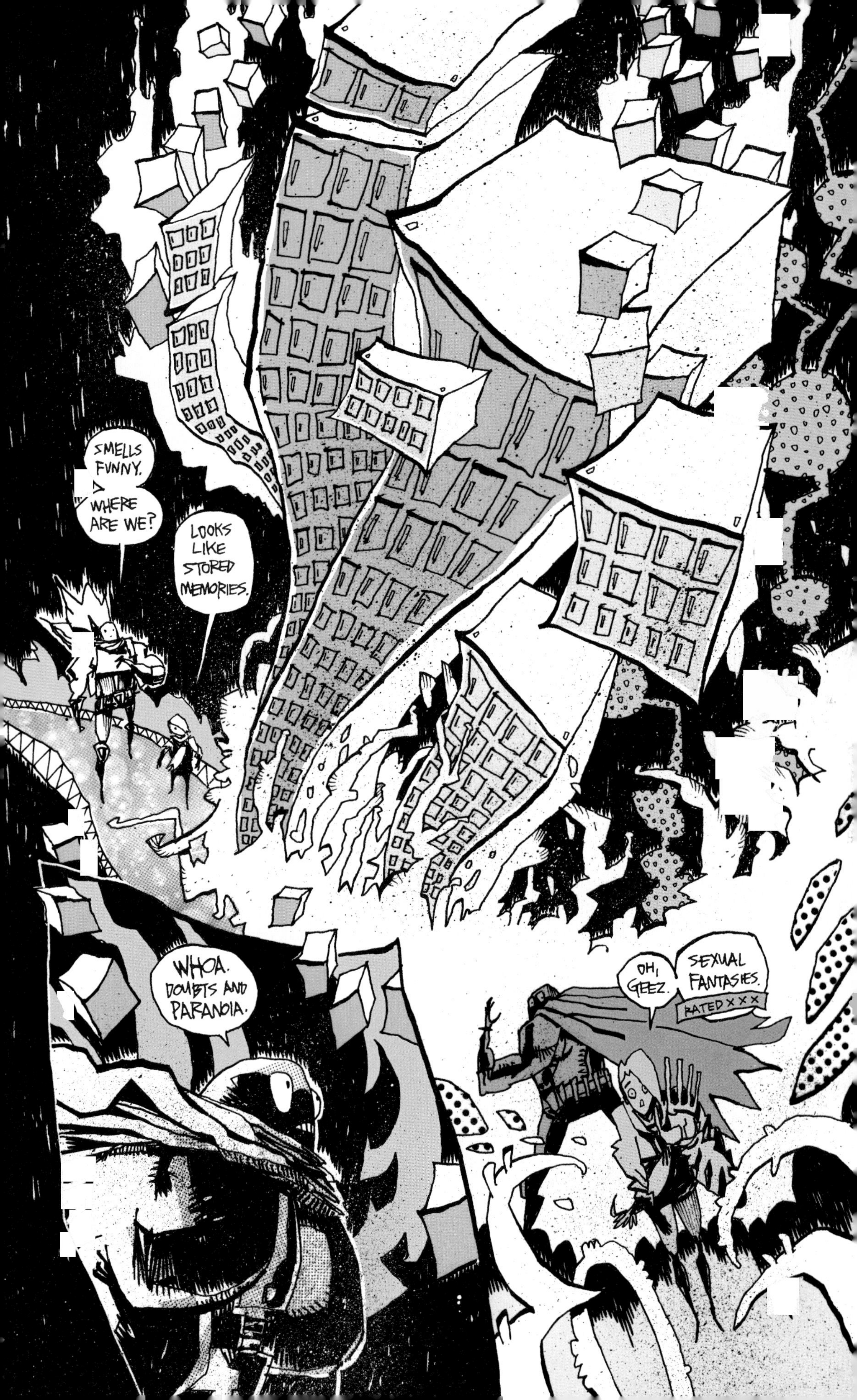
SMELLS FUNNY.
WHERE ARE WE?
LOOKS LIKE STORED MEMORIES.
WHOA. DOUBTS AND PARANOIA.
OH, GEEZ.
SEXUAL FANTASIES.
RATED XXX

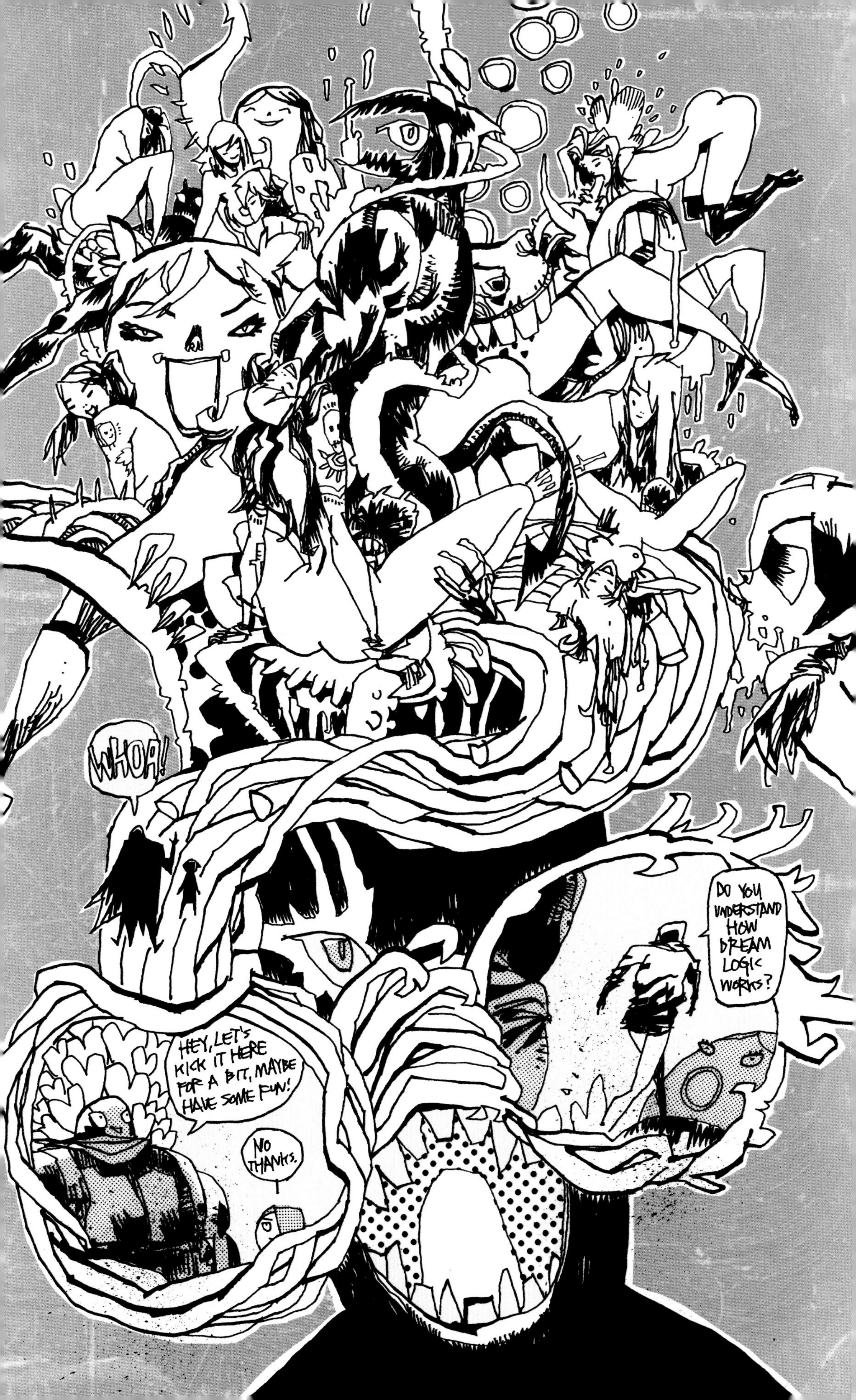
WHOA!
DO YOU UNDERSTAND HOW DREAM LOGIC WORKS?
HEY, LET'S KICK IT HERE FOR A BIT, MAYBE HAVE SOME FUN!
NO THANKS.

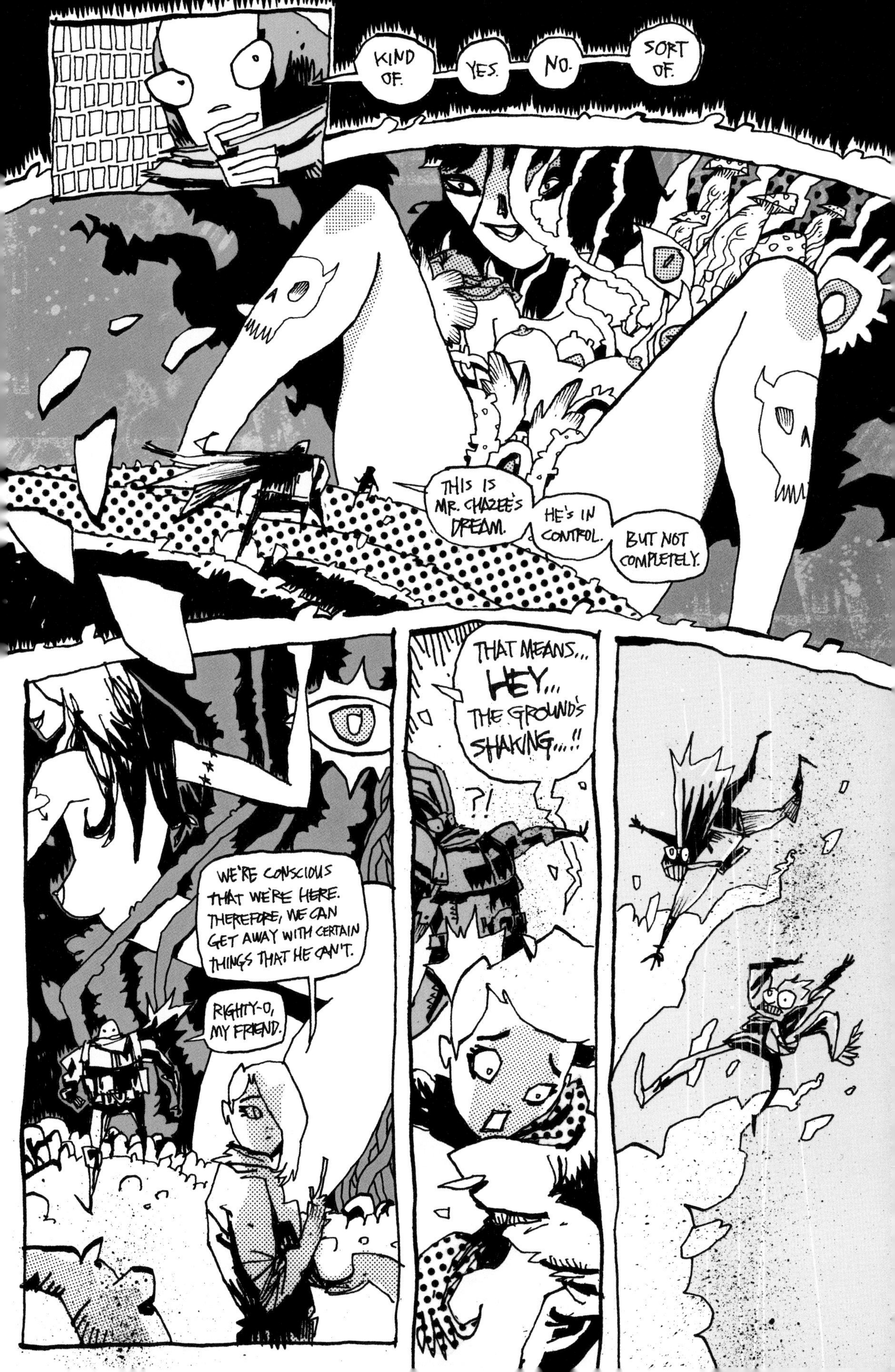
KIND OF.
YES.
NO.
SORT OF.
THIS IS MR. CHAZEE'S DREAM.
HE'S IN CONTROL.
BUT NOT COMPLETELY.
WE'RE CONSCIOUS THAT WE'RE HERE. THEREFORE, WE CAN GET AWAY WITH CERTAIN THINGS THAT HE CAN'T.
RIGHTY-O, MY FRIEND.
THAT MEANS... HEY... THE GROUND'S SHAKING...!!
?!

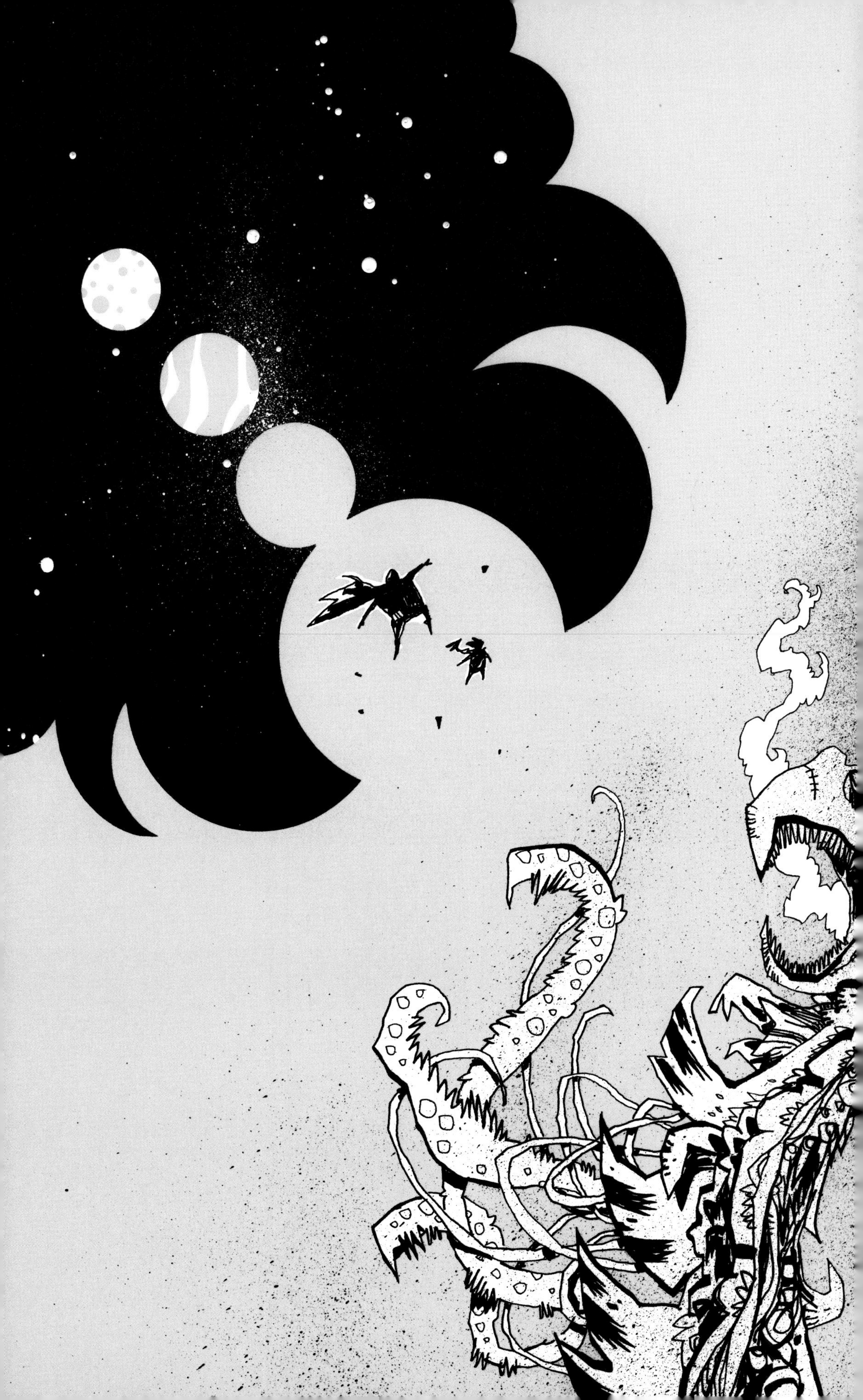

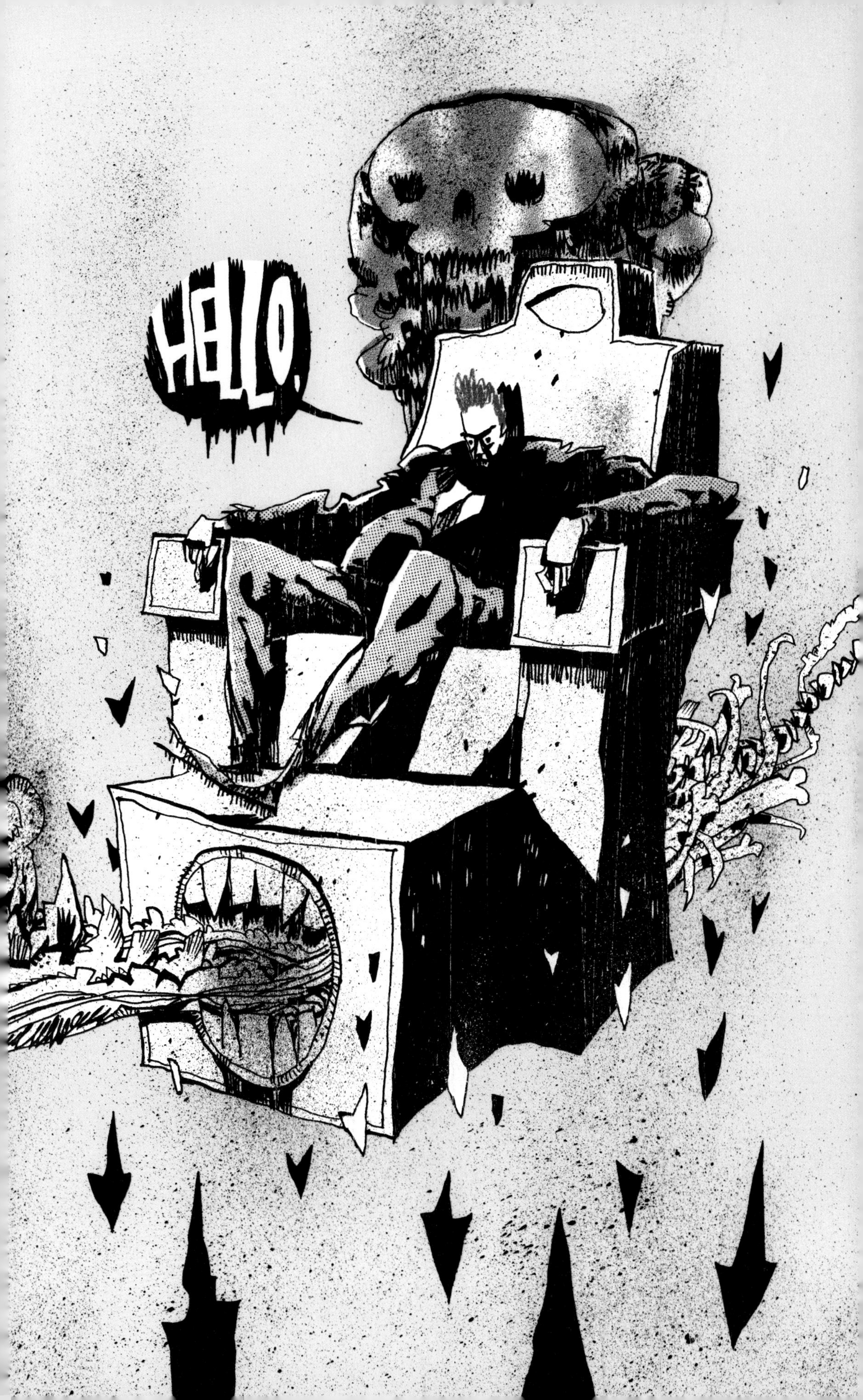
HELLO.

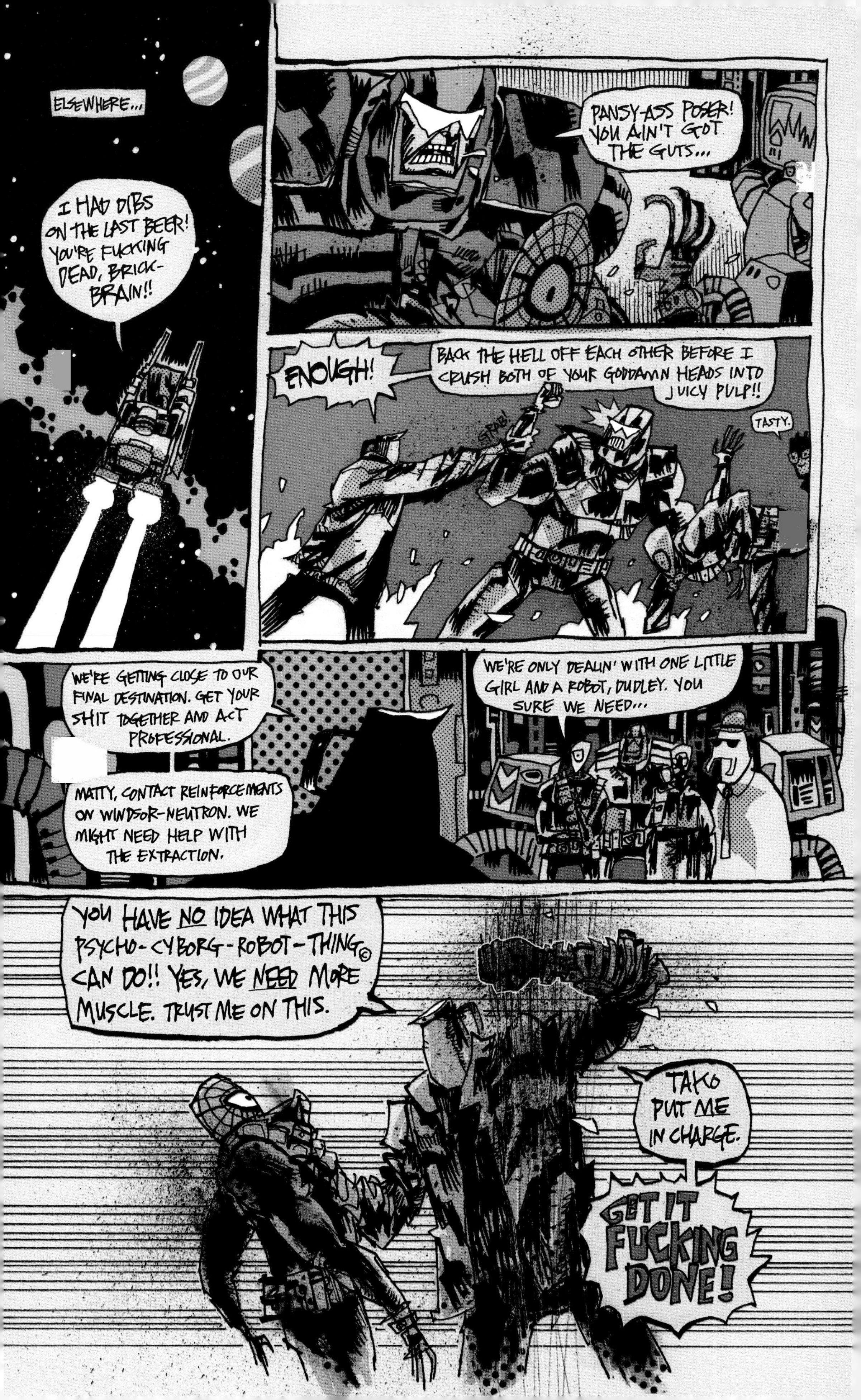
ELSEWHERE...
I HAD DIBS ON THE LAST BEER! YOU'RE FUCKING DEAD, BRICK-BRAIN!!
PANSY-ASS POSER! YOU AIN'T GOT THE GUTS...
ENOUGH!
BACK THE HELL OFF EACH OTHER BEFORE I CRUSH BOTH OF YOUR GODDAMN HEADS INTO JUICY PULP!!
TASTY.
WE'RE GETTING CLOSE TO OUR FINAL DESTINATION. GET YOUR SHIT TOGETHER AND ACT PROFESSIONAL.
MATTY, CONTACT REINFORCEMENTS ON WINDSOR-NEUTRON. WE MIGHT NEED HELP WITH THE EXTRACTION.
WE'RE ONLY DEALIN' WITH ONE LITTLE GIRL AND A ROBOT, DUDLEY. YOU SURE WE NEED...
YOU HAVE NO IDEA WHAT THIS PSYCHO-CYBORG-ROBOT-THING© CAN DO!! YES, WE NEED MORE MUSCLE. TRUST ME ON THIS.
TAKO PUT ME IN CHARGE.
GET IT FUCKING DONE!

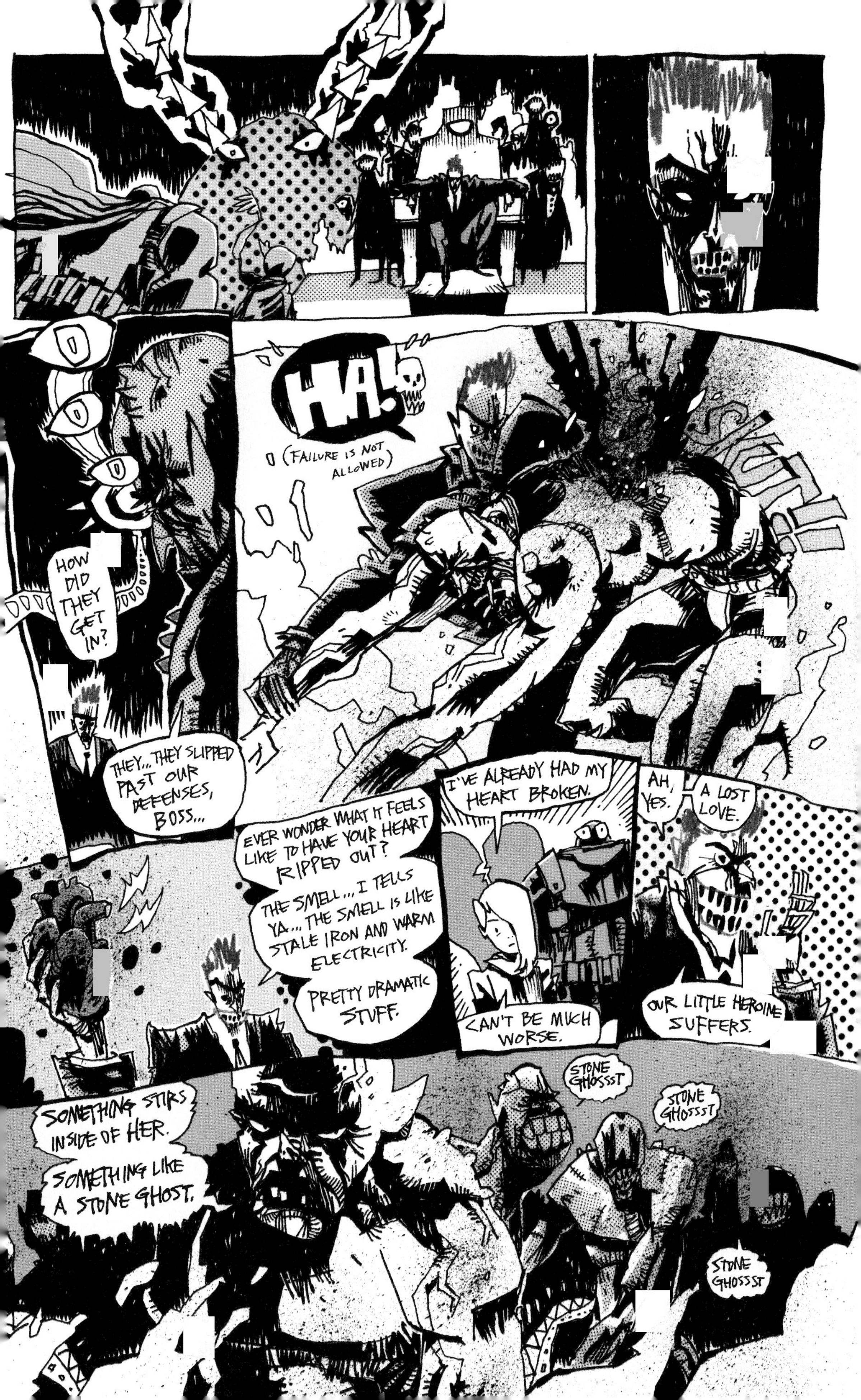
HOW DID THEY GET IN?
THEY... THEY SLIPPED PAST OUR DEFENSES, BOSS...
HA!
(FAILURE IS NOT ALLOWED)
EVER WONDER WHAT IT FEELS LIKE TO HAVE YOUR HEART RIPPED OUT?
THE SMELL... I TELLS YA... THE SMELL IS LIKE STALE IRON AND WARM ELECTRICITY.
PRETTY DRAMATIC STUFF.
I'VE ALREADY HAD MY HEART BROKEN.
CAN'T BE MUCH WORSE.
AH, YES.
A LOST LOVE.
OUR LITTLE HEROINE SUFFERS.
SOMETHING STIRS INSIDE OF HER.
SOMETHING LIKE A STONE GHOST.
STONE GHOSSST
STONE GHOSSST
STONE GHOSSST

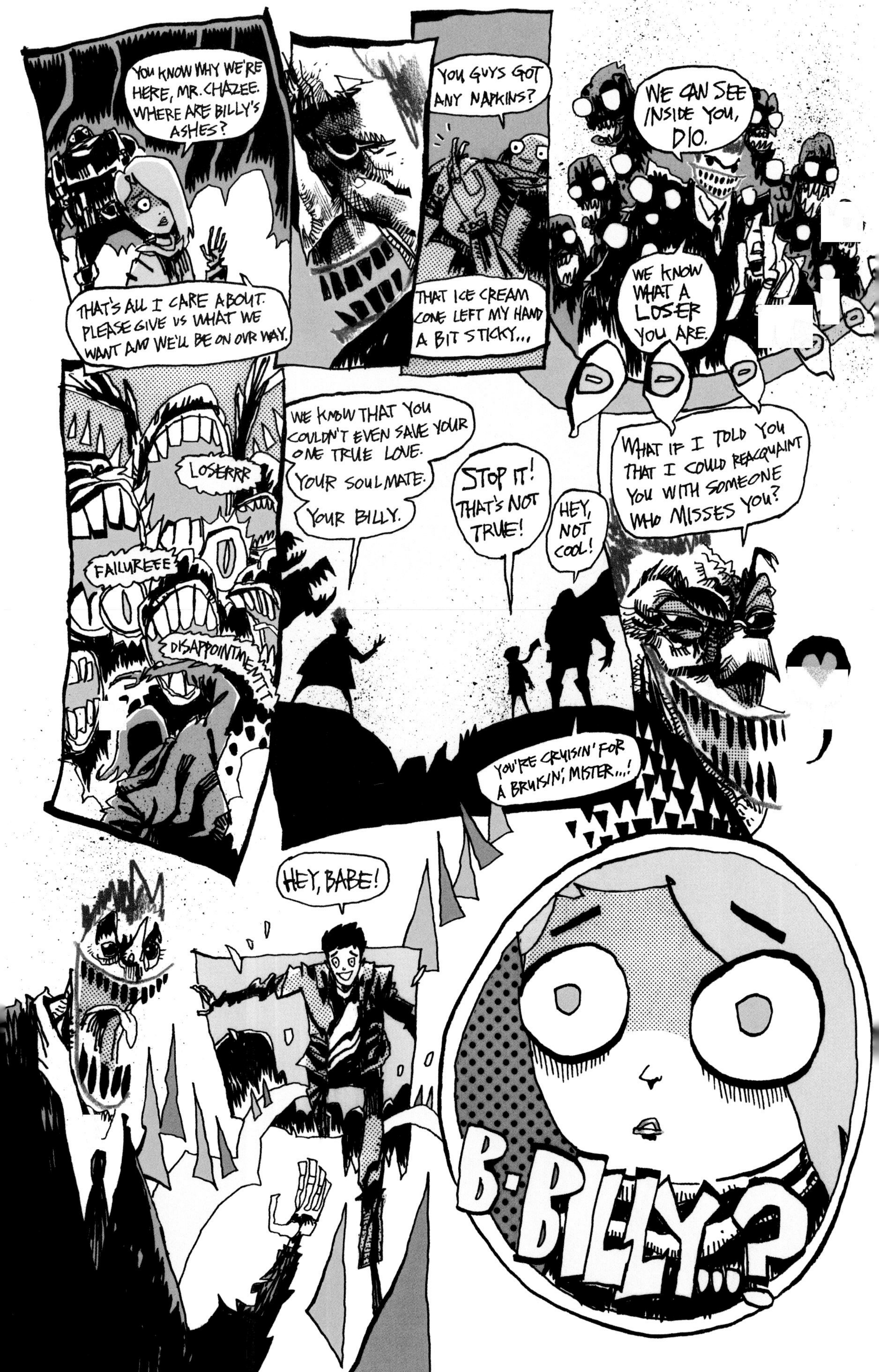
YOU KNOW WHY WE'RE HERE, MR. CHAZEE. WHERE ARE BILLY'S ASHES?
THAT'S ALL I CARE ABOUT. PLEASE GIVE US WHAT WE WANT AND WE'LL BE ON OUR WAY.
YOU GUYS GOT ANY NAPKINS?
THAT ICE CREAM CONE LEFT MY HAND A BIT STICKY...
WE CAN SEE INSIDE YOU, DIO.
WE KNOW WHAT A LOSER YOU ARE.
LOSERRR
FAILUREEE
DISAPPOINTMENTTT
WE KNOW THAT YOU COULDN'T EVEN SAVE YOUR ONE TRUE LOVE.
YOUR SOULMATE.
YOUR BILLY.
STOP IT! THAT'S NOT TRUE!
HEY, NOT COOL!
WHAT IF I TOLD YOU THAT I COULD REACQUAINT YOU WITH SOMEONE WHO MISSES YOU?
YOU'RE CRUISIN' FOR A BRUISIN', MISTER...!
HEY, BABE!
B-BILLY...?

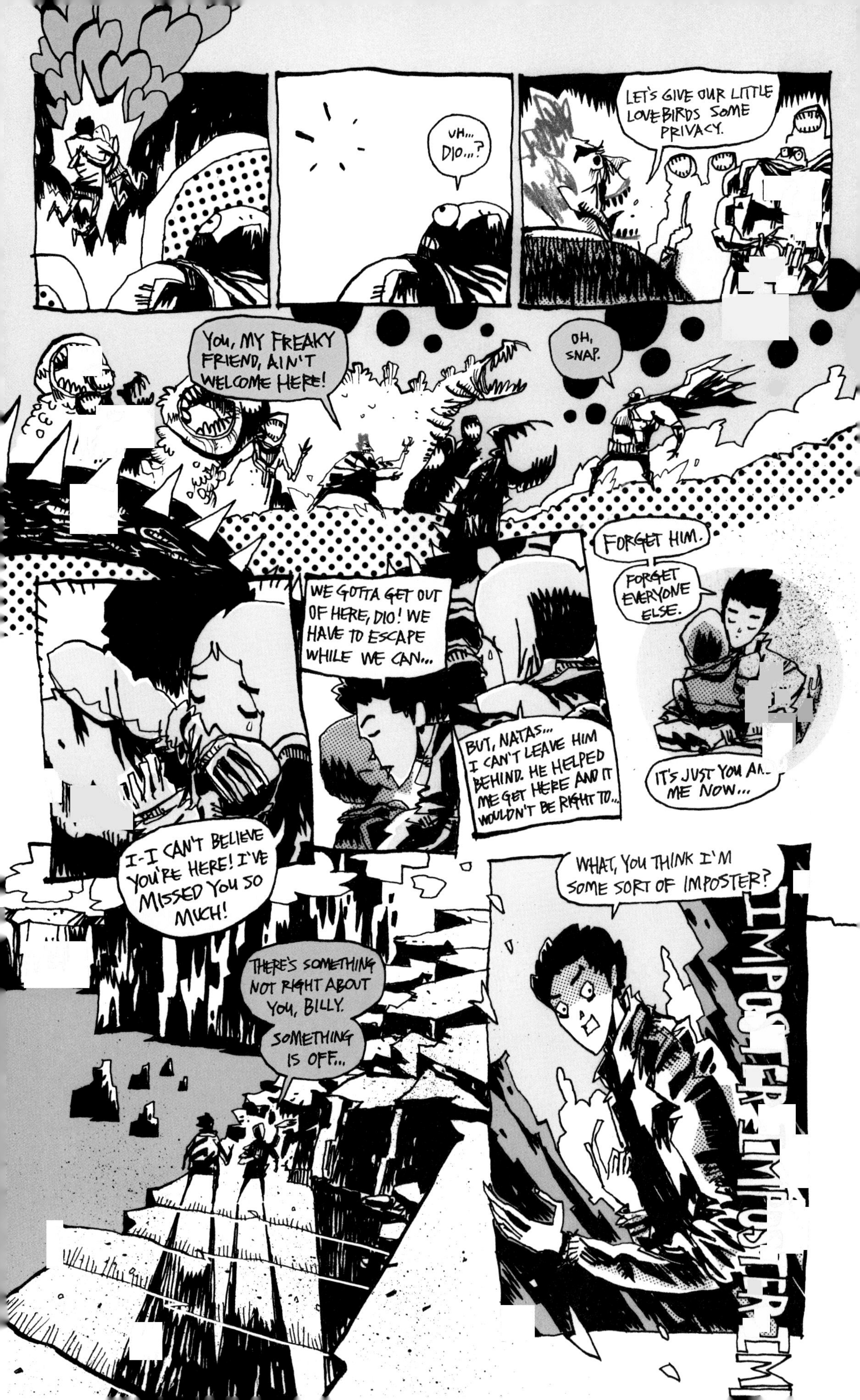
UH... DIO...?
LET'S GIVE OUR LITTLE LOVEBIRDS SOME PRIVACY.
YOU, MY FREAKY FRIEND, AIN'T WELCOME HERE!
OH, SNAP.
WE GOTTA GET OUT OF HERE, DIO! WE HAVE TO ESCAPE WHILE WE CAN...
BUT, NATAS... I CAN'T LEAVE HIM BEHIND. HE HELPED ME GET HERE AND IT WOULDN'T BE RIGHT TO...
FORGET HIM.
FORGET EVERYONE ELSE.
IT'S JUST YOU AN
ME NOW...
I-I CAN'T BELIEVE YOU'RE HERE! I'VE MISSED YOU SO MUCH!
THERE'S SOMETHING NOT RIGHT ABOUT YOU, BILLY.
SOMETHING IS OFF...
WHAT, YOU THINK I'M SOME SORT OF IMPOSTER?
IMPOSTER

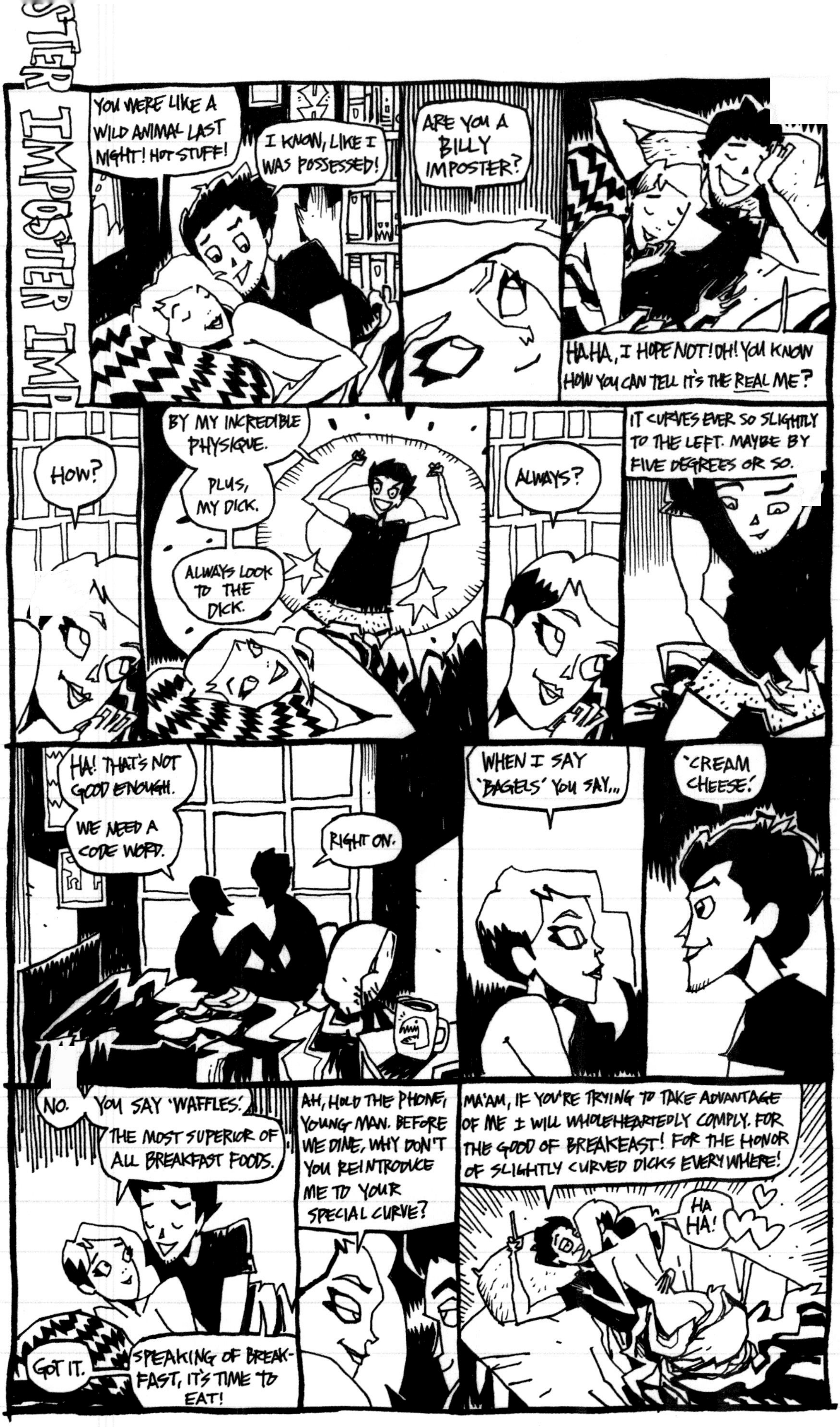
STER IMPOSTER IMPOSTER IMP
YOU WERE LIKE A WILD ANIMAL LAST NIGHT! HOT STUFF!
I KNOW, LIKE I WAS POSSESSED!
ARE YOU A BILLY IMPOSTER?
HA HA, I HOPE NOT! OH! YOU KNOW HOW YOU CAN TELL IT'S THE REAL ME?
HOW?
BY MY INCREDIBLE PHYSIQUE.
PLUS, MY DICK.
ALWAYS LOOK TO THE DICK.
ALWAYS?
IT CURVES EVER SO SLIGHTLY TO THE LEFT. MAYBE BY FIVE DEGREES OR SO.
HA! THAT'S NOT GOOD ENOUGH.
WE NEED A CODE WORD.
RIGHT ON.
WHEN I SAY 'BAGELS' YOU SAY...
'CREAM CHEESE.'
NO.
YOU SAY 'WAFFLES.'
THE MOST SUPERIOR OF ALL BREAKFAST FOODS.
GOT IT.
SPEAKING OF BREAK-FAST, IT'S TIME TO EAT!
AH, HOLD THE PHONE, YOUNG MAN. BEFORE WE DINE, WHY DON'T YOU REINTRODUCE ME TO YOUR SPECIAL CURVE?
MA'AM, IF YOU'RE TRYING TO TAKE ADVANTAGE OF ME I WILL WHOLEHEARTEDLY COMPLY. FOR THE GOOD OF BREAKFAST! FOR THE HONOR OF SLIGHTLY CURVED DICKS EVERYWHERE!
HA HA!

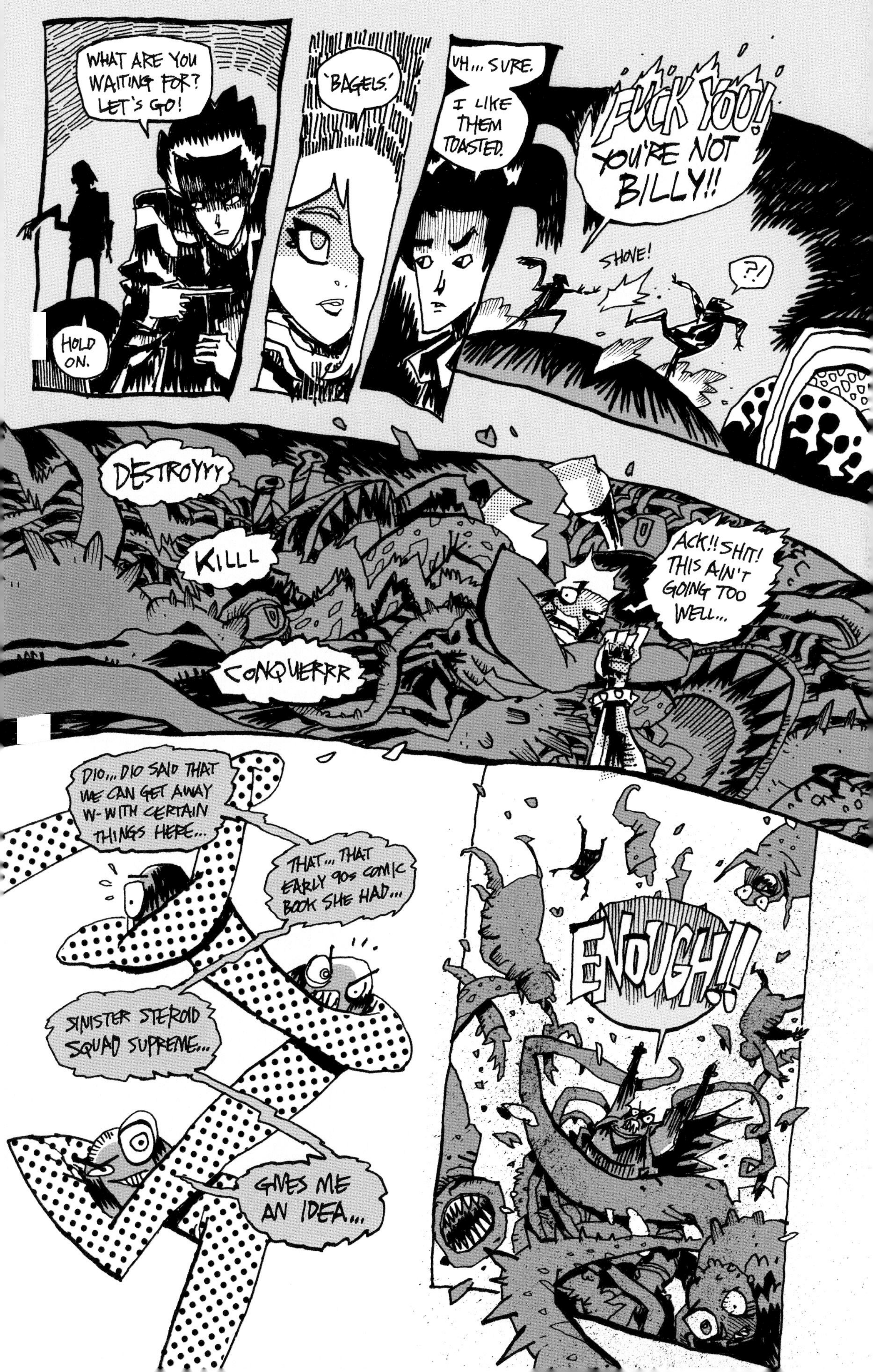
WHAT ARE YOU WAITING FOR? LET'S GO!
HOLD ON.
`BAGELS.'
UH... SURE.
I LIKE THEM TOASTED.
FUCK YOU! YOU'RE NOT BILLY!!
SHOVE!
?!
DESTROYYY
KILLL
CONQUERRR
ACK!! SHIT! THIS AIN'T GOING TOO WELL...
DIO... DIO SAID THAT WE CAN GET AWAY W-WITH CERTAIN THINGS HERE...
THAT... THAT EARLY 90s COMIC BOOK SHE HAD...
SINISTER STEROID SQUAD SUPREME...
GIVES ME AN IDEA...
ENOUGH!!

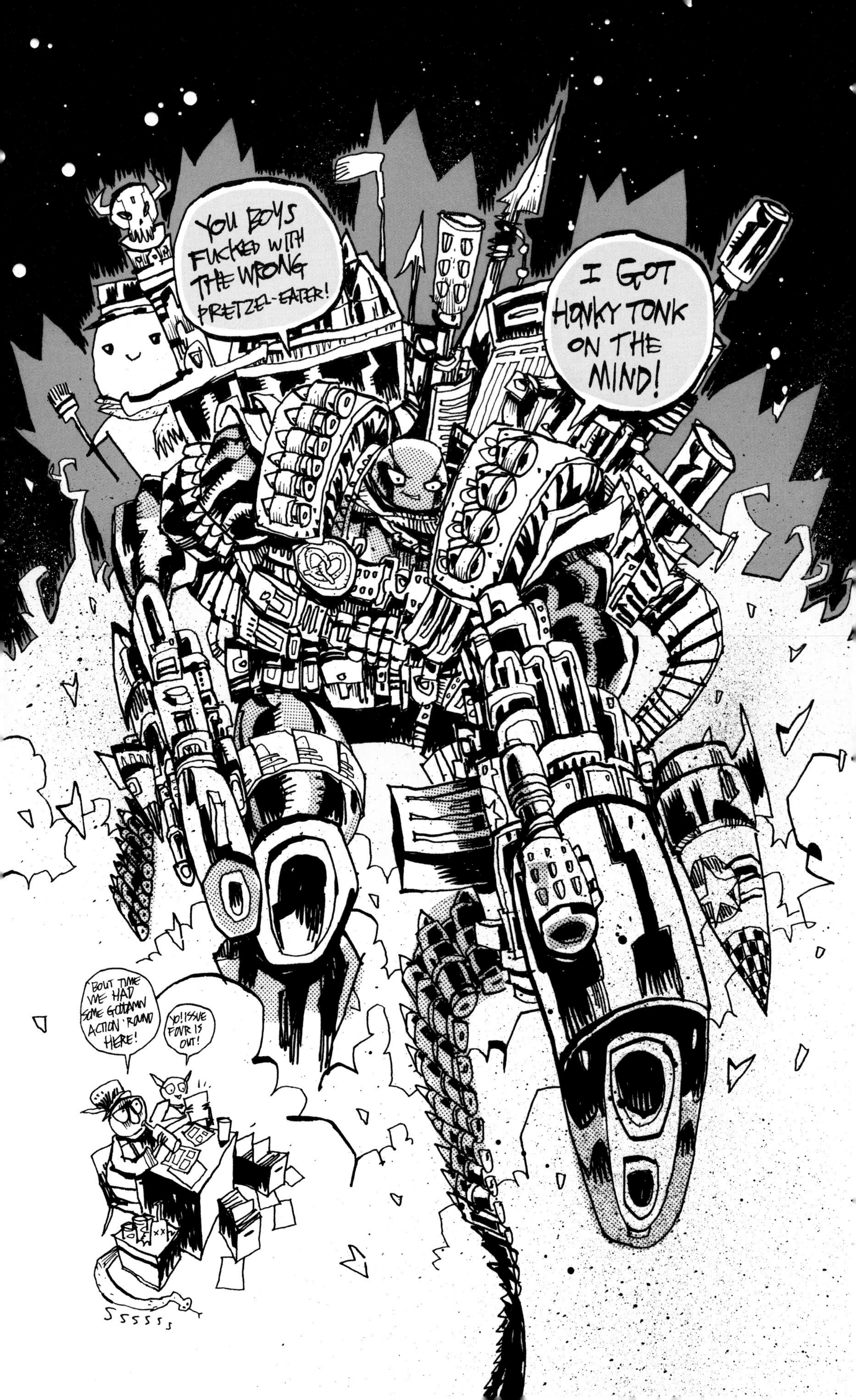
YOU BOYS FUCKED WITH THE WRONG PRETZEL-EATER!
I GOT HONKY TONK ON THE MIND!
'BOUT TIME WE HAD SOME GODDAMN ACTION 'ROUND HERE!
YO! ISSUE FOUR IS OUT!
SSSSSS

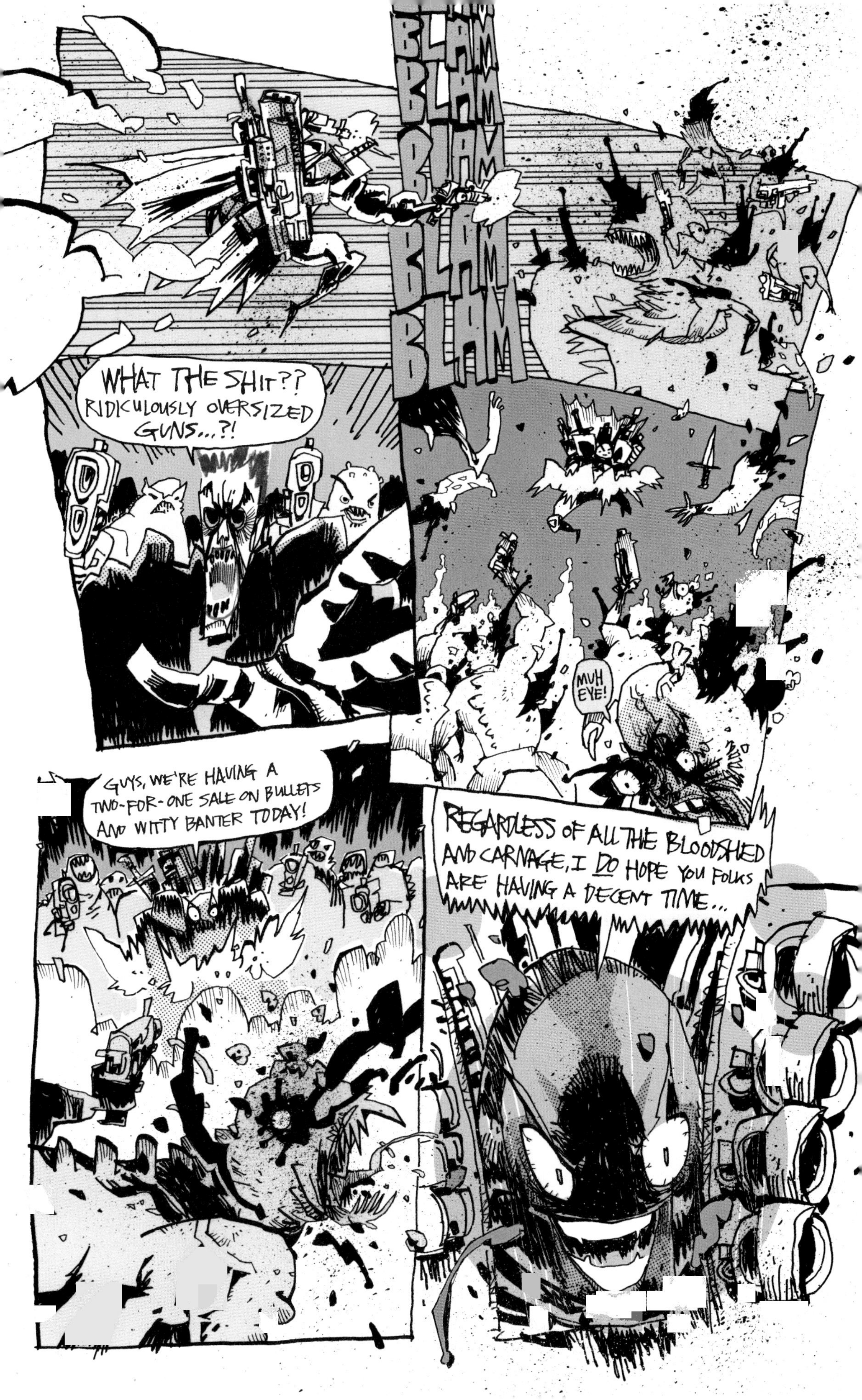
BLAM
BLAM
BLAM
BLAM
BLAM
WHAT THE SHIT?? RIDICULOUSLY OVERSIZED GUNS...?!
MUH EYE!
GUYS, WE'RE HAVING A TWO-FOR-ONE SALE ON BULLETS AND WITTY BANTER TODAY!
REGARDLESS OF ALL THE BLOODSHED AND CARNAGE, I DO HOPE YOU FOLKS ARE HAVING A DECENT TIME...

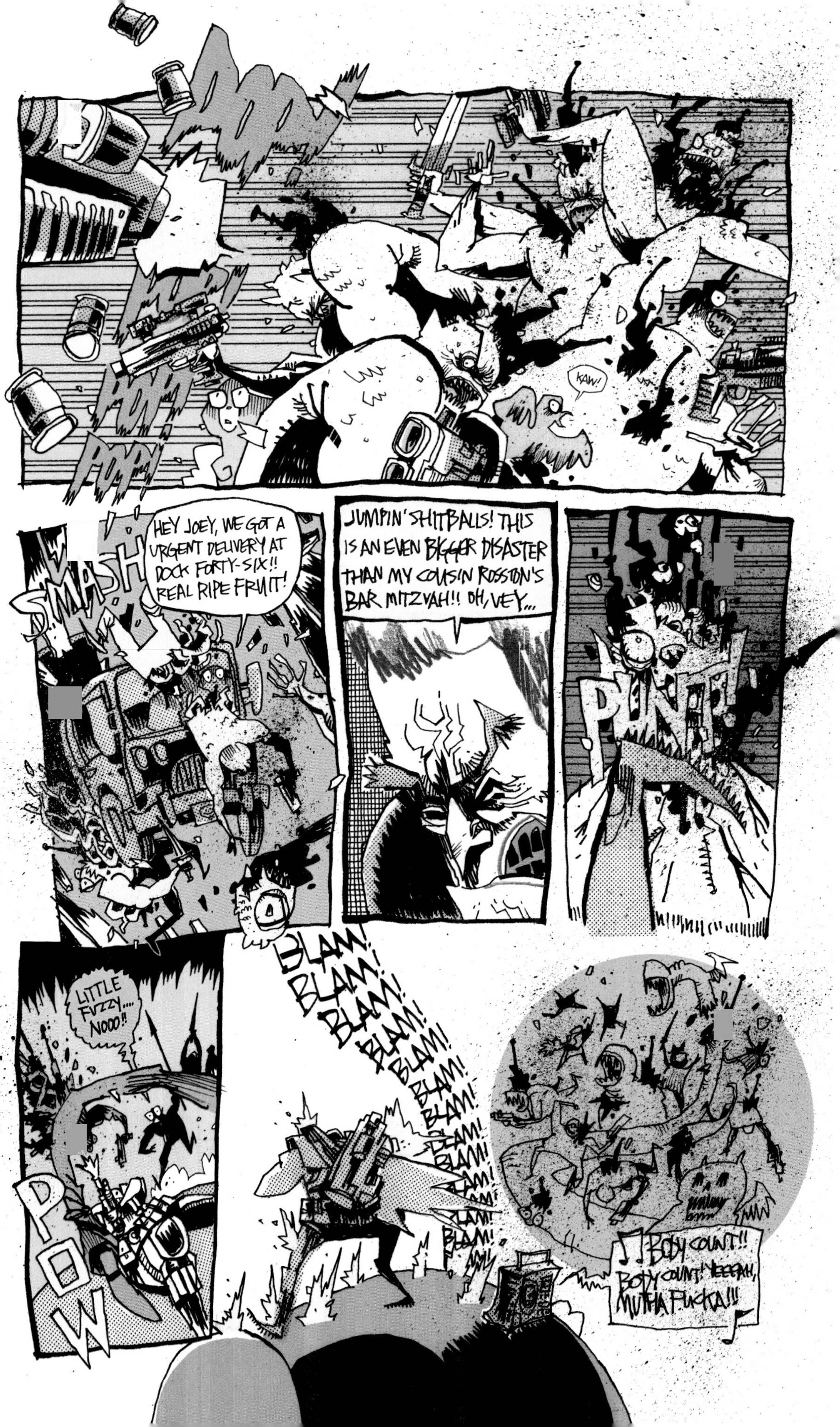
POP!
KAW!
SMASH
HEY JOEY, WE GOT A URGENT DELIVERY AT DOCK FORTY-SIX!! REAL RIPE FRUIT!
JUMPIN' SHITBALLS! THIS IS AN EVEN BIGGER DISASTER THAN MY COUSIN ROSSTON'S BAR MITZVAH!! OH, VEY...
PUNT!
LITTLE FUZZY.... NOOO!!
POW
BLAM! BLAM! BLAM! BLAM! BLAM! BLAM! BLAM! BLAM! BLAM! BLAM! BLAM! BLAM!
BODY COUNT!! BODY COUNT! YEEEAH, MUTHA FUCKA!!

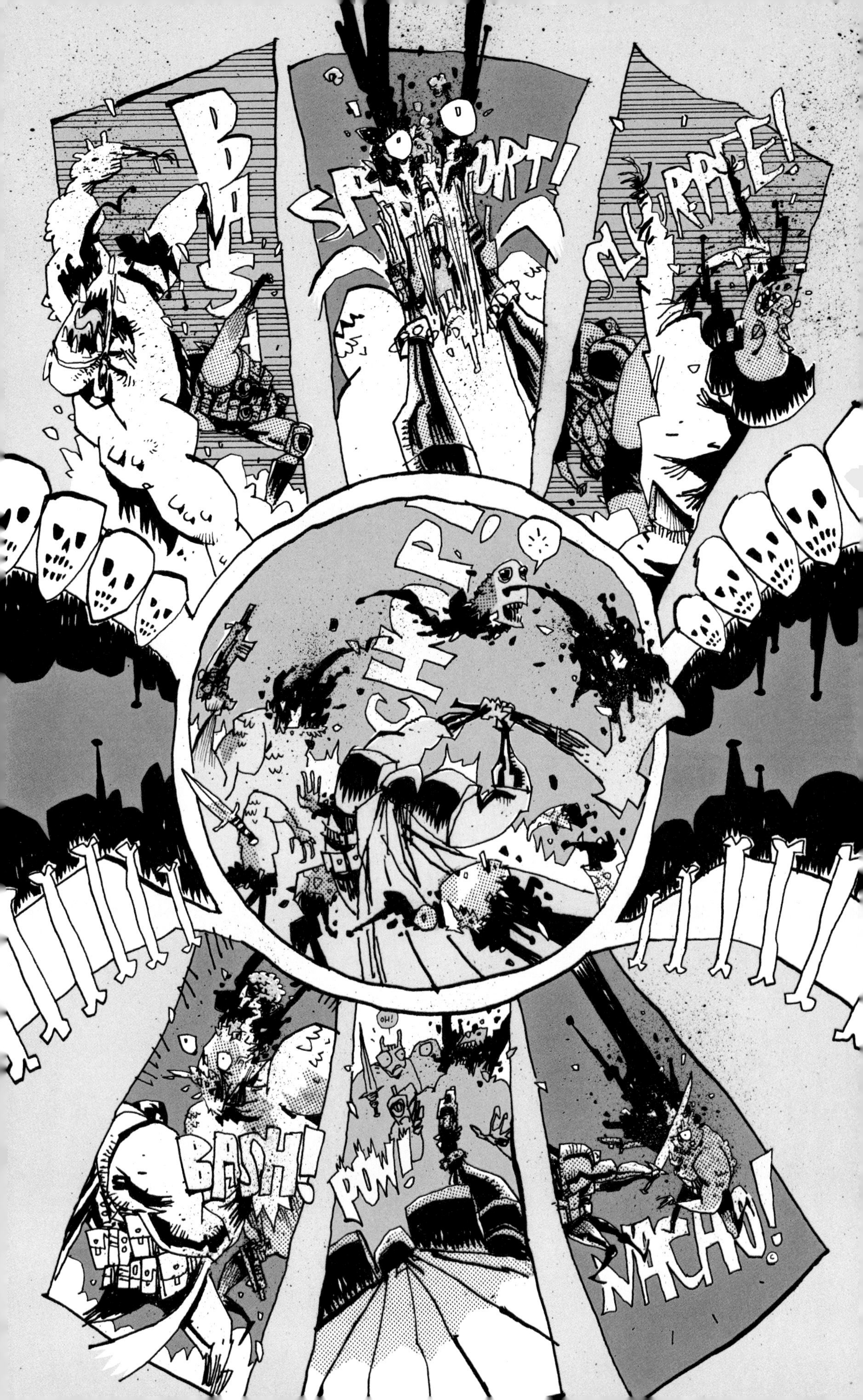
BASH
BASH!
OH!
POW!
NACHO!

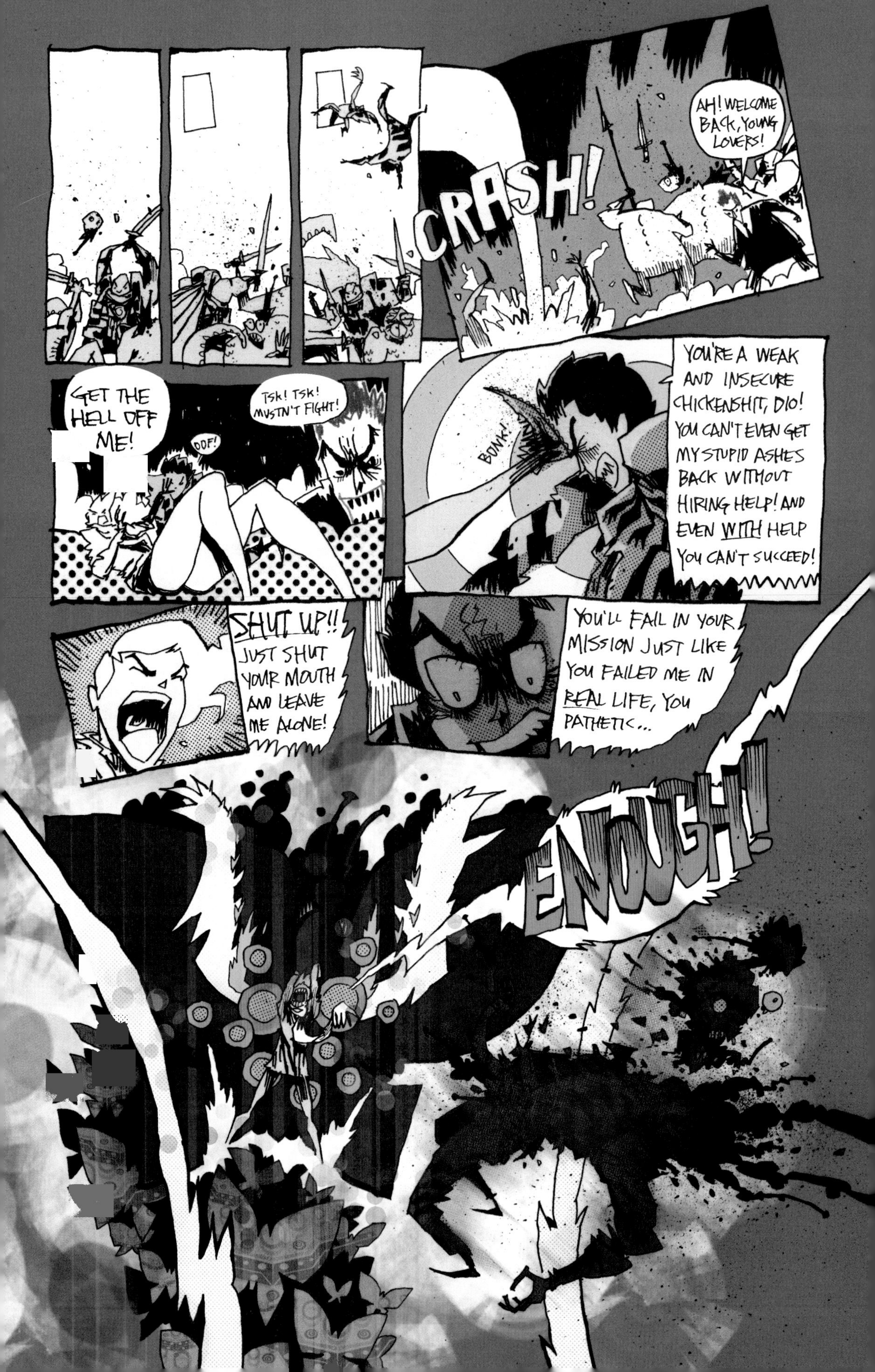
CRASH!
AH! WELCOME BACK, YOUNG LOVERS!
GET THE HELL OFF ME!
TSK! TSK! MUSTN'T FIGHT!
OOF!
BONK!
YOU'RE A WEAK AND INSECURE CHICKENSHIT, DIO! YOU CAN'T EVEN GET MY STUPID ASHES BACK WITHOUT HIRING HELP! AND EVEN WITH HELP YOU CAN'T SUCCEED!
SHUT UP!! JUST SHUT YOUR MOUTH AND LEAVE ME ALONE!
YOU'LL FAIL IN YOUR MISSION JUST LIKE YOU FAILED ME IN REAL LIFE, YOU PATHETIC...
ENOUGH!

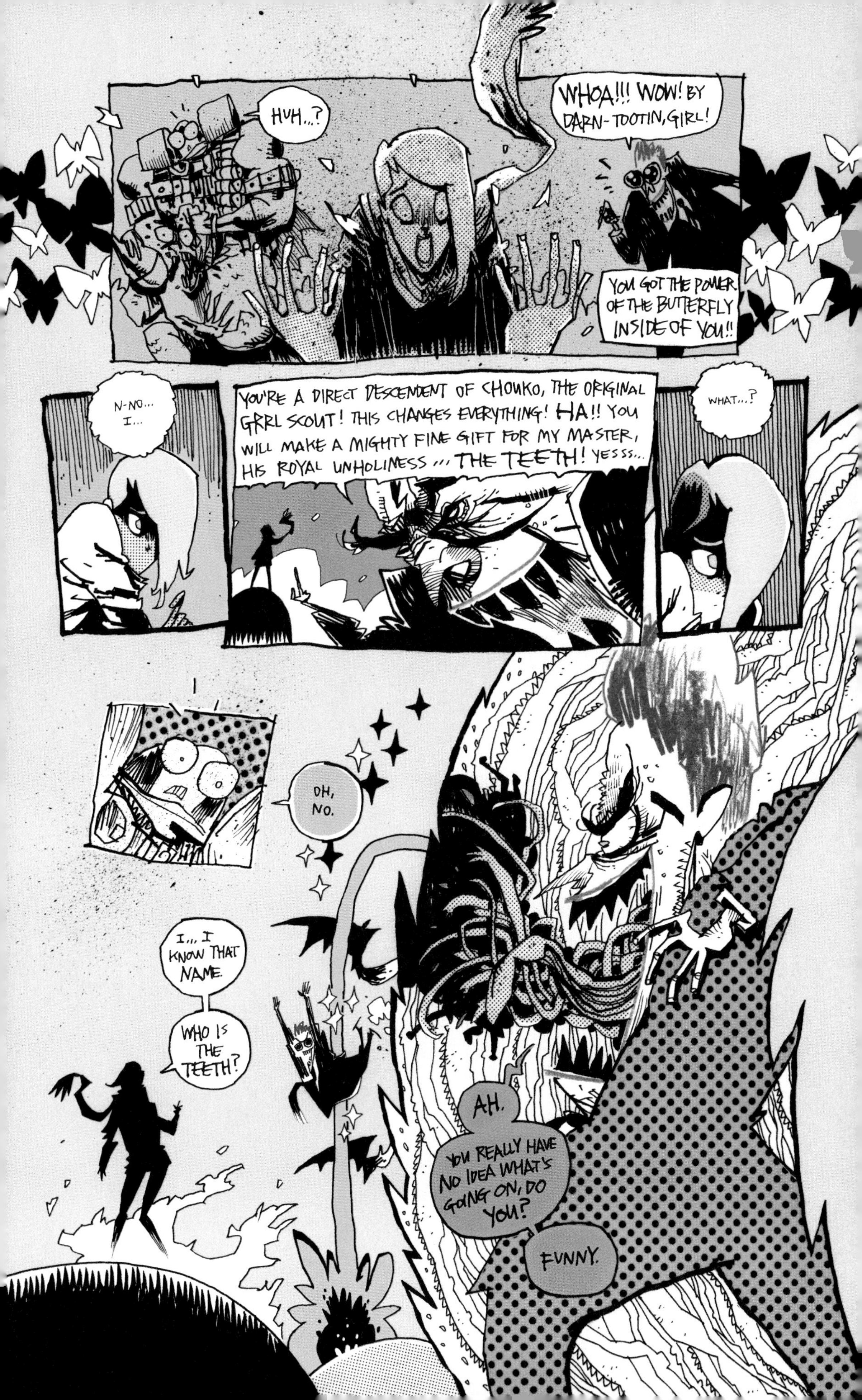
HUH...?
WHOA!!! WOW! BY DARN-TOOTIN, GIRL!
YOU GOT THE POWER OF THE BUTTERFLY INSIDE OF YOU!!
N-NO... I...
YOU'RE A DIRECT DESCENDENT OF CHOUKO, THE ORIGINAL GRRL SCOUT! THIS CHANGES EVERYTHING! HA!! YOU WILL MAKE A MIGHTY FINE GIFT FOR MY MASTER, HIS ROYAL UNHOLINESS ... THE TEETH! YESSS...
WHAT...?
OH, NO.
I... I KNOW THAT NAME.
WHO IS THE TEETH?
AH.
YOU REALLY HAVE NO IDEA WHAT'S GOING ON, DO YOU?
FUNNY.

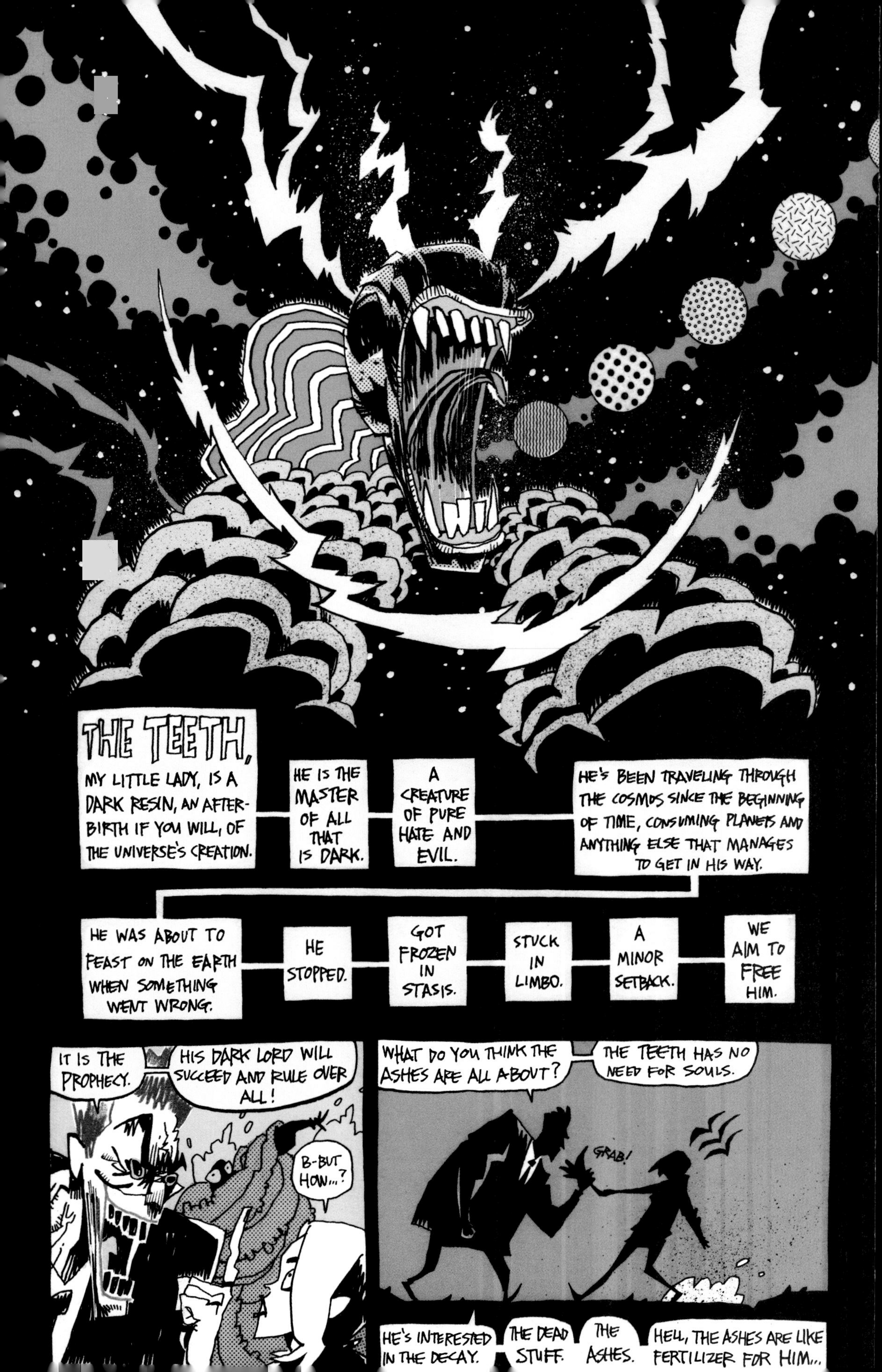
THE TEETH,
MY LITTLE LADY, IS A DARK RESIN, AN AFTER-BIRTH IF YOU WILL, OF THE UNIVERSE'S CREATION.
HE IS THE MASTER OF ALL THAT IS DARK.
A CREATURE OF PURE HATE AND EVIL.
HE'S BEEN TRAVELING THROUGH THE COSMOS SINCE THE BEGINNING OF TIME, CONSUMING PLANETS AND ANYTHING ELSE THAT MANAGES TO GET IN HIS WAY.
HE WAS ABOUT TO FEAST ON THE EARTH WHEN SOMETHING WENT WRONG.
HE STOPPED.
GOT FROZEN IN STASIS.
STUCK IN LIMBO.
A MINOR SETBACK.
WE AIM TO FREE HIM.
IT IS THE PROPHECY.
HIS DARK LORD WILL SUCCEED AND RULE OVER ALL!
B-BUT HOW...?
WHAT DO YOU THINK THE ASHES ARE ALL ABOUT?
THE TEETH HAS NO NEED FOR SOULS.
GRAB!
HE'S INTERESTED IN THE DECAY.
THE DEAD STUFF.
THE ASHES.
HELL, THE ASHES ARE LIKE FERTILIZER FOR HIM...

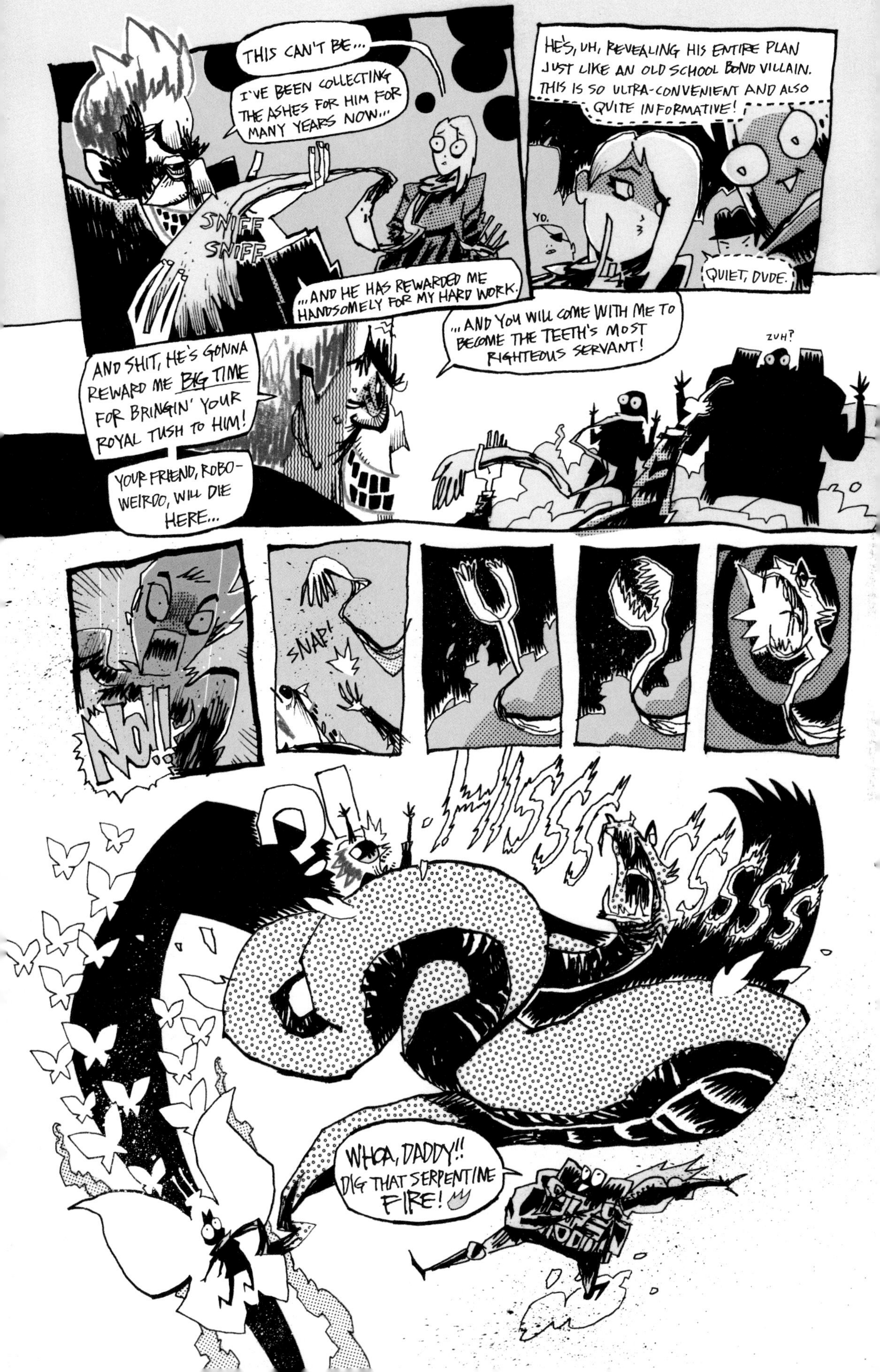
THIS CAN'T BE...
I'VE BEEN COLLECTING THE ASHES FOR HIM FOR MANY YEARS NOW...
SNIFF SNIFF
...AND HE HAS REWARDED ME HANDSOMELY FOR MY HARD WORK.
HE'S, UH, REVEALING HIS ENTIRE PLAN JUST LIKE AN OLD SCHOOL BOND VILLAIN. THIS IS SO ULTRA-CONVENIENT AND ALSO QUITE INFORMATIVE!
YO.
QUIET, DUDE.
AND SHIT, HE'S GONNA REWARD ME BIG TIME FOR BRINGIN' YOUR ROYAL TUSH TO HIM!
YOUR FRIEND, ROBO-WEIRDO, WILL DIE HERE...
...AND YOU WILL COME WITH ME TO BECOME THE TEETH'S MOST RIGHTEOUS SERVANT!
ZUH?
NO!!
SNAP!
HISSSSSS
WHOA, DADDY!! DIG THAT SERPENTINE FIRE!

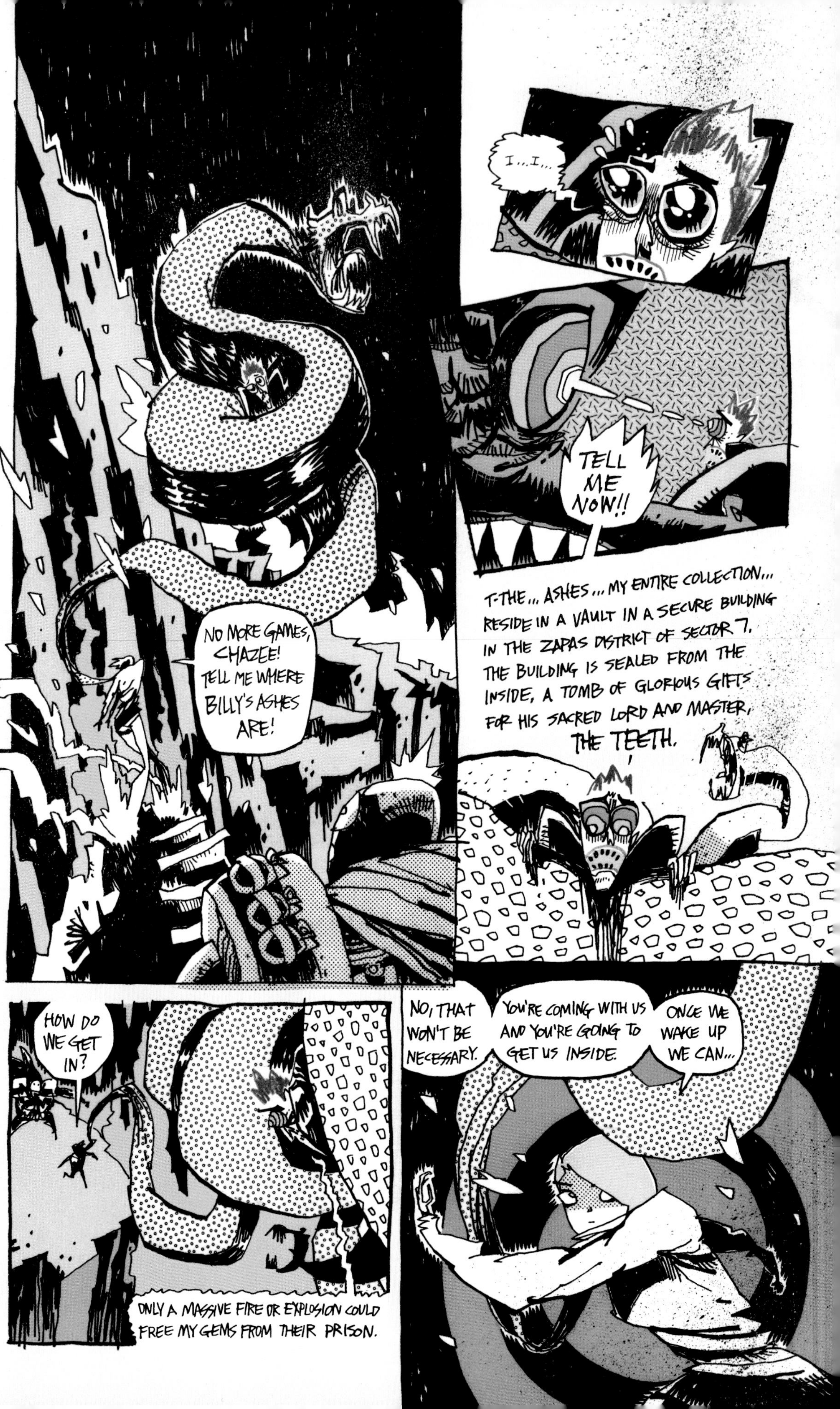

I...I...
TELL ME NOW!!
T-THE... ASHES... MY ENTIRE COLLECTION... RESIDE IN A VAULT IN A SECURE BUILDING IN THE ZAPAS DISTRICT OF SECTOR 7. THE BUILDING IS SEALED FROM THE INSIDE, A TOMB OF GLORIOUS GIFTS FOR HIS SACRED LORD AND MASTER, THE TEETH.
NO MORE GAMES, CHAZEE! TELL ME WHERE BILLY'S ASHES ARE!
HOW DO WE GET IN?
ONLY A MASSIVE FIRE OR EXPLOSION COULD FREE MY GEMS FROM THEIR PRISON.
NO, THAT WON'T BE NECESSARY.
YOU'RE COMING WITH US AND YOU'RE GOING TO GET US INSIDE.
ONCE WE WAKE UP WE CAN...

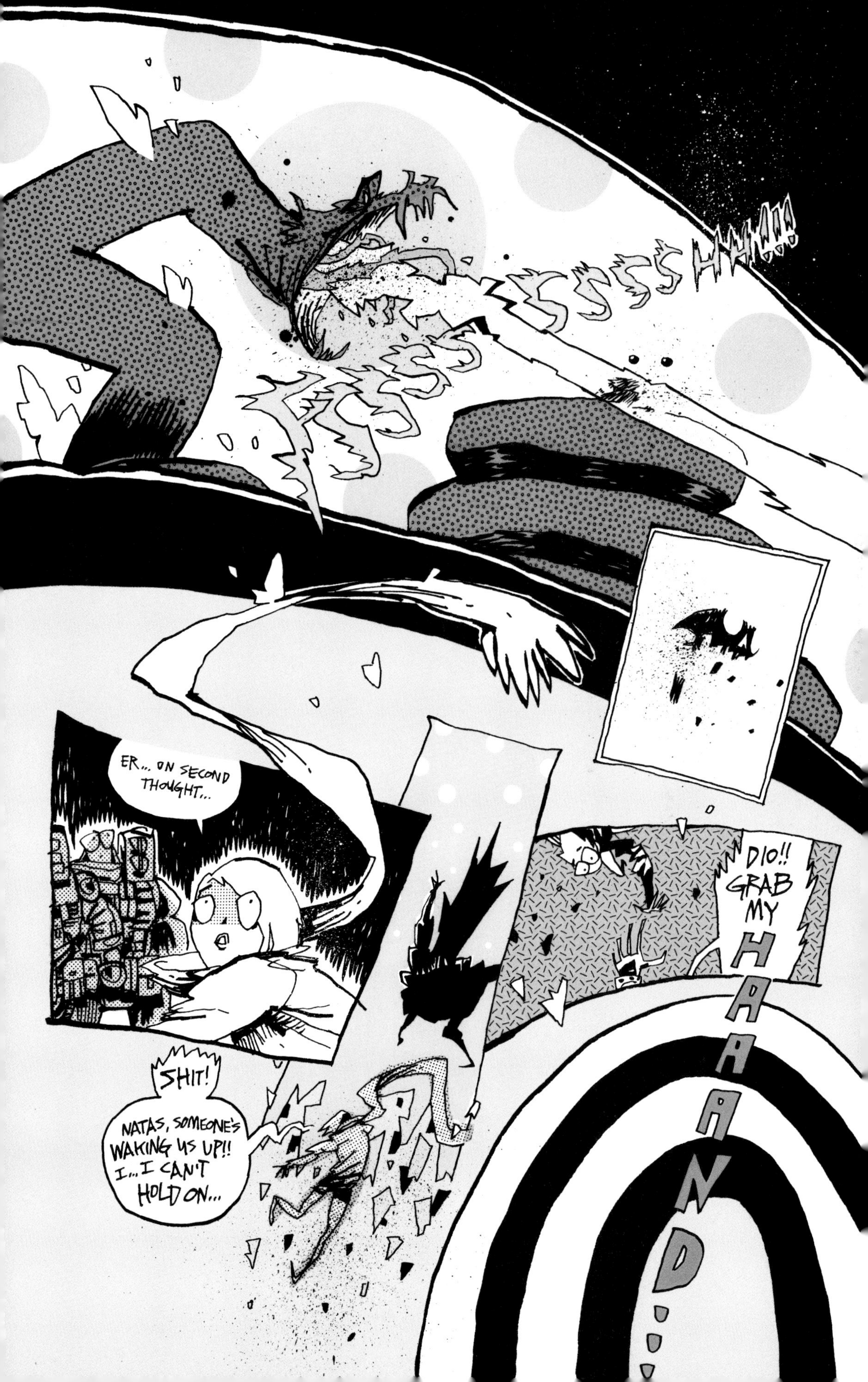
SSSSSHHH!!!
HSSSSSS
ER... ON SECOND THOUGHT...
DIO!! GRAB MY HAAAAND...
SHIT!
NATAS, SOMEONE'S WAKING US UP!! I... I CAN'T HOLD ON...

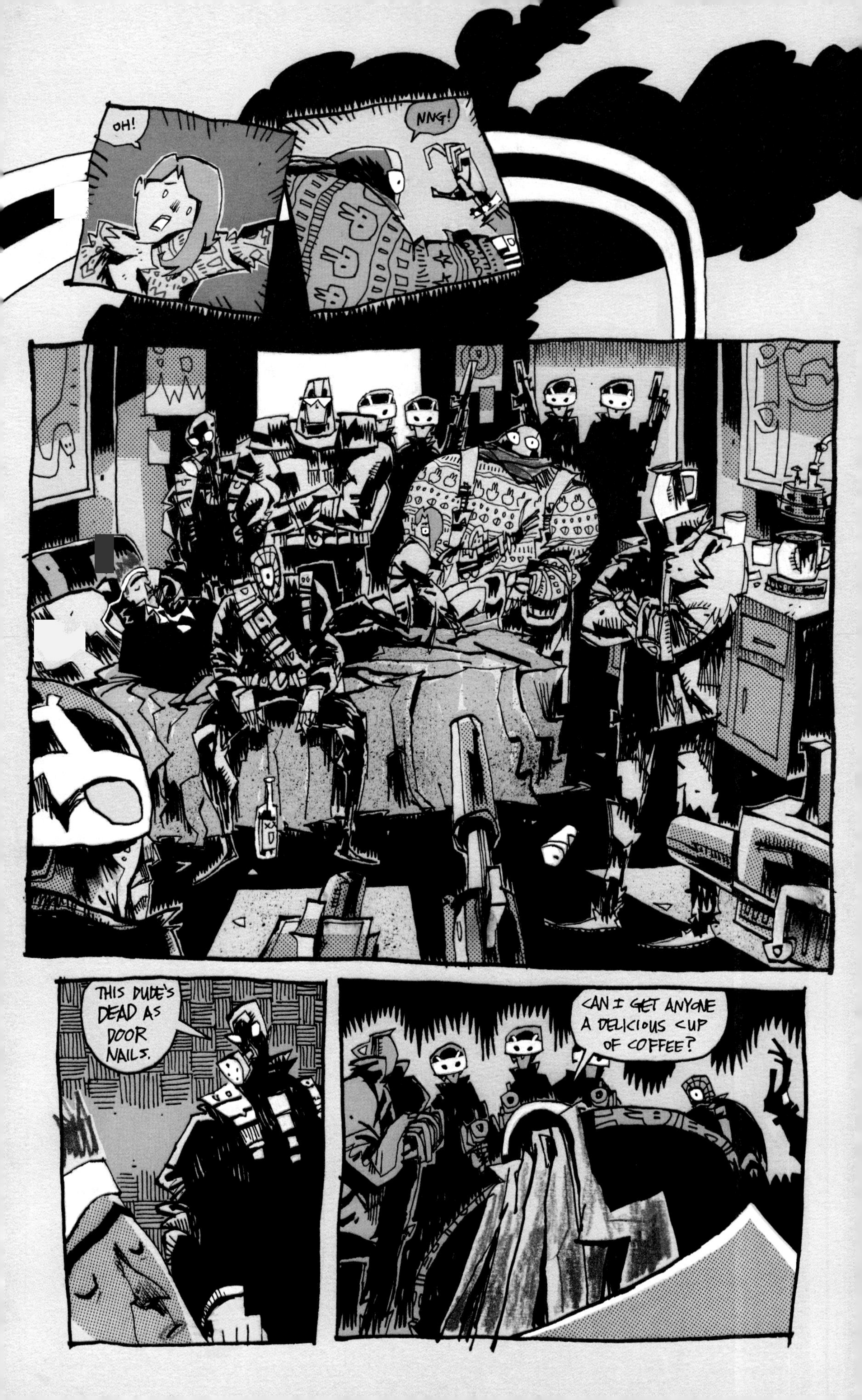
OH!
NNG!
THIS DUDE'S DEAD AS DOOR NAILS.
CAN I GET ANYONE A DELICIOUS CUP OF COFFEE?

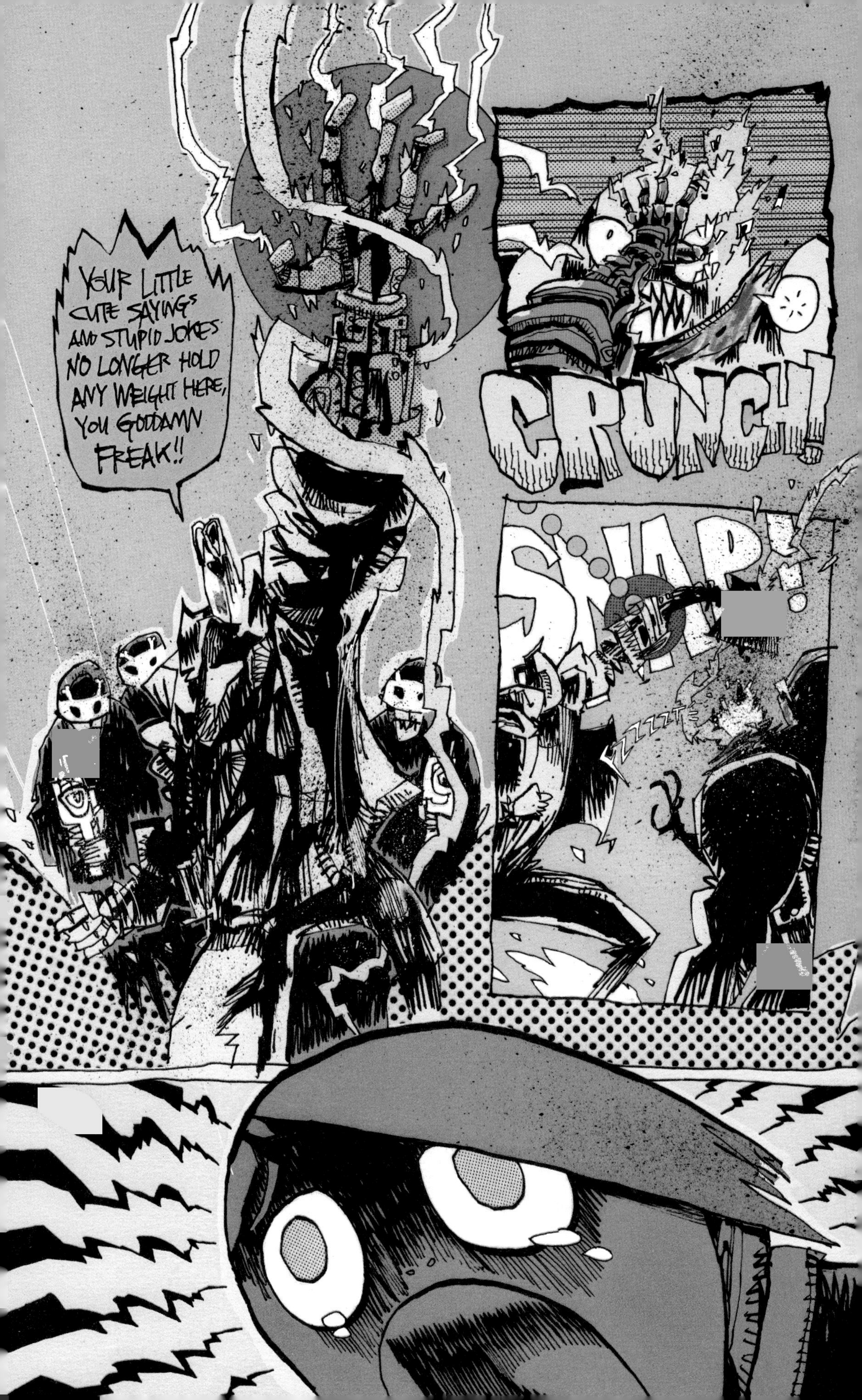
YOUR LITTLE CUTE SAYINGS AND STUPID JOKES NO LONGER HOLD ANY WEIGHT HERE, YOU GODDAMN FREAK!!
CRUNCH!
SNAP!
ZZZZZT

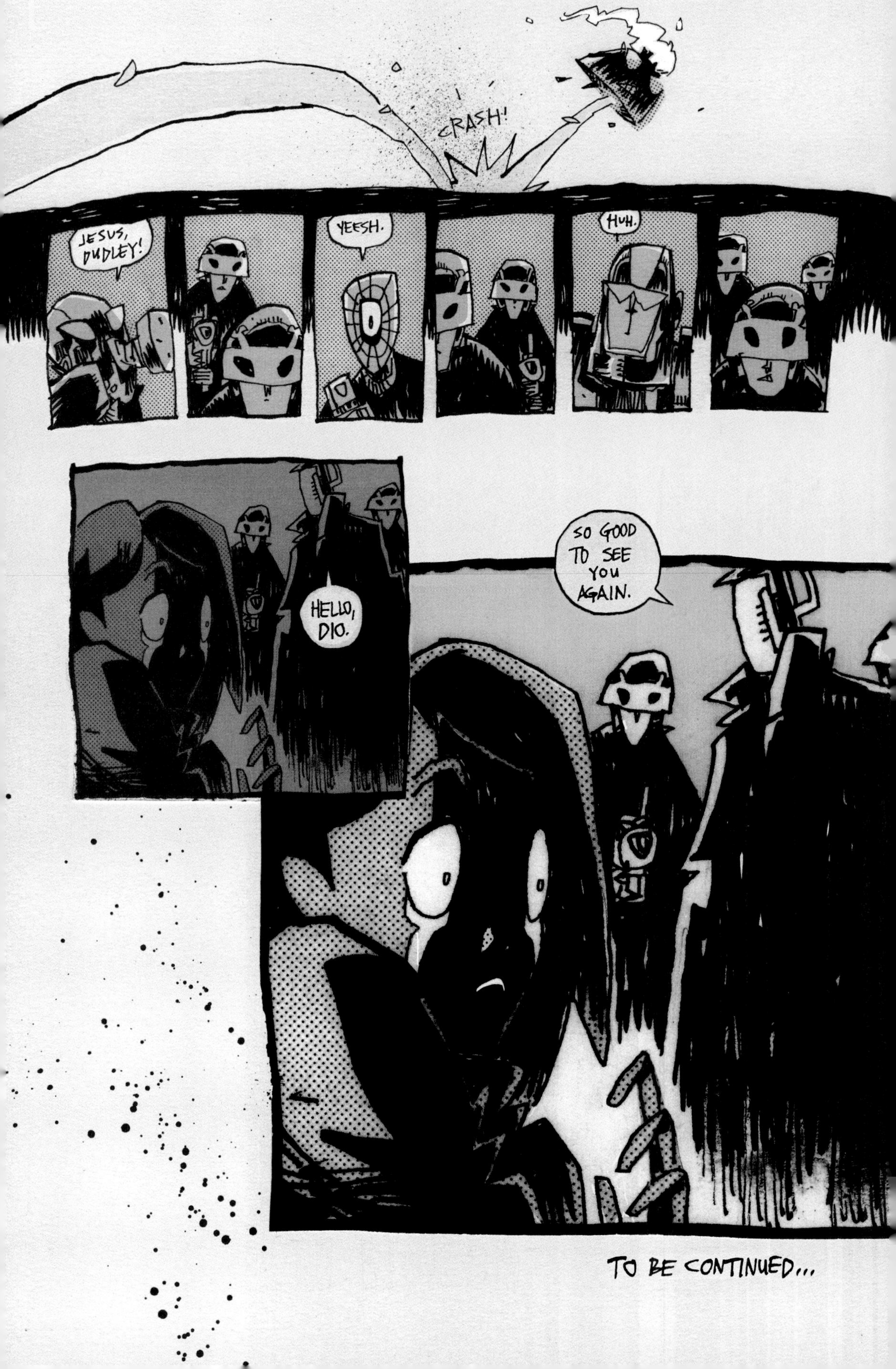
CRASH!
JESUS, DUDLEY!
YEESH.
HUH.
HELLO, DIO.
SO GOOD TO SEE YOU AGAIN.
TO BE CONTINUED...

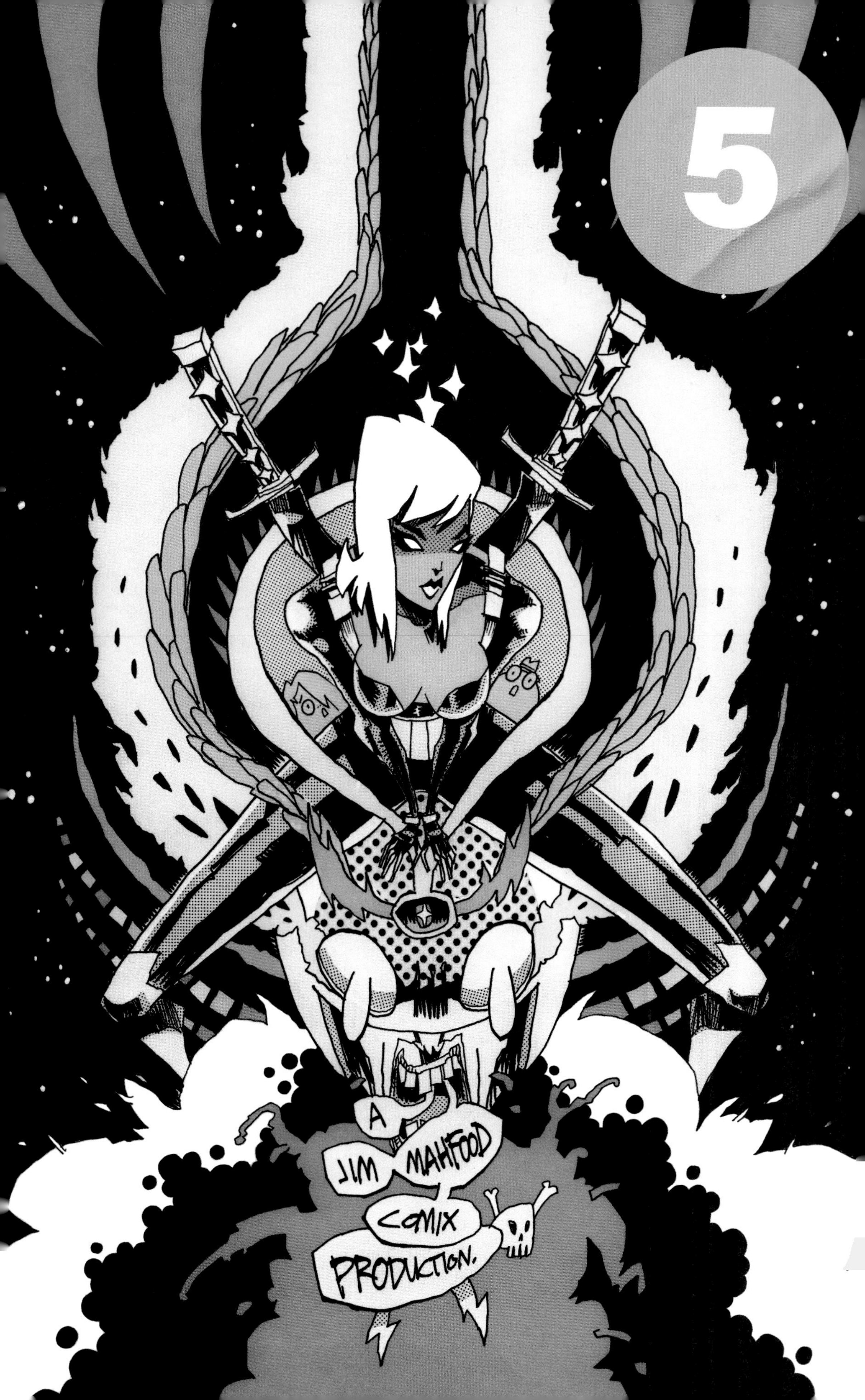
5
A
JIM MAHFOOD
COMIX
PRODUCTION.

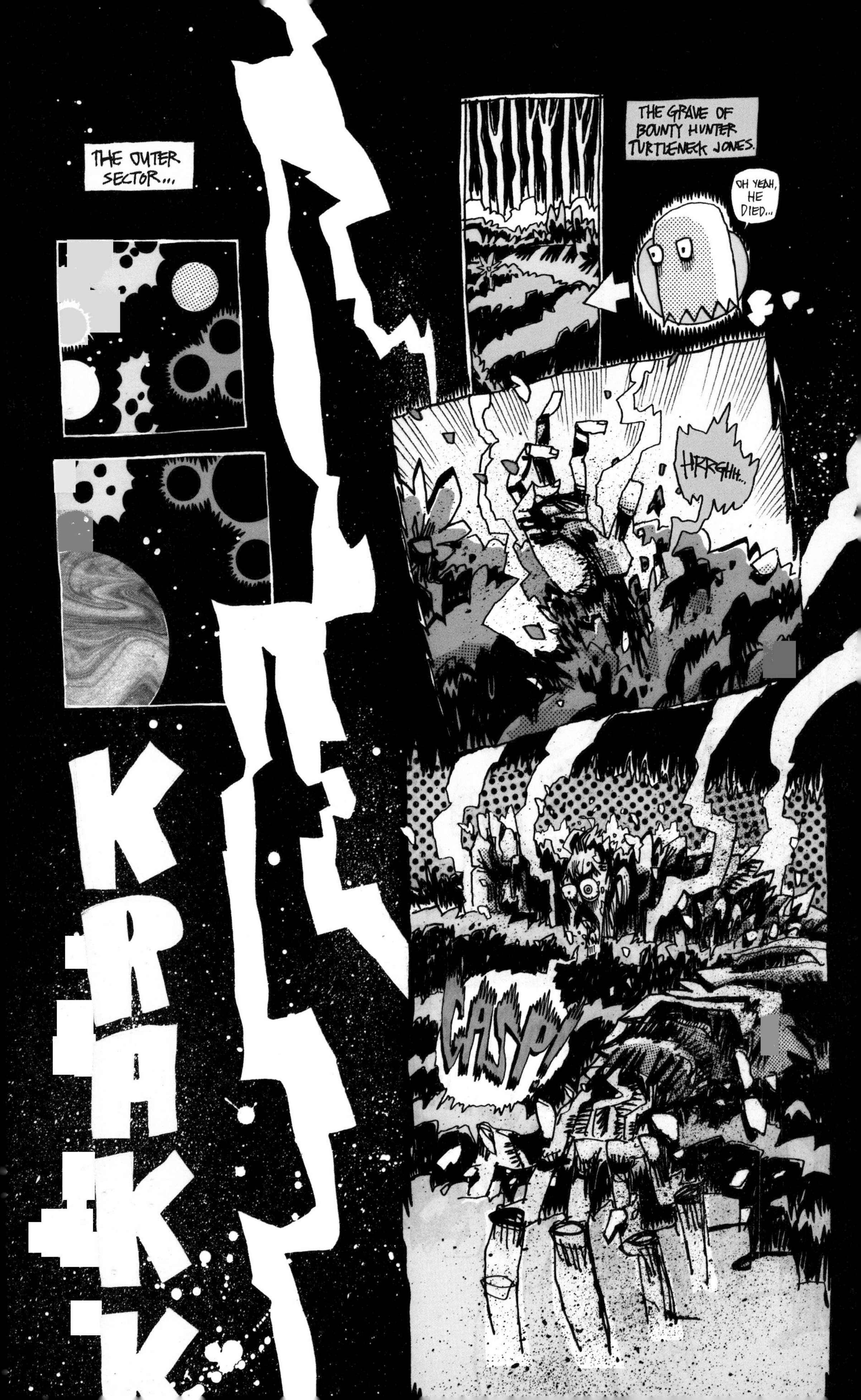
THE OUTER SECTOR...
THE GRAVE OF BOUNTY HUNTER TURTLENECK JONES.
OH YEAH, HE DIED...
HRRGHH...
GASP!
KRAKKK

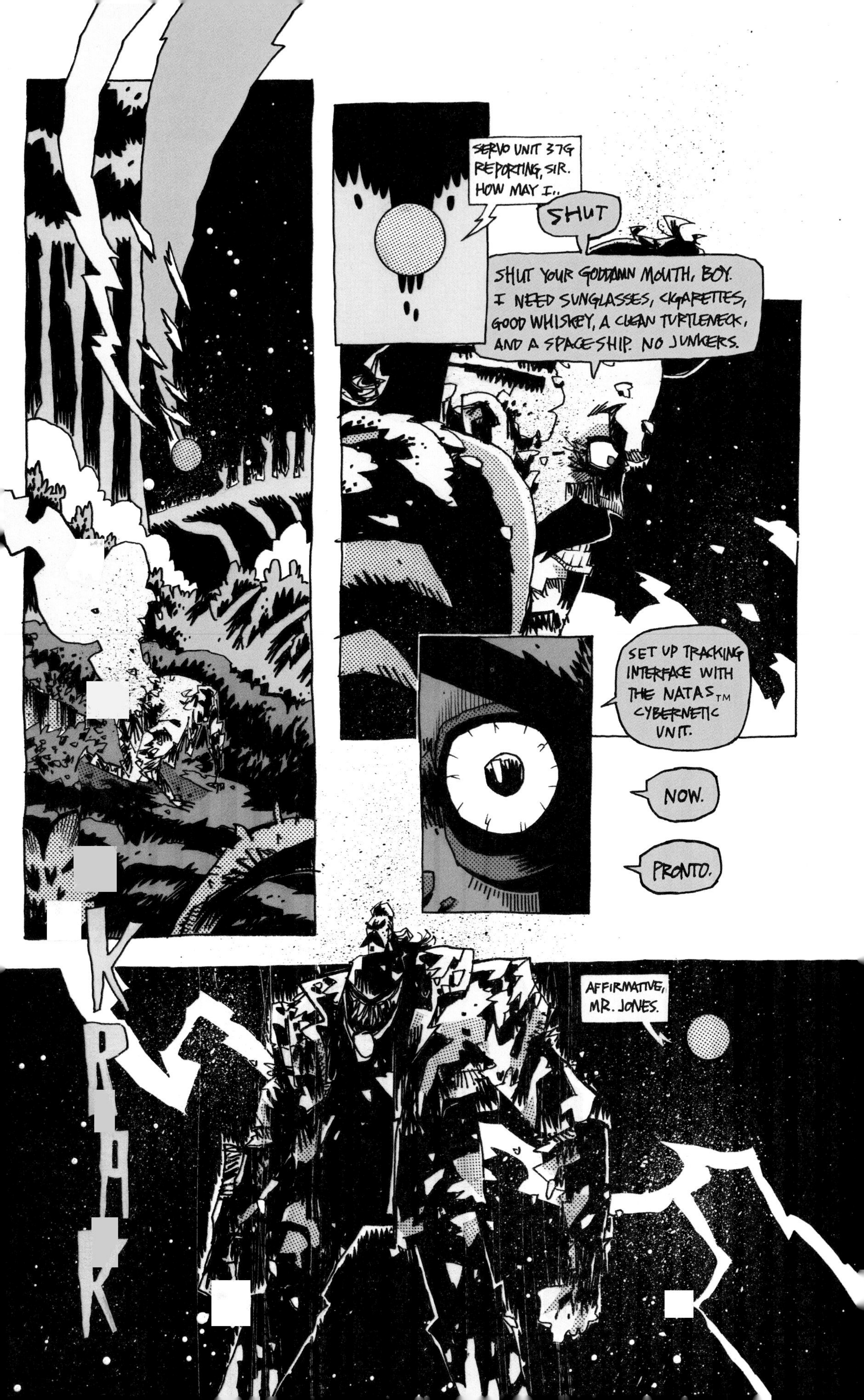
SERVO UNIT 37G REPORTING, SIR. HOW MAY I..
SHUT
SHUT YOUR GODDAMN MOUTH, BOY. I NEED SUNGLASSES, CIGARETTES, GOOD WHISKEY, A CLEAN TURTLENECK, AND A SPACESHIP. NO JUNKERS.
SET UP TRACKING INTERFACE WITH THE NATAS™ CYBERNETIC UNIT.
NOW.
PRONTO.
AFFIRMATIVE, MR. JONES.

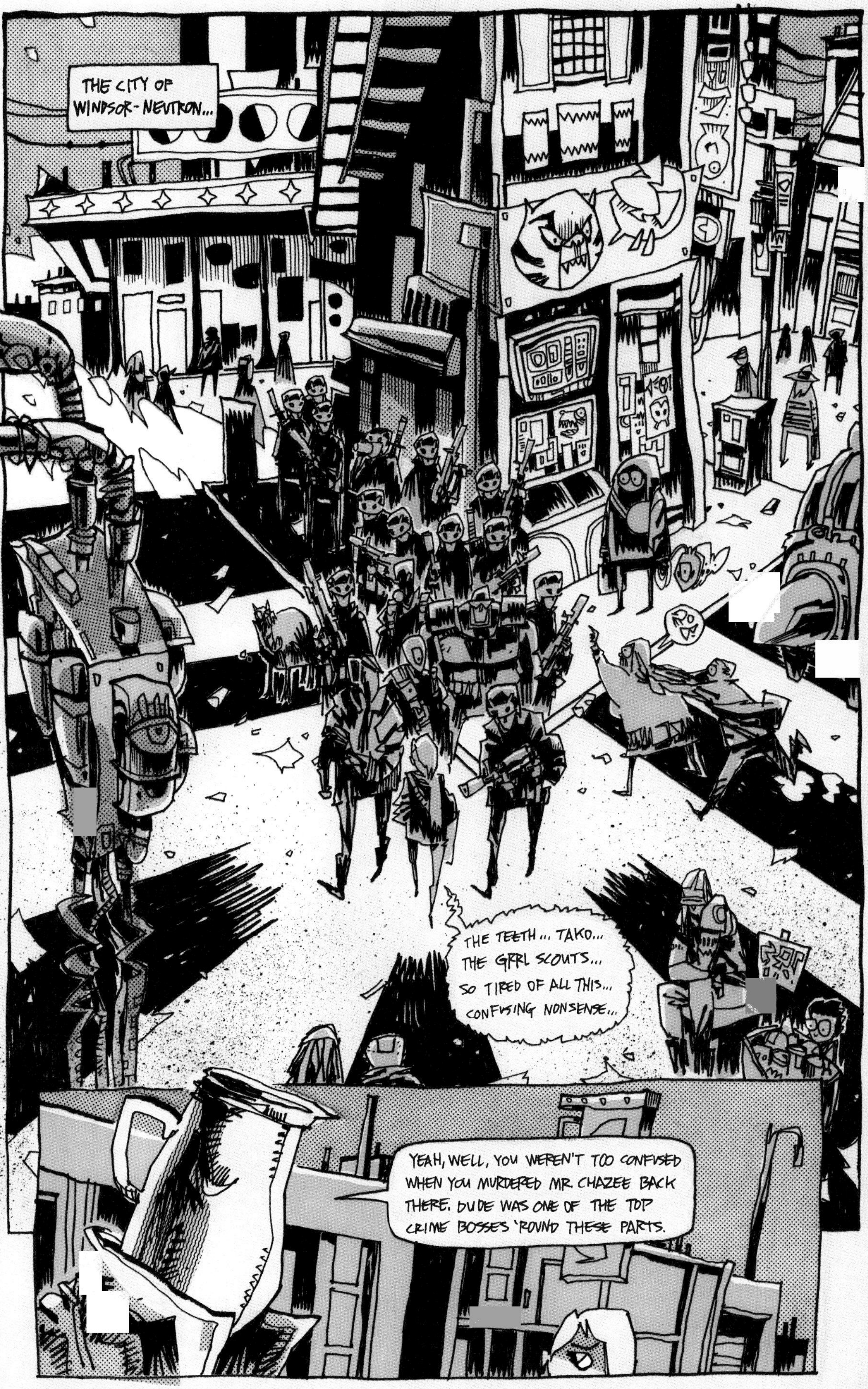
THE CITY OF WINDSOR-NEUTRON...
THE TEETH... TAKO... THE GRRL SCOUTS... SO TIRED OF ALL THIS... CONFUSING NONSENSE...
YEAH, WELL, YOU WEREN'T TOO CONFUSED WHEN YOU MURDERED MR. CHAZEE BACK THERE. DUDE WAS ONE OF THE TOP CRIME BOSSES 'ROUND THESE PARTS.

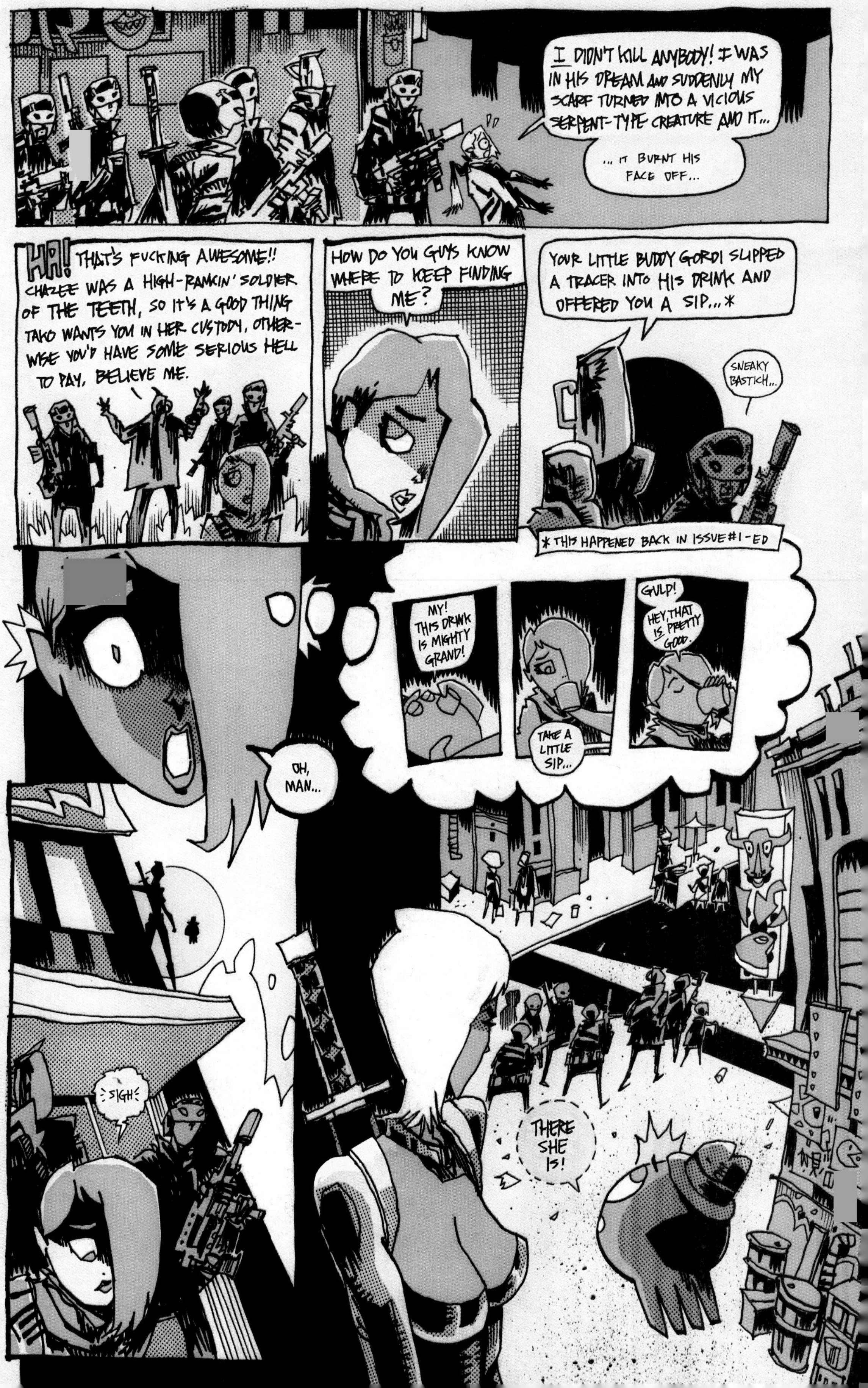
I DIDN'T KILL ANYBODY! I WAS IN HIS DREAM AND SUDDENLY MY SCARF TURNED INTO A VICIOUS SERPENT-TYPE CREATURE AND IT...
...IT BURNT HIS FACE OFF...
HA! THAT'S FUCKING AWESOME!! CHAZEE WAS A HIGH-RANKIN' SOLDIER OF THE TEETH, SO IT'S A GOOD THING TAKO WANTS YOU IN HER CUSTODY, OTHERWISE YOU'D HAVE SOME SERIOUS HELL TO PAY, BELIEVE ME.
HOW DO YOU GUYS KNOW WHERE TO KEEP FINDING ME?
YOUR LITTLE BUDDY GORDI SLIPPED A TRACER INTO HIS DRINK AND OFFERED YOU A SIP...*
SNEAKY BASTICH...
* THIS HAPPENED BACK IN ISSUE #1 -ED
MY! THIS DRINK IS MIGHTY GRAND!
TAKE A LITTLE SIP...
GULP!
HEY, THAT IS PRETTY GOOD.
OH, MAN...
SIGH
THERE SHE IS!

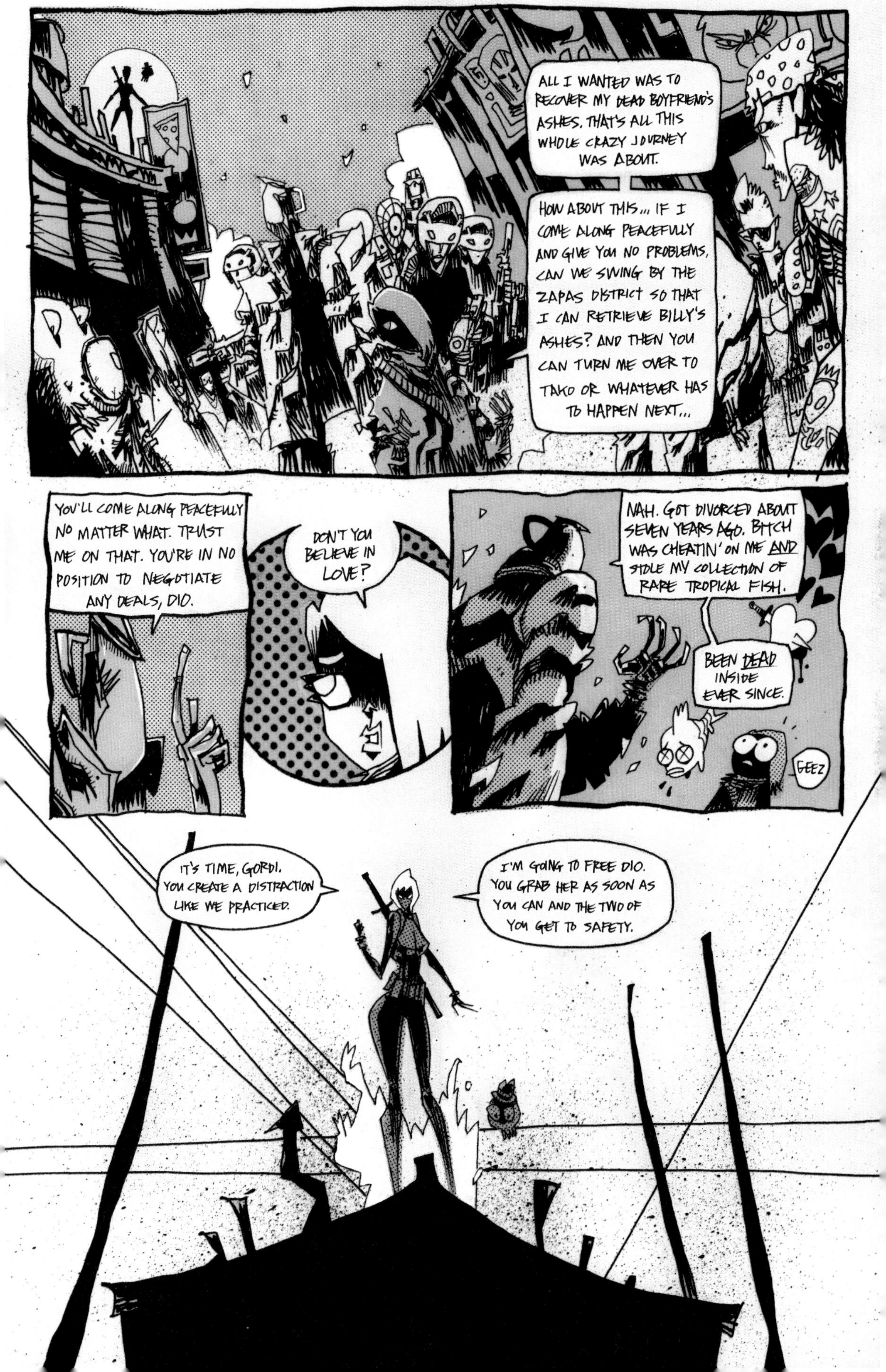
ALL I WANTED WAS TO RECOVER MY DEAD BOYFRIEND'S ASHES. THAT'S ALL THIS WHOLE CRAZY JOURNEY WAS ABOUT.
HOW ABOUT THIS... IF I COME ALONG PEACEFULLY AND GIVE YOU NO PROBLEMS, CAN WE SWING BY THE ZAPAS DISTRICT SO THAT I CAN RETRIEVE BILLY'S ASHES? AND THEN YOU CAN TURN ME OVER TO TAKO OR WHATEVER HAS TO HAPPEN NEXT...
YOU'LL COME ALONG PEACEFULLY NO MATTER WHAT. TRUST ME ON THAT. YOU'RE IN NO POSITION TO NEGOTIATE ANY DEALS, DIO.
DON'T YOU BELIEVE IN LOVE?
NAH. GOT DIVORCED ABOUT SEVEN YEARS AGO. BITCH WAS CHEATIN' ON ME AND STOLE MY COLLECTION OF RARE TROPICAL FISH.
BEEN DEAD INSIDE EVER SINCE.
GEEZ
IT'S TIME, GORDI. YOU CREATE A DISTRACTION LIKE WE PRACTICED.
I'M GOING TO FREE DIO. YOU GRAB HER AS SOON AS YOU CAN AND THE TWO OF YOU GET TO SAFETY.

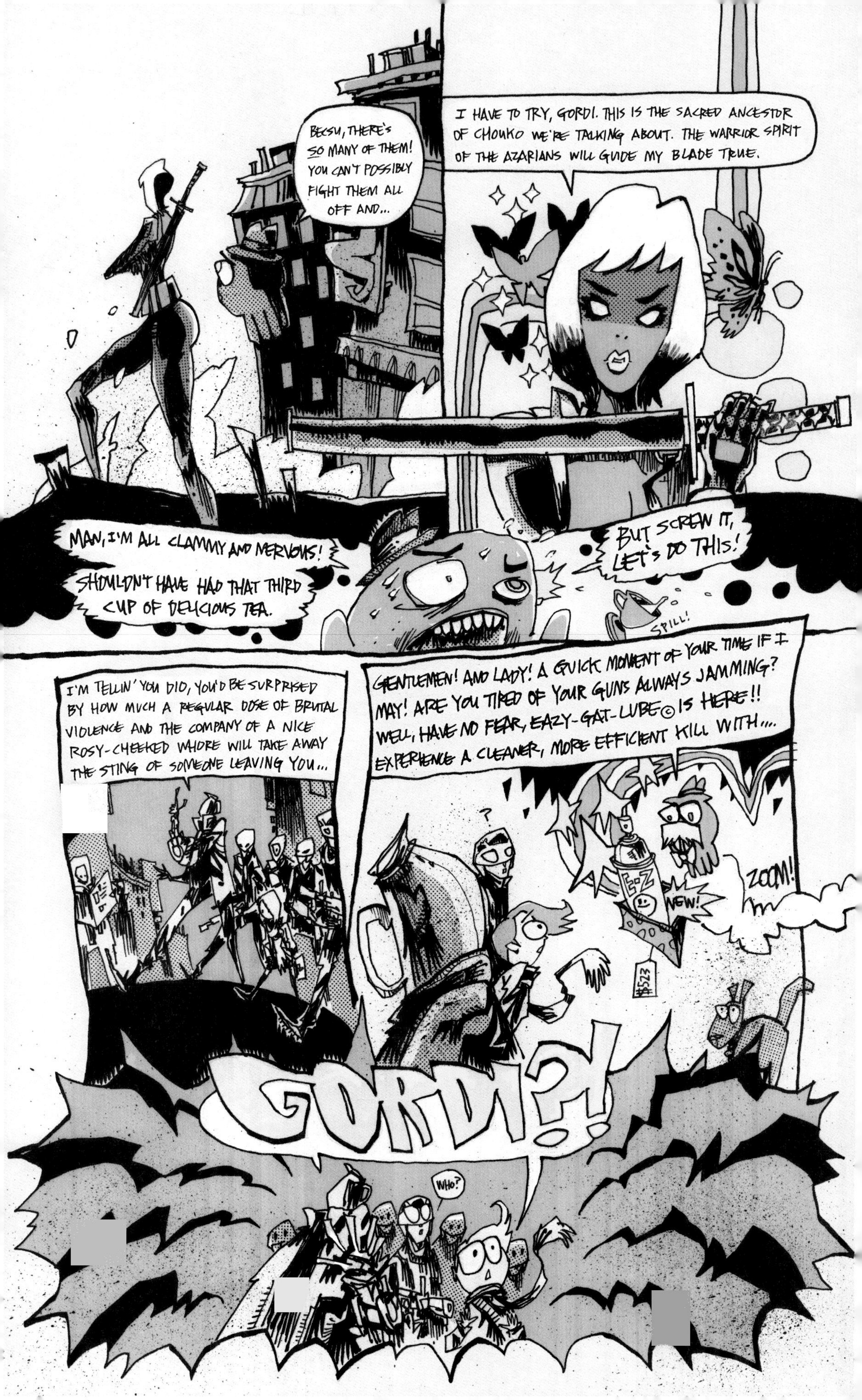
BECSU, THERE'S SO MANY OF THEM! YOU CAN'T POSSIBLY FIGHT THEM ALL OFF AND...
I HAVE TO TRY, GORDI. THIS IS THE SACRED ANCESTOR OF CHOUKO WE'RE TALKING ABOUT. THE WARRIOR SPIRIT OF THE AZARIANS WILL GUIDE MY BLADE TRUE.
MAN, I'M ALL CLAMMY AND NERVOUS!
SHOULDN'T HAVE HAD THAT THIRD CUP OF DELICIOUS TEA.
BUT SCREW IT, LET'S DO THIS!
SPILL!
I'M TELLIN' YOU DIO, YOU'D BE SURPRISED BY HOW MUCH A REGULAR DOSE OF BRUTAL VIOLENCE AND THE COMPANY OF A NICE ROSY-CHEEKED WHORE WILL TAKE AWAY THE STING OF SOMEONE LEAVING YOU...
GENTLEMEN! AND LADY! A QUICK MOMENT OF YOUR TIME IF I MAY! ARE YOU TIRED OF YOUR GUNS ALWAYS JAMMING? WELL, HAVE NO FEAR, EAZY-GAT-LUBE© IS HERE!! EXPERIENCE A CLEANER, MORE EFFICIENT KILL WITH....
?
E-Z
NEW!
ZOOM!
$5.23
GORDI?!
WHO?

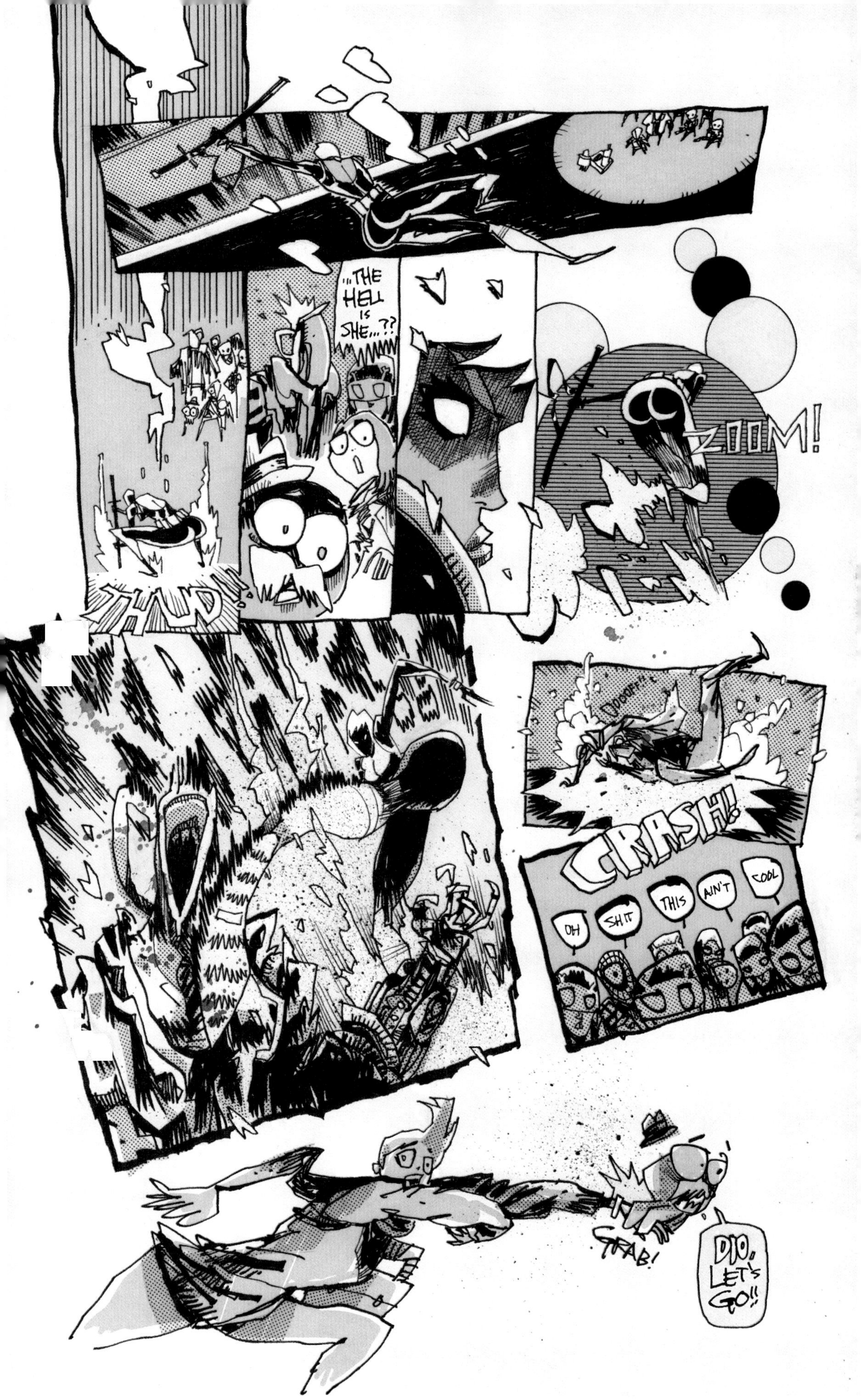
THUD!
...THE HELL IS SHE...??
ZOOM!
CRASH!
OH
SHIT
THIS
AIN'T
COOL
GRAB!
DIO, LET'S GO!!

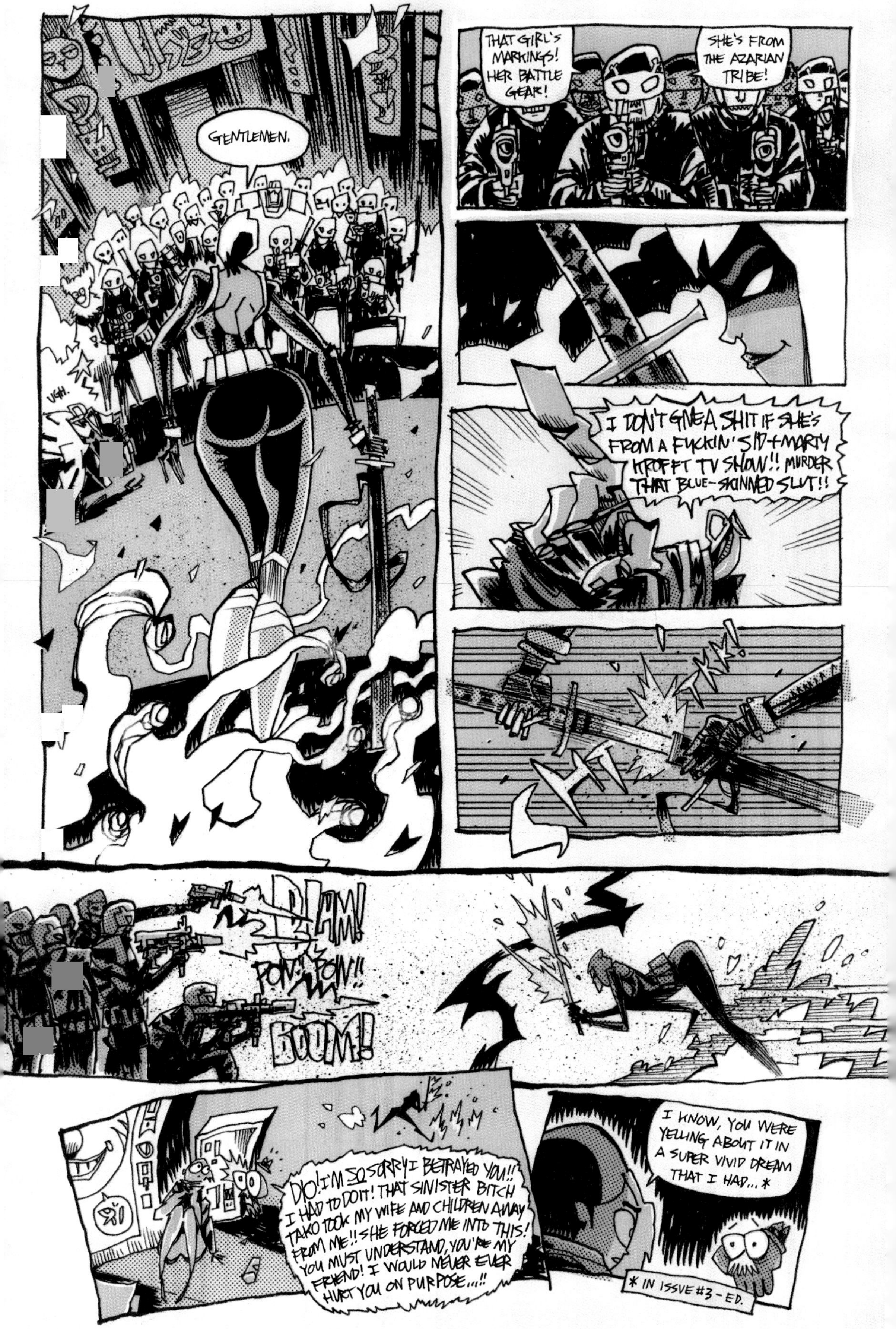
GENTLEMEN.
UGH.
THAT GIRL'S MARKINGS! HER BATTLE GEAR!
SHE'S FROM THE AZARIAN TRIBE!
I DON'T GIVE A SHIT IF SHE'S FROM A FUCKIN' SID + MARTY KROFFT TV SHOW!! MURDER THAT BLUE-SKINNED SLUT!!
BLAM!
POW! POW!!
BOOM!
DIO! I'M SO SORRY I BETRAYED YOU!! I HAD TO DO IT! THAT SINISTER BITCH TAKO TOOK MY WIFE AND CHILDREN AWAY FROM ME!! SHE FORCED ME INTO THIS! YOU MUST UNDERSTAND, YOU'RE MY FRIEND! I WOULD NEVER EVER HURT YOU ON PURPOSE...!!
I KNOW, YOU WERE YELLING ABOUT IT IN A SUPER VIVID DREAM THAT I HAD... *
* IN ISSUE #3 - ED.

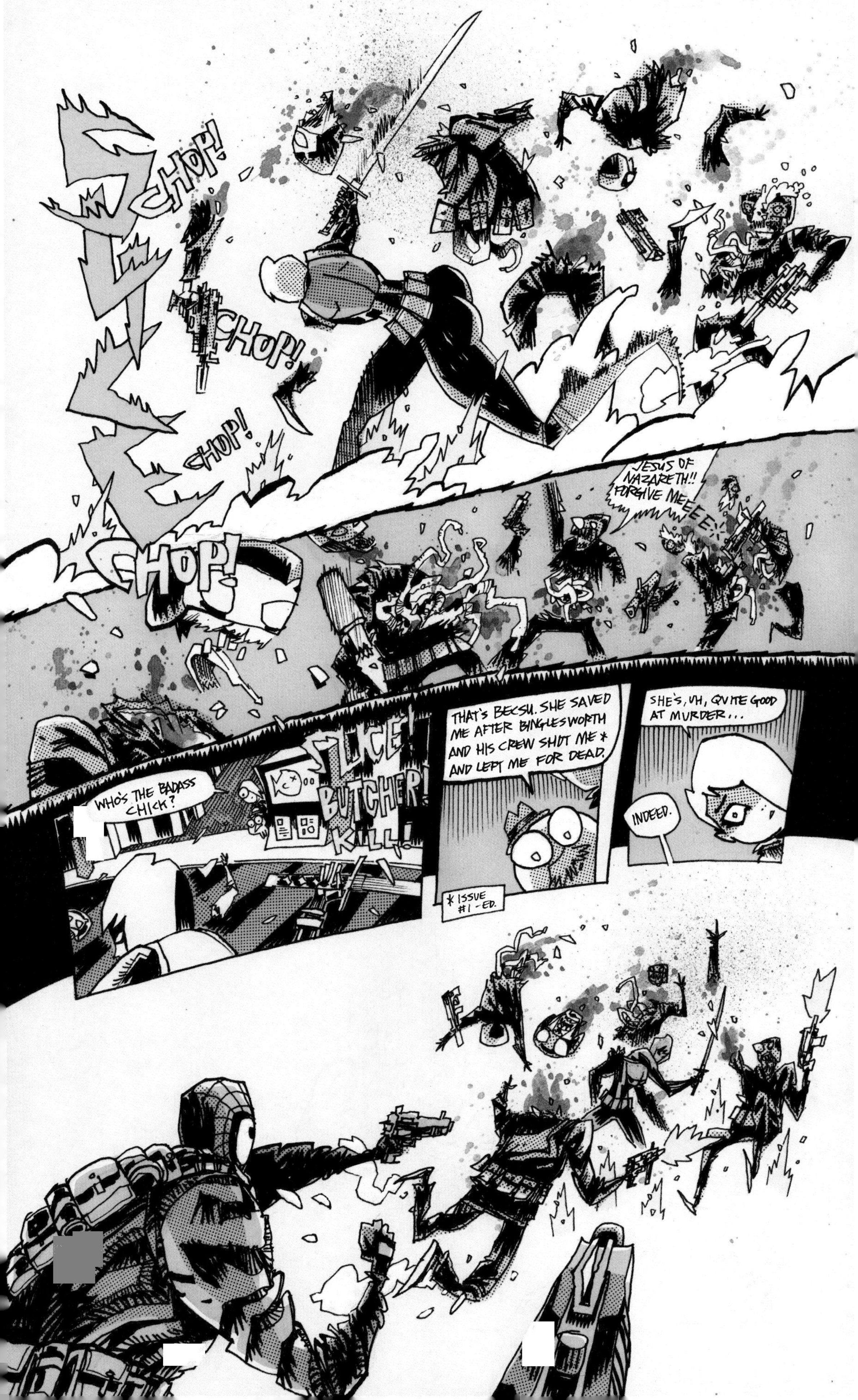
CHOP!
CHOP!
CHOP!
CHOP!
JESUS OF NAZARETH!! FORGIVE MEEEE!
SLICE! BUTCHER! KILL!
WHO'S THE BADASS CHICK?
THAT'S BECSU. SHE SAVED ME AFTER BINGLESWORTH AND HIS CREW SHOT ME * AND LEFT ME FOR DEAD.
* ISSUE #1 - ED.
SHE'S, UH, QUITE GOOD AT MURDER...
INDEED.

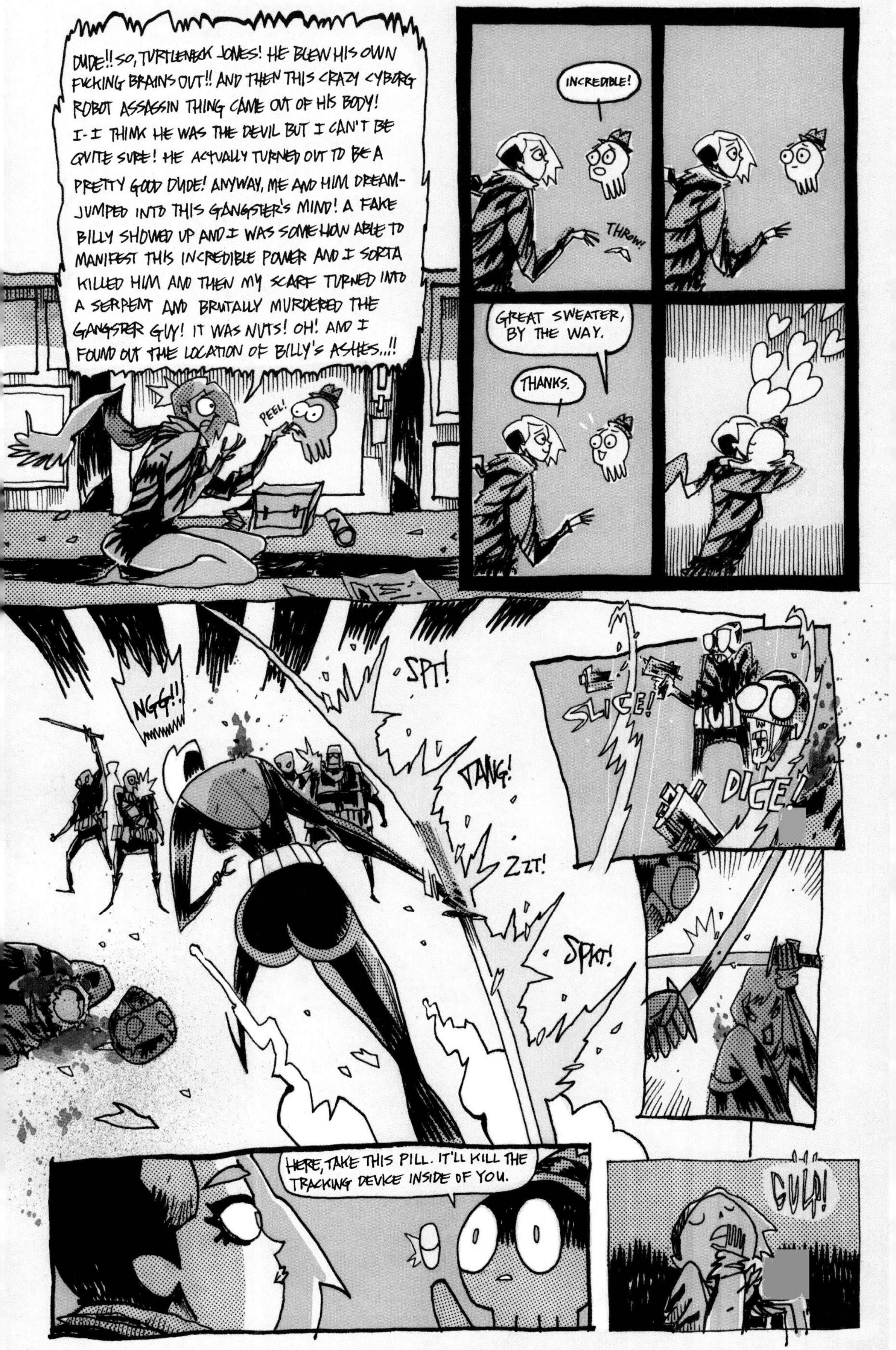

DUDE!! SO, TURTLENECK JONES! HE BLEW HIS OWN FUCKING BRAINS OUT!! AND THEN THIS CRAZY CYBORG ROBOT ASSASSIN THING CAME OUT OF HIS BODY! I- I THINK HE WAS THE DEVIL BUT I CAN'T BE QUITE SURE! HE ACTUALLY TURNED OUT TO BE A PRETTY GOOD DUDE! ANYWAY, ME AND HIM DREAM-JUMPED INTO THIS GANGSTER'S MIND! A FAKE BILLY SHOWED UP AND I WAS SOMEHOW ABLE TO MANIFEST THIS INCREDIBLE POWER AND I SORTA KILLED HIM AND THEN MY SCARF TURNED INTO A SERPENT AND BRUTALLY MURDERED THE GANGSTER GUY! IT WAS NUTS! OH! AND I FOUND OUT THE LOCATION OF BILLY'S ASHES..!!
PEEL!
INCREDIBLE!
THROW!
GREAT SWEATER, BY THE WAY.
THANKS.
NGG!!
SPT!
TANG!
ZZT!
SPKT!
SLICE!
DICE!
HERE, TAKE THIS PILL. IT'LL KILL THE TRACKING DEVICE INSIDE OF YOU.
GULP!

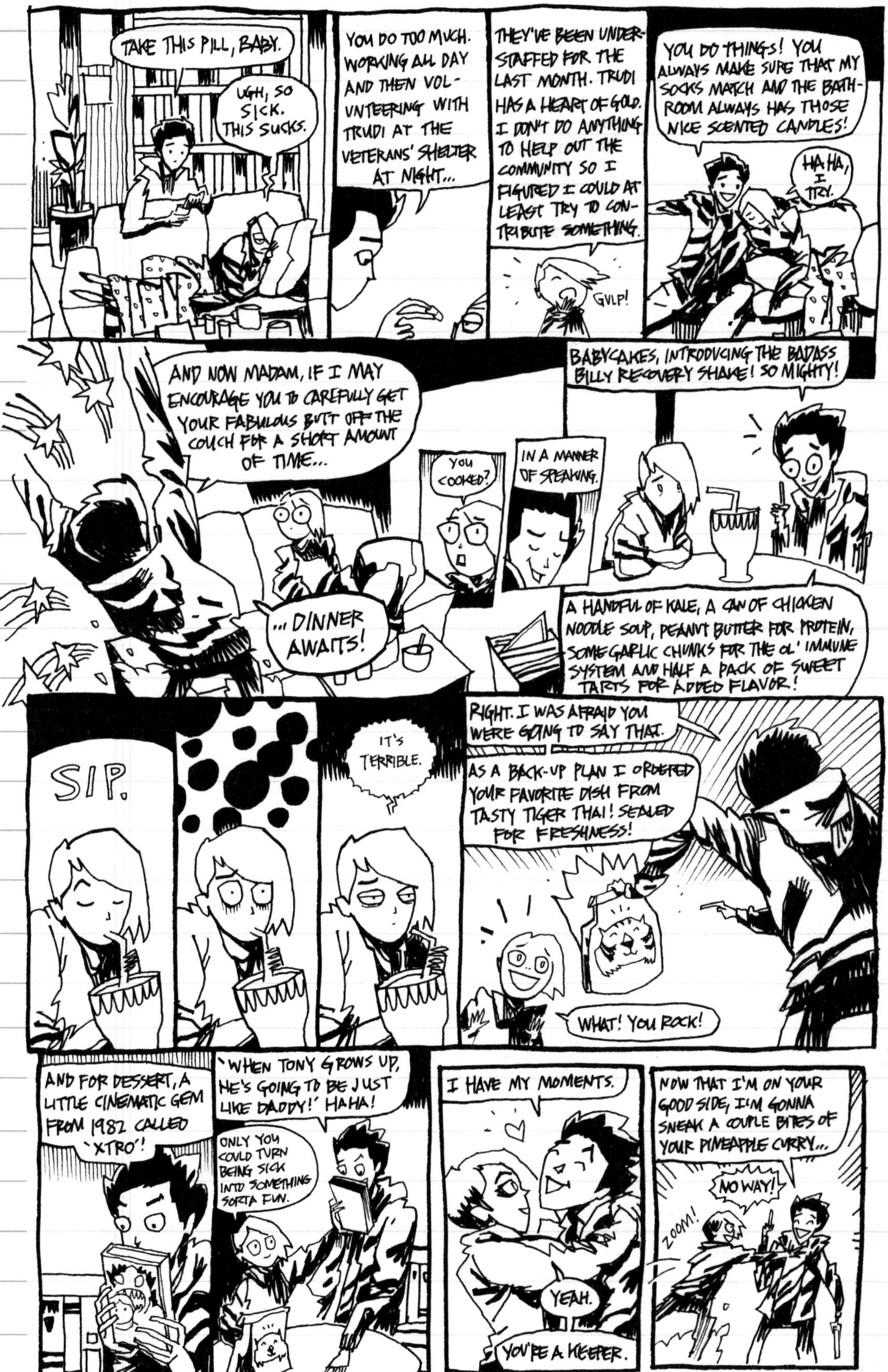
TAKE THIS PILL, BABY.
UGH, SO SICK. THIS SUCKS.
YOU DO TOO MUCH. WORKING ALL DAY AND THEN VOLUNTEERING WITH TRUDI AT THE VETERANS' SHELTER AT NIGHT...
THEY'VE BEEN UNDERSTAFFED FOR THE LAST MONTH. TRUDI HAS A HEART OF GOLD. I DON'T DO ANYTHING TO HELP OUT THE COMMUNITY SO I FIGURED I COULD AT LEAST TRY TO CONTRIBUTE SOMETHING.
GULP!
YOU DO THINGS! YOU ALWAYS MAKE SURE THAT MY SOCKS MATCH AND THE BATHROOM ALWAYS HAS THOSE NICE SCENTED CANDLES!
HA HA, I TRY.
AND NOW MADAM, IF I MAY ENCOURAGE YOU TO CAREFULLY GET YOUR FABULOUS BUTT OFF THE COUCH FOR A SHORT AMOUNT OF TIME...
...DINNER AWAITS!
YOU COOKED?
IN A MANNER OF SPEAKING.
BABYCAKES, INTRODUCING THE BADASS BILLY RECOVERY SHAKE! SO MIGHTY!
A HANDFUL OF KALE, A CAN OF CHICKEN NOODLE SOUP, PEANUT BUTTER FOR PROTEIN, SOME GARLIC CHUNKS FOR THE OL' IMMUNE SYSTEM AND HALF A PACK OF SWEET TARTS FOR ADDED FLAVOR!
SIP.
IT'S TERRIBLE.
RIGHT. I WAS AFRAID YOU WERE GOING TO SAY THAT.
AS A BACK-UP PLAN I ORDERED YOUR FAVORITE DISH FROM TASTY TIGER THAI! SEALED FOR FRESHNESS!
WHAT! YOU ROCK!
AND FOR DESSERT, A LITTLE CINEMATIC GEM FROM 1982 CALLED `XTRO'!
`WHEN TONY GROWS UP, HE'S GOING TO BE JUST LIKE DADDY!' HAHA!
ONLY YOU COULD TURN BEING SICK INTO SOMETHING SORTA FUN.
I HAVE MY MOMENTS.
YEAH.
YOU'RE A KEEPER.
NOW THAT I'M ON YOUR GOOD SIDE, I'M GONNA SNEAK A COUPLE BITES OF YOUR PINEAPPLE CURRY...
NO WAY!
ZOOM!

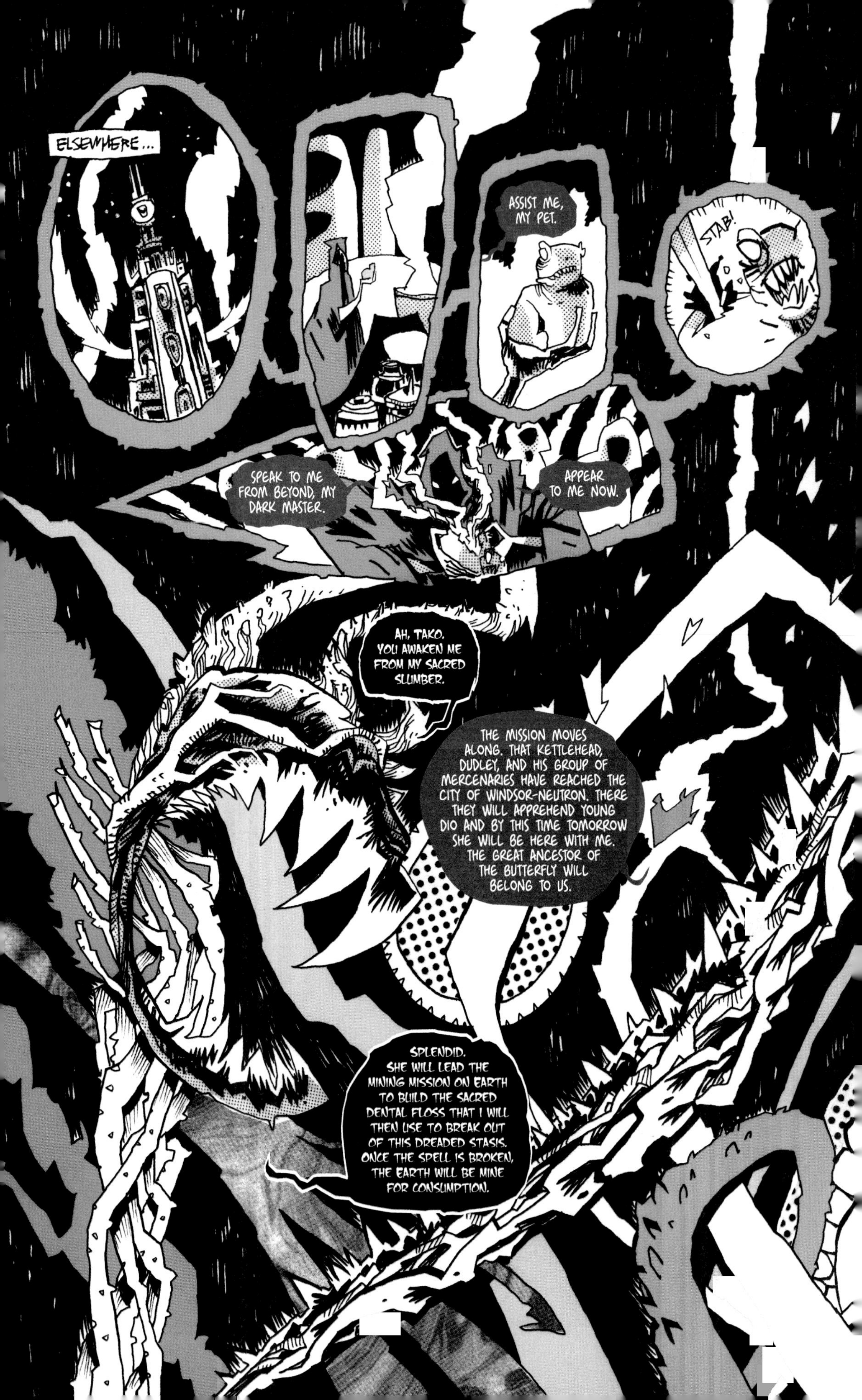
ELSEWHERE...
ASSIST ME, MY PET.
STAB!
SPEAK TO ME FROM BEYOND, MY DARK MASTER.
APPEAR TO ME NOW.
AH, TAKO. YOU AWAKEN ME FROM MY SACRED SLUMBER.
THE MISSION MOVES ALONG. THAT KETTLEHEAD, DUDLEY, AND HIS GROUP OF MERCENARIES HAVE REACHED THE CITY OF WINDSOR-NEUTRON. THERE THEY WILL APPREHEND YOUNG DIO AND BY THIS TIME TOMORROW SHE WILL BE HERE WITH ME. THE GREAT ANCESTOR OF THE BUTTERFLY WILL BELONG TO US.
SPLENDID. SHE WILL LEAD THE MINING MISSION ON EARTH TO BUILD THE SACRED DENTAL FLOSS THAT I WILL THEN USE TO BREAK OUT OF THIS DREADED STASIS. ONCE THE SPELL IS BROKEN, THE EARTH WILL BE MINE FOR CONSUMPTION.

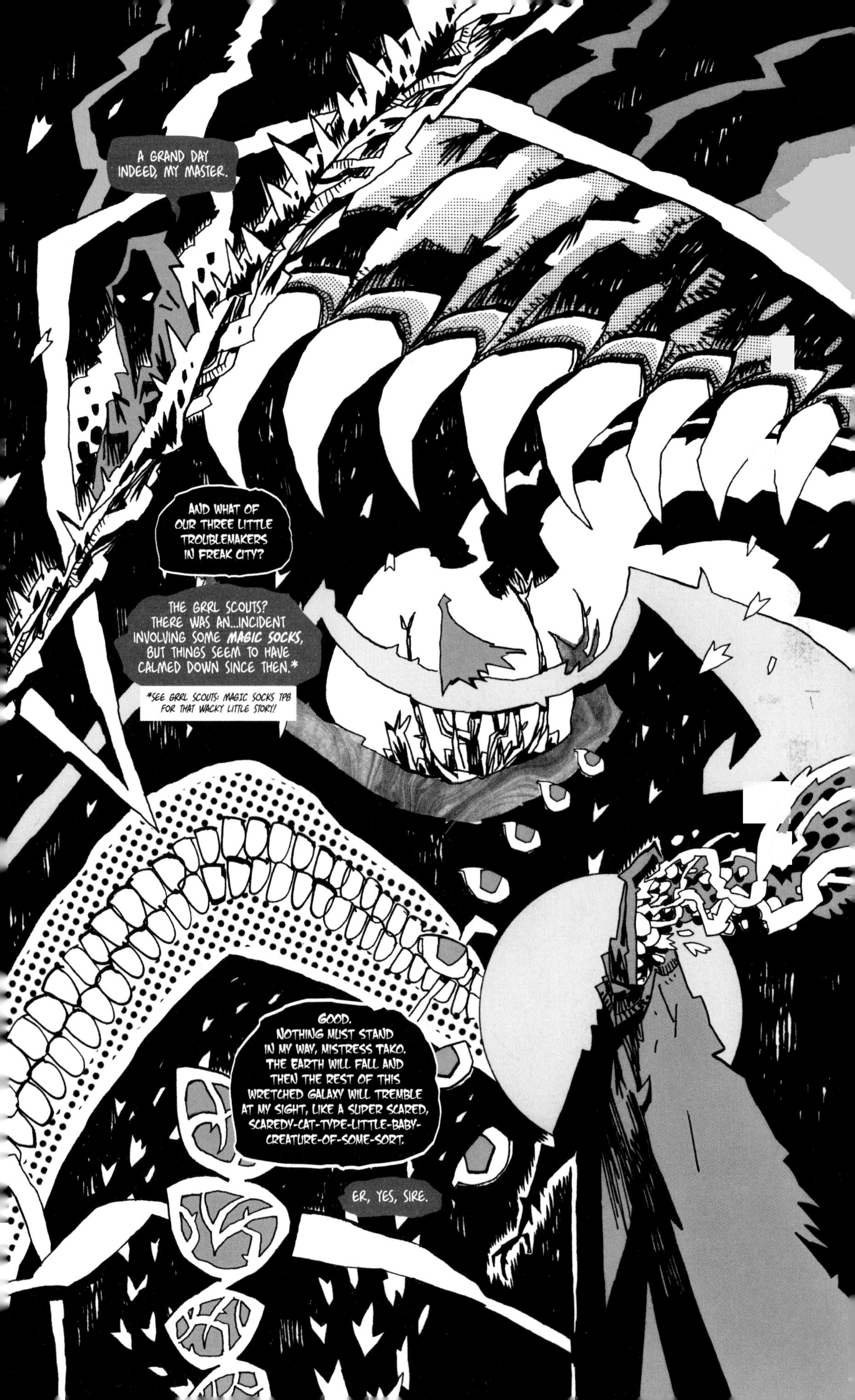

A GRAND DAY INDEED, MY MASTER.
AND WHAT OF OUR THREE LITTLE TROUBLEMAKERS IN FREAK CITY?
THE GRRL SCOUTS? THERE WAS AN...INCIDENT INVOLVING SOME MAGIC SOCKS, BUT THINGS SEEM TO HAVE CALMED DOWN SINCE THEN.*
*SEE GRRL SCOUTS: MAGIC SOCKS TPB FOR THAT WACKY LITTLE STORY!
GOOD. NOTHING MUST STAND IN MY WAY, MISTRESS TAKO. THE EARTH WILL FALL AND THEN THE REST OF THIS WRETCHED GALAXY WILL TREMBLE AT MY SIGHT, LIKE A SUPER SCARED, SCAREDY-CAT-TYPE-LITTLE-BABY-CREATURE-OF-SOME-SORT.
ER, YES, SIRE.

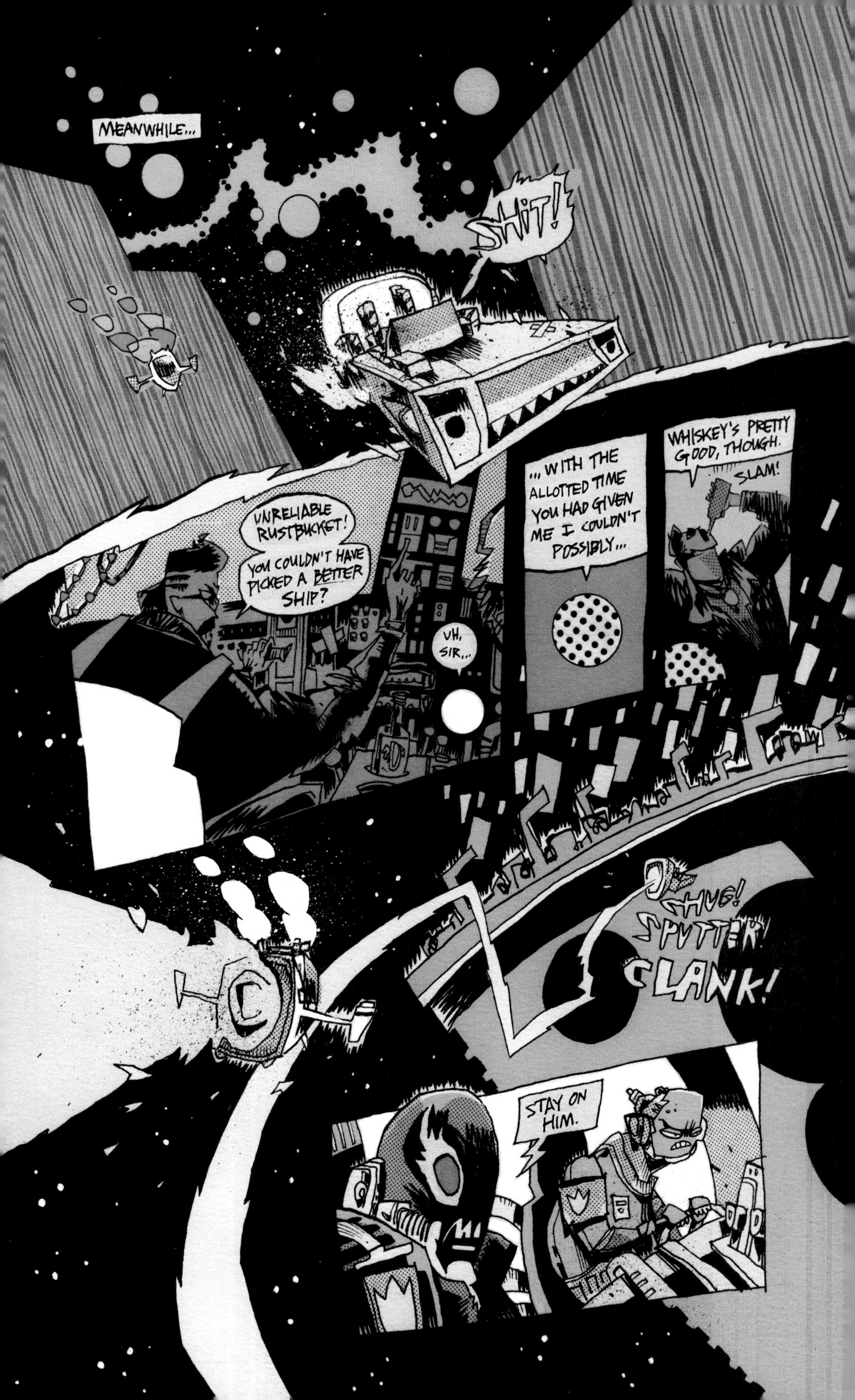
MEANWHILE...
SHIT!
UNRELIABLE RUSTBUCKET!
YOU COULDN'T HAVE PICKED A BETTER SHIP?
UH, SIR...
...WITH THE ALLOTTED TIME YOU HAD GIVEN ME I COULDN'T POSSIBLY...
WHISKEY'S PRETTY GOOD, THOUGH.
SLAM!
CHUG!
SPUTTER
CLANK!
STAY ON HIM.

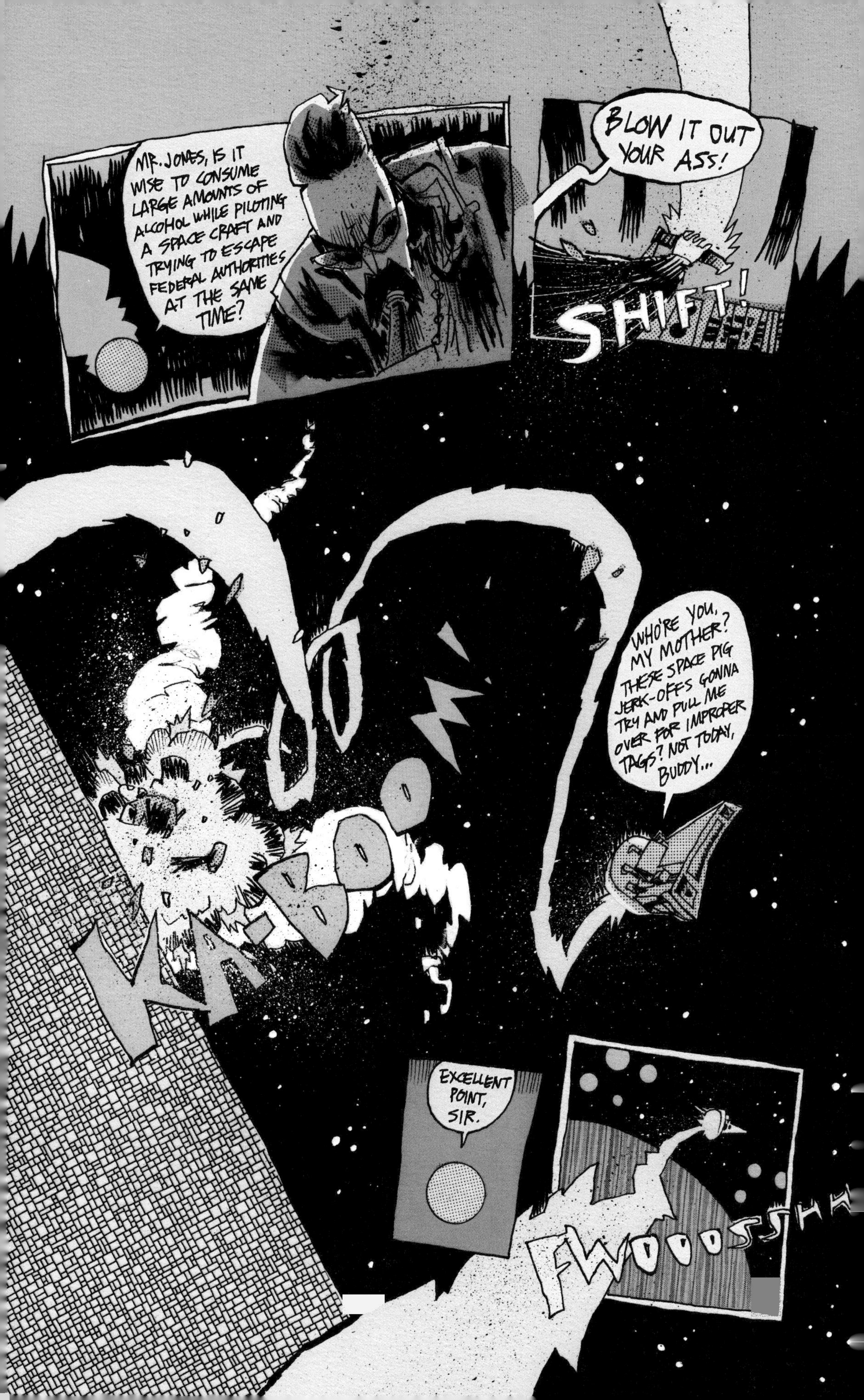

MR. JONES, IS IT WISE TO CONSUME LARGE AMOUNTS OF ALCOHOL WHILE PILOTING A SPACE CRAFT AND TRYING TO ESCAPE FEDERAL AUTHORITIES AT THE SAME TIME?
BLOW IT OUT YOUR ASS!
SHIFT!
WHO'RE YOU, MY MOTHER? THESE SPACE PIG JERK-OFFS GONNA TRY AND PULL ME OVER FOR IMPROPER TAGS? NOT TODAY, BUDDY...
KA-BOOOOM
EXCELLENT POINT, SIR.
FWOOOSSHH

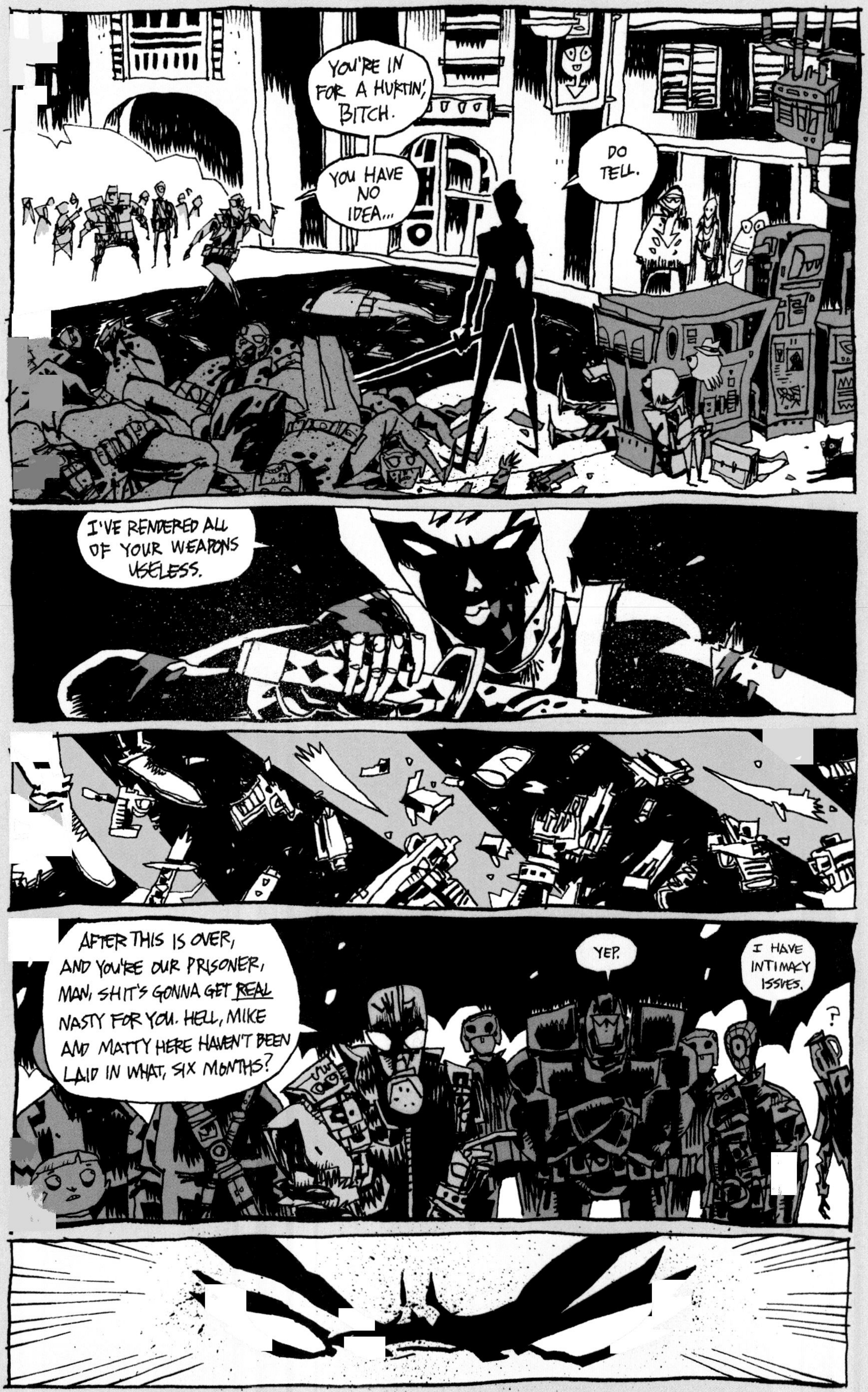
YOU'RE IN FOR A HURTIN', BITCH.
YOU HAVE NO IDEA...
DO TELL.
I'VE RENDERED ALL OF YOUR WEAPONS USELESS.
AFTER THIS IS OVER, AND YOU'RE OUR PRISONER, MAN, SHIT'S GONNA GET REAL NASTY FOR YOU. HELL, MIKE AND MATTY HERE HAVEN'T BEEN LAID IN WHAT, SIX MONTHS?
YEP.
I HAVE INTIMACY ISSUES.
?

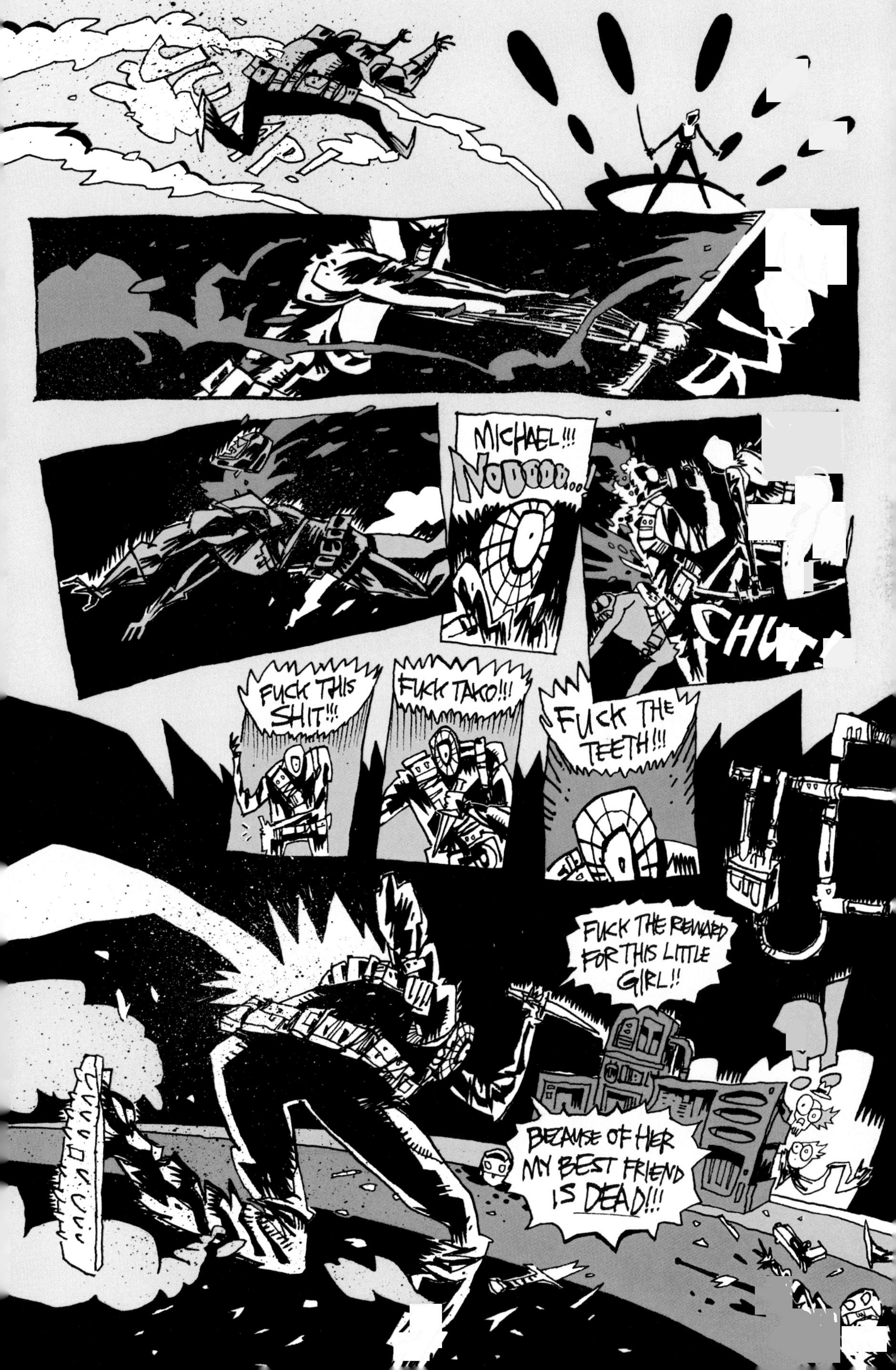
MICHAEL!!!
NOOOOO...
FUCK THIS SHIT!!!
FUCK TAKO!!!
FUCK THE TEETH!!!
FUCK THE REWARD FOR THIS LITTLE GIRL!!
BECAUSE OF HER MY BEST FRIEND IS DEAD!!!

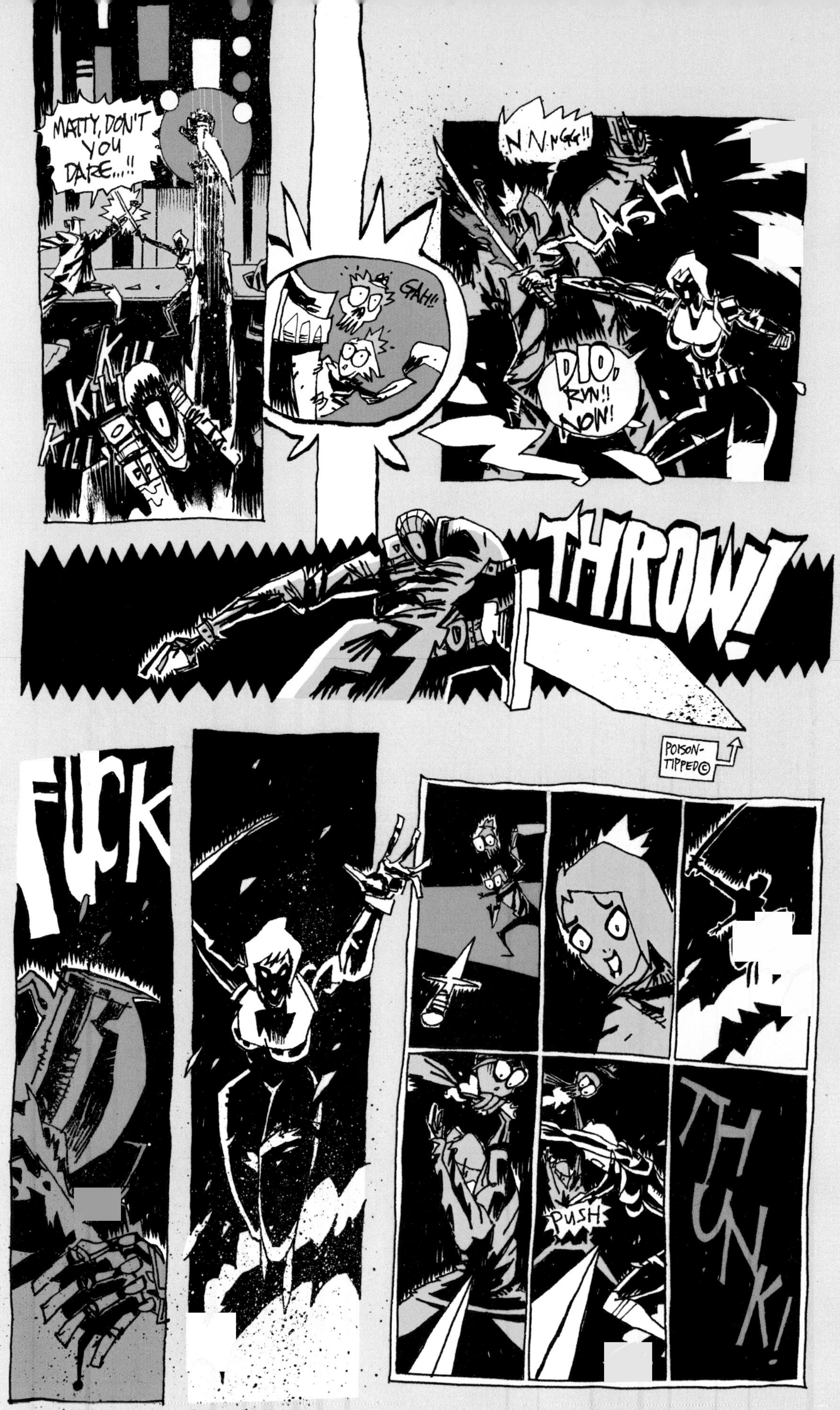
MATTY, DON'T YOU DARE...!!
KILL KILL KILL
GAH!!
N N.NGG!!
DIO, RUN!! NOW!
THROW!
POISON-TIPPED©
FUCK
PUSH
THUNK!

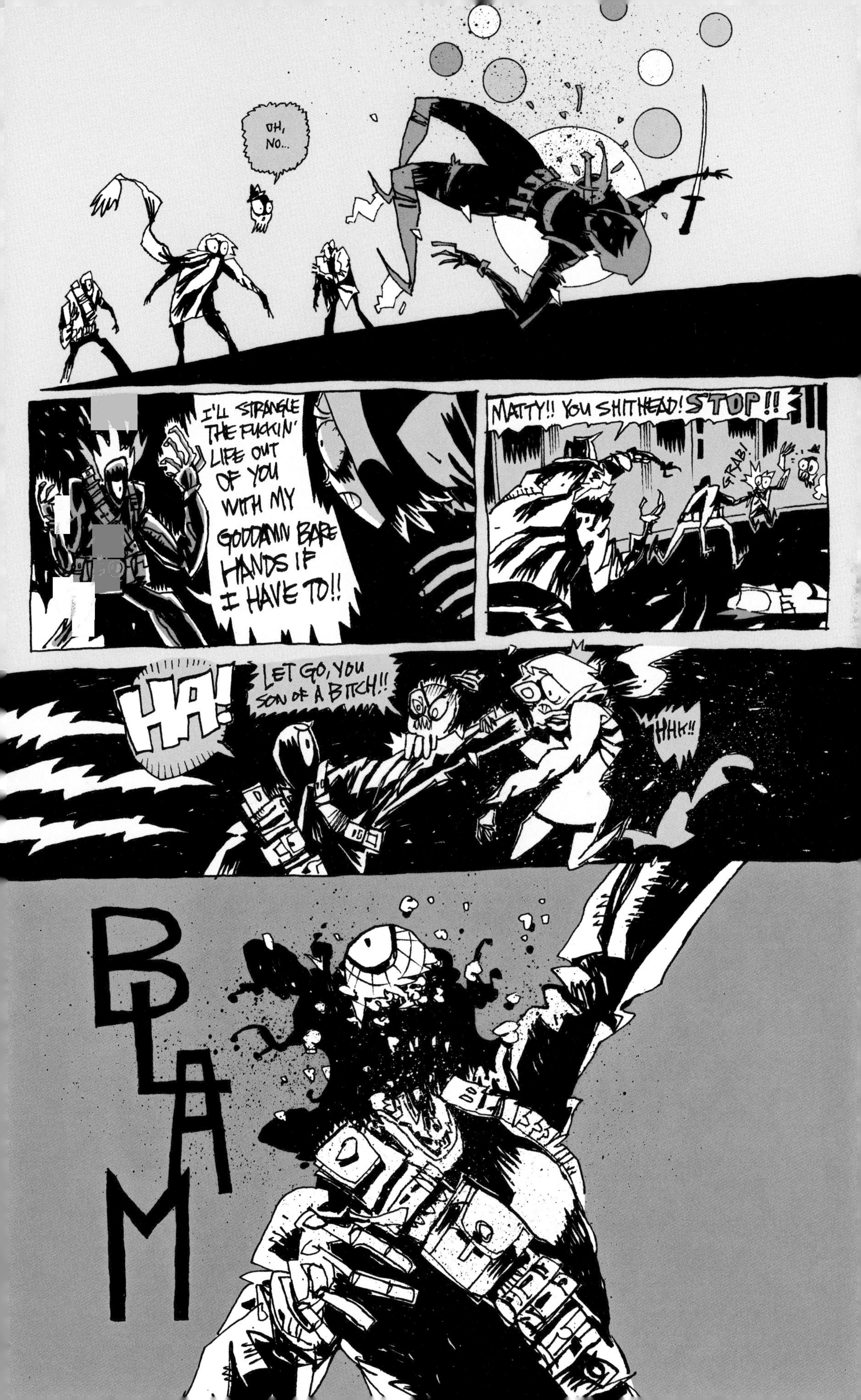
OH, NO...
I'LL STRANGLE THE FUCKIN' LIFE OUT OF YOU WITH MY GODDAMN BARE HANDS IF I HAVE TO!!
MATTY!! YOU SHITHEAD! STOP!!
GRAB!
HA!
LET GO, YOU SON OF A BITCH!!
HHK!!
BLAM

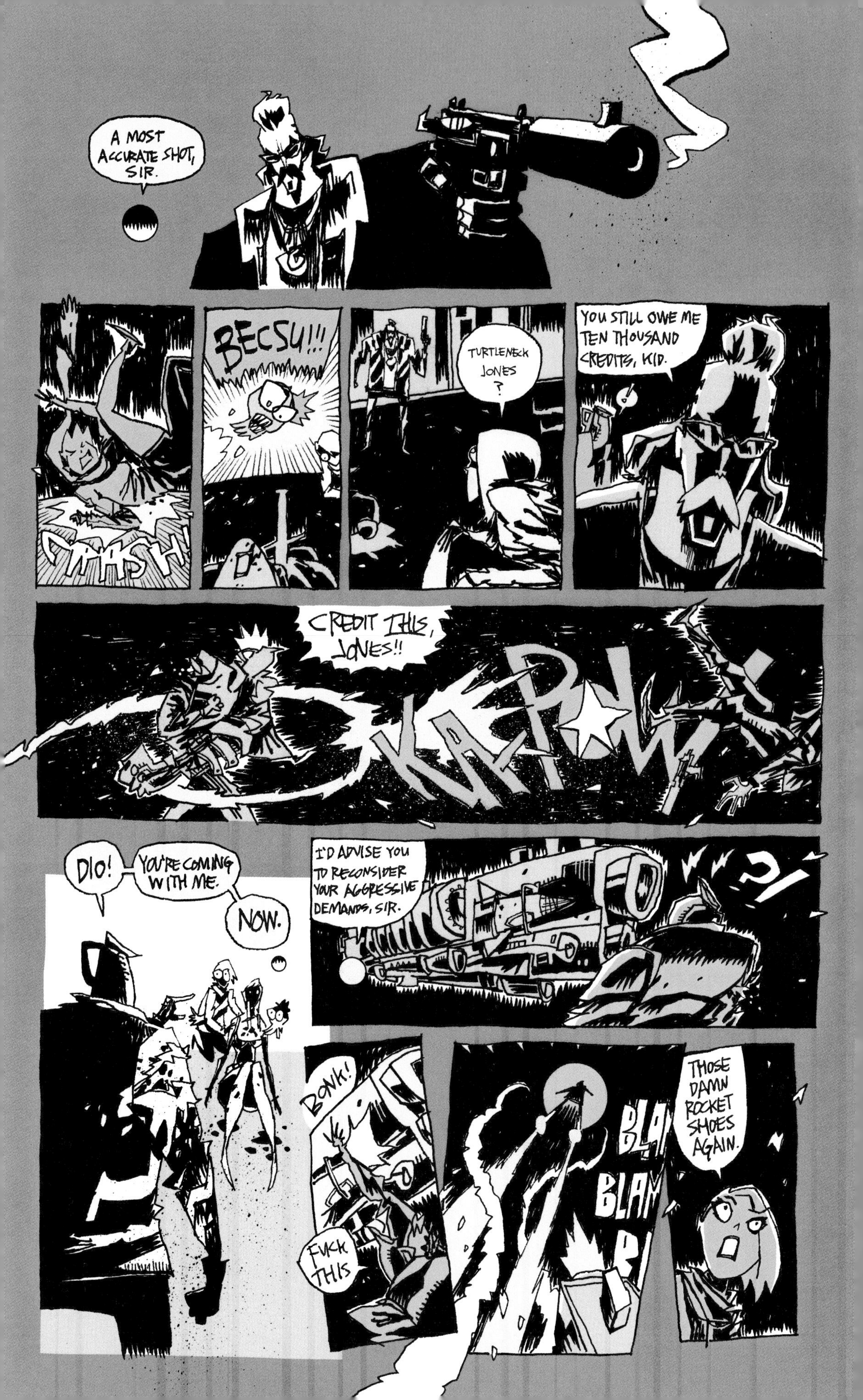
A MOST ACCURATE SHOT, SIR.
CRASH!
BECSU!!!
TURTLENECK JONES ?
YOU STILL OWE ME TEN THOUSAND CREDITS, KID.
CREDIT THIS, JONES!!
KA-POW
DIO!
YOU'RE COMING WITH ME.
NOW.
I'D ADVISE YOU TO RECONSIDER YOUR AGGRESSIVE DEMANDS, SIR.
?!
BONK!
FUCK THIS
BLAM
BLAM
THOSE DAMN ROCKET SHOES AGAIN.

DVDLEY.... THAT FUCKIN' KETTLEHEAD ASSHOLE.

MR. JONES! ARE YOU ALRIGHT, SIR?

WE GOT ANY WHISKEY LEFT?

NEGATIVE, SIR.

MY SENSORS INDICATE TOXICOLOGY READINGS OF A FATAL DOSE THAT...

PUT A LID ON IT, CHROME-DOME.

YOU-YOU SAVED MY LIFE! I'M SO SORRY THIS HAPPENED! HOW CAN WE...

A-ALL IN THE LINE OF DUTY, MY LITTLE BUTTERFLY. IT IS A T-TRUE... HKK... HONOR TO MEET YOU...

...EVEN FOR SUCH A BRIEF MOMENT OF TIME.

WE CAN GET YOU TO A HOSPITAL! WE CAN MAKE THIS RIGHT...

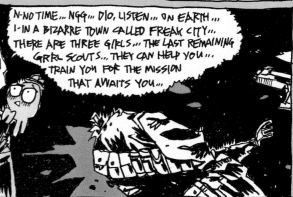

N-NO TIME... NGG... DIO, LISTEN... ON EARTH... I-IN A BIZARRE TOWN CALLED FREAK CITY... THERE ARE THREE GIRLS... THE LAST REMAINING GRRL SCOUTS... THEY CAN HELP YOU... TRAIN YOU FOR THE MISSION THAT AWAITS YOU...

WAIT, WHAT...?

...Y-YOU WILL NOT FAIL IN YOUR SACRED JOURNEY...

...I... HKK... I KNOW THIS TO BE TRUEEEE

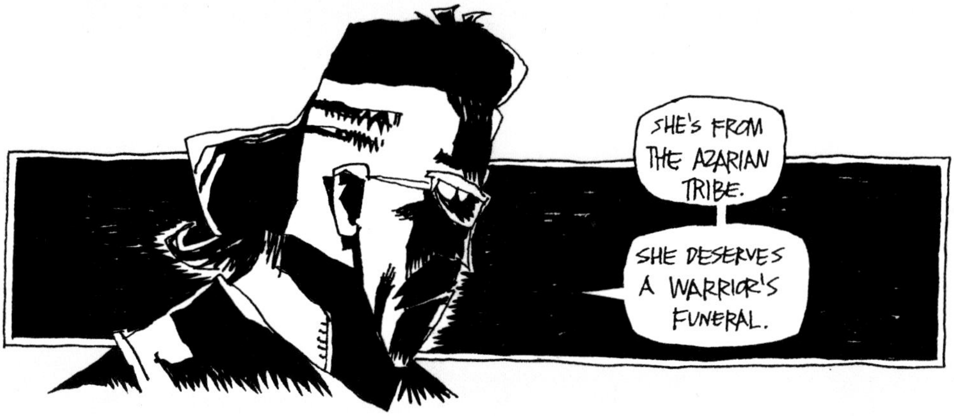
SHE'S FROM THE AZARIAN TRIBE.
SHE DESERVES A WARRIOR'S FUNERAL.

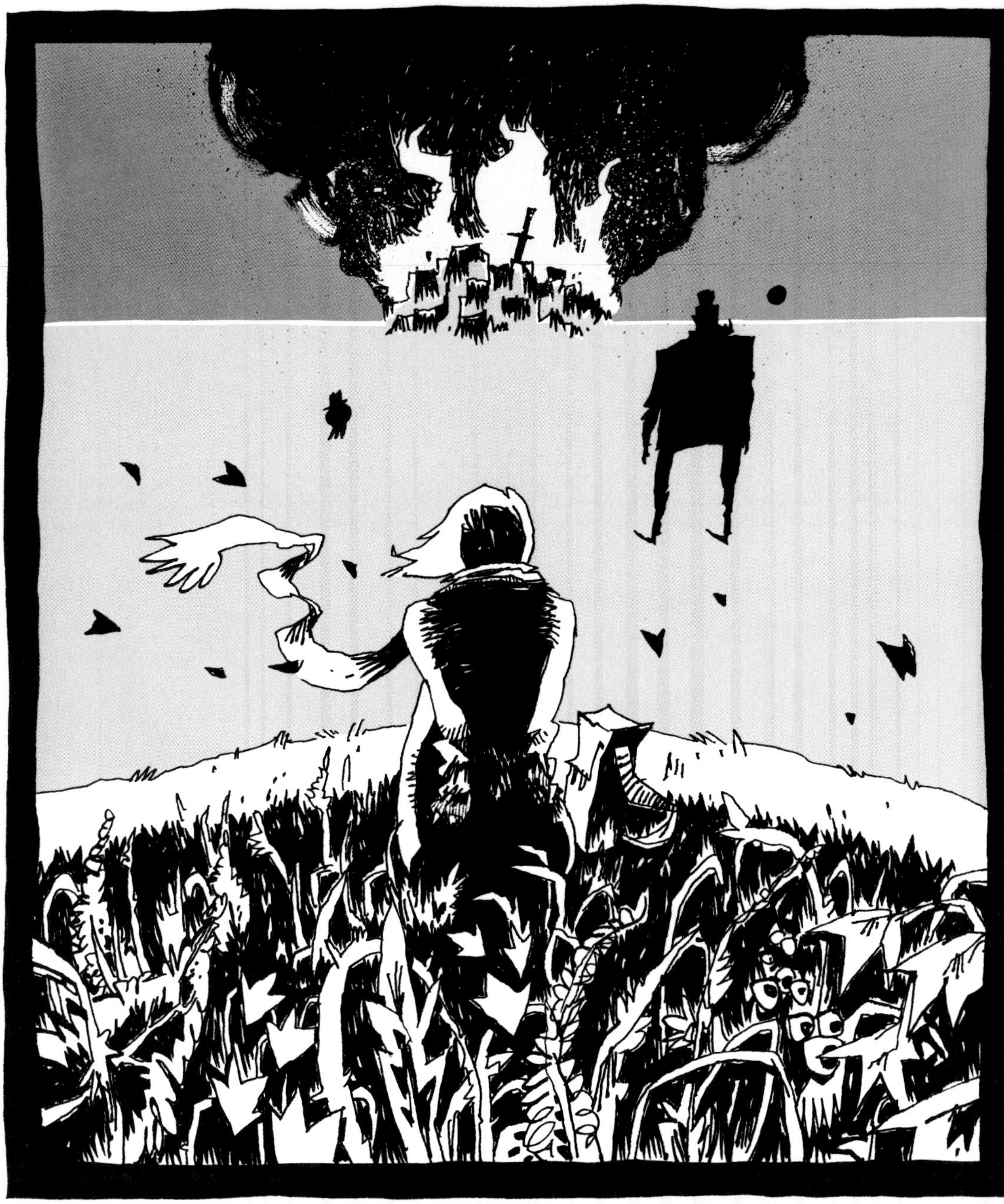

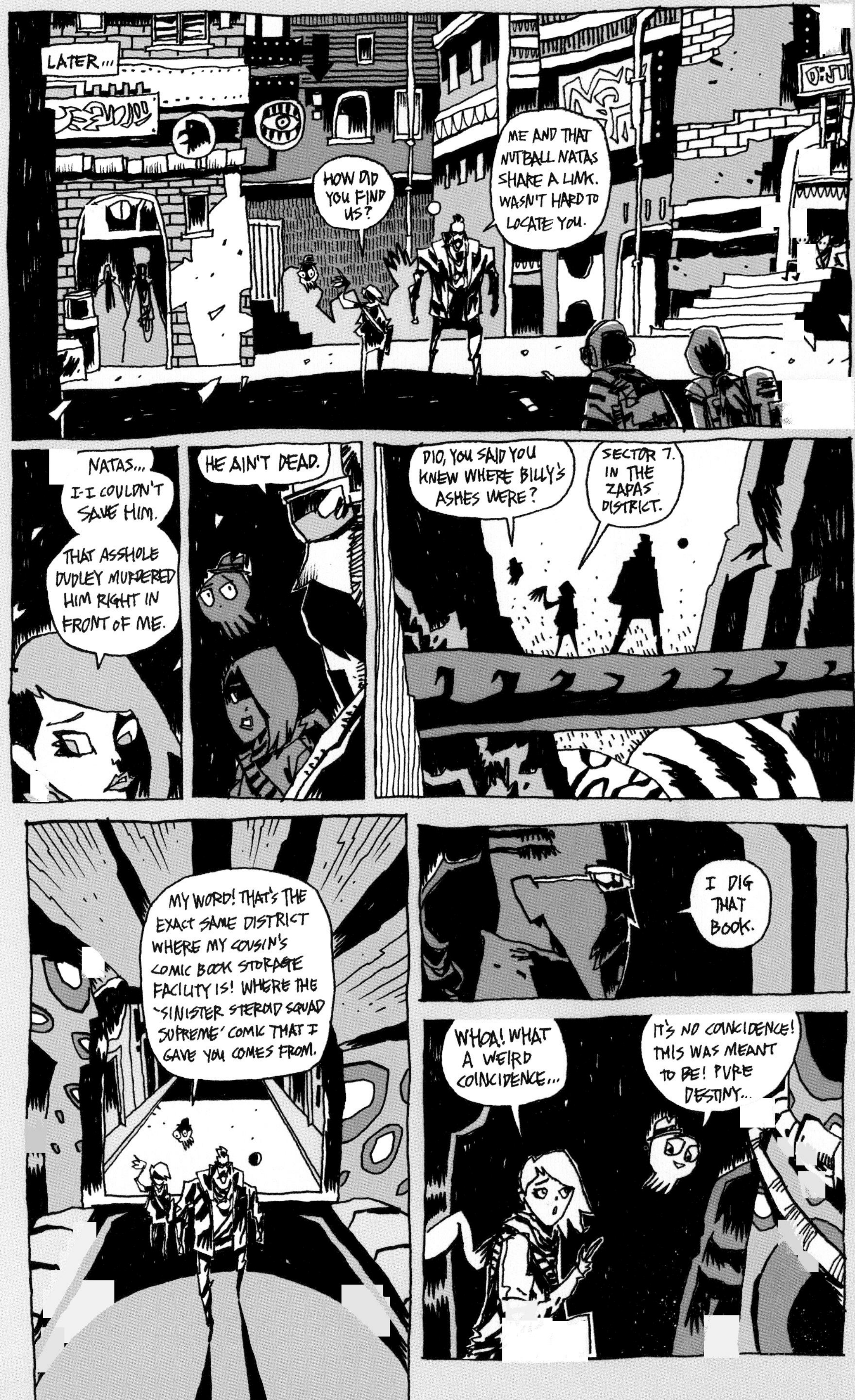
LATER...
HOW DID YOU FIND US?
ME AND THAT NUTBALL NATAS SHARE A LINK. WASN'T HARD TO LOCATE YOU.
NATAS... I-I COULDN'T SAVE HIM.
THAT ASSHOLE DUDLEY MURDERED HIM RIGHT IN FRONT OF ME.
HE AIN'T DEAD.
DIO, YOU SAID YOU KNEW WHERE BILLY'S ASHES WERE?
SECTOR 7. IN THE ZAPAS DISTRICT.
MY WORD! THAT'S THE EXACT SAME DISTRICT WHERE MY COUSIN'S COMIC BOOK STORAGE FACILITY IS! WHERE THE 'SINISTER STEROID SQUAD SUPREME' COMIC THAT I GAVE YOU COMES FROM.
I DIG THAT BOOK.
WHOA! WHAT A WEIRD COINCIDENCE...
IT'S NO COINCIDENCE! THIS WAS MEANT TO BE! PURE DESTINY...

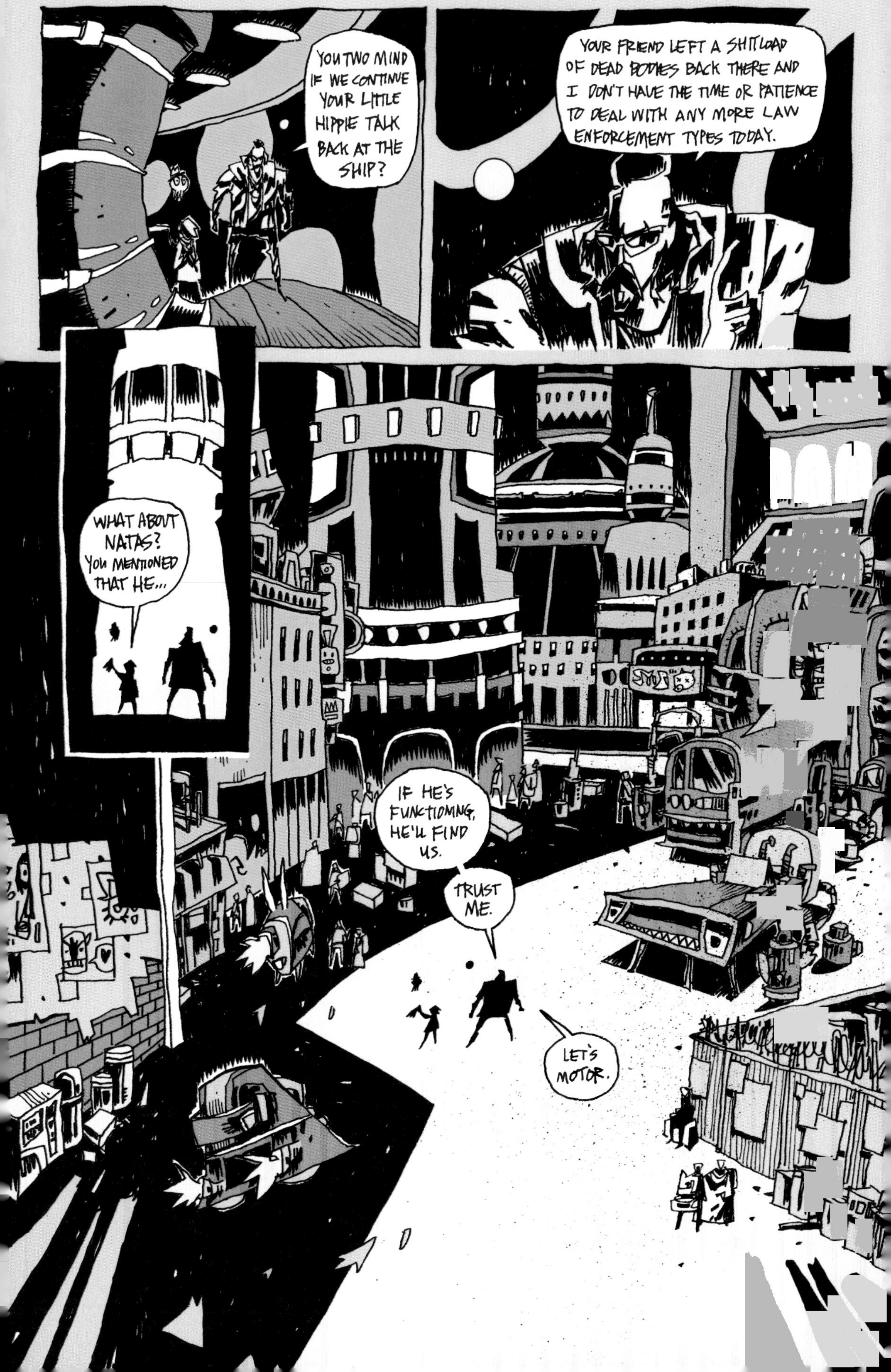
YOU TWO MIND IF WE CONTINUE YOUR LITTLE HIPPIE TALK BACK AT THE SHIP?
YOUR FRIEND LEFT A SHITLOAD OF DEAD BODIES BACK THERE AND I DON'T HAVE THE TIME OR PATIENCE TO DEAL WITH ANY MORE LAW ENFORCEMENT TYPES TODAY.
WHAT ABOUT NATAS? YOU MENTIONED THAT HE...
IF HE'S FUNCTIONING, HE'LL FIND US.
TRUST ME.
LET'S MOTOR.

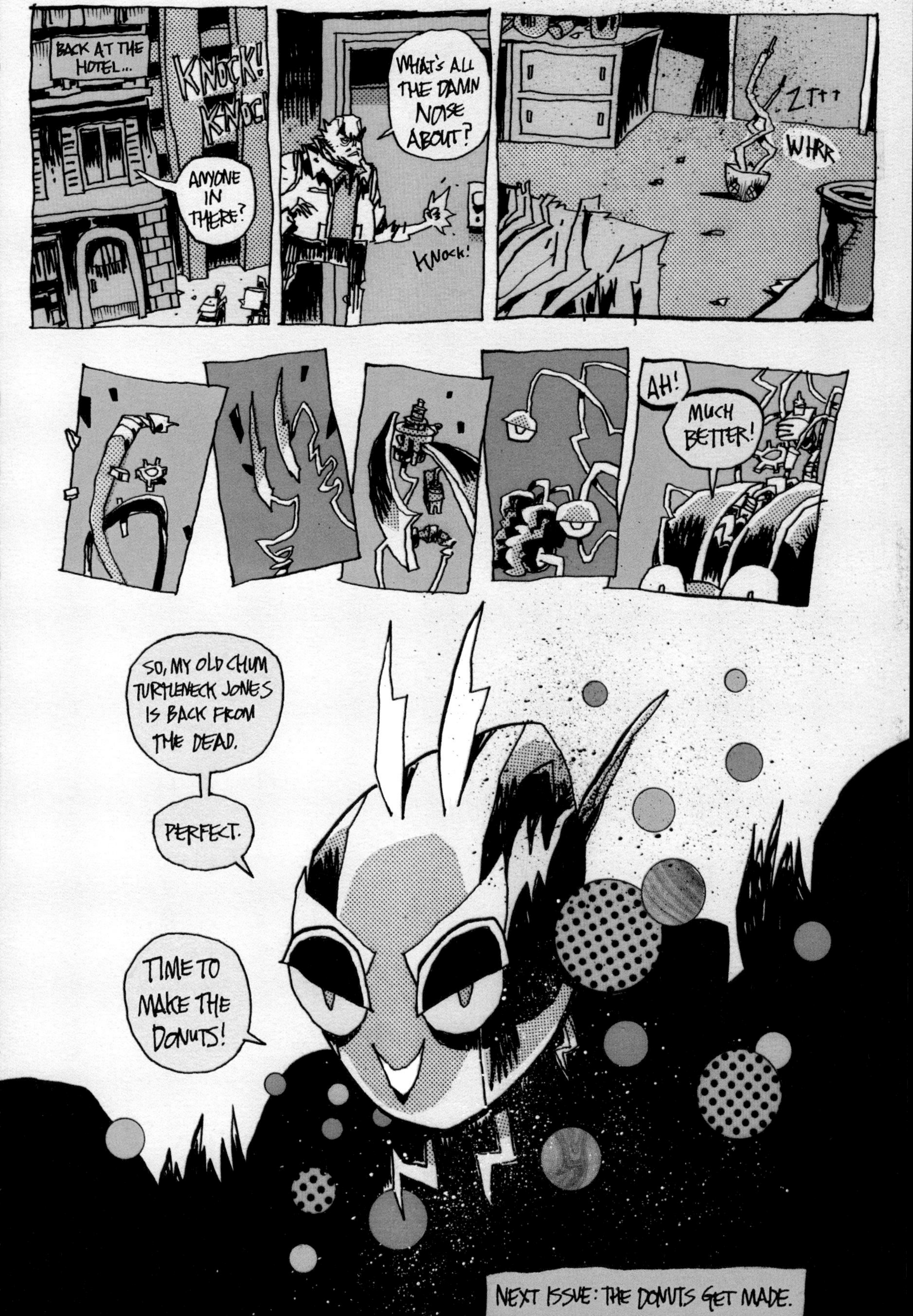
BACK AT THE HOTEL...
KNOCK!
KNOC!
ANYONE IN THERE?
WHAT'S ALL THE DAMN NOISE ABOUT?
KNOCK!
ZTTT
WHRR
AH!
MUCH BETTER!
SO, MY OLD CHUM TURTLENECK JONES IS BACK FROM THE DEAD.
PERFECT.
TIME TO MAKE THE DONUTS!
NEXT ISSUE: THE DONUTS GET MADE.

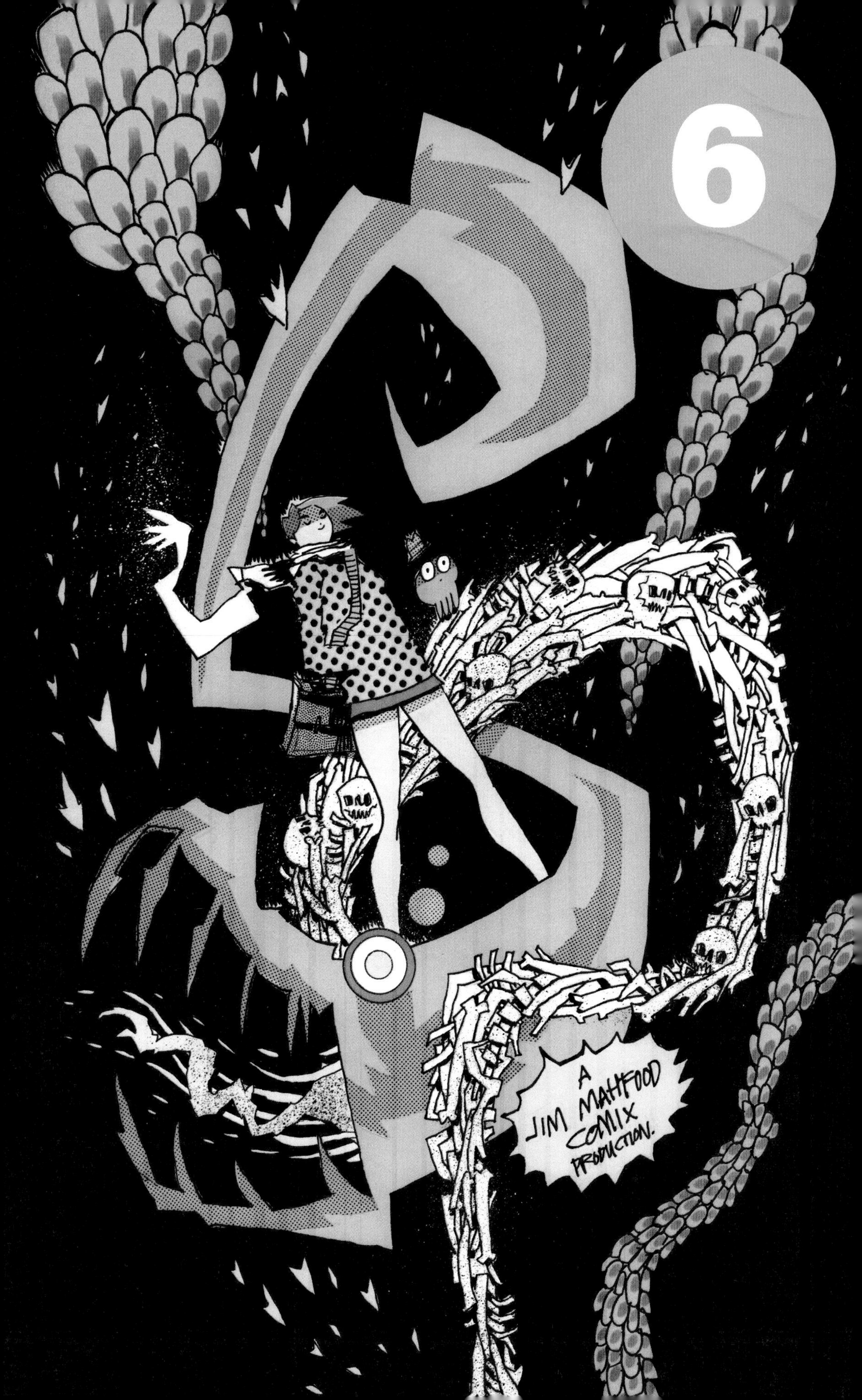
6
A JIM MAHFOOD COMIX PRODUCTION.

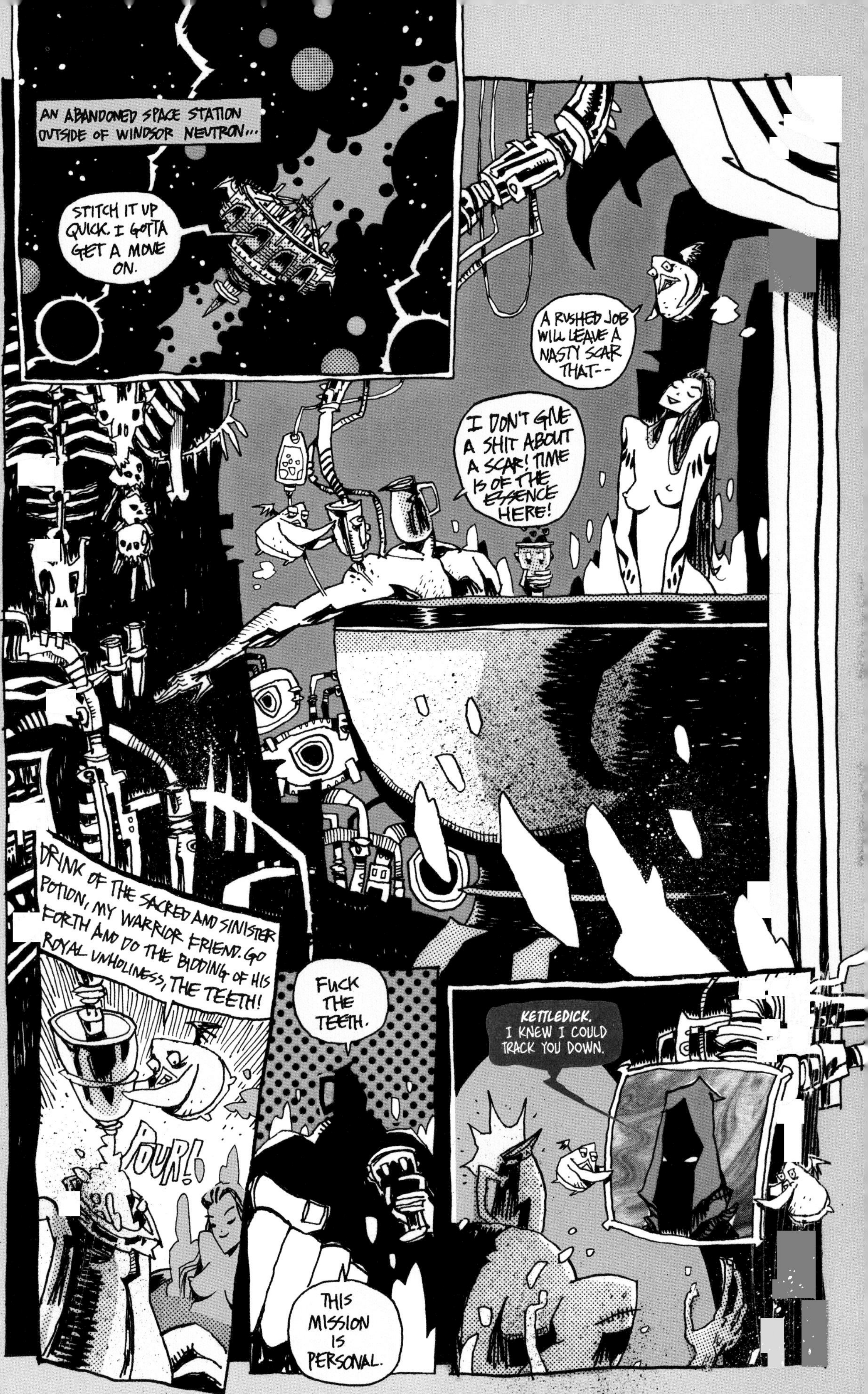
AN ABANDONED SPACE STATION OUTSIDE OF WINDSOR NEUTRON...
STITCH IT UP QUICK. I GOTTA GET A MOVE ON.
A RUSHED JOB WILL LEAVE A NASTY SCAR THAT--
I DON'T GIVE A SHIT ABOUT A SCAR! TIME IS OF THE ESSENCE HERE!
DRINK OF THE SACRED AND SINISTER POTION, MY WARRIOR FRIEND. GO FORTH AND DO THE BIDDING OF HIS ROYAL UNHOLINESS, THE TEETH!
POUR!
FUCK THE TEETH.
THIS MISSION IS PERSONAL.
KETTLEDICK. I KNEW I COULD TRACK YOU DOWN.

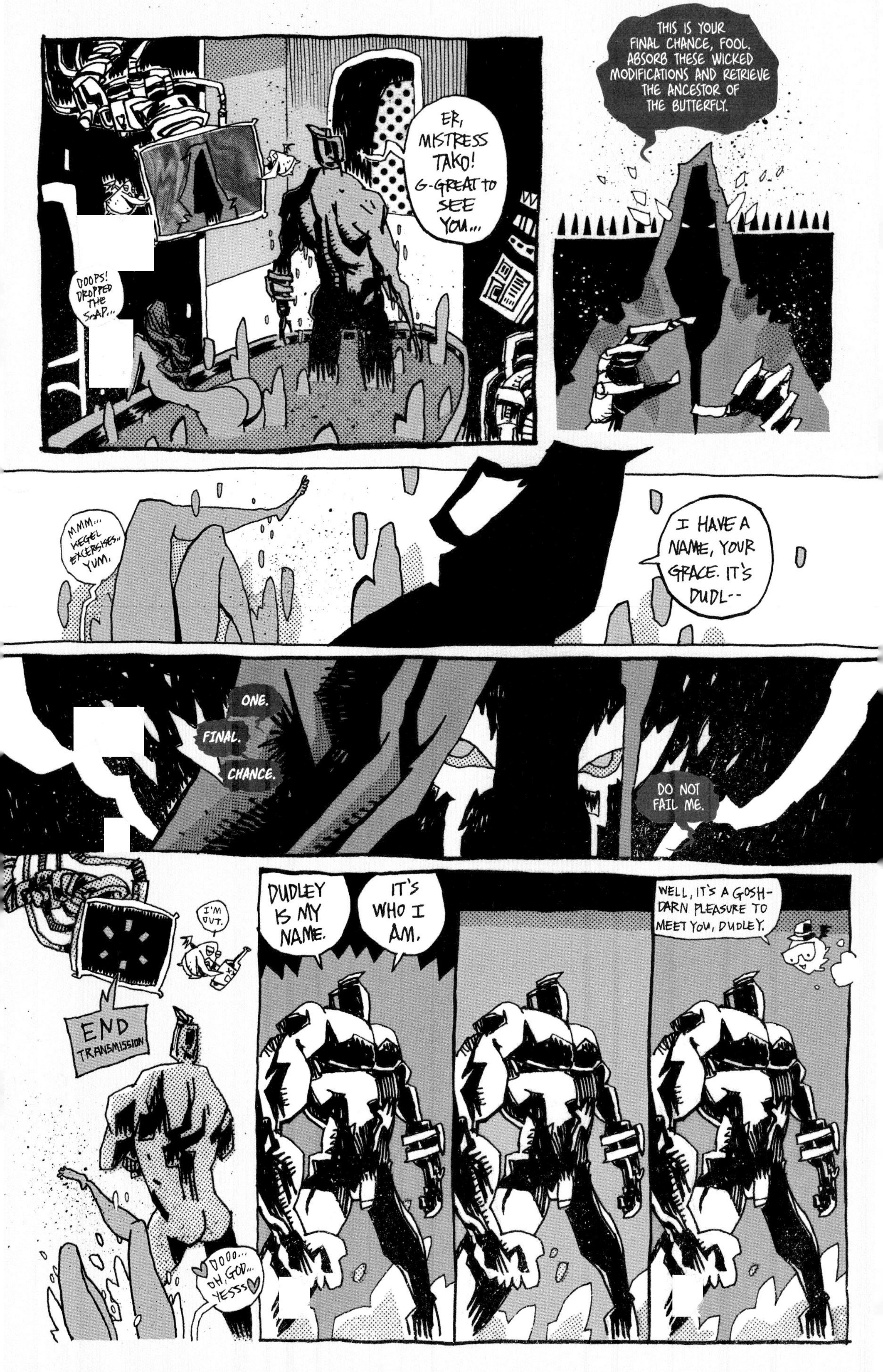
ER, MISTRESS TAKO! G-GREAT TO SEE YOU...
OOOPS! DROPPED THE SOAP...
THIS IS YOUR FINAL CHANCE, FOOL. ABSORB THESE WICKED MODIFICATIONS AND RETRIEVE THE ANCESTOR OF THE BUTTERFLY.
MMM... KEGEL EXCERSISES... YUM.
I HAVE A NAME, YOUR GRACE. IT'S DUDL--
ONE.
FINAL.
CHANCE.
DO NOT FAIL ME.
I'M OUT.
END TRANSMISSION
OOOO... OH, GOD... YESSS
DUDLEY IS MY NAME.
IT'S WHO I AM.
WELL, IT'S A GOSH-DARN PLEASURE TO MEET YOU, DUDLEY.

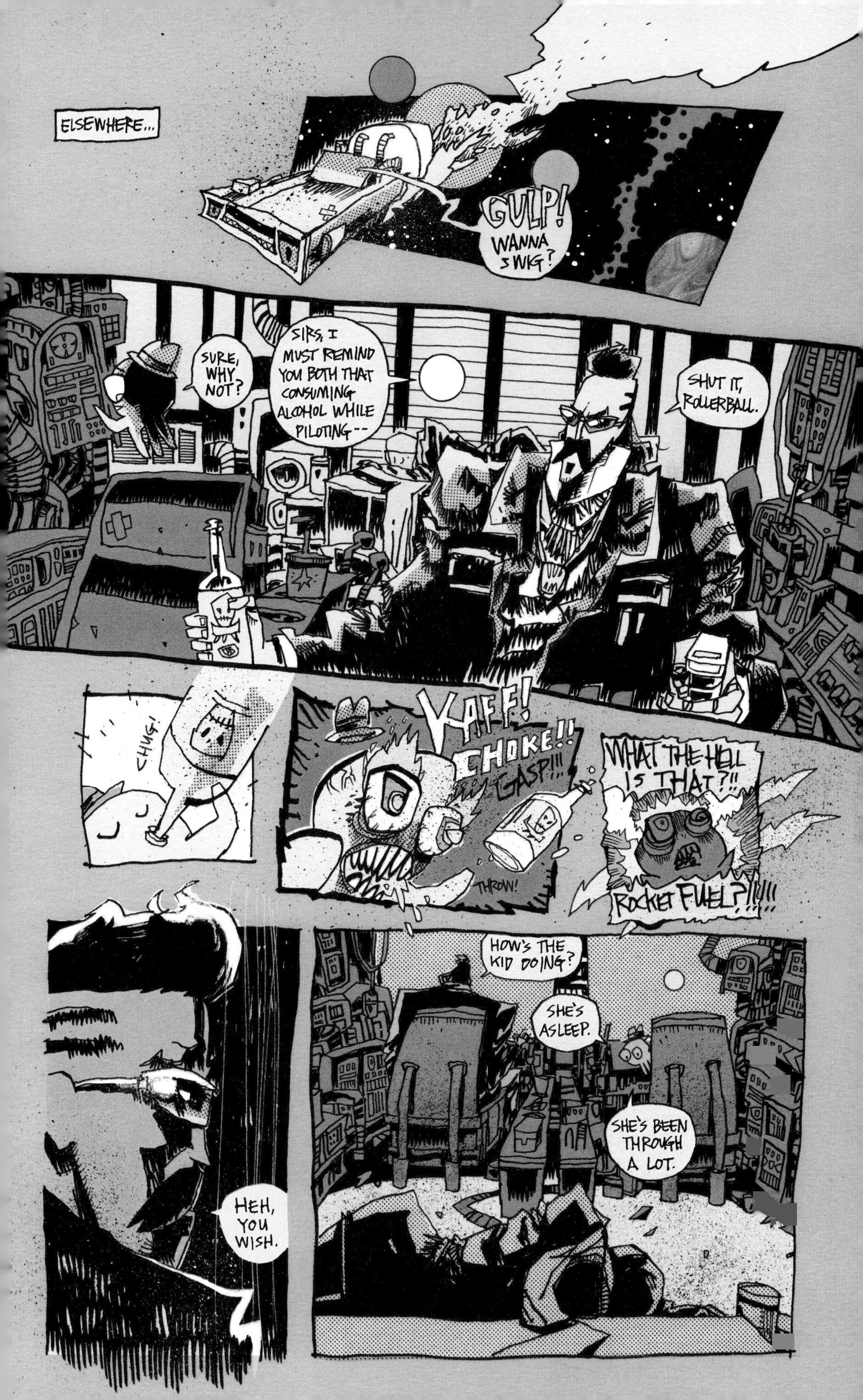
ELSEWHERE...
GULP!
WANNA SWIG?
SURE, WHY NOT?
SIRS, I MUST REMIND YOU BOTH THAT CONSUMING ALCOHOL WHILE PILOTING--
SHUT IT, ROLLERBALL.
CHUG!
KAFF!
CHOKE!!
GASP!!!
THROW!
WHAT THE HELL IS THAT?!!
ROCKET FUEL?!!!!!
HOW'S THE KID DOING?
SHE'S ASLEEP.
SHE'S BEEN THROUGH A LOT.
HEH, YOU WISH.

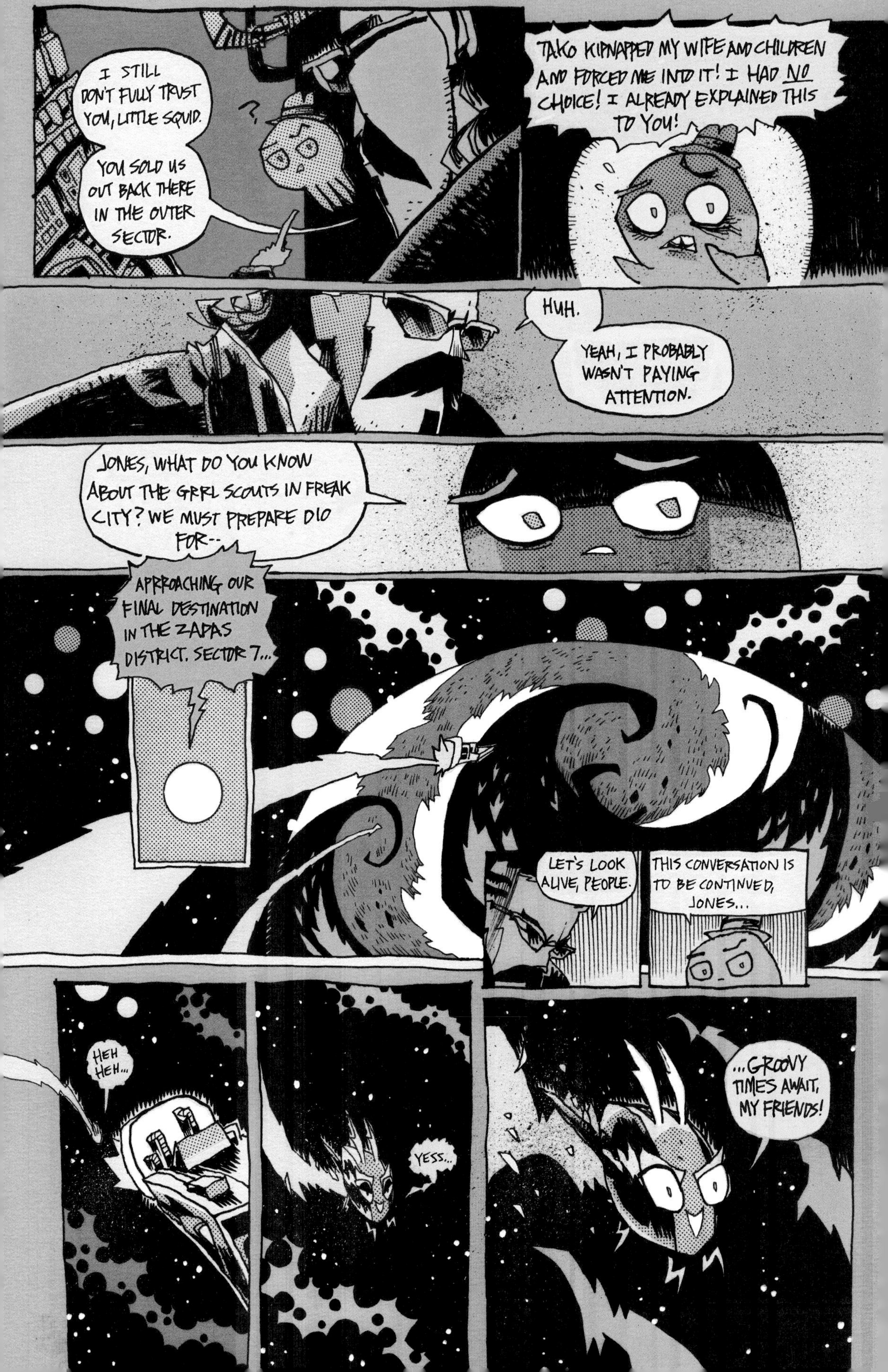
I STILL DON'T FULLY TRUST YOU, LITTLE SQUID.
YOU SOLD US OUT BACK THERE IN THE OUTER SECTOR.
TAKO KIDNAPPED MY WIFE AND CHILDREN AND FORCED ME INTO IT! I HAD NO CHOICE! I ALREADY EXPLAINED THIS TO YOU!
HUH.
YEAH, I PROBABLY WASN'T PAYING ATTENTION.
JONES, WHAT DO YOU KNOW ABOUT THE GRRL SCOUTS IN FREAK CITY? WE MUST PREPARE DIO FOR--
APPROACHING OUR FINAL DESTINATION IN THE ZAPAS DISTRICT. SECTOR 7...
LET'S LOOK ALIVE, PEOPLE.
THIS CONVERSATION IS TO BE CONTINUED, JONES...
HEH HEH...
YESS...
...GROOVY TIMES AWAIT, MY FRIENDS!

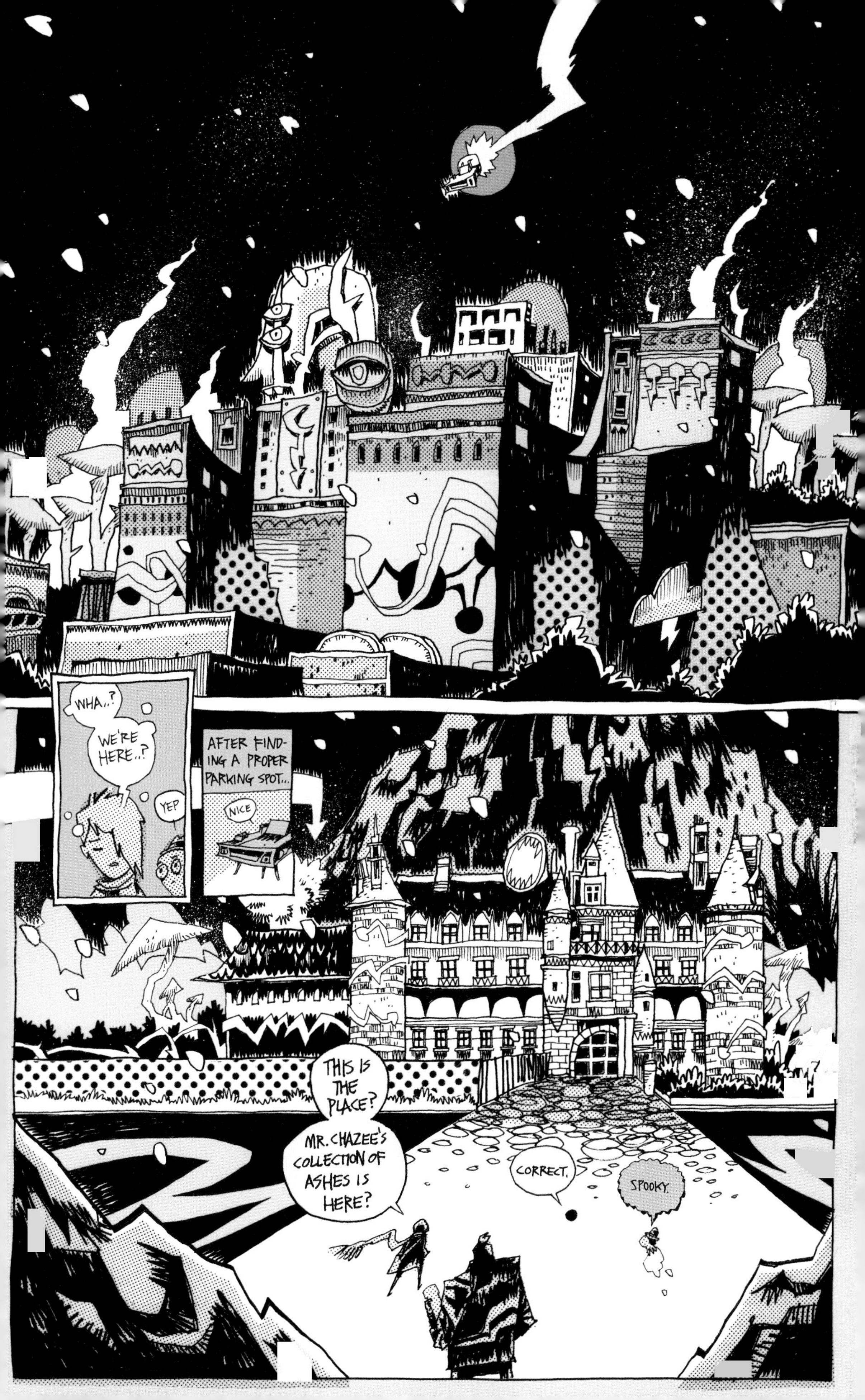
WHA..?
WE'RE HERE..?
YEP
AFTER FINDING A PROPER PARKING SPOT...
NICE
THIS IS THE PLACE?
MR. CHAZEE'S COLLECTION OF ASHES IS HERE?
CORRECT.
SPOOKY.

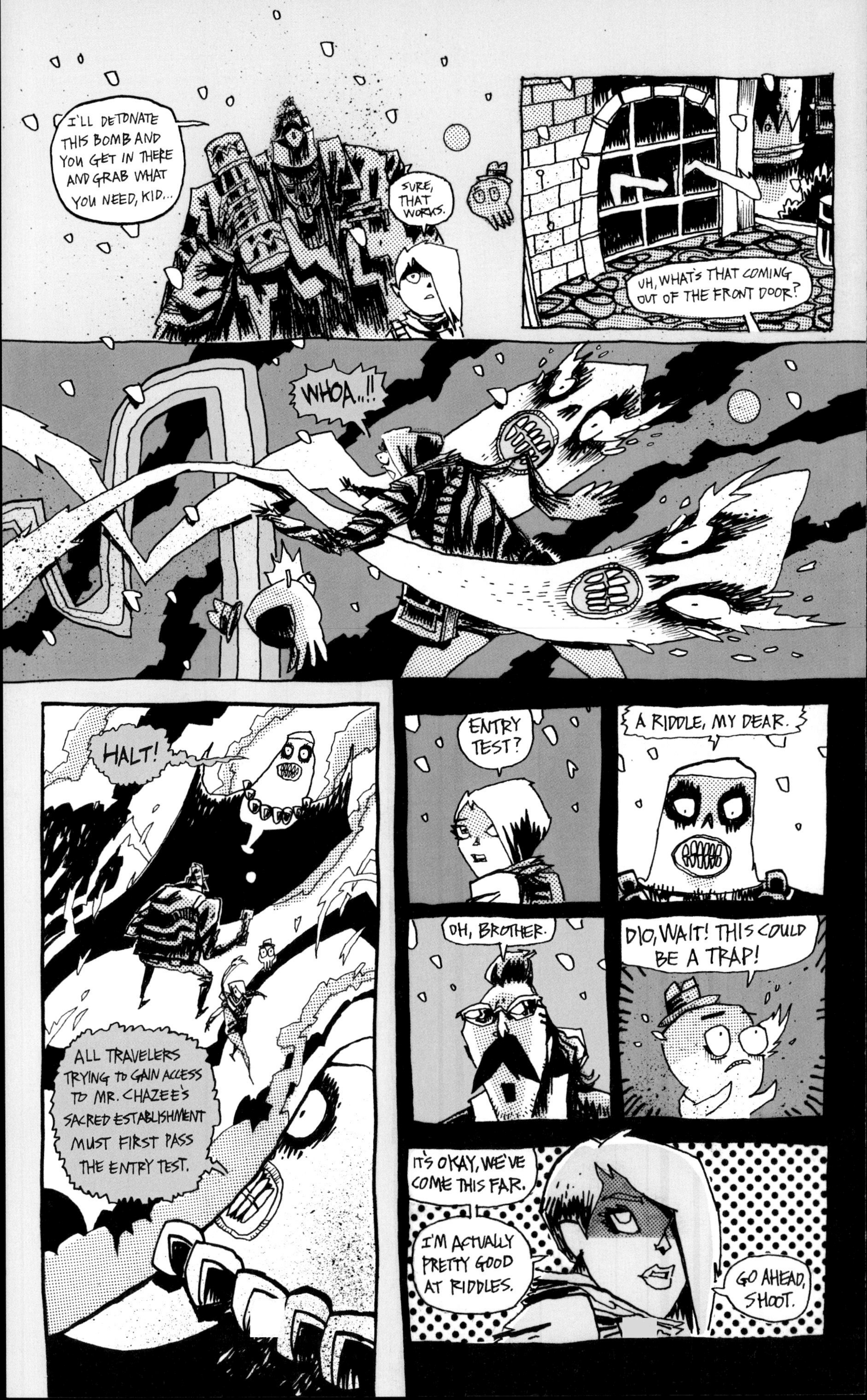
I'LL DETONATE THIS BOMB AND YOU GET IN THERE AND GRAB WHAT YOU NEED, KID...
SURE, THAT WORKS.
UH, WHAT'S THAT COMING OUT OF THE FRONT DOOR?
WHOA...!!
HALT!
ALL TRAVELERS TRYING TO GAIN ACCESS TO MR. CHAZEE'S SACRED ESTABLISHMENT MUST FIRST PASS THE ENTRY TEST.
ENTRY TEST?
A RIDDLE, MY DEAR.
OH, BROTHER.
DIO, WAIT! THIS COULD BE A TRAP!
IT'S OKAY, WE'VE COME THIS FAR.
I'M ACTUALLY PRETTY GOOD AT RIDDLES.
GO AHEAD, SHOOT.

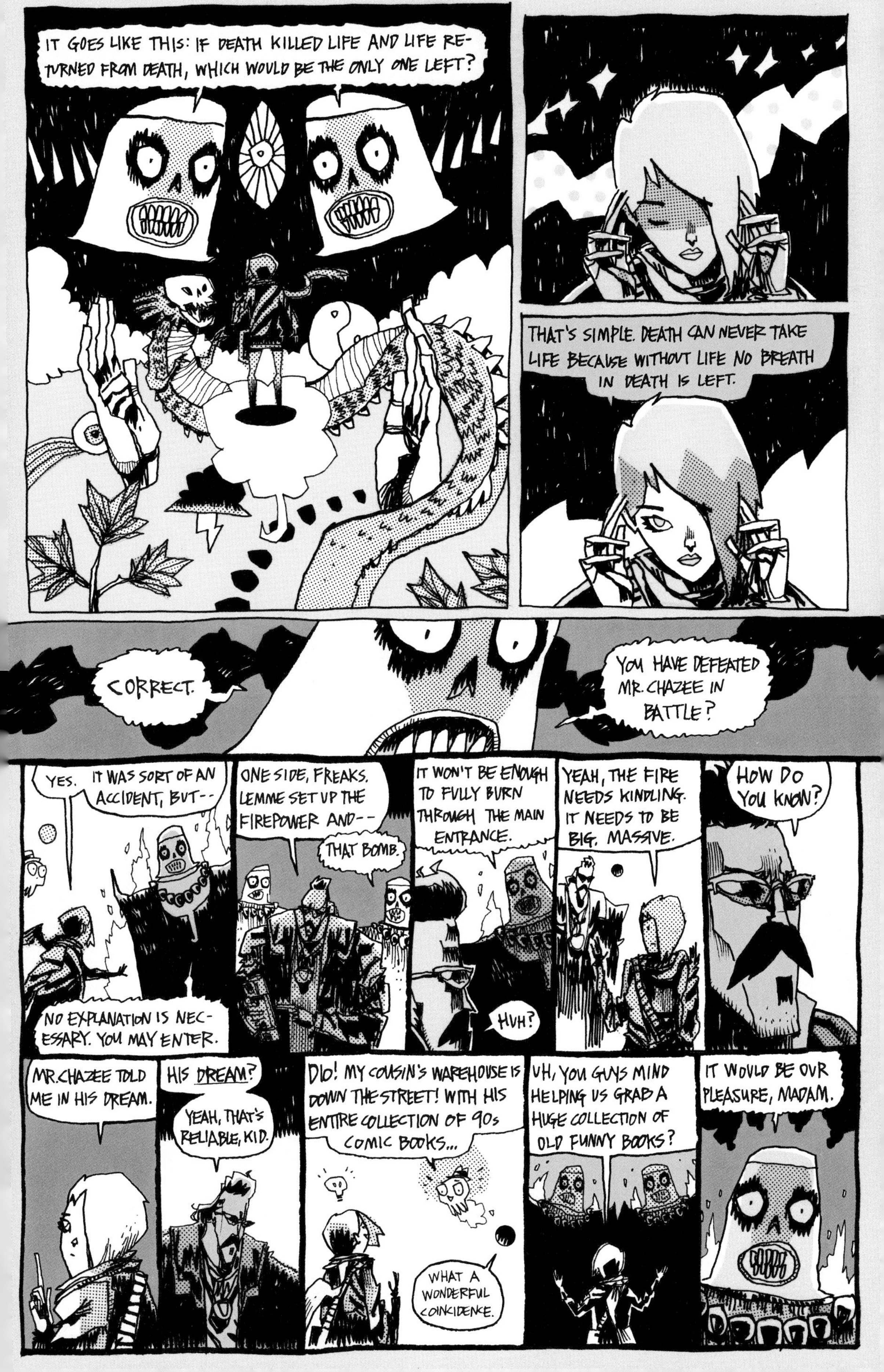
IT GOES LIKE THIS: IF DEATH KILLED LIFE AND LIFE RE-TURNED FROM DEATH, WHICH WOULD BE THE ONLY ONE LEFT?
THAT'S SIMPLE. DEATH CAN NEVER TAKE LIFE BECAUSE WITHOUT LIFE NO BREATH IN DEATH IS LEFT.
CORRECT.
YOU HAVE DEFEATED MR. CHAZEE IN BATTLE?
YES.
IT WAS SORT OF AN ACCIDENT, BUT--
NO EXPLANATION IS NEC-ESSARY. YOU MAY ENTER.
ONE SIDE, FREAKS. LEMME SET UP THE FIREPOWER AND--
THAT BOMB.
IT WON'T BE ENOUGH TO FULLY BURN THROUGH THE MAIN ENTRANCE.
HUH?
YEAH, THE FIRE NEEDS KINDLING. IT NEEDS TO BE BIG. MASSIVE.
HOW DO YOU KNOW?
MR. CHAZEE TOLD ME IN HIS DREAM.
HIS DREAM?
YEAH, THAT'S RELIABLE, KID.
DIO! MY COUSIN'S WAREHOUSE IS DOWN THE STREET! WITH HIS ENTIRE COLLECTION OF 90s COMIC BOOKS...
WHAT A WONDERFUL COINCIDENCE.
UH, YOU GUYS MIND HELPING US GRAB A HUGE COLLECTION OF OLD FUNNY BOOKS?
IT WOULD BE OUR PLEASURE, MADAM.

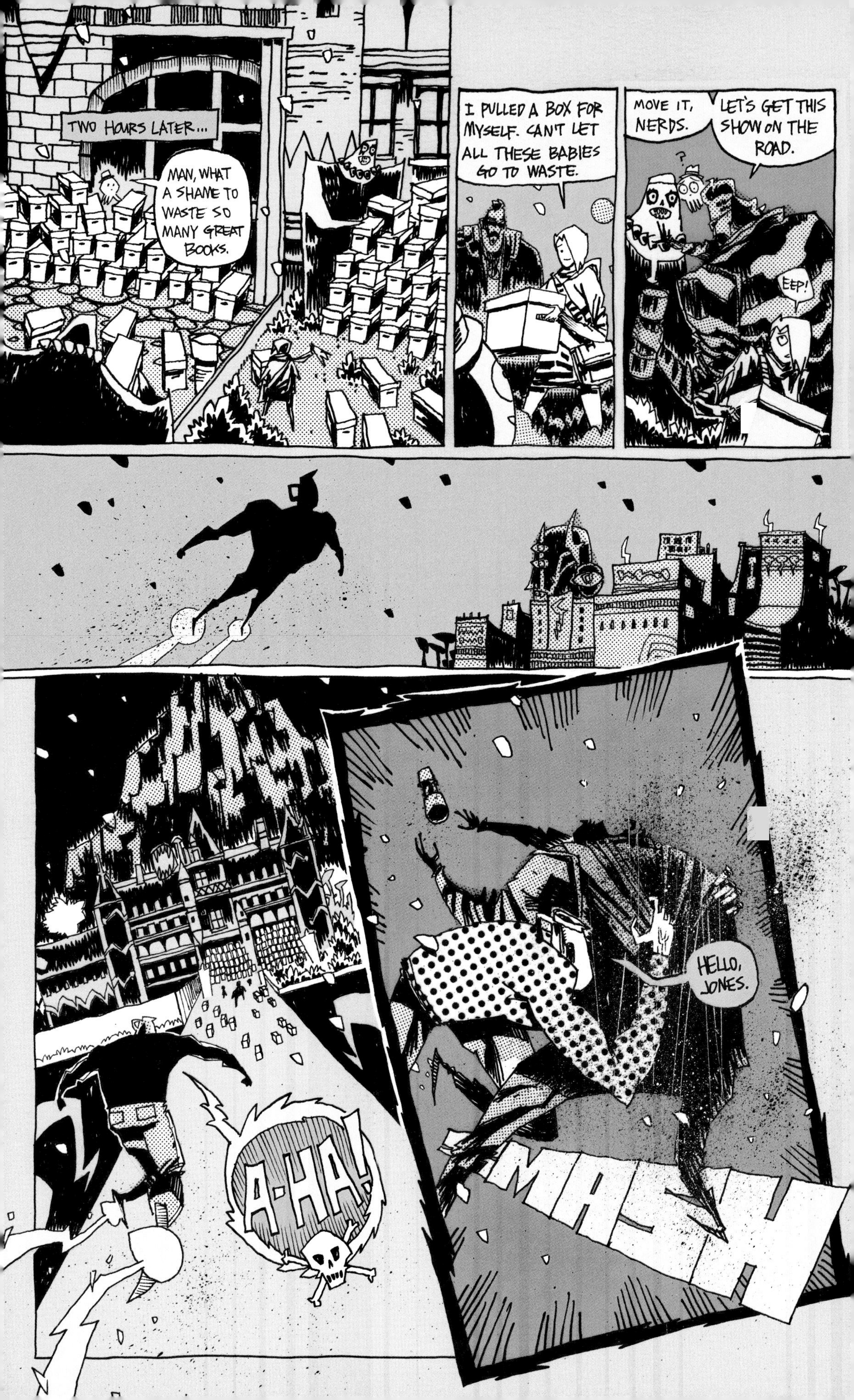
TWO HOURS LATER...
MAN, WHAT A SHAME TO WASTE SO MANY GREAT BOOKS.
I PULLED A BOX FOR MYSELF. CAN'T LET ALL THESE BABIES GO TO WASTE.
MOVE IT, NERDS.
?
LET'S GET THIS SHOW ON THE ROAD.
EEP!
A-HA!
HELLO, JONES.
MASH

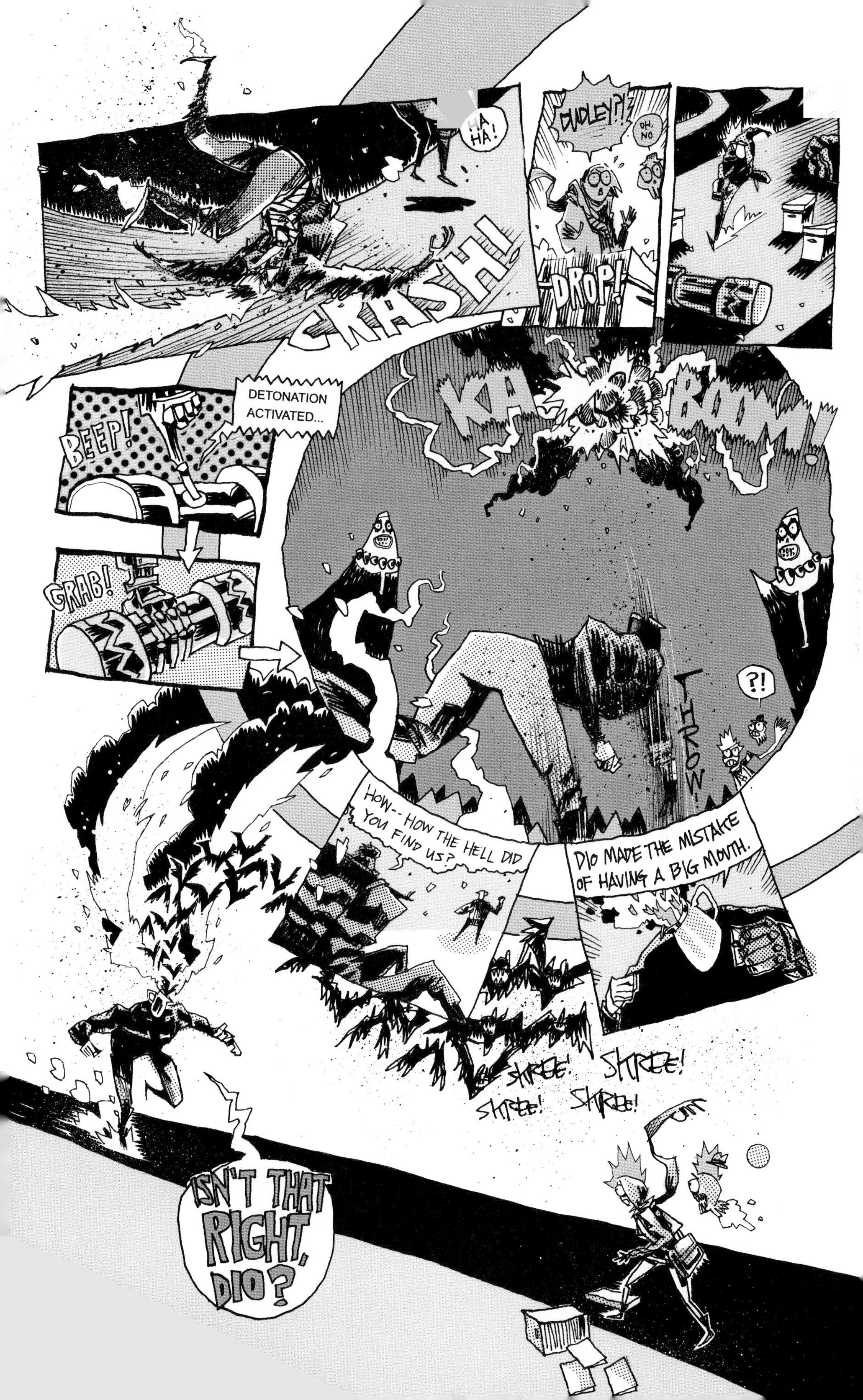
HA HA!
CRASH!
DUDLEY?!
OH, NO
DROP!
BEEP!
DETONATION ACTIVATED...
GRAB!
KA-BOOM!
THROW!
?!
HOW-- HOW THE HELL DID YOU FIND US?
DIO MADE THE MISTAKE OF HAVING A BIG MOUTH.
SKREE! SKREE!
SKREE! SKREE!
ISN'T THAT RIGHT, DIO?

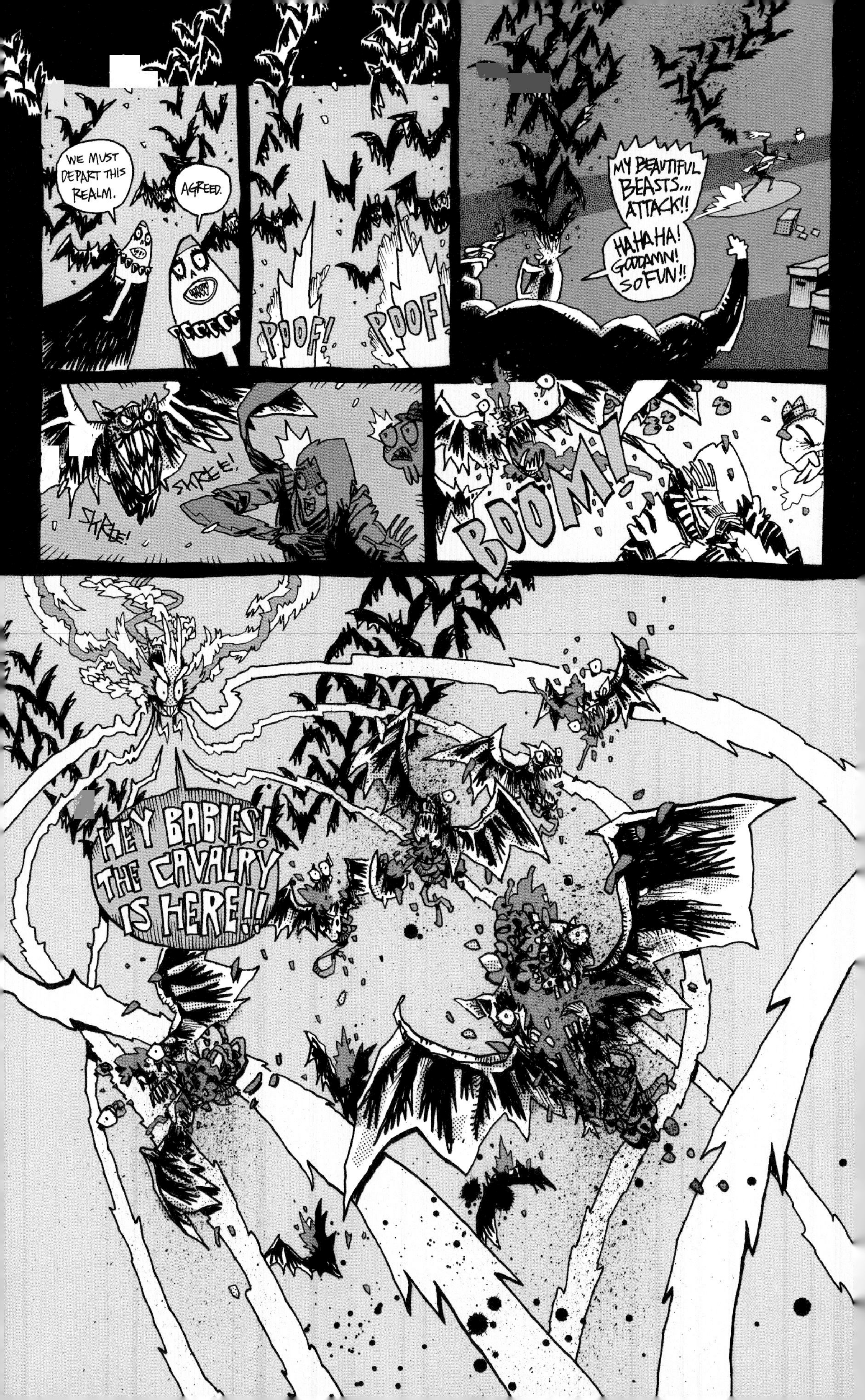
WE MUST DEPART THIS REALM.
AGREED.
POOF!
POOF!
MY BEAUTIFUL BEASTS... ATTACK!!
HAHAHA! GODDAMN! SO FUN!!
SKREEE!
SKREE!
BOOM!
HEY BABIES! THE CAVALRY IS HERE!!

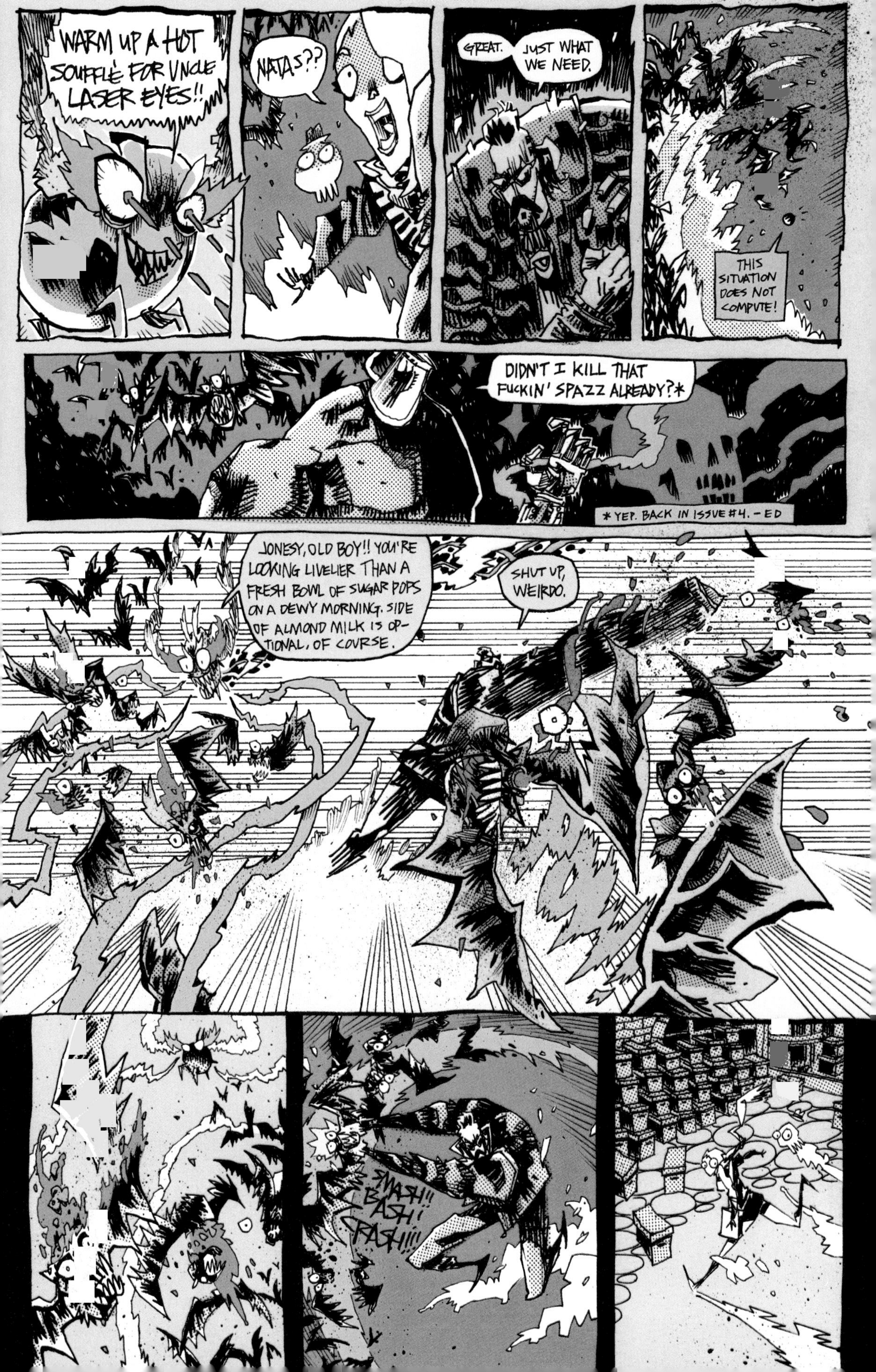
WARM UP A HOT SOUFFLÉ FOR UNCLE LASER EYES!!
NATAS??
GREAT.
JUST WHAT WE NEED.
THIS SITUATION DOES NOT COMPUTE!
DIDN'T I KILL THAT FUCKIN' SPAZZ ALREADY?*
* YEP. BACK IN ISSUE #4. - ED
JONESY, OLD BOY!! YOU'RE LOOKING LIVELIER THAN A FRESH BOWL OF SUGAR POPS ON A DEWY MORNING. SIDE OF ALMOND MILK IS OPTIONAL, OF COURSE.
SHUT UP, WEIRDO.
SMASH!! BASH! CRASH!!!

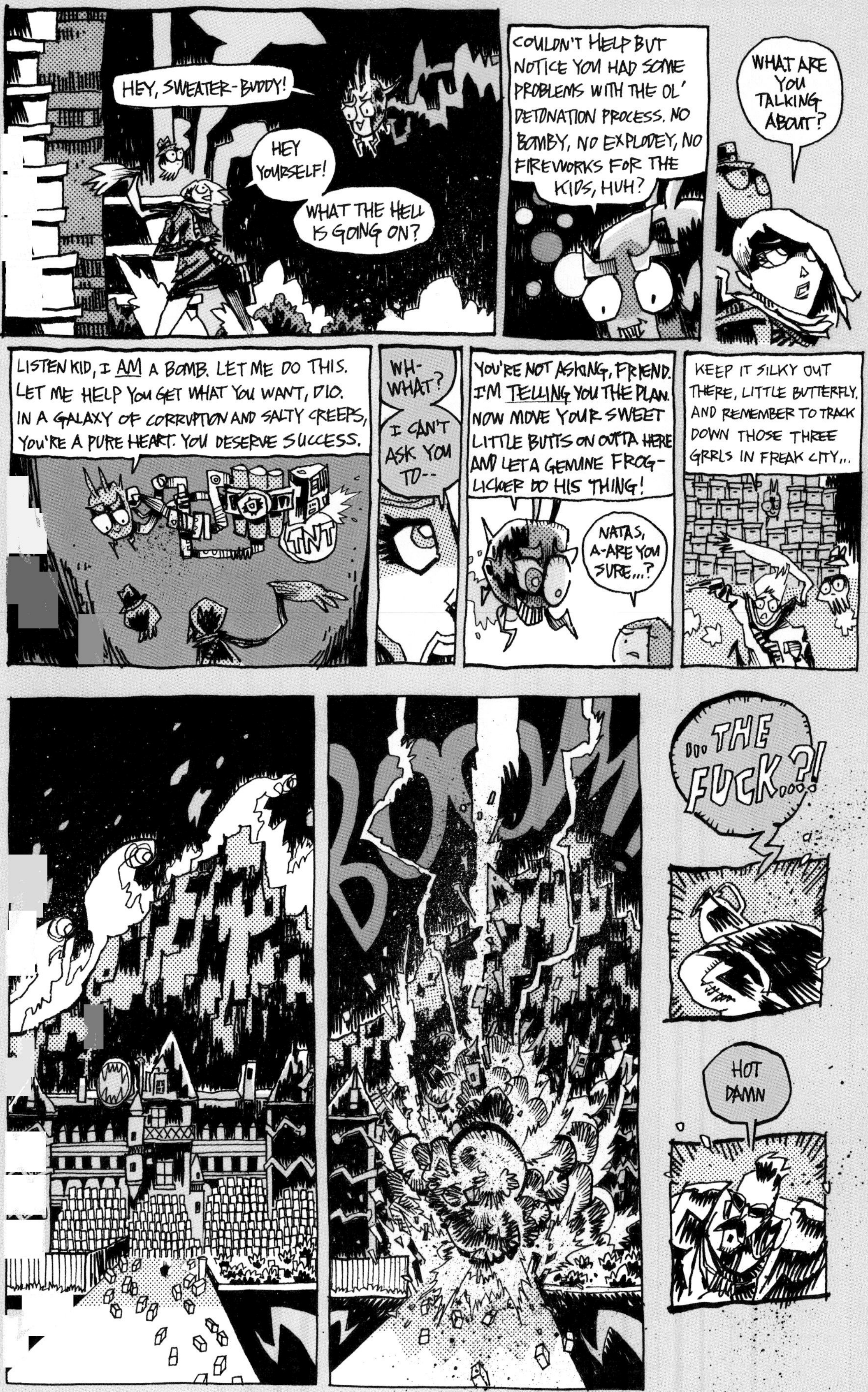
HEY, SWEATER-BUDDY!
HEY YOURSELF!
WHAT THE HELL IS GOING ON?
COULDN'T HELP BUT NOTICE YOU HAD SOME PROBLEMS WITH THE OL' DETONATION PROCESS. NO BOMBY, NO EXPLODEY, NO FIREWORKS FOR THE KIDS, HUH?
WHAT ARE YOU TALKING ABOUT?
LISTEN KID, I AM A BOMB. LET ME DO THIS. LET ME HELP YOU GET WHAT YOU WANT, DIO. IN A GALAXY OF CORRUPTION AND SALTY CREEPS, YOU'RE A PURE HEART. YOU DESERVE SUCCESS.
TNT
WH-WHAT?
I CAN'T ASK YOU TO--
YOU'RE NOT ASKING, FRIEND. I'M TELLING YOU THE PLAN. NOW MOVE YOUR SWEET LITTLE BUTTS ON OUTTA HERE AND LET A GENUINE FROG-LICKER DO HIS THING!
NATAS, A-ARE YOU SURE...?
KEEP IT SILKY OUT THERE, LITTLE BUTTERFLY, AND REMEMBER TO TRACK DOWN THOSE THREE GRRLS IN FREAK CITY...
BOOM!
...THE FUCK...?!
HOT DAMN

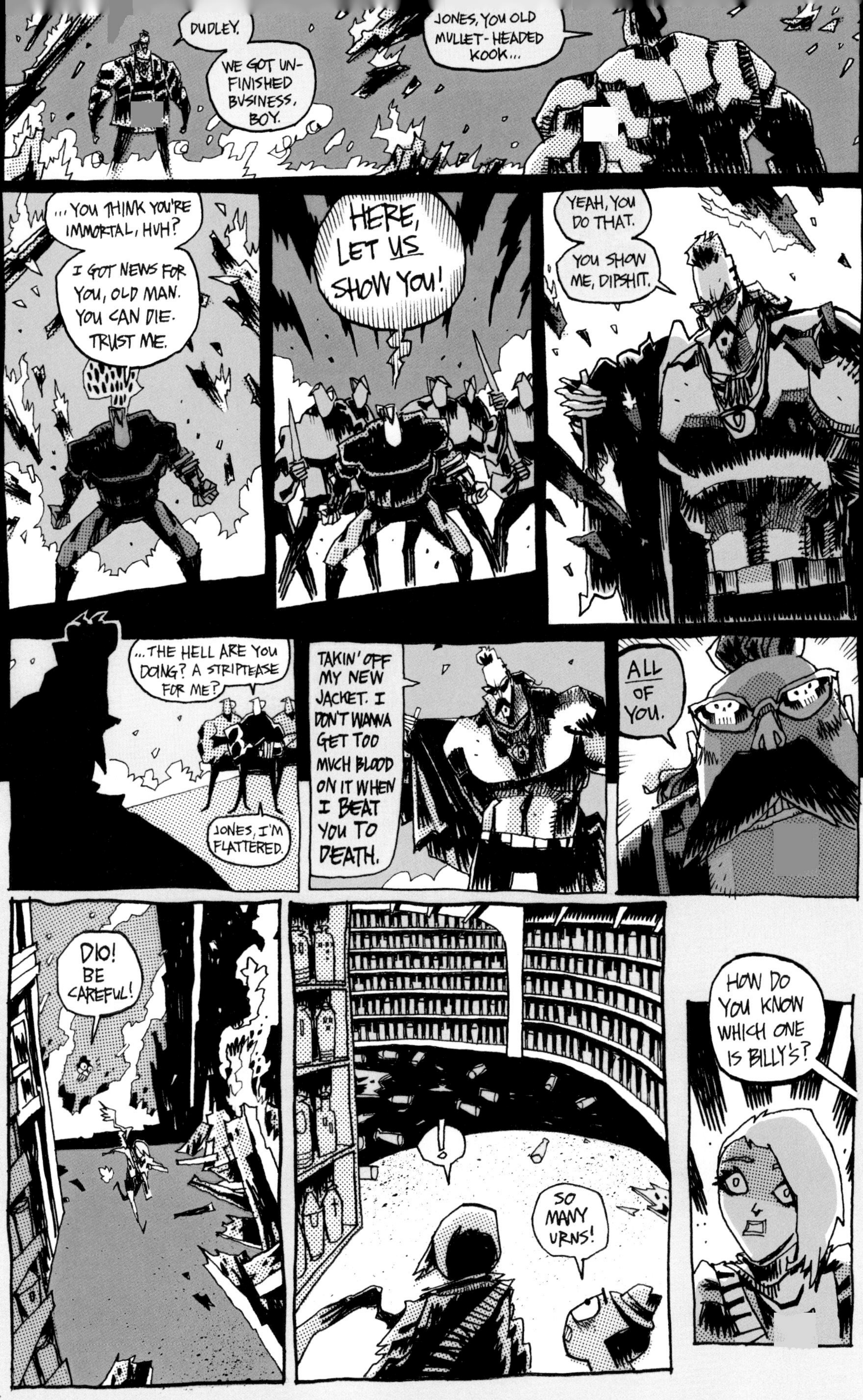
DUDLEY.
WE GOT UNFINISHED BUSINESS, BOY.
JONES, YOU OLD MULLET-HEADED KOOK...
...YOU THINK YOU'RE IMMORTAL, HUH?
I GOT NEWS FOR YOU, OLD MAN. YOU CAN DIE. TRUST ME.
HERE, LET US SHOW YOU!
YEAH, YOU DO THAT.
YOU SHOW ME, DIPSHIT.
...THE HELL ARE YOU DOING? A STRIPTEASE FOR ME?
JONES, I'M FLATTERED.
TAKIN' OFF MY NEW JACKET. I DON'T WANNA GET TOO MUCH BLOOD ON IT WHEN I BEAT YOU TO DEATH.
ALL OF YOU.
DIO! BE CAREFUL!
!
SO MANY URNS!
HOW DO YOU KNOW WHICH ONE IS BILLY'S?

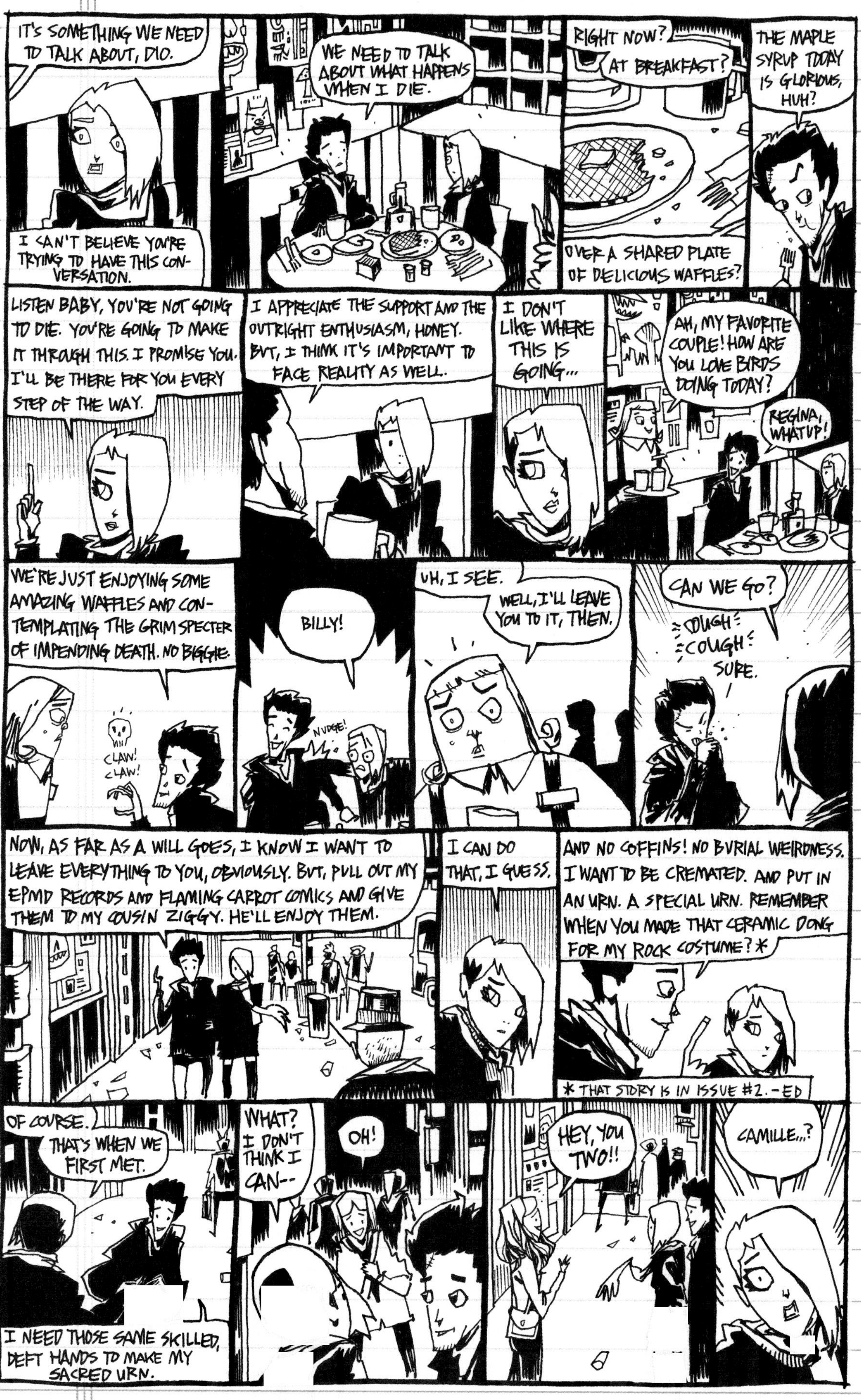
IT'S SOMETHING WE NEED TO TALK ABOUT, DIO.
I CAN'T BELIEVE YOU'RE TRYING TO HAVE THIS CONVERSATION.
WE NEED TO TALK ABOUT WHAT HAPPENS WHEN I DIE.
RIGHT NOW?
AT BREAKFAST?
OVER A SHARED PLATE OF DELICIOUS WAFFLES?
THE MAPLE SYRUP TODAY IS GLORIOUS, HUH?
LISTEN BABY, YOU'RE NOT GOING TO DIE. YOU'RE GOING TO MAKE IT THROUGH THIS. I PROMISE YOU. I'LL BE THERE FOR YOU EVERY STEP OF THE WAY.
I APPRECIATE THE SUPPORT AND THE OUTRIGHT ENTHUSIASM, HONEY. BUT, I THINK IT'S IMPORTANT TO FACE REALITY AS WELL.
I DON'T LIKE WHERE THIS IS GOING...
AH, MY FAVORITE COUPLE! HOW ARE YOU LOVE BIRDS DOING TODAY?
REGINA, WHATUP!
WE'RE JUST ENJOYING SOME AMAZING WAFFLES AND CONTEMPLATING THE GRIM SPECTER OF IMPENDING DEATH. NO BIGGIE.
CLAW! CLAW!
BILLY!
NUDGE!
UH, I SEE.
WELL, I'LL LEAVE YOU TO IT, THEN.
CAN WE GO?
COUGH COUGH
SURE.
NOW, AS FAR AS A WILL GOES, I KNOW I WANT TO LEAVE EVERYTHING TO YOU, OBVIOUSLY. BUT, PULL OUT MY EPMD RECORDS AND FLAMING CARROT COMICS AND GIVE THEM TO MY COUSIN ZIGGY. HE'LL ENJOY THEM.
I CAN DO THAT, I GUESS.
AND NO COFFINS! NO BURIAL WEIRDNESS. I WANT TO BE CREMATED. AND PUT IN AN URN. A SPECIAL URN. REMEMBER WHEN YOU MADE THAT CERAMIC DONG FOR MY ROCK COSTUME?*
* THAT STORY IS IN ISSUE #2. –ED
OF COURSE.
THAT'S WHEN WE FIRST MET.
I NEED THOSE SAME SKILLED, DEFT HANDS TO MAKE MY SACRED URN.
WHAT? I DON'T THINK I CAN--
OH!
HEY, YOU TWO!!
CAMILLE...?

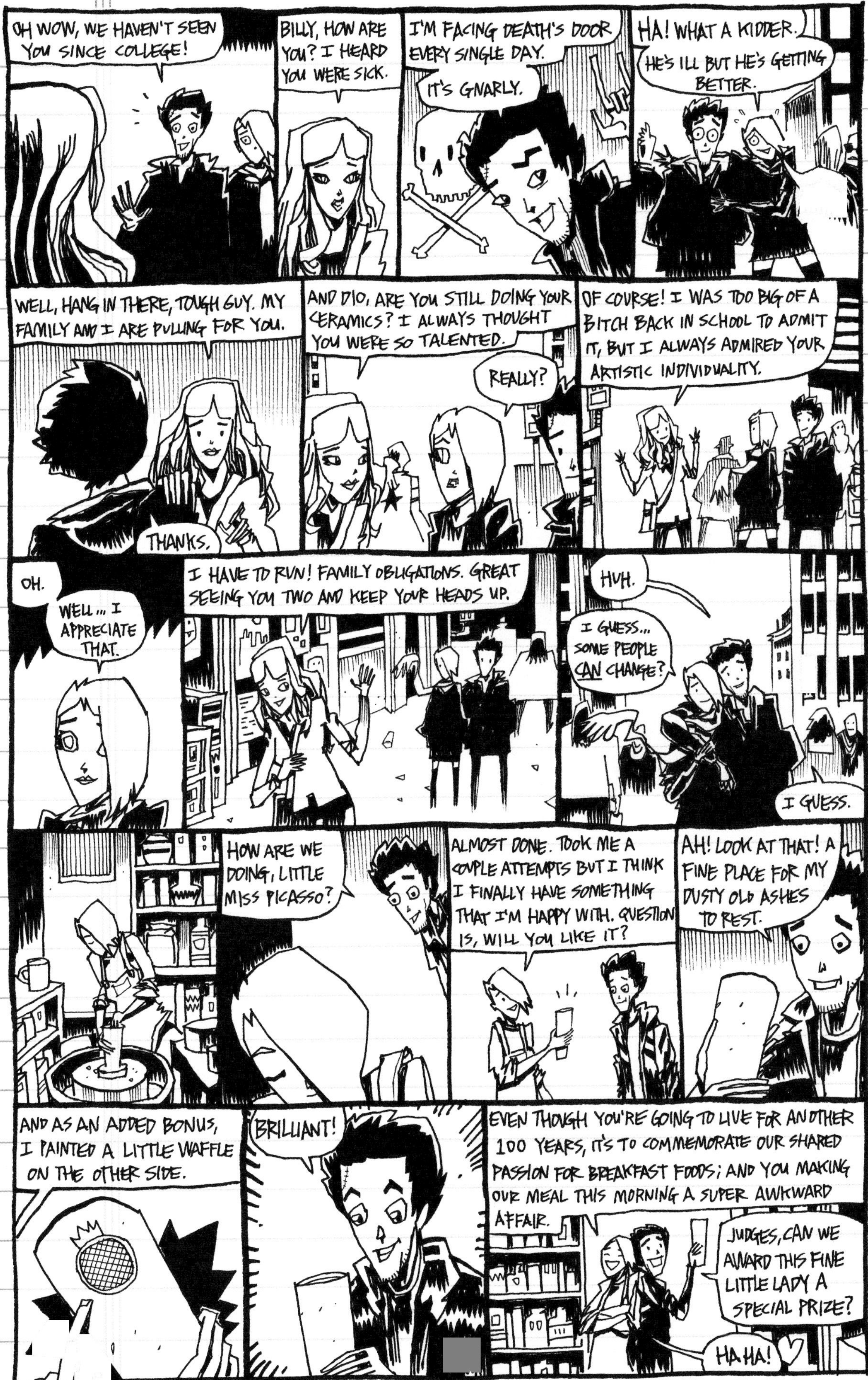

OH WOW, WE HAVEN'T SEEN YOU SINCE COLLEGE!
BILLY, HOW ARE YOU? I HEARD YOU WERE SICK.
I'M FACING DEATH'S DOOR EVERY SINGLE DAY.
IT'S GNARLY.
HA! WHAT A KIDDER.
HE'S ILL BUT HE'S GETTING BETTER.
WELL, HANG IN THERE, TOUGH GUY. MY FAMILY AND I ARE PULLING FOR YOU.
THANKS.
AND DIO, ARE YOU STILL DOING YOUR CERAMICS? I ALWAYS THOUGHT YOU WERE SO TALENTED.
REALLY?
OF COURSE! I WAS TOO BIG OF A BITCH BACK IN SCHOOL TO ADMIT IT, BUT I ALWAYS ADMIRED YOUR ARTISTIC INDIVIDUALITY.
OH.
WELL... I APPRECIATE THAT.
I HAVE TO RUN! FAMILY OBLIGATIONS. GREAT SEEING YOU TWO AND KEEP YOUR HEADS UP.
HUH.
I GUESS... SOME PEOPLE CAN CHANGE?
I GUESS.
HOW ARE WE DOING, LITTLE MISS PICASSO?
ALMOST DONE. TOOK ME A COUPLE ATTEMPTS BUT I THINK I FINALLY HAVE SOMETHING THAT I'M HAPPY WITH. QUESTION IS, WILL YOU LIKE IT?
AH! LOOK AT THAT! A FINE PLACE FOR MY DUSTY OLD ASHES TO REST.
AND AS AN ADDED BONUS, I PAINTED A LITTLE WAFFLE ON THE OTHER SIDE.
BRILLIANT!
EVEN THOUGH YOU'RE GOING TO LIVE FOR ANOTHER 100 YEARS, IT'S TO COMMEMORATE OUR SHARED PASSION FOR BREAKFAST FOODS; AND YOU MAKING OUR MEAL THIS MORNING A SUPER AWKWARD AFFAIR.
JUDGES, CAN WE AWARD THIS FINE LITTLE LADY A SPECIAL PRIZE?
HA HA!

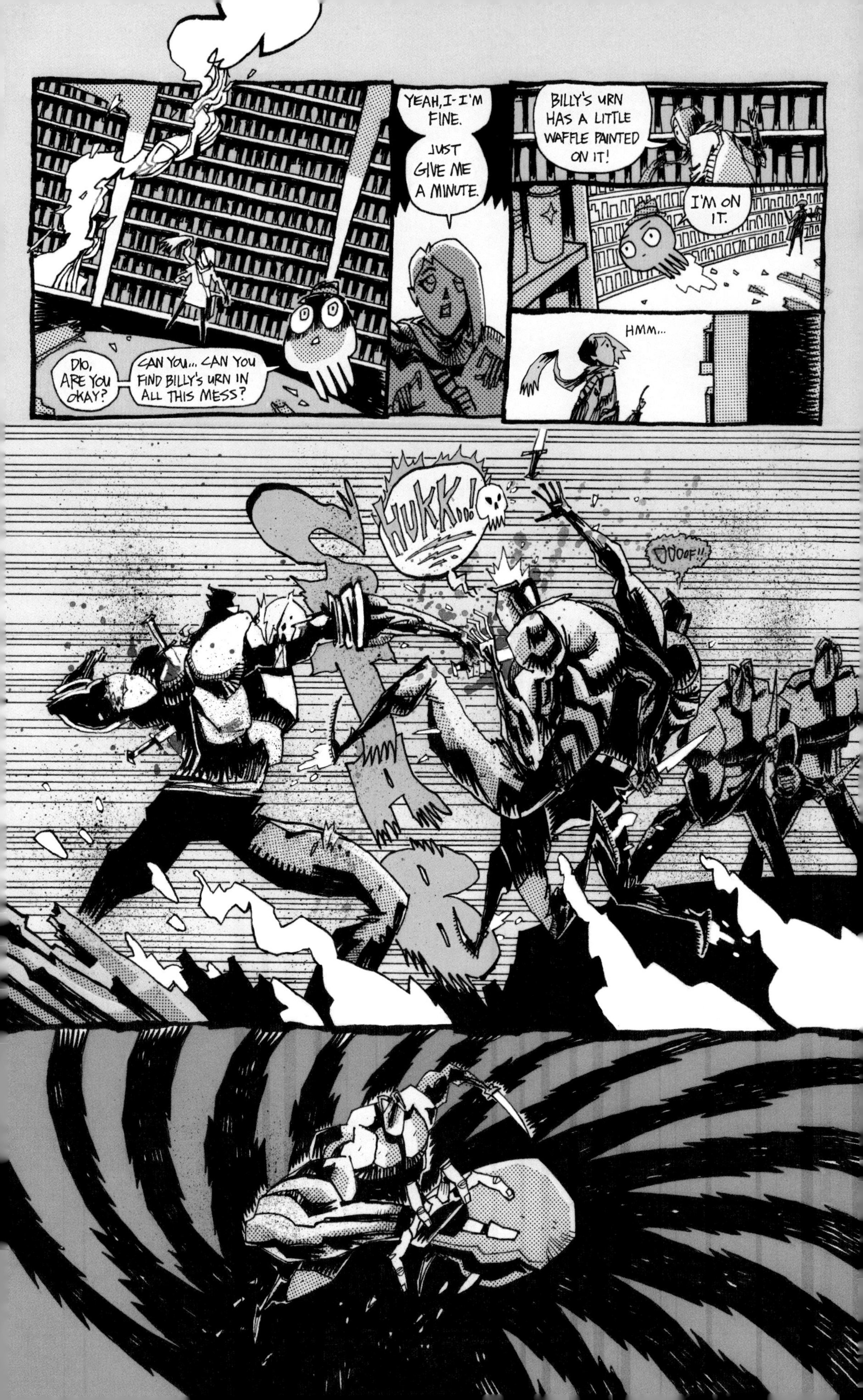
DIO, ARE YOU OKAY?
CAN YOU... CAN YOU FIND BILLY'S URN IN ALL THIS MESS?
YEAH, I-I'M FINE.
JUST GIVE ME A MINUTE.
BILLY'S URN HAS A LITTLE WAFFLE PAINTED ON IT!
I'M ON IT.
HMM...
HUKK..!
OOOF!!

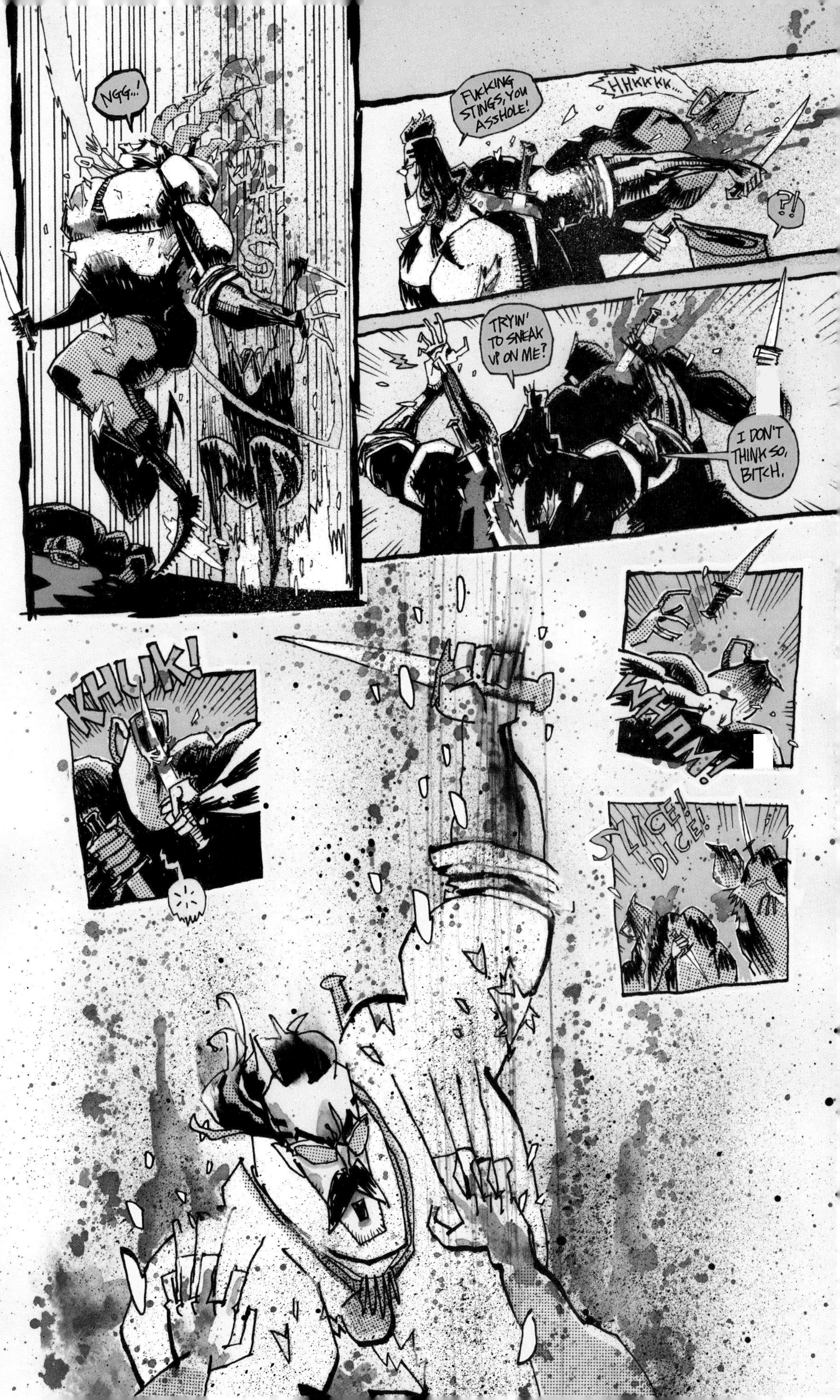
NGG...!
FUCKING STINGS, YOU ASSHOLE!
HHKKKKK...
?!
TRYIN' TO SNEAK UP ON ME?
I DON'T THINK SO, BITCH.
KHUK!
WHAM!
SLICE! DICE!

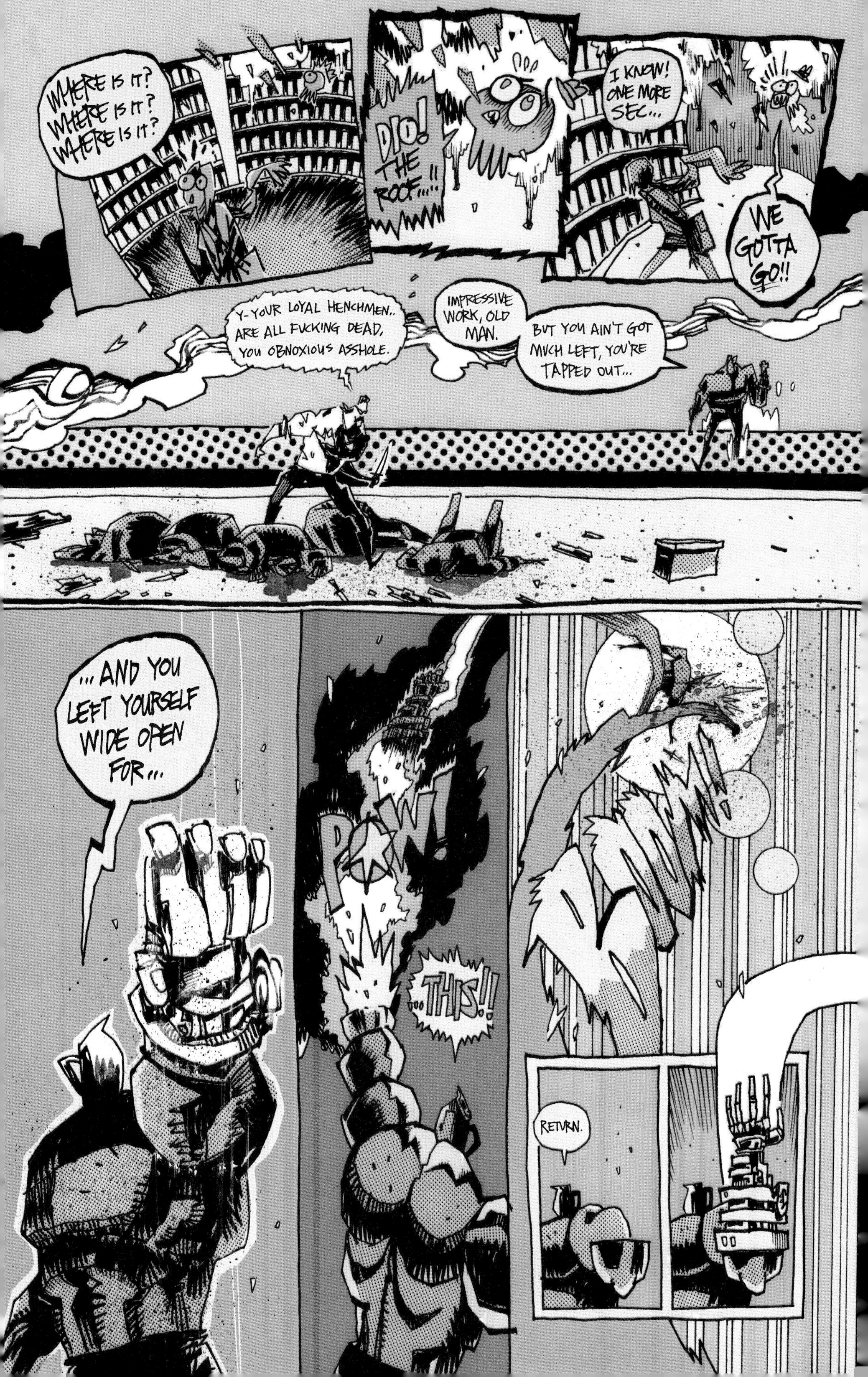
WHERE IS IT? WHERE IS IT? WHERE IS IT?
DIO! THE ROOF...!!
I KNOW! ONE MORE SEC...
WE GOTTA GO!!
Y-YOUR LOYAL HENCHMEN.. ARE ALL FUCKING DEAD, YOU OBNOXIOUS ASSHOLE.
IMPRESSIVE WORK, OLD MAN.
BUT YOU AIN'T GOT MUCH LEFT, YOU'RE TAPPED OUT...
...AND YOU LEFT YOURSELF WIDE OPEN FOR...
POW!
...THIS!!
RETURN.

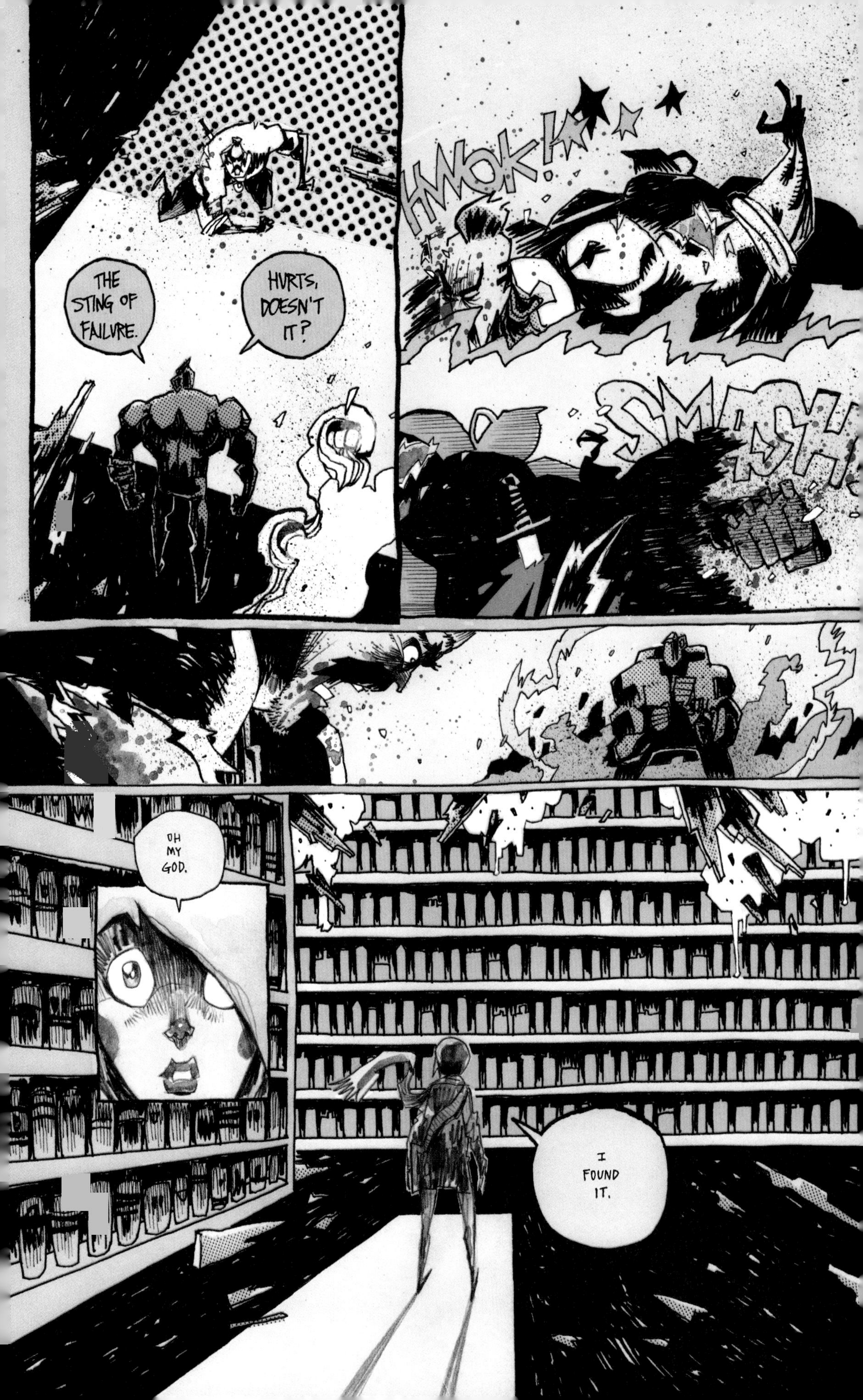
THE STING OF FAILURE.
HURTS, DOESN'T IT?
THWOK!
SMASH
OH MY GOD.
I FOUND IT.

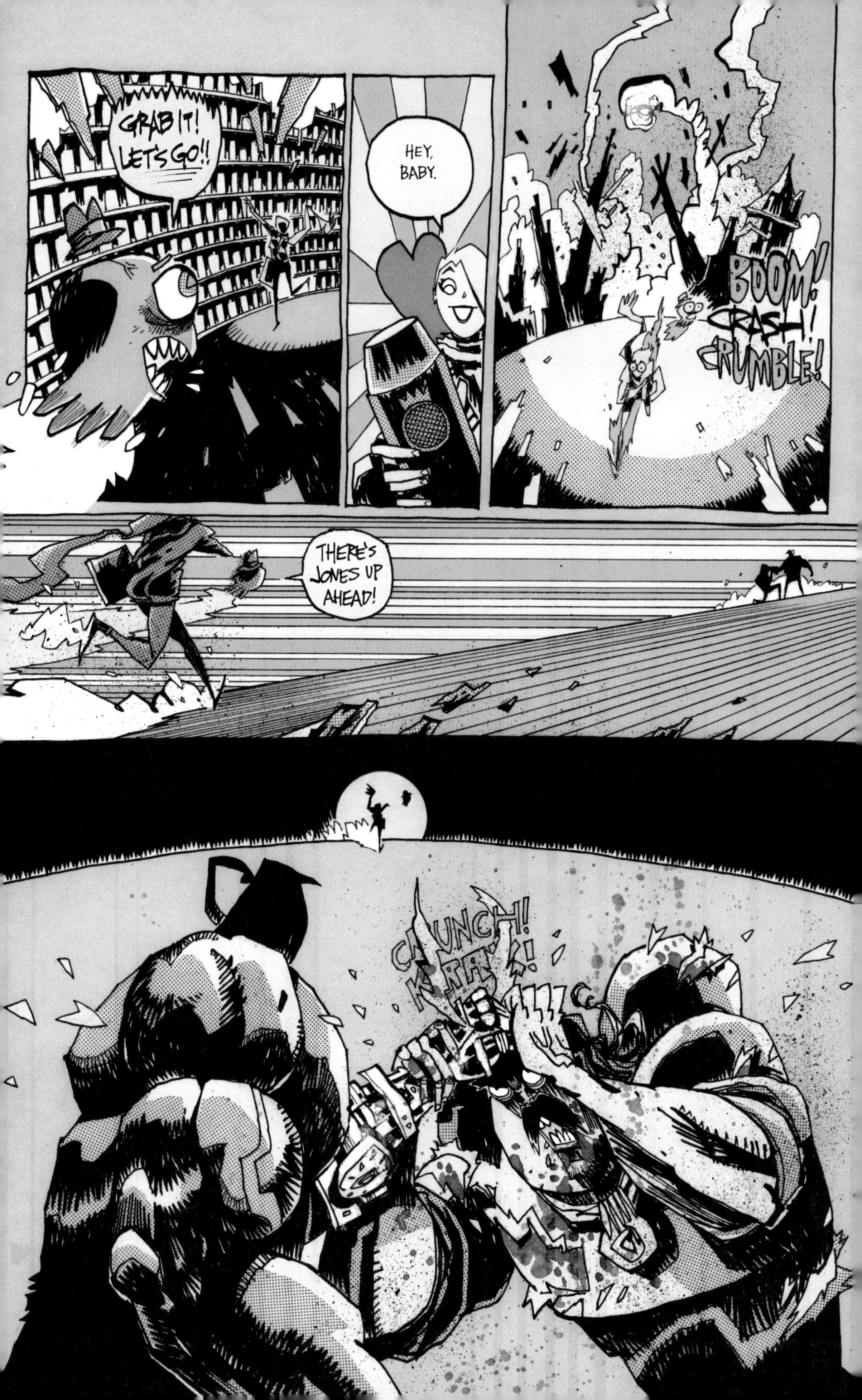
GRAB IT! LET'S GO!!
HEY, BABY.
BOOM! CRASH! CRUMBLE!
THERE'S JONES UP AHEAD!
CRUNCH! KRAK!

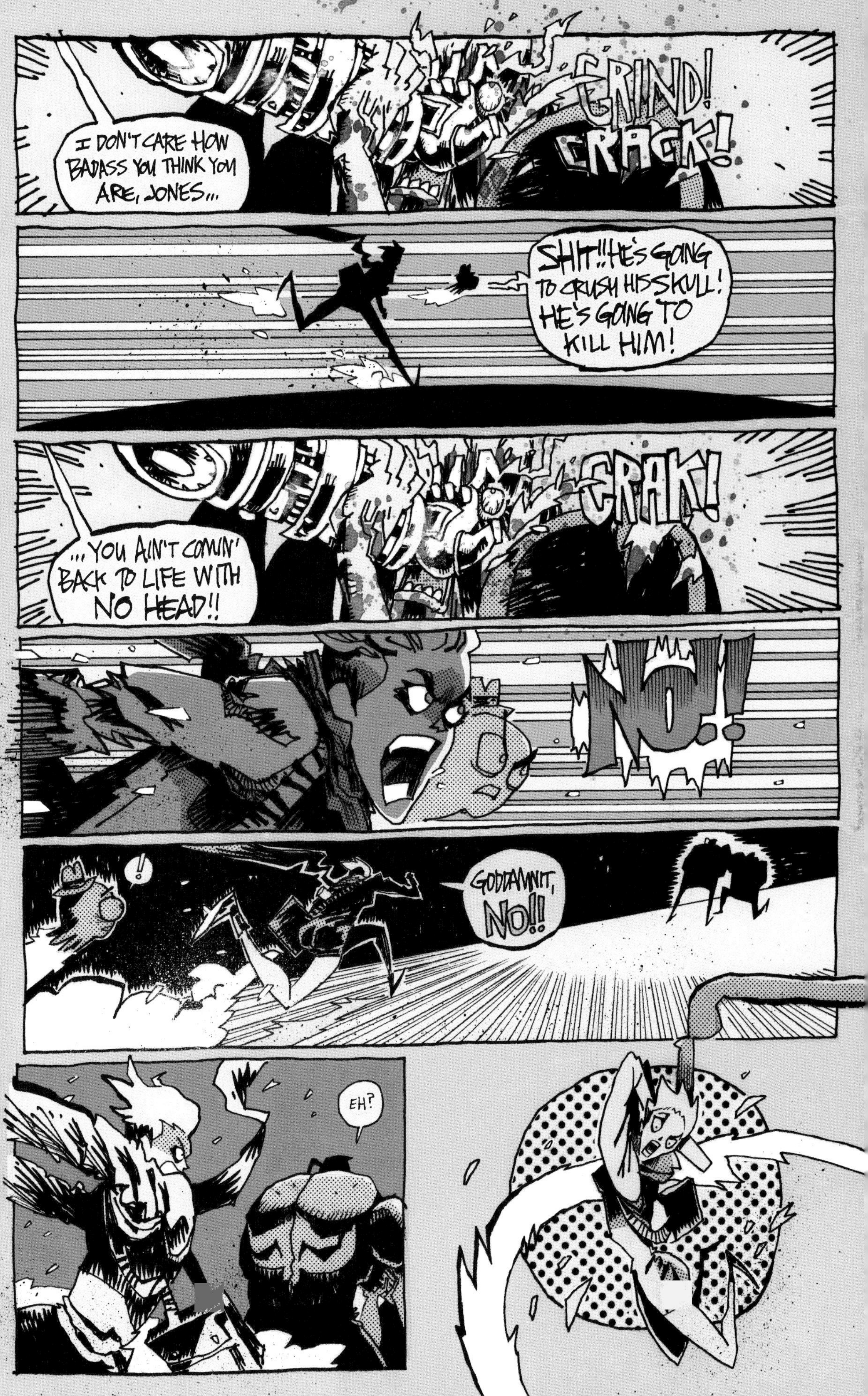
I DON'T CARE HOW BADASS YOU THINK YOU ARE, JONES...
GRIND!
CRACK!
SHIT!! HE'S GOING TO CRUSH HIS SKULL! HE'S GOING TO KILL HIM!
CRAK!
...YOU AIN'T COMIN' BACK TO LIFE WITH NO HEAD!!
NO!!
!
GODDAMNIT, NO!!
EH?

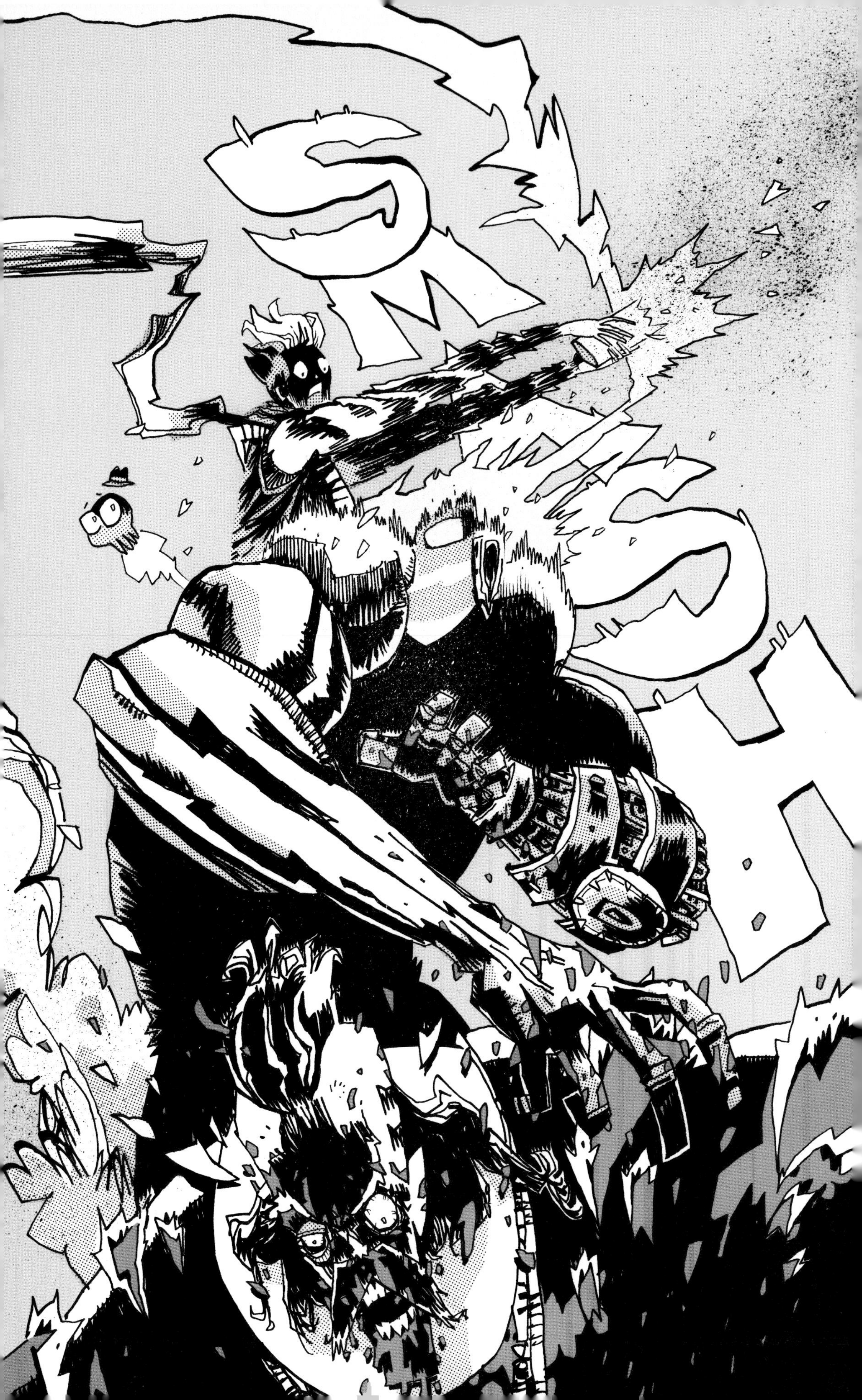
SM
SH

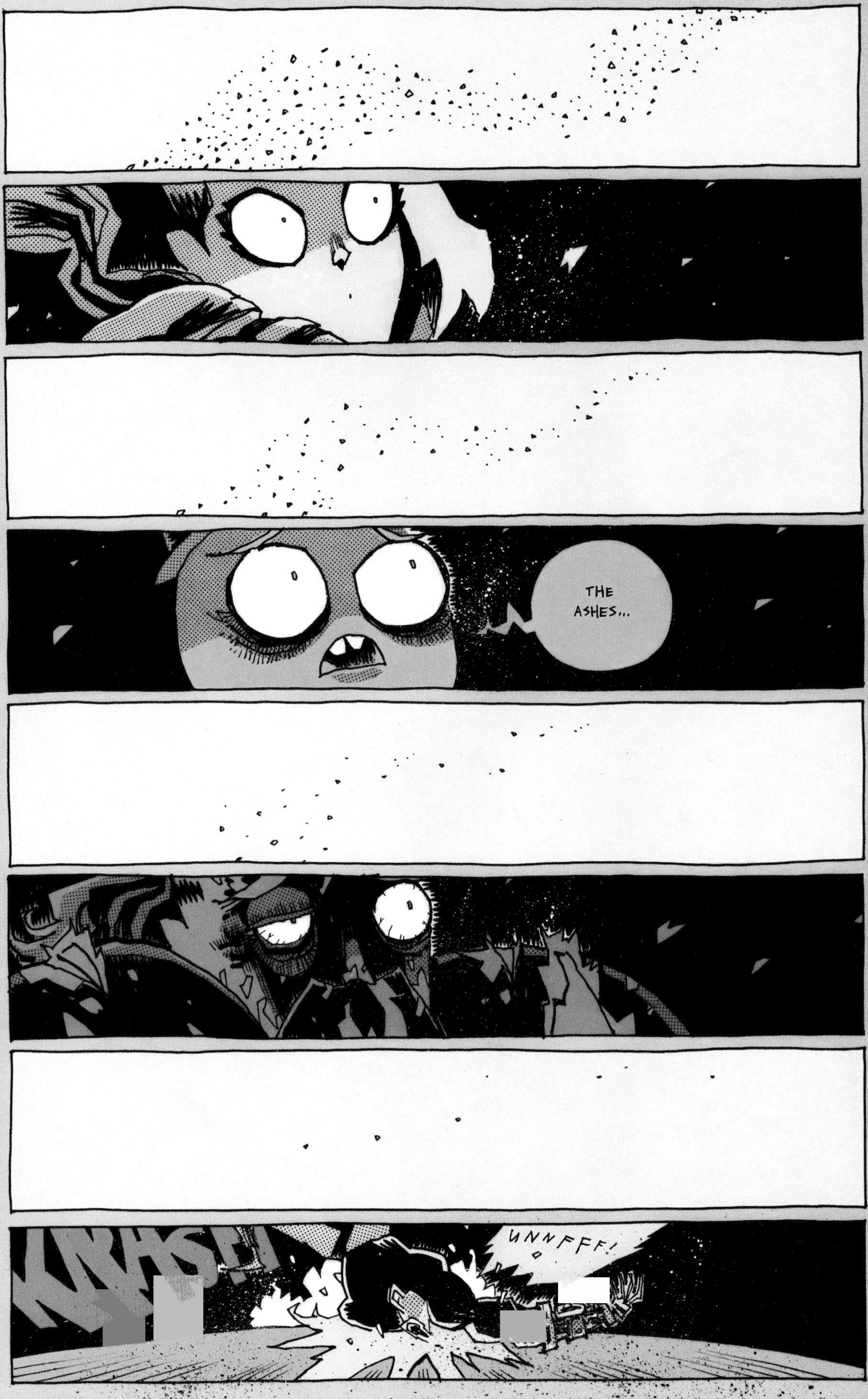
THE ASHES...
KRASH!
UNNFFF!

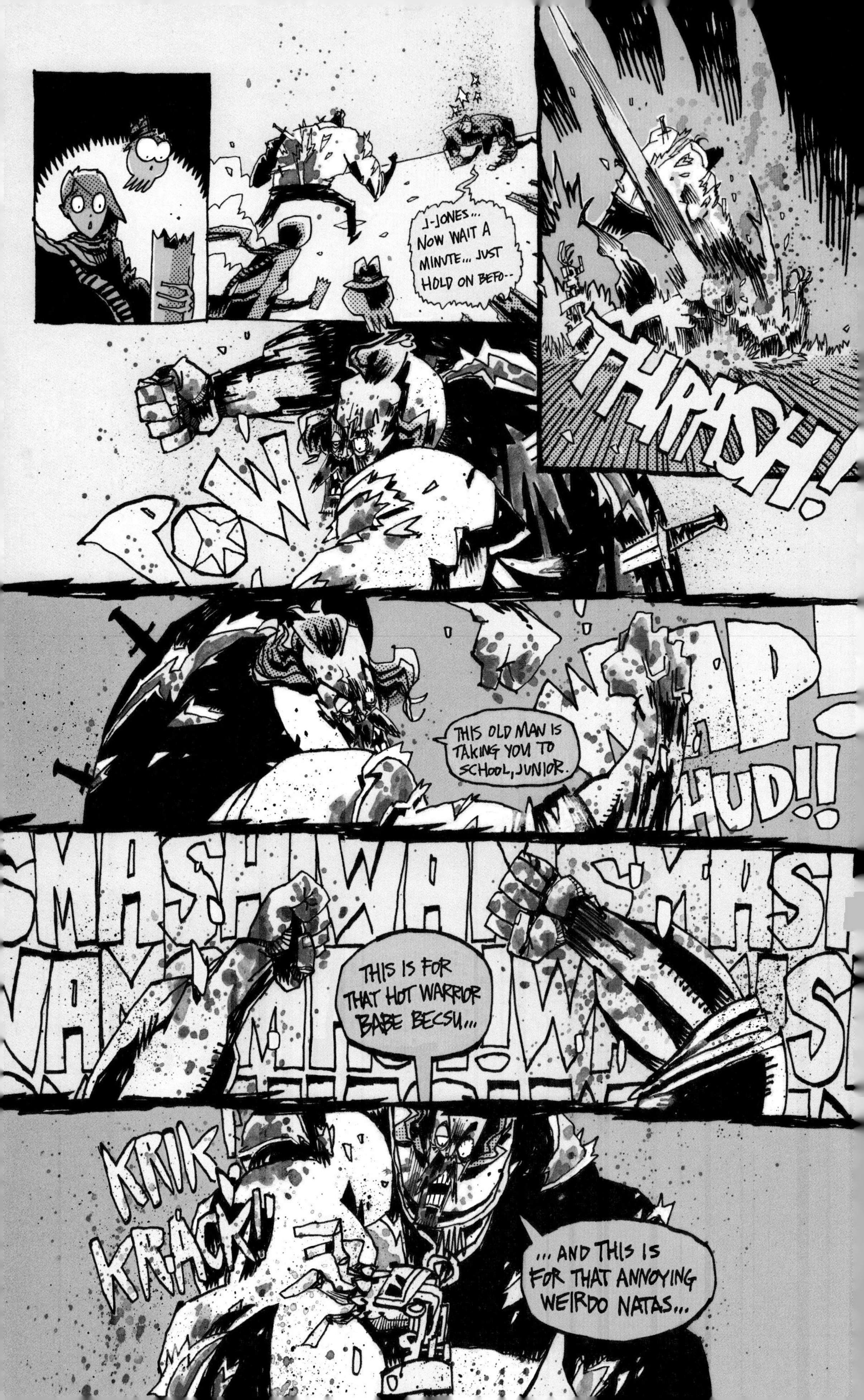
J-JONES... NOW WAIT A MINUTE... JUST HOLD ON BEFO--
THRASH!
POW
THIS OLD MAN IS TAKING YOU TO SCHOOL, JUNIOR.
THUD!!
THIS IS FOR THAT HOT WARRIOR BABE BECSU...
KRIK!
KRACK!
... AND THIS IS FOR THAT ANNOYING WEIRDO NATAS...

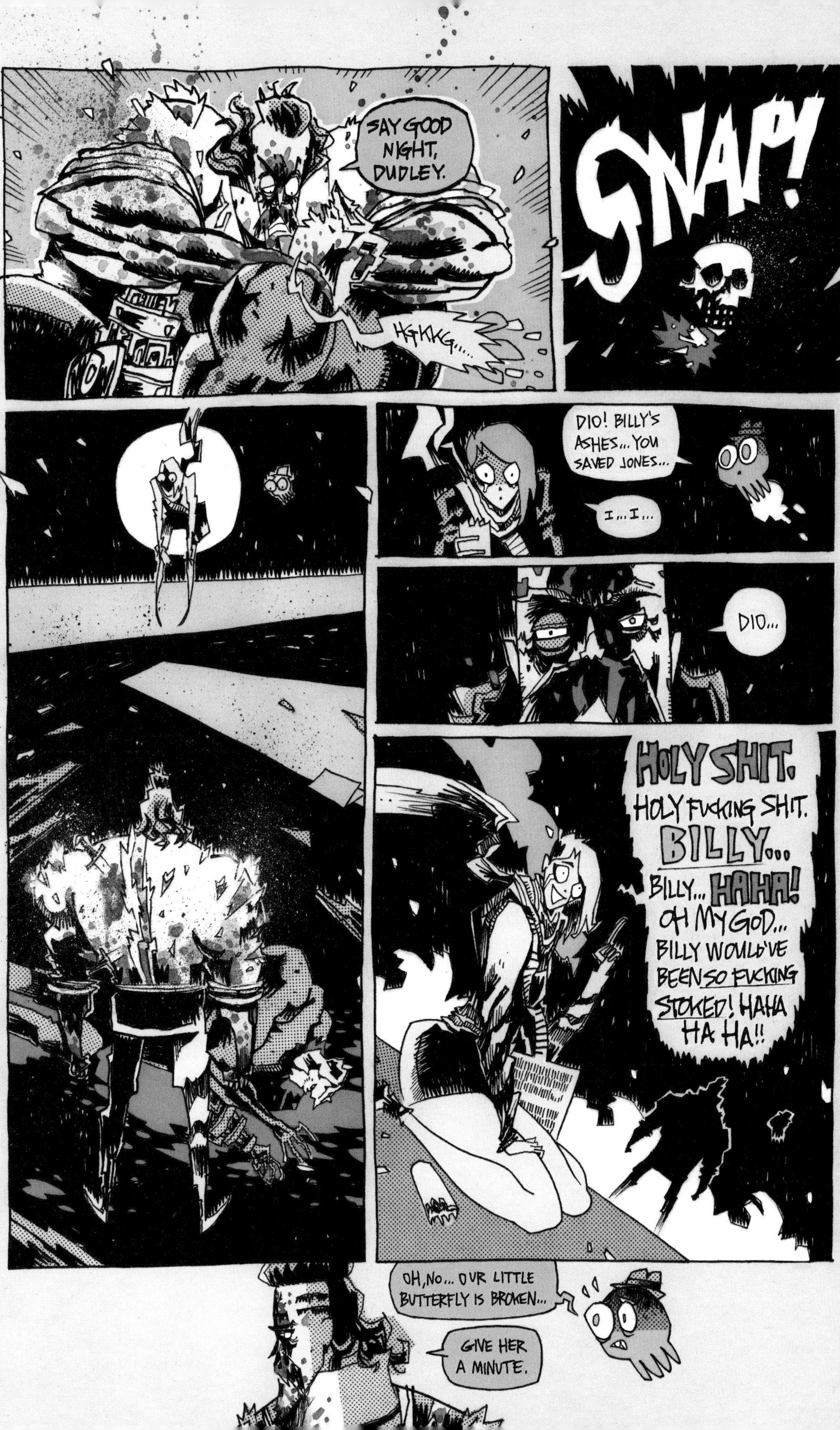
SAY GOOD NIGHT, DUDLEY.
HGKKG....
SNAP!
DIO! BILLY'S ASHES... YOU SAVED JONES...
I... I...
DIO...
HOLY SHIT.
HOLY FUCKING SHIT. BILLY...
BILLY... HAHA! OH MY GOD... BILLY WOULD'VE BEEN SO FUCKING STOKED! HAHA HA HA!!
OH, NO... OUR LITTLE BUTTERFLY IS BROKEN...
GIVE HER A MINUTE.

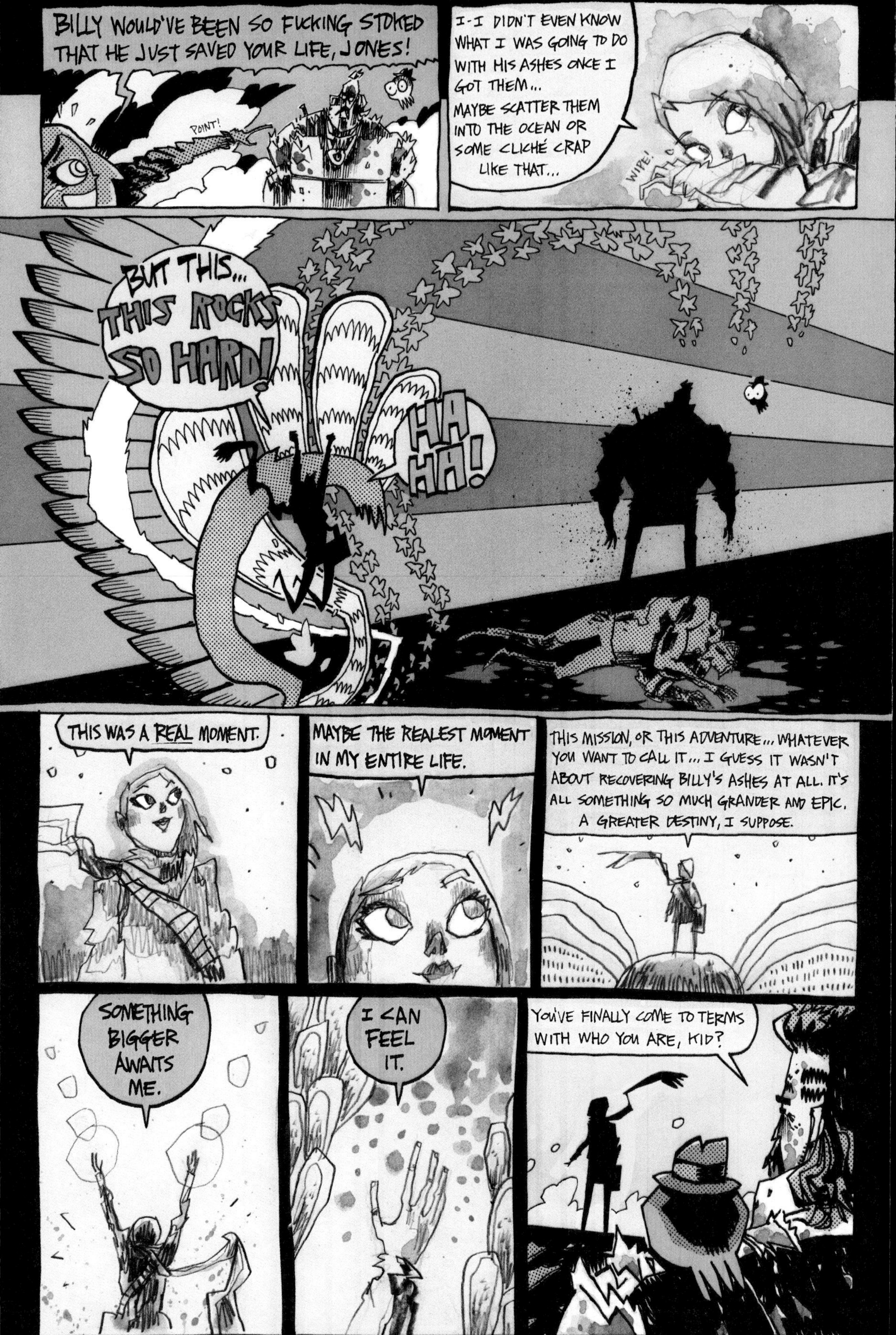
BILLY WOULD'VE BEEN SO FUCKING STOKED THAT HE JUST SAVED YOUR LIFE, JONES!
POINT!
I-I DIDN'T EVEN KNOW WHAT I WAS GOING TO DO WITH HIS ASHES ONCE I GOT THEM... MAYBE SCATTER THEM INTO THE OCEAN OR SOME CLICHÉ CRAP LIKE THAT...
WIPE!
BUT THIS... THIS ROCKS SO HARD!
HA HA!
THIS WAS A REAL MOMENT.
MAYBE THE REALEST MOMENT IN MY ENTIRE LIFE.
THIS MISSION, OR THIS ADVENTURE... WHATEVER YOU WANT TO CALL IT... I GUESS IT WASN'T ABOUT RECOVERING BILLY'S ASHES AT ALL. IT'S ALL SOMETHING SO MUCH GRANDER AND EPIC. A GREATER DESTINY, I SUPPOSE.
SOMETHING BIGGER AWAITS ME.
I CAN FEEL IT.
YOU'VE FINALLY COME TO TERMS WITH WHO YOU ARE, KID?

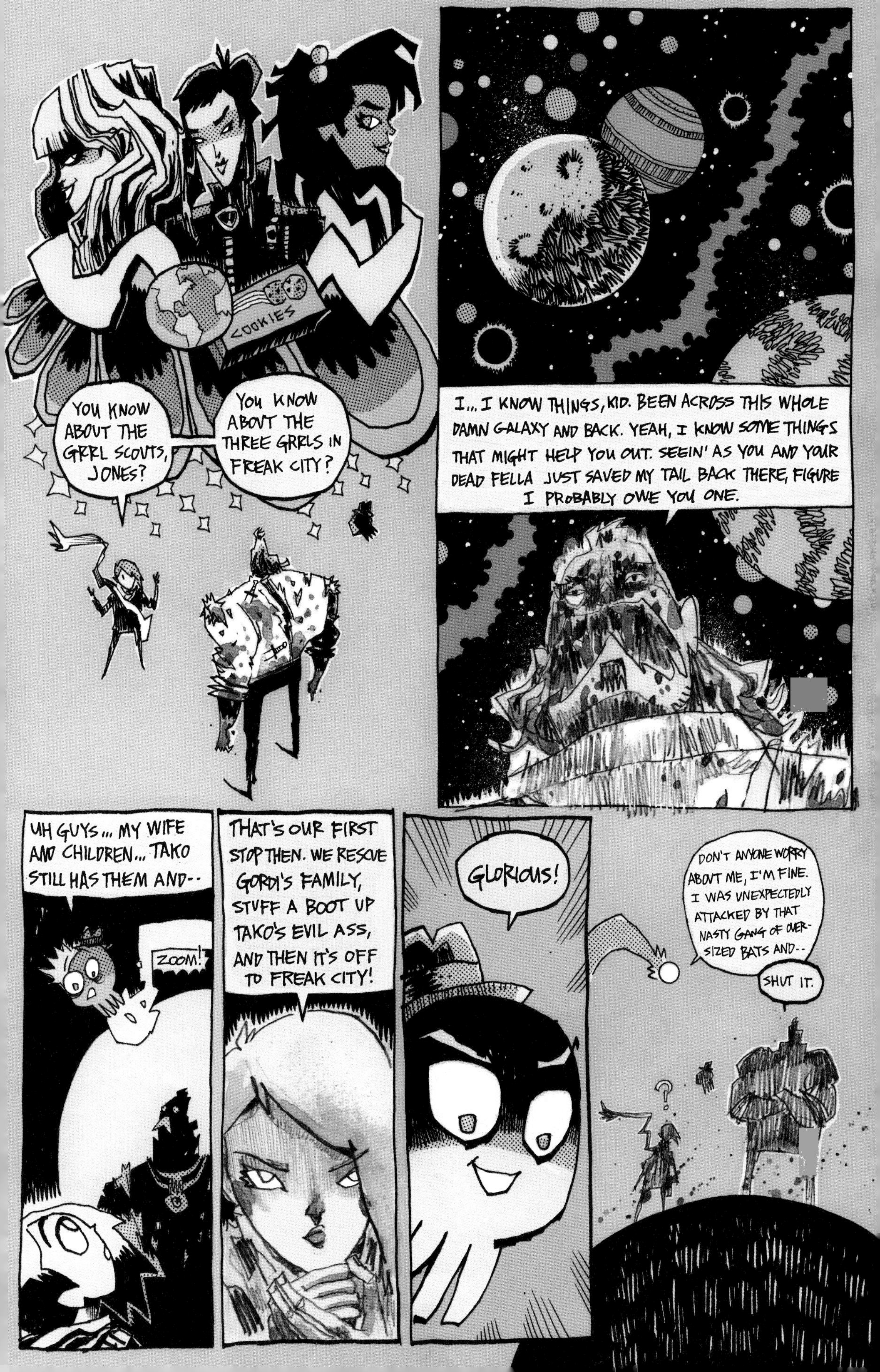
COOKIES
YOU KNOW ABOUT THE GRRL SCOUTS, JONES?
YOU KNOW ABOUT THE THREE GRRLS IN FREAK CITY?
I... I KNOW THINGS, KID. BEEN ACROSS THIS WHOLE DAMN GALAXY AND BACK. YEAH, I KNOW SOME THINGS THAT MIGHT HELP YOU OUT. SEEIN' AS YOU AND YOUR DEAD FELLA JUST SAVED MY TAIL BACK THERE, FIGURE I PROBABLY OWE YOU ONE.
UH GUYS... MY WIFE AND CHILDREN... TAKO STILL HAS THEM AND--
ZOOM!
THAT'S OUR FIRST STOP THEN. WE RESCUE GORDI'S FAMILY, STUFF A BOOT UP TAKO'S EVIL ASS, AND THEN IT'S OFF TO FREAK CITY!
GLORIOUS!
DON'T ANYONE WORRY ABOUT ME, I'M FINE. I WAS UNEXPECTEDLY ATTACKED BY THAT NASTY GANG OF OVER-SIZED BATS AND--
SHUT IT.

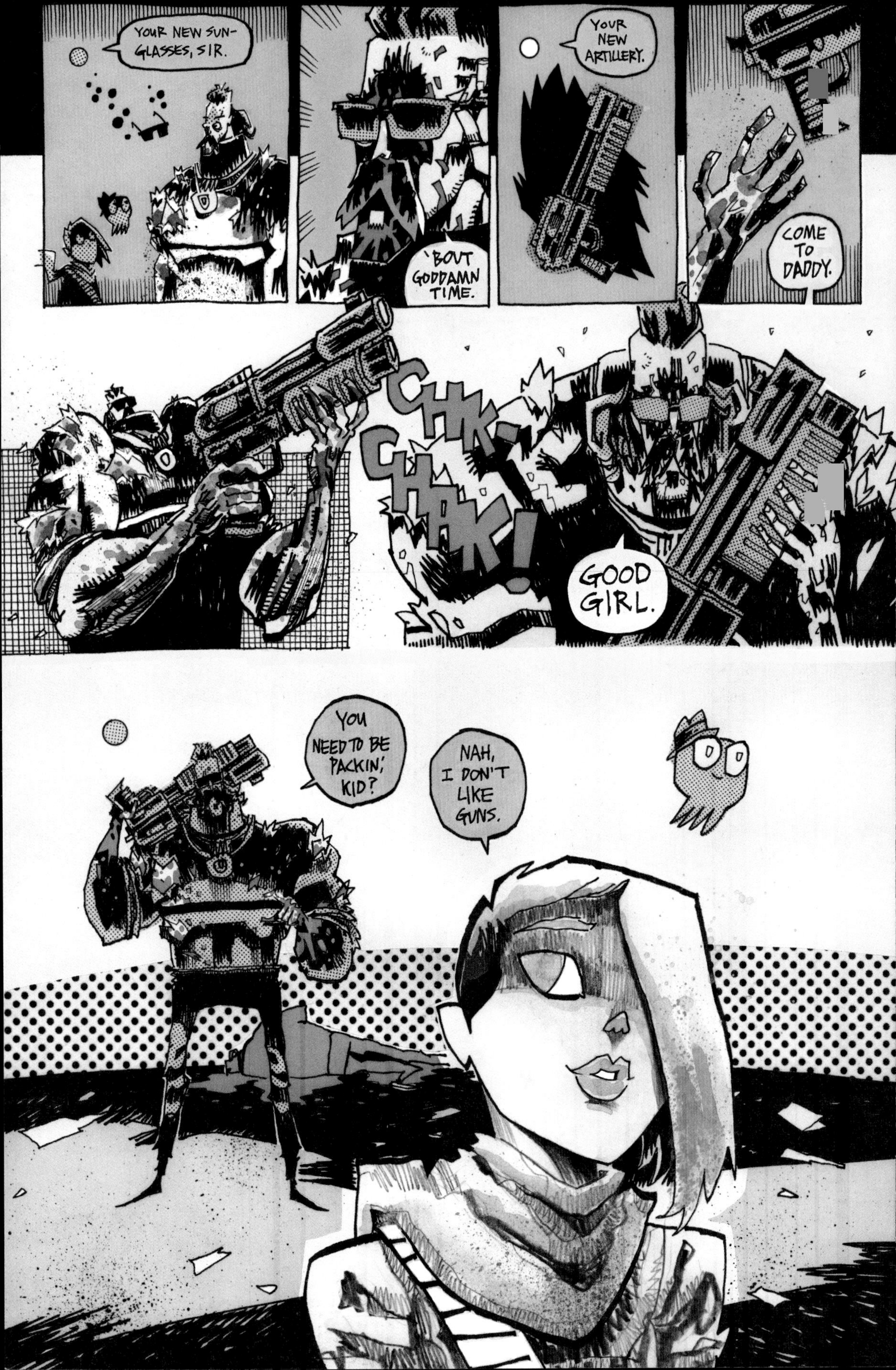
YOUR NEW SUN-GLASSES, SIR.
'BOUT GODDAMN TIME.
YOUR NEW ARTILLERY.
COME TO DADDY.
CHK-CHAK!
GOOD GIRL.
YOU NEED TO BE PACKIN', KID?
NAH, I DON'T LIKE GUNS.

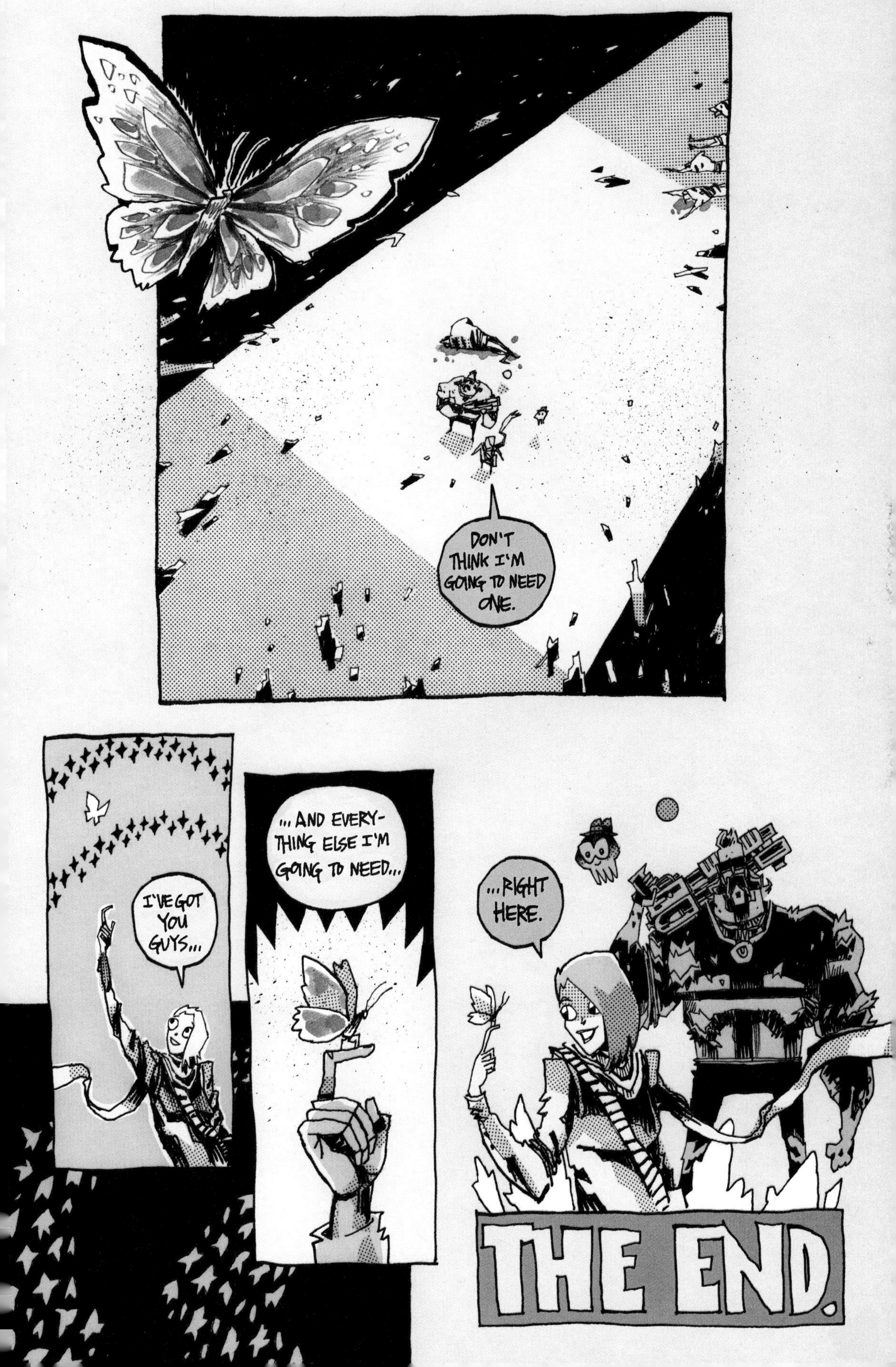
DON'T THINK I'M GOING TO NEED ONE.
I'VE GOT YOU GUYS...
...AND EVERY-THING ELSE I'M GOING TO NEED...
...RIGHT HERE.
THE END.

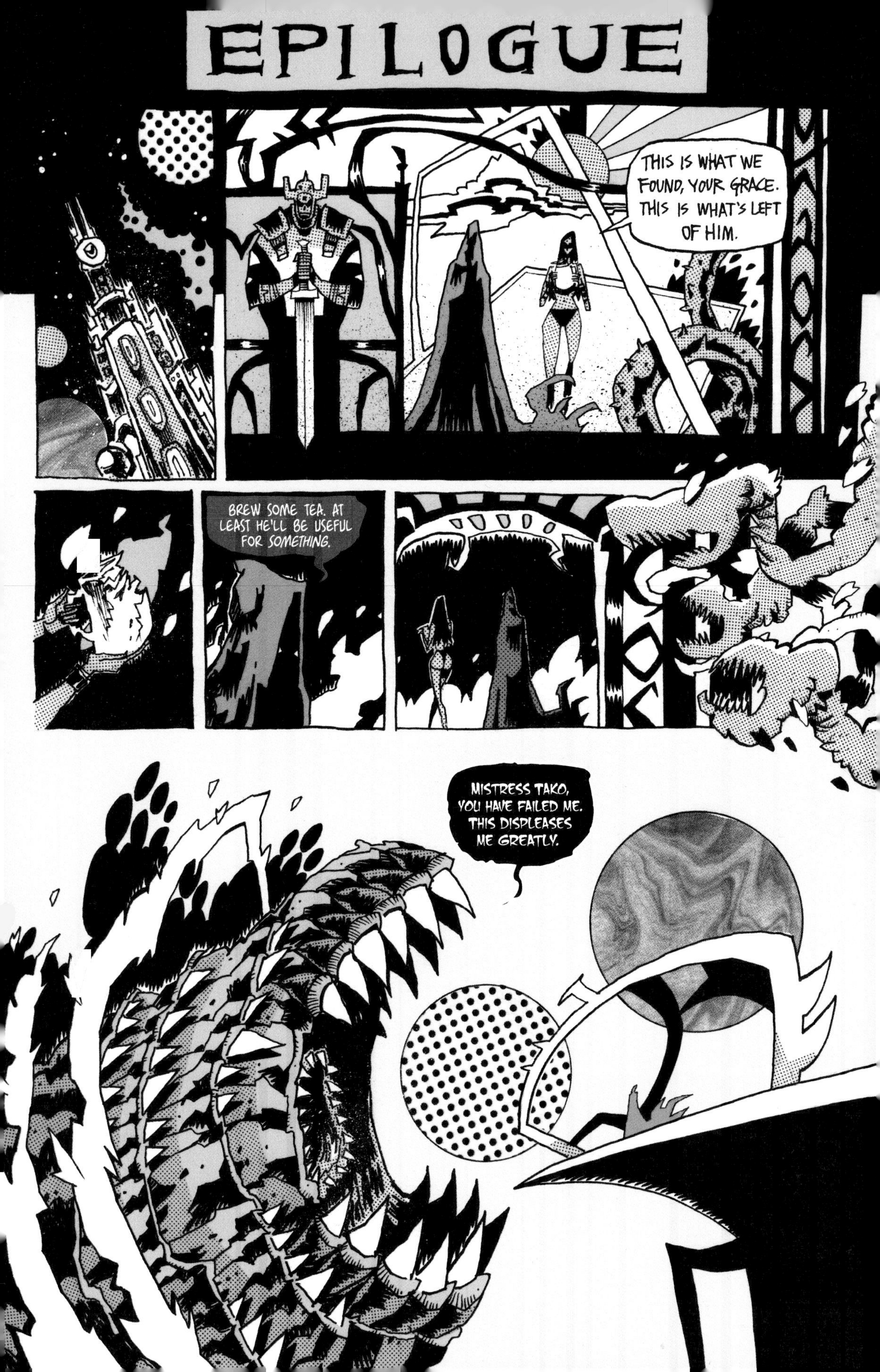
EPILOGUE
THIS IS WHAT WE FOUND, YOUR GRACE. THIS IS WHAT'S LEFT OF HIM.
BREW SOME TEA. AT LEAST HE'LL BE USEFUL FOR SOMETHING.
MISTRESS TAKO, YOU HAVE FAILED ME. THIS DISPLEASES ME GREATLY.

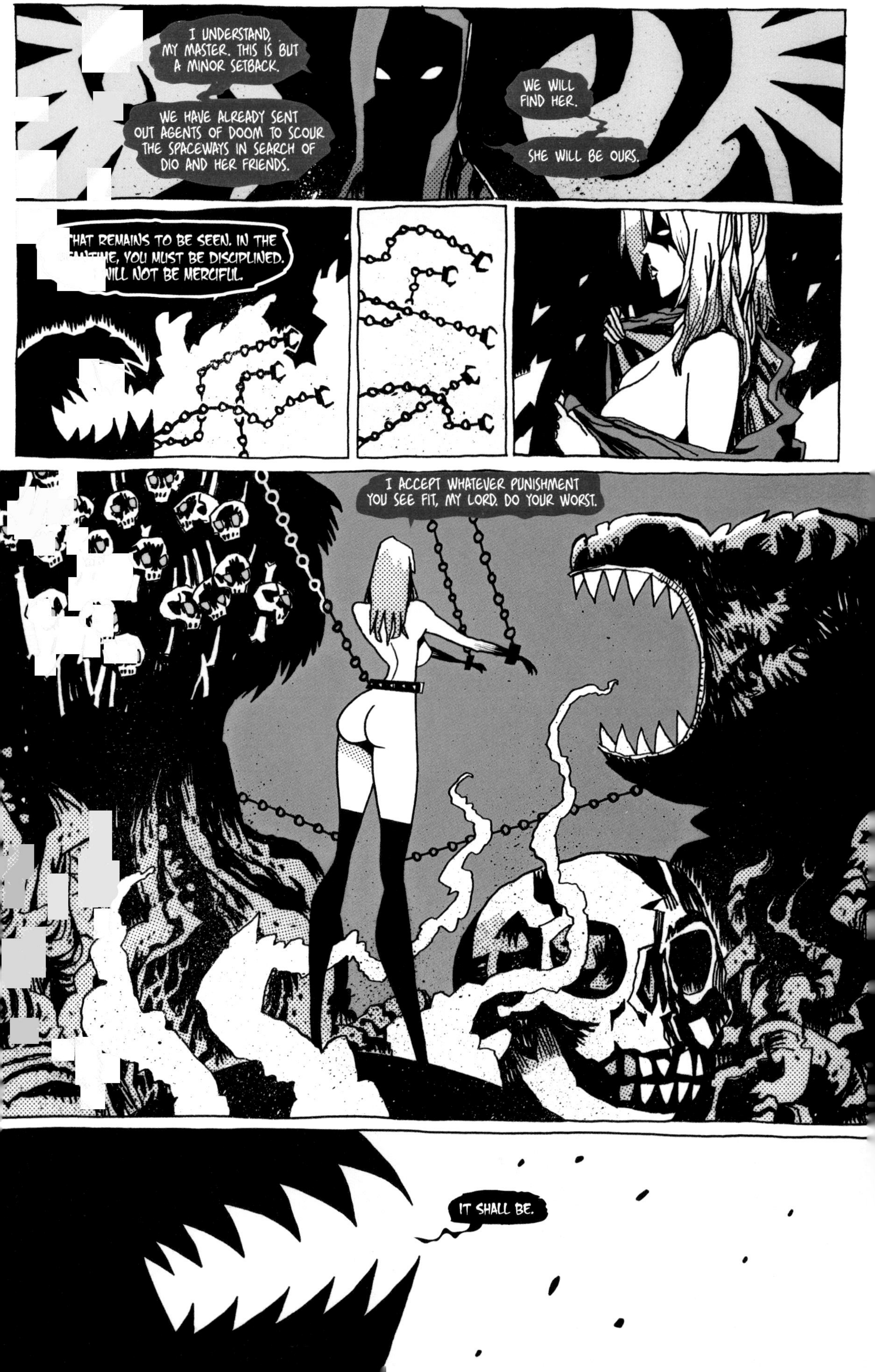
I UNDERSTAND, MY MASTER. THIS IS BUT A MINOR SETBACK.
WE HAVE ALREADY SENT OUT AGENTS OF DOOM TO SCOUR THE SPACEWAYS IN SEARCH OF DIO AND HER FRIENDS.
WE WILL FIND HER.
SHE WILL BE OURS.
THAT REMAINS TO BE SEEN. IN THE
ANTIME, YOU MUST BE DISCIPLINED.
WILL NOT BE MERCIFUL.
I ACCEPT WHATEVER PUNISHMENT YOU SEE FIT, MY LORD. DO YOUR WORST.
IT SHALL BE.

BONUS
COMICS.

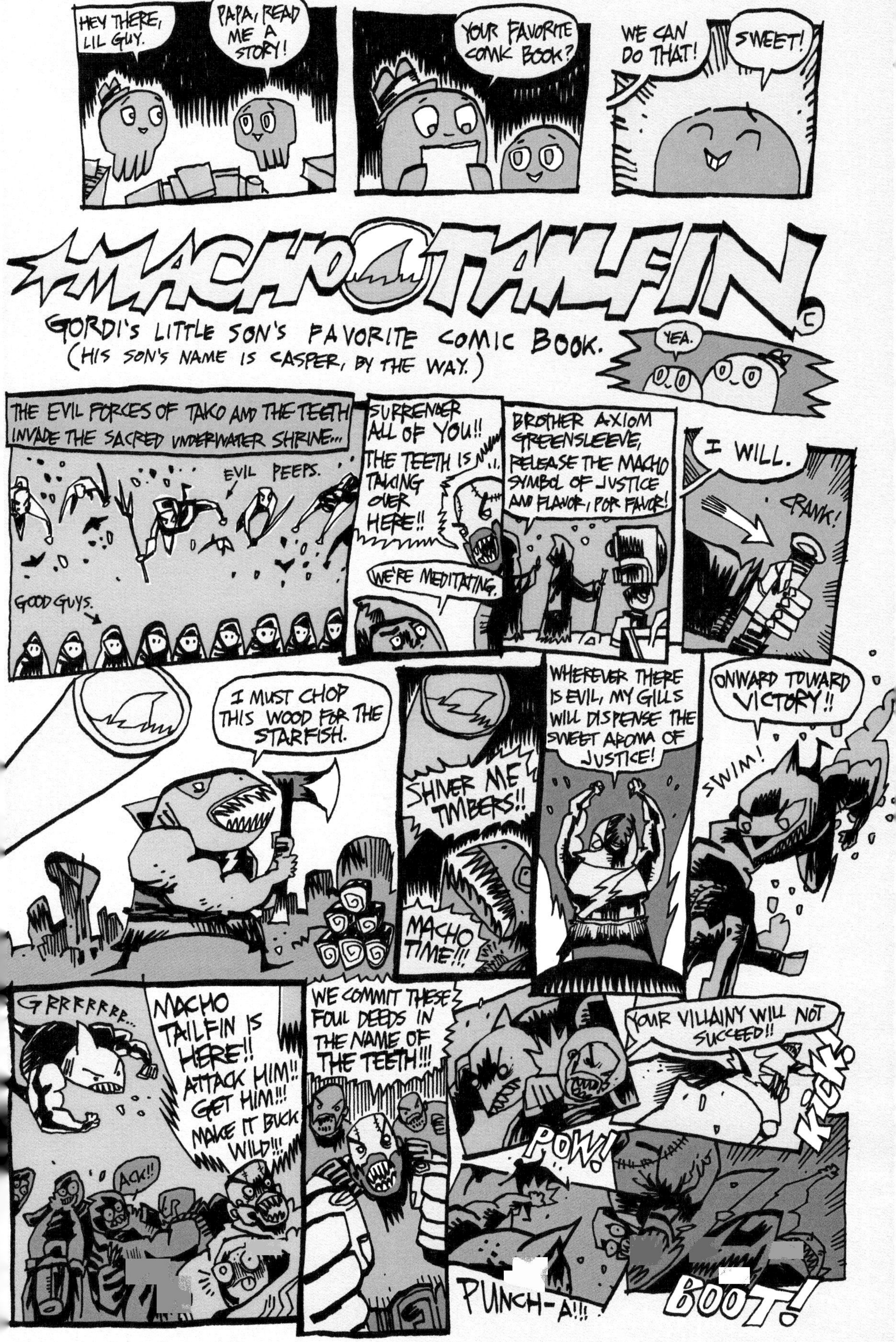
HEY THERE, LIL GUY.
PAPA, READ ME A STORY!!
YOUR FAVORITE COMIC BOOK?
WE CAN DO THAT!
SWEET!
MACHO TAILFIN.
GORDI'S LITTLE SON'S FAVORITE COMIC BOOK.
(HIS SON'S NAME IS CASPER, BY THE WAY.)
YEA.
THE EVIL FORCES OF TAKO AND THE TEETH INVADE THE SACRED UNDERWATER SHRINE...
EVIL PEEPS.
GOOD GUYS.
SURRENDER ALL OF YOU!! THE TEETH IS TAKING OVER HERE!!
WE'RE MEDITATING.
BROTHER AXIOM GREENSLEEVE, RELEASE THE MACHO SYMBOL OF JUSTICE AND FLAVOR, POR FAVOR!
I WILL.
CRANK!
I MUST CHOP THIS WOOD FOR THE STARFISH.
SHIVER ME TIMBERS!!
MACHO TIME!!!
WHEREVER THERE IS EVIL, MY GILLS WILL DISPENSE THE SWEET AROMA OF JUSTICE!
ONWARD TOWARD VICTORY!!
SWIM!
GRRRRRRR...
MACHO TAILFIN IS HERE!! ATTACK HIM!! GET HIM!!! MAKE IT BUCK WILD!!!
ACK!!
WE COMMIT THESE FOUL DEEDS IN THE NAME OF THE TEETH!!!
YOUR VILLAINY WILL NOT SUCCEED!!
KICK!
POW!
PUNCH-A!!!
BOOT!

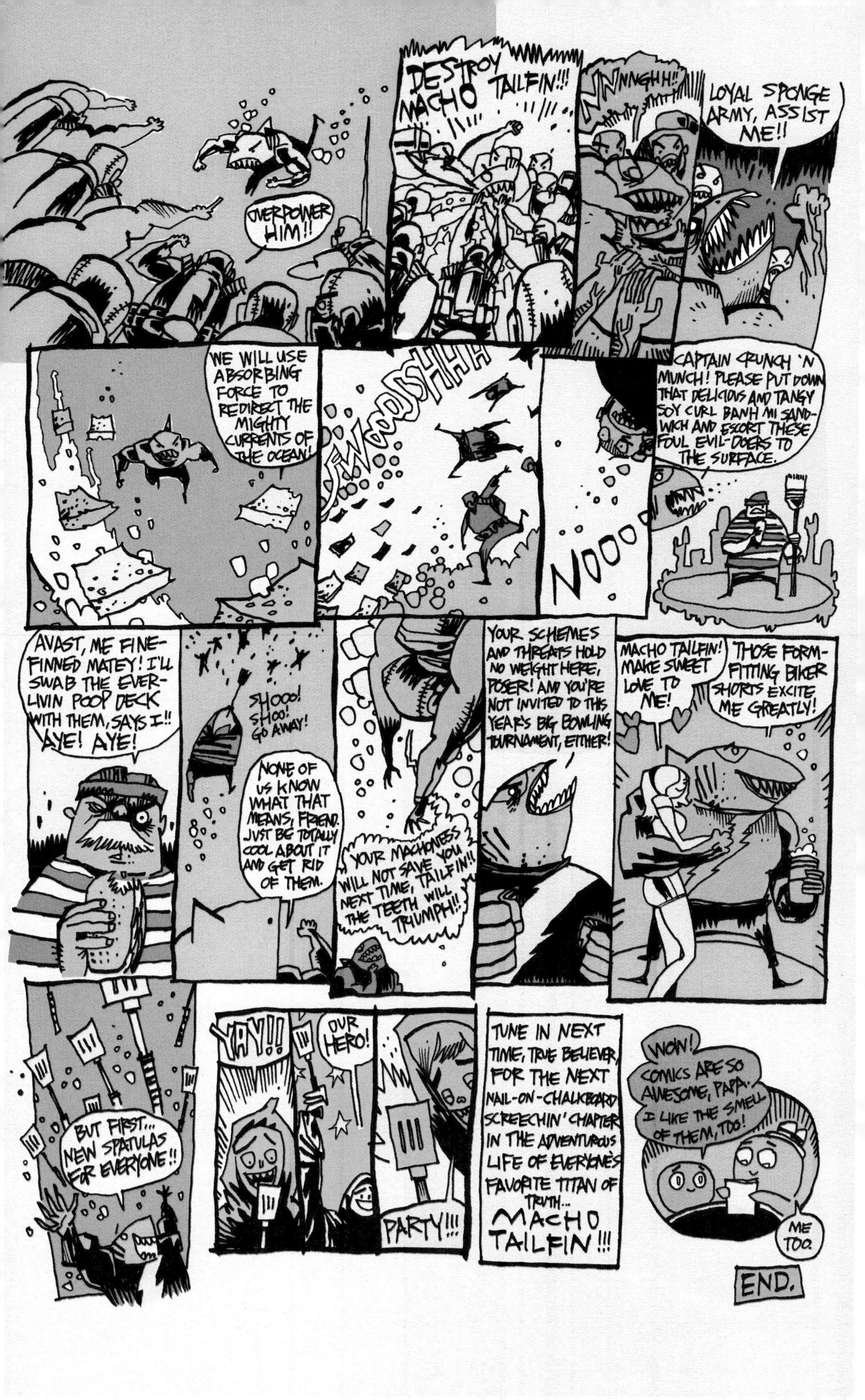
OVERPOWER HIM!!
DESTROY MACHO TAILFIN!!!
NNNNGHH!!
LOYAL SPONGE ARMY, ASSIST ME!!
WE WILL USE ABSORBING FORCE TO REDIRECT THE MIGHTY CURRENTS OF THE OCEAN!
FWOOOSHHH
NOOOO
CAPTAIN CRUNCH 'N MUNCH! PLEASE PUT DOWN THAT DELICIOUS AND TANGY SOY CURL BANH MI SANDWICH AND ESCORT THESE FOUL EVIL-DOERS TO THE SURFACE.
AVAST, ME FINE-FINNED MATEY! I'LL SWAB THE EVER-LIVIN POOP DECK WITH THEM, SAYS I!! AYE! AYE!
SHOOO! SHOO! GO AWAY!
NONE OF US KNOW WHAT THAT MEANS, FRIEND. JUST BE TOTALLY COOL ABOUT IT AND GET RID OF THEM.
YOUR MACHONESS WILL NOT SAVE YOU NEXT TIME, TAILFIN!! THE TEETH WILL TRIUMPH!!
YOUR SCHEMES AND THREATS HOLD NO WEIGHT HERE, POSER! AND YOU'RE NOT INVITED TO THIS YEAR'S BIG BOWLING TOURNAMENT, EITHER!
MACHO TAILFIN! MAKE SWEET LOVE TO ME!
THOSE FORM-FITTING BIKER SHORTS EXCITE ME GREATLY!
BUT FIRST... NEW SPATULAS FOR EVERYONE!!
YAY!!
OUR HERO!
PARTY!!!
TUNE IN NEXT TIME, TRUE BELIEVER, FOR THE NEXT NAIL-ON-CHALKBOARD SCREECHIN' CHAPTER IN THE ADVENTUROUS LIFE OF EVERYONE'S FAVORITE TITAN OF TRUTH... MACHO TAILFIN!!!
WOW! COMICS ARE SO AWESOME, PAPA. I LIKE THE SMELL OF THEM, TOO!
ME TOO.
END.

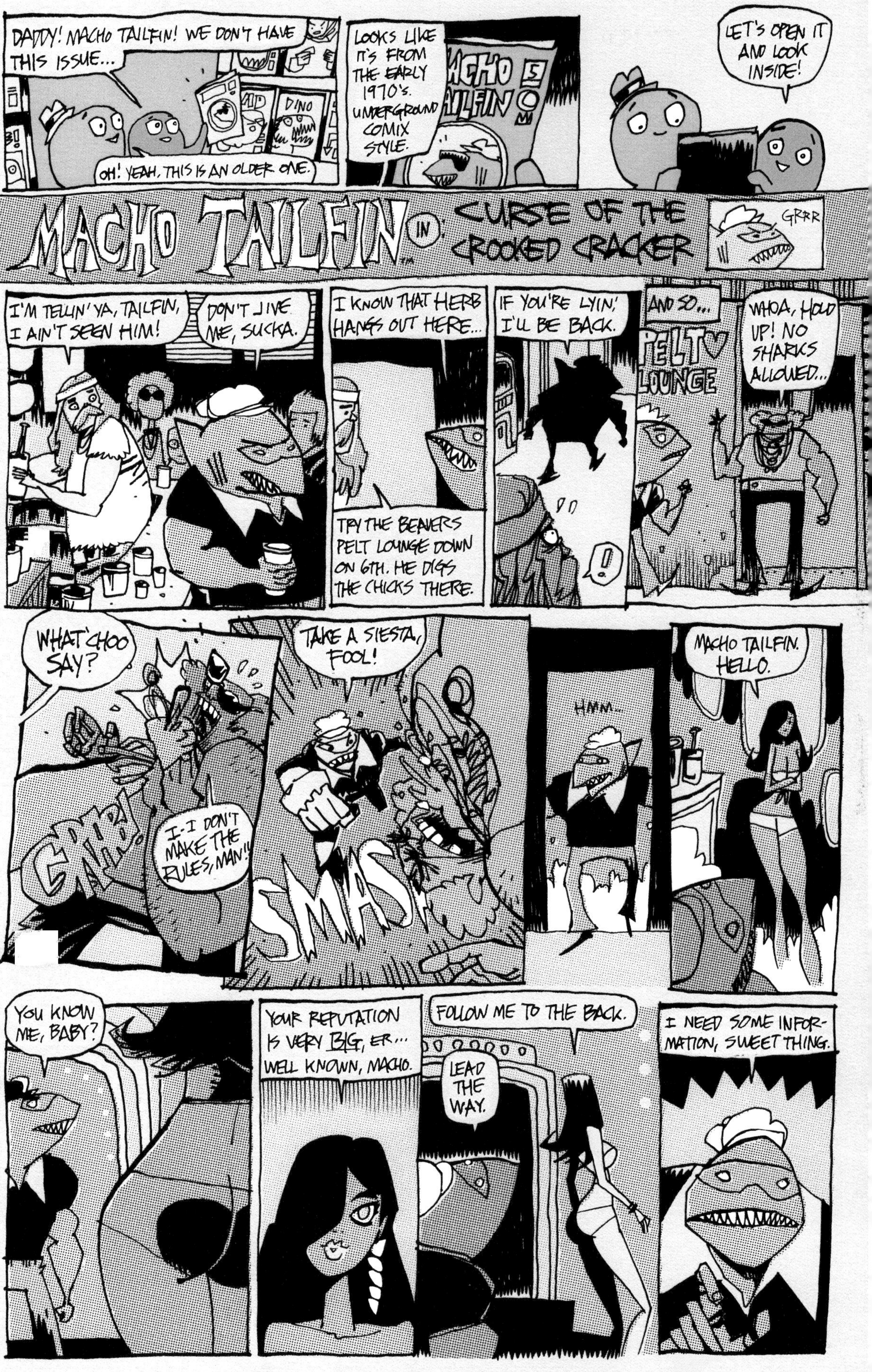
DADDY! MACHO TAILFIN! WE DON'T HAVE THIS ISSUE...
OH! YEAH, THIS IS AN OLDER ONE.
LOOKS LIKE IT'S FROM THE EARLY 1970'S. UNDERGROUND COMIX STYLE.
MACHO 5 TAILFIN
LET'S OPEN IT AND LOOK INSIDE!
MACHO TAILFIN IN: CURSE OF THE CROOKED CRACKER
GRRR
I'M TELLIN' YA, TAILFIN, I AIN'T SEEN HIM!
DON'T JIVE ME, SUCKA.
I KNOW THAT HERB HANGS OUT HERE...
TRY THE BEAVERS PELT LOUNGE DOWN ON 6TH. HE DIGS THE CHICKS THERE.
IF YOU'RE LYIN', I'LL BE BACK.
!
AND SO...
PELT LOUNGE
WHOA, HOLD UP! NO SHARKS ALLOWED...
WHAT'CHOO SAY?
GRAB!
I-I DON'T MAKE THE RULES, MAN!!
TAKE A SIESTA, FOOL!
SMASH
HMM...
MACHO TAILFIN. HELLO.
YOU KNOW ME, BABY?
YOUR REPUTATION IS VERY BIG, ER... WELL KNOWN, MACHO.
FOLLOW ME TO THE BACK.
LEAD THE WAY.
I NEED SOME INFORMATION, SWEET THING.

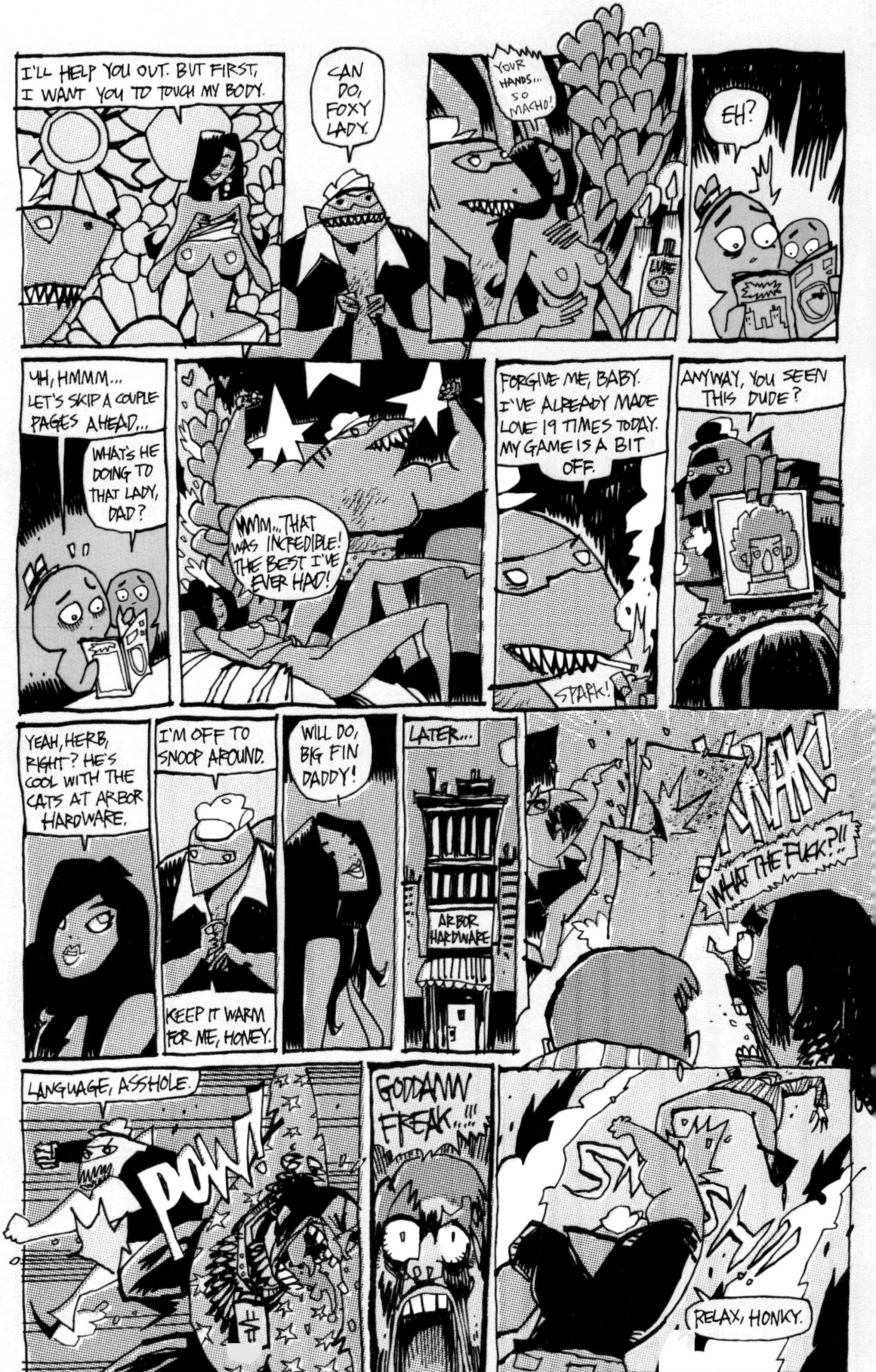
I'LL HELP YOU OUT. BUT FIRST, I WANT YOU TO TOUCH MY BODY.
CAN DO, FOXY LADY.
YOUR HANDS... SO MACHO!
LUBE
EH?
UH, HMMM... LET'S SKIP A COUPLE PAGES AHEAD...
WHAT'S HE DOING TO THAT LADY, DAD?
MMM... THAT WAS INCREDIBLE! THE BEST I'VE EVER HAD!
FORGIVE ME, BABY. I'VE ALREADY MADE LOVE 19 TIMES TODAY. MY GAME IS A BIT OFF.
SPARK!
ANYWAY, YOU SEEN THIS DUDE?
YEAH, HERB, RIGHT? HE'S COOL WITH THE CATS AT ARBOR HARDWARE.
I'M OFF TO SNOOP AROUND.
KEEP IT WARM FOR ME, HONEY.
WILL DO, BIG FIN DADDY!
LATER...
ARBOR HARDWARE
WHAT THE FUCK?!!
LANGUAGE, ASSHOLE.
POW!
GODDAMN FREAK...!!!
RELAX, HONKY.

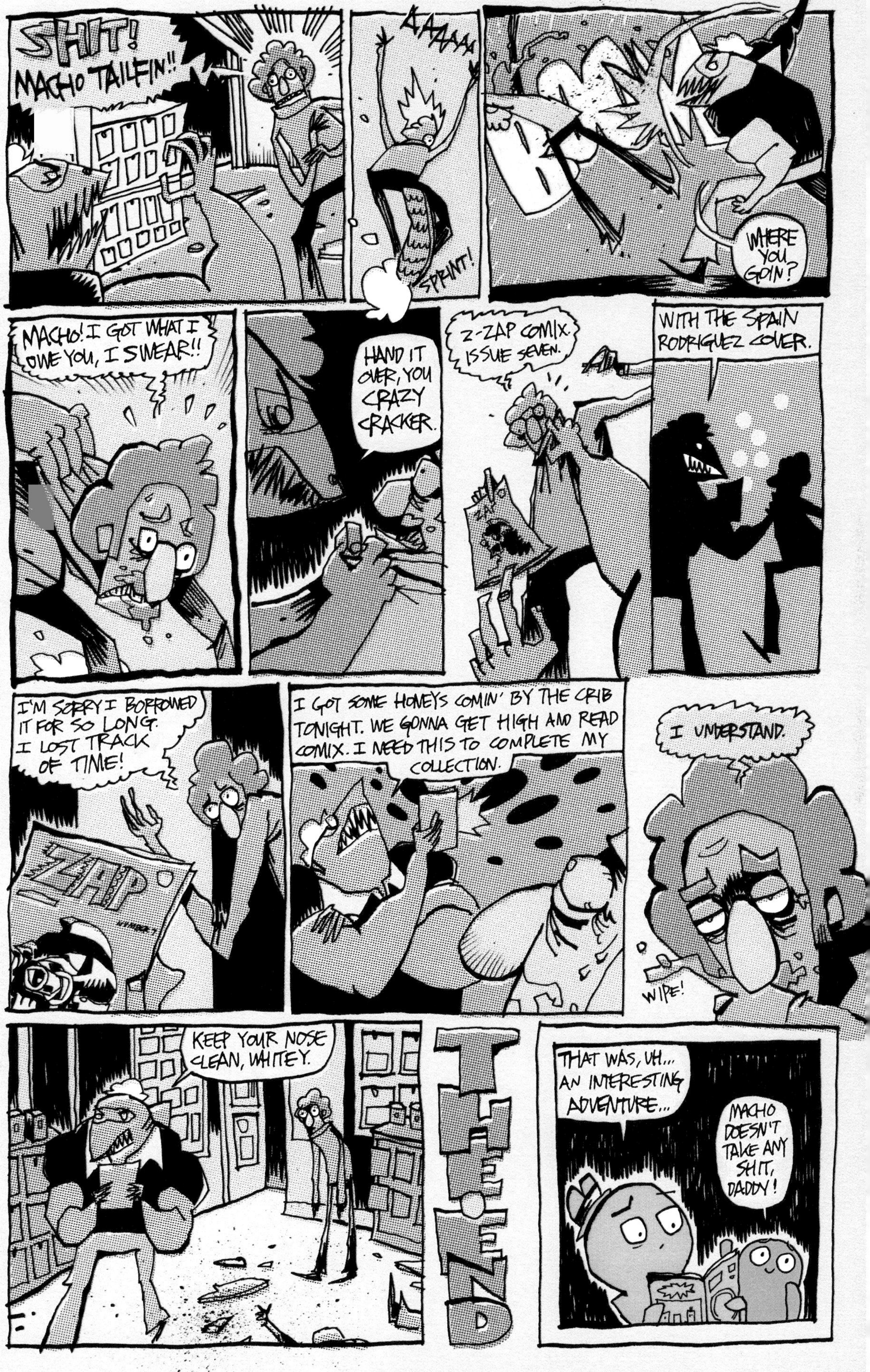
SHIT!
MACHO TAILFIN!!
AAAAAA
SPRINT!
WHERE YOU GOIN?
MACHO! I GOT WHAT I OWE YOU, I SWEAR!!
HAND IT OVER, YOU CRAZY CRACKER.
Z-ZAP COMIX. ISSUE SEVEN.
ZAP
WITH THE SPAIN RODRIGUEZ COVER.
I'M SORRY I BORROWED IT FOR SO LONG. I LOST TRACK OF TIME!
ZAP
I GOT SOME HONEYS COMIN' BY THE CRIB TONIGHT. WE GONNA GET HIGH AND READ COMIX. I NEED THIS TO COMPLETE MY COLLECTION.
I UNDERSTAND.
WIPE!
KEEP YOUR NOSE CLEAN, WHITEY.
THE END
THAT WAS, UH... AN INTERESTING ADVENTURE...
MACHO DOESN'T TAKE ANY SHIT, DADDY!

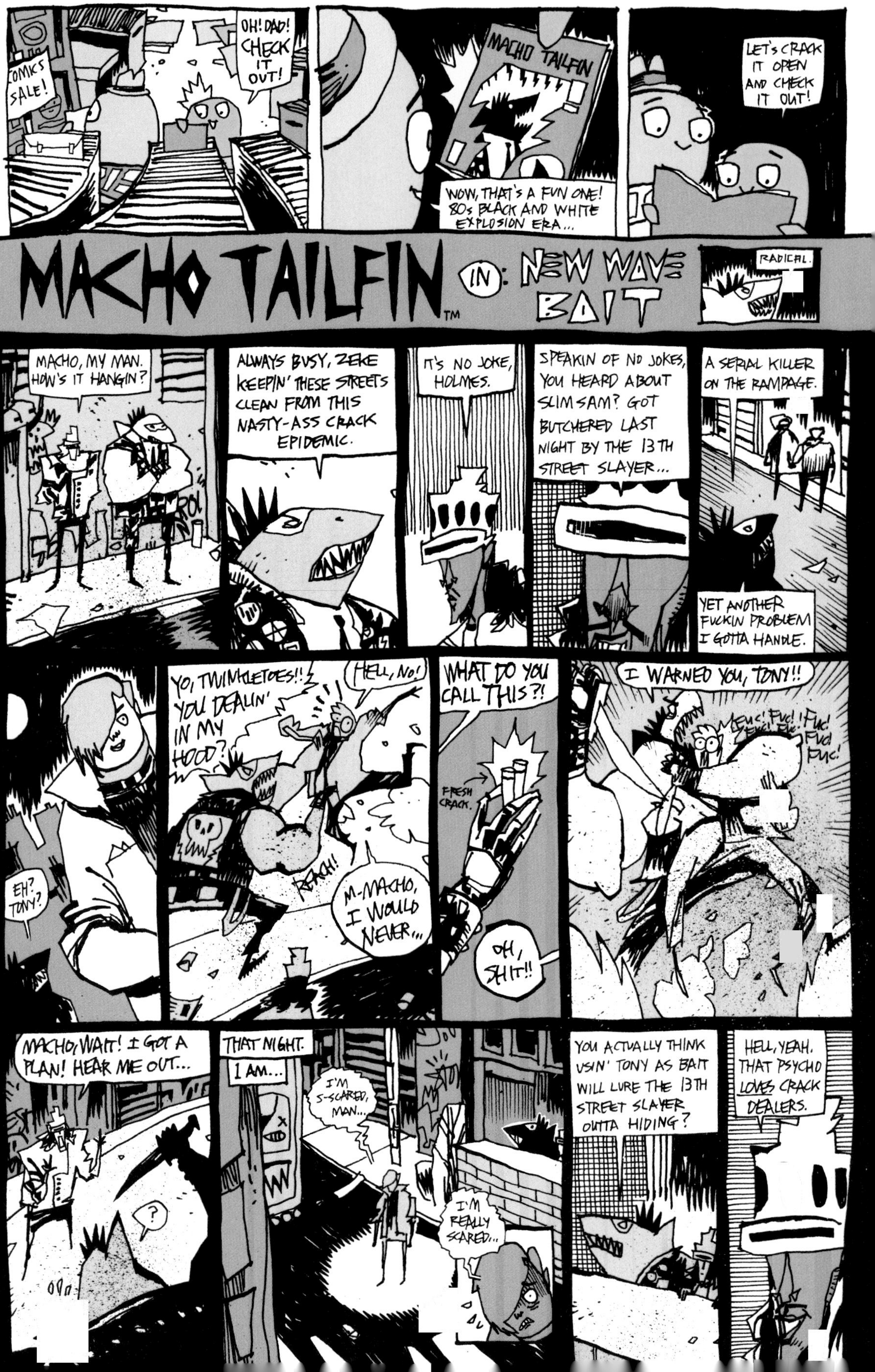
COMICS SALE!
OH! DAD! CHECK IT OUT!
MACHO TAILFIN
WOW, THAT'S A FUN ONE! 80s BLACK AND WHITE EXPLOSION ERA...
LET'S CRACK IT OPEN AND CHECK IT OUT!
MACHO TAILFIN™ IN: NEW WAVE BAIT
RADICAL.
MACHO, MY MAN. HOW'S IT HANGIN?
ALWAYS BUSY, ZEKE KEEPIN' THESE STREETS CLEAN FROM THIS NASTY-ASS CRACK EPIDEMIC.
IT'S NO JOKE, HOLMES.
SPEAKIN OF NO JOKES, YOU HEARD ABOUT SLIM SAM? GOT BUTCHERED LAST NIGHT BY THE 13TH STREET SLAYER...
A SERIAL KILLER ON THE RAMPAGE.
YET ANOTHER FUCKIN PROBLEM I GOTTA HANDLE.
EH? TONY?
YO, TWINKLETOES!! YOU DEALIN' IN MY HOOD?
HELL, NO!
REACH!
M-MACHO, I WOULD NEVER...
WHAT DO YOU CALL THIS?!
FRESH CRACK.
OH, SHIT!!
I WARNED YOU, TONY!!
MACHO, WAIT! I GOT A PLAN! HEAR ME OUT...
?
THAT NIGHT.
1 AM...
I'M S-SCARED, MAN...
I'M REALLY SCARED...
YOU ACTUALLY THINK USIN' TONY AS BAIT WILL LURE THE 13TH STREET SLAYER OUTTA HIDING?
HELL, YEAH. THAT PSYCHO LOVES CRACK DEALERS.

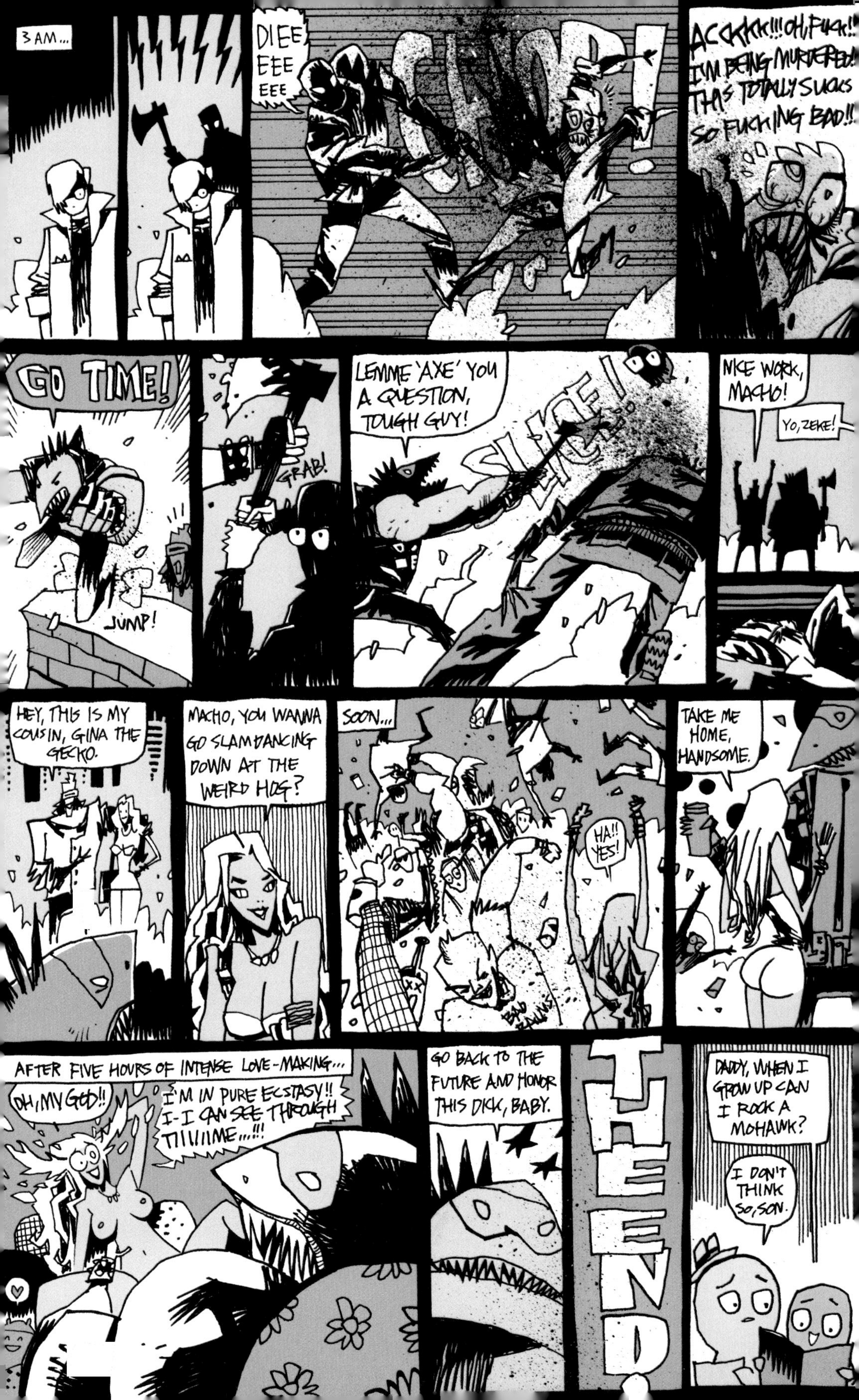
3 AM...
DIEEEEEEEE
CHOP!
ACCKKKK!!! OH, FUCK!! I'M BEING MURDERED!! THIS TOTALLY SUCKS SO FUCKING BAD!!
GO TIME!
JUMP!
GRAB!
LEMME 'AXE' YOU A QUESTION, TOUGH GUY!
SLICE!
NICE WORK, MACHO!
YO, ZEKE!
HEY, THIS IS MY COUSIN, GINA THE GECKO.
MACHO, YOU WANNA GO SLAMDANCING DOWN AT THE WEIRD HOG?
SOON...
HA!! YES!
BAD BRAINS
TAKE ME HOME, HANDSOME.
AFTER FIVE HOURS OF INTENSE LOVE-MAKING...
OH, MY GOD!!
I'M IN PURE ECSTASY!! I-I CAN SEE THROUGH TIIIIIME...!!!
GO BACK TO THE FUTURE AND HONOR THIS DICK, BABY.
THE END
DADDY, WHEN I GROW UP CAN I ROCK A MOHAWK?
I DON'T THINK SO, SON.

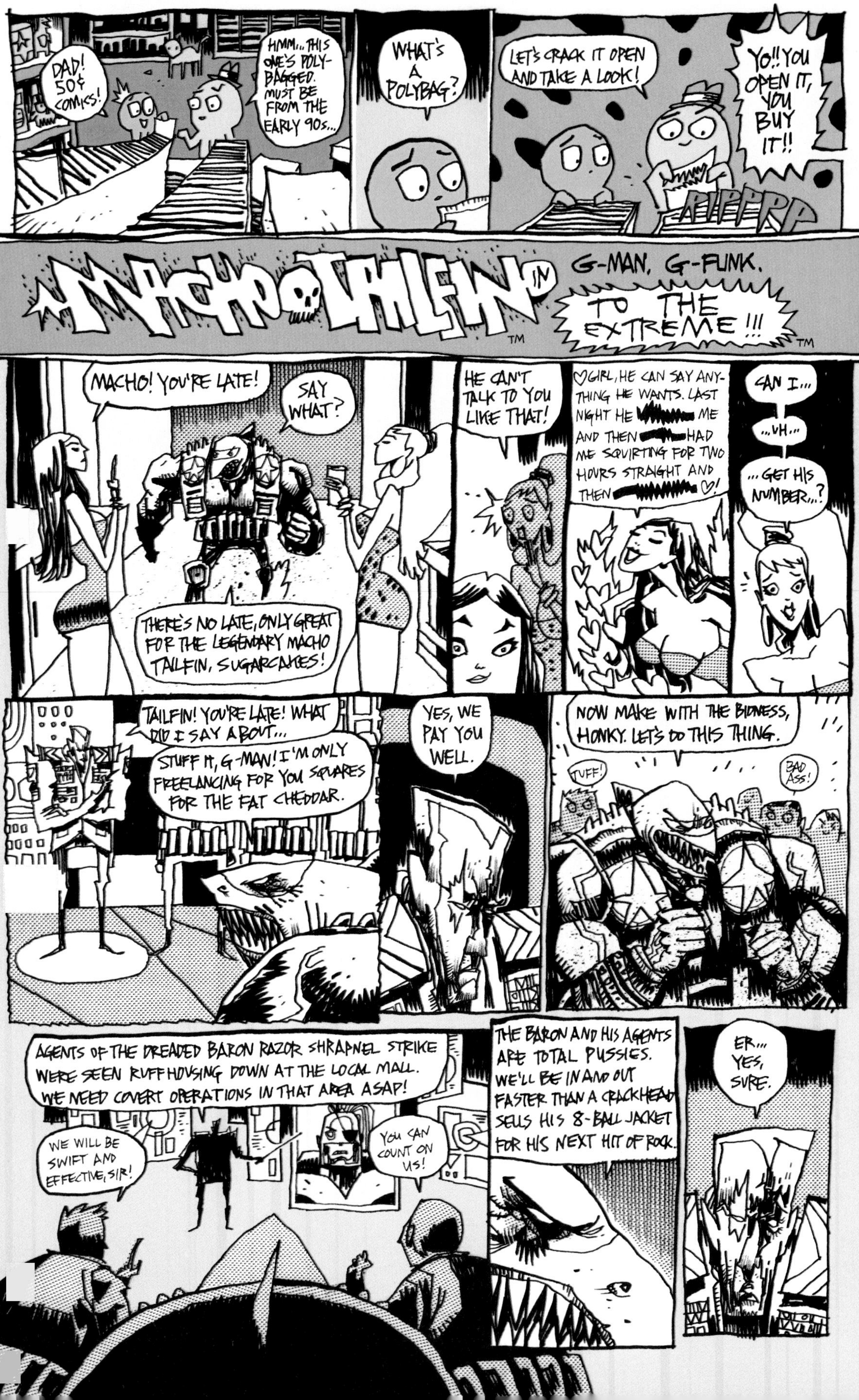
DAD! 50¢ COMICS!
HMM... THIS ONE'S POLY-BAGGED. MUST BE FROM THE EARLY 90s...
WHAT'S A POLYBAG?
LET'S CRACK IT OPEN AND TAKE A LOOK!
RIPPPP
YO!! YOU OPEN IT, YOU BUY IT!!
MACHO TAILFIN IN
G-MAN, G-FUNK, TO THE EXTREME!!! TM
TM
MACHO! YOU'RE LATE!
SAY WHAT?
THERE'S NO LATE, ONLY GREAT FOR THE LEGENDARY MACHO TAILFIN, SUGARCAKES!
HE CAN'T TALK TO YOU LIKE THAT!
♡GIRL, HE CAN SAY ANYTHING HE WANTS. LAST NIGHT HE [redacted] ME AND THEN [redacted] HAD ME SQUIRTING FOR TWO HOURS STRAIGHT AND THEN [redacted]♡!
CAN I...
...UH...
...GET HIS NUMBER...?
TAILFIN! YOU'RE LATE! WHAT DID I SAY ABOUT...
STUFF IT, G-MAN! I'M ONLY FREELANCING FOR YOU SQUARES FOR THE FAT CHEDDAR.
YES, WE PAY YOU WELL.
NOW MAKE WITH THE BIDNESS, HONKY. LET'S DO THIS THING.
TUFF!
BAD ASS!
AGENTS OF THE DREADED BARON RAZOR SHRAPNEL STRIKE WERE SEEN RUFFHOUSING DOWN AT THE LOCAL MALL. WE NEED COVERT OPERATIONS IN THAT AREA ASAP!
WE WILL BE SWIFT AND EFFECTIVE, SIR!
YOU CAN COUNT ON US!
THE BARON AND HIS AGENTS ARE TOTAL PUSSIES. WE'LL BE IN AND OUT FASTER THAN A CRACKHEAD SELLS HIS 8-BALL JACKET FOR HIS NEXT HIT OF ROCK.
ER... YES, SURE.

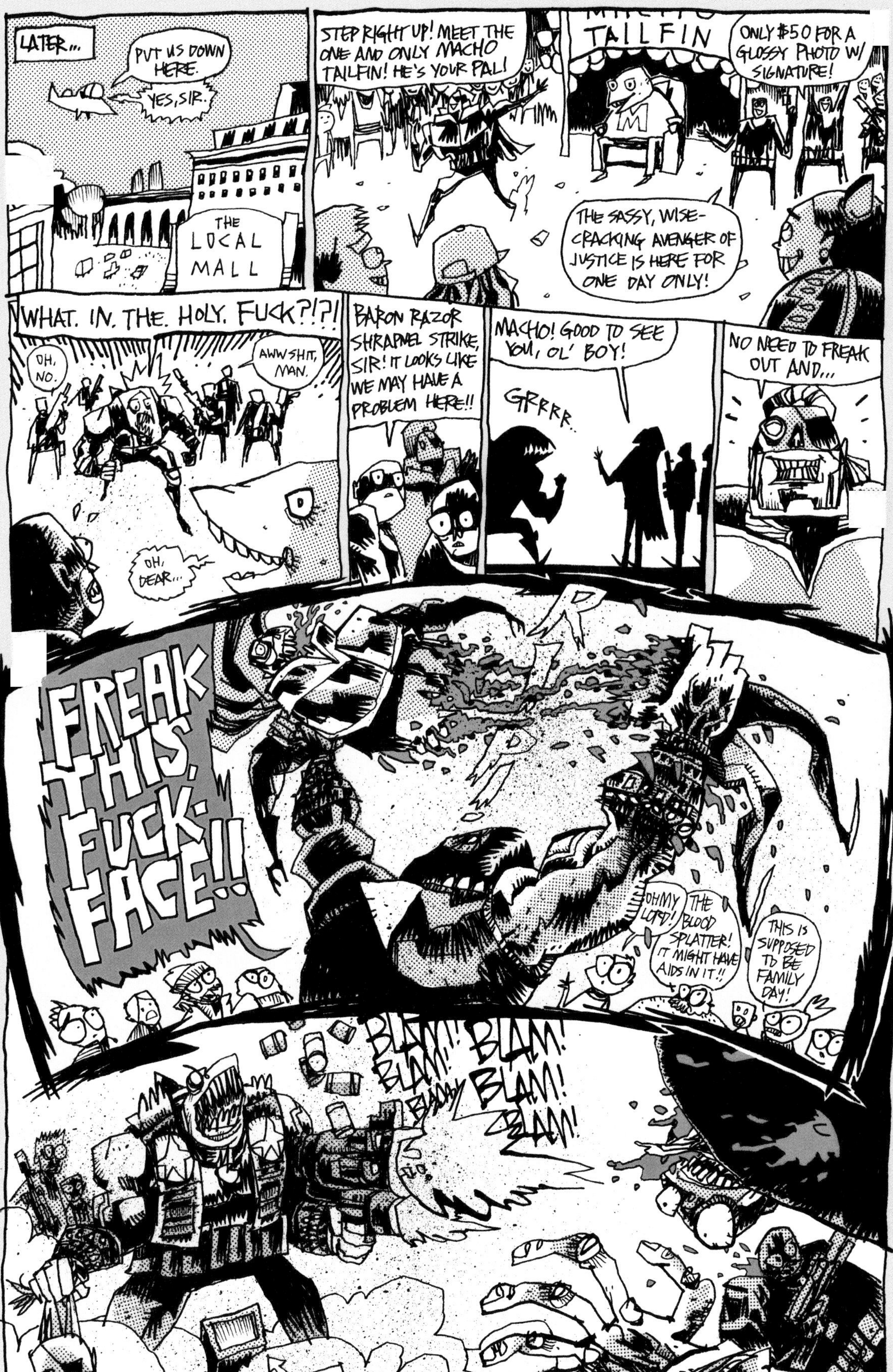
LATER...
PUT US DOWN HERE.
YES, SIR.
THE LOCAL MALL
STEP RIGHT UP! MEET THE ONE AND ONLY MACHO TAILFIN! HE'S YOUR PAL!
TAILFIN
ONLY $50 FOR A GLOSSY PHOTO W/ SIGNATURE!
THE SASSY, WISE-CRACKING AVENGER OF JUSTICE IS HERE FOR ONE DAY ONLY!
WHAT. IN. THE. HOLY. FUCK?!?!
OH, NO.
AWW SHIT, MAN.
OH, DEAR...
BARON RAZOR SHRAPNEL STRIKE, SIR! IT LOOKS LIKE WE MAY HAVE A PROBLEM HERE!!
MACHO! GOOD TO SEE YOU, OL' BOY!
GRRRR.
NO NEED TO FREAK OUT AND...
FREAK THIS, FUCK-FACE!!
OHMY LORD!
THE BLOOD SPLATTER! IT MIGHT HAVE AIDS IN IT!!
THIS IS SUPPOSED TO BE FAMILY DAY!
BLAM! BLAM! BLAM! BLAM! BLAM! BLAM!
SMOKE MACHINE.
$100.

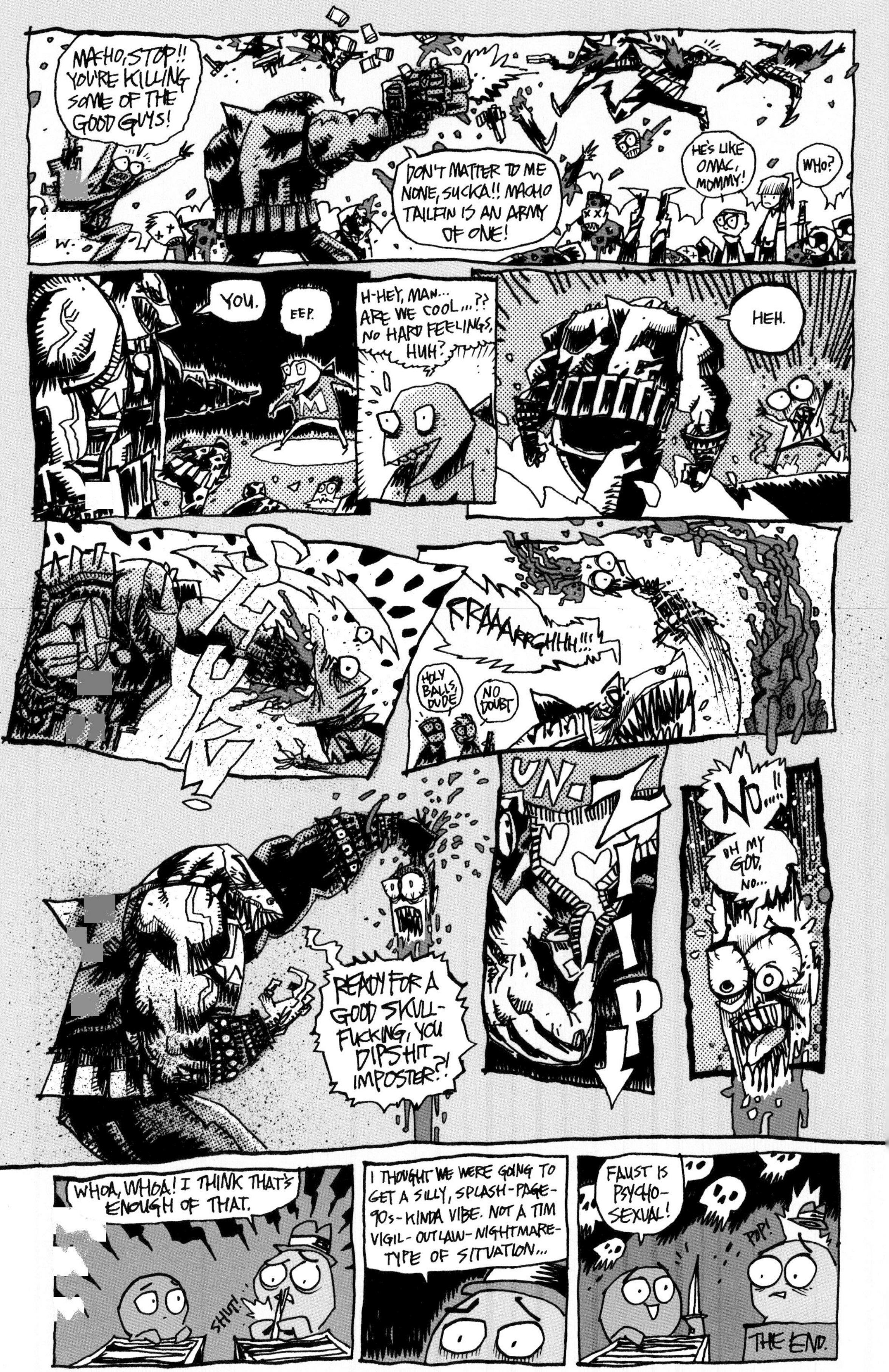
MACHO, STOP!! YOU'RE KILLING SOME OF THE GOOD GUYS!
DON'T MATTER TO ME NONE, SUCKA!! MACHO TAILFIN IS AN ARMY OF ONE!
HE'S LIKE OMAC, MOMMY!
WHO?
YOU.
EEP.
H-HEY, MAN... ARE WE COOL...?? NO HARD FEELINGS, HUH?
HEH.
FRAAAARRGHHH!!!
HOLY BALLS, DUDE
NO DOUBT
UN-
ZIP
READY FOR A GOOD SKULL-FUCKING, YOU DIPSHIT IMPOSTER?!
NO...!!
OH MY GOD, NO...
WHOA, WHOA! I THINK THAT'S ENOUGH OF THAT.
SHUT!
I THOUGHT WE WERE GOING TO GET A SILLY, SPLASH-PAGE-90s-KINDA VIBE. NOT A TIM VIGIL-OUTLAW-NIGHTMARE-TYPE OF SITUATION...
FAUST IS PSYCHO-SEXUAL!
POP!
THE END.

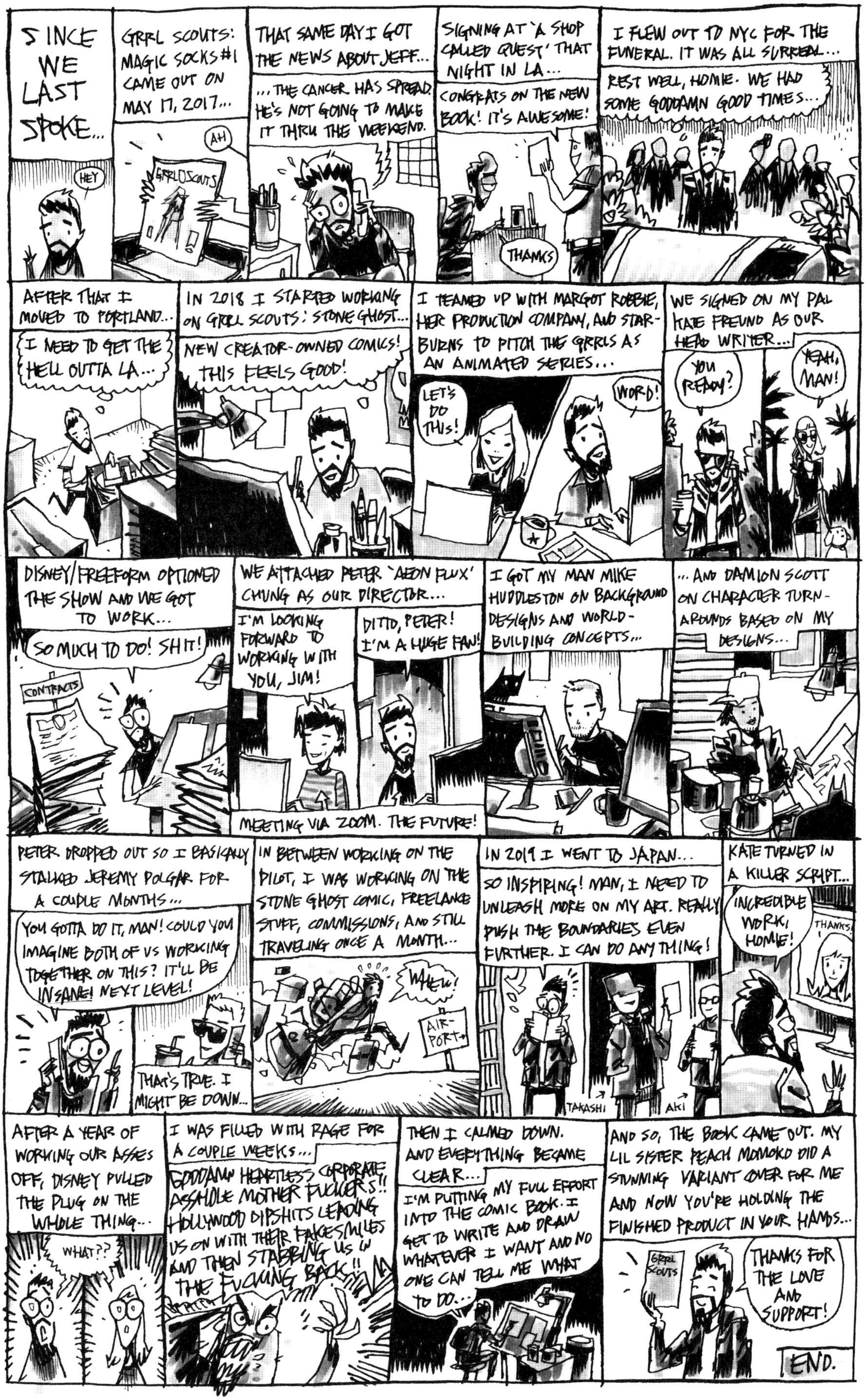
SINCE WE LAST SPOKE...
HEY
GRRL SCOUTS: MAGIC SOCKS #1 CAME OUT ON MAY 17, 2017...
AH
GRRL SCOUTS
THAT SAME DAY I GOT THE NEWS ABOUT JEFF...
...THE CANCER HAS SPREAD. HE'S NOT GOING TO MAKE IT THRU THE WEEKEND.
SIGNING AT A SHOP CALLED 'QUEST' THAT NIGHT IN LA...
CONGRATS ON THE NEW BOOK! IT'S AWESOME!
THANKS
I FLEW OUT TO NYC FOR THE FUNERAL. IT WAS ALL SURREAL...
REST WELL, HOMIE. WE HAD SOME GODDAMN GOOD TIMES...
AFTER THAT I MOVED TO PORTLAND...
I NEED TO GET THE HELL OUTTA LA...
IN 2018 I STARTED WORKING ON GRRL SCOUTS: STONE GHOST...
NEW CREATOR-OWNED COMICS! THIS FEELS GOOD!
I TEAMED UP WITH MARGOT ROBBIE, HER PRODUCTION COMPANY, AND STARBURNS TO PITCH THE GRRLS AS AN ANIMATED SERIES...
LET'S DO THIS!
WORD!
WE SIGNED ON MY PAL KATE FREUND AS OUR HEAD WRITER...
YOU READY?
YEAH, MAN!
DISNEY/FREEFORM OPTIONED THE SHOW AND WE GOT TO WORK...
SO MUCH TO DO! SHIT!
CONTRACTS
WE ATTACHED PETER 'AEON FLUX' CHUNG AS OUR DIRECTOR...
I'M LOOKING FORWARD TO WORKING WITH YOU, JIM!
DITTO, PETER! I'M A HUGE FAN!
MEETING VIA ZOOM. THE FUTURE!
I GOT MY MAN MIKE HUDDLESTON ON BACKGROUND DESIGNS AND WORLD-BUILDING CONCEPTS...
...AND DAMION SCOTT ON CHARACTER TURN-AROUNDS BASED ON MY DESIGNS...
PETER DROPPED OUT SO I BASICALLY STALKED JEREMY POLGAR FOR A COUPLE MONTHS...
YOU GOTTA DO IT, MAN! COULD YOU IMAGINE BOTH OF US WORKING TOGETHER ON THIS? IT'LL BE INSANE! NEXT LEVEL!
THAT'S TRUE. I MIGHT BE DOWN...
IN BETWEEN WORKING ON THE PILOT, I WAS WORKING ON THE STONE GHOST COMIC, FREELANCE STUFF, COMMISSIONS, AND STILL TRAVELING ONCE A MONTH...
WHEW!
AIR-PORT
IN 2019 I WENT TO JAPAN...
SO INSPIRING! MAN, I NEED TO UNLEASH MORE ON MY ART. REALLY PUSH THE BOUNDARIES EVEN FURTHER. I CAN DO ANYTHING!
TAKASHI
AKI
KATE TURNED IN A KILLER SCRIPT...
INCREDIBLE WORK, HOMIE!
THANKS!
AFTER A YEAR OF WORKING OUR ASSES OFF, DISNEY PULLED THE PLUG ON THE WHOLE THING...
WHAT??
I WAS FILLED WITH RAGE FOR A COUPLE WEEKS...
GODDAMN HEARTLESS CORPORATE ASSHOLE MOTHER FUCKERS!! HOLLYWOOD DIPSHITS LEADING US ON WITH THEIR FAKE SMILES AND THEN STABBING US IN THE FUCKING BACK!!
THEN I CALMED DOWN. AND EVERYTHING BECAME CLEAR...
I'M PUTTING MY FULL EFFORT INTO THE COMIC BOOK. I GET TO WRITE AND DRAW WHATEVER I WANT AND NO ONE CAN TELL ME WHAT TO DO...
AND SO, THE BOOK CAME OUT. MY LIL SISTER PEACH MOMOKO DID A STUNNING VARIANT COVER FOR ME AND NOW YOU'RE HOLDING THE FINISHED PRODUCT IN YOUR HANDS...
GRRL SCOUTS
THANKS FOR THE LOVE AND SUPPORT!
END.

JIM MAHFOOD

LOCAL COMIC SHOP DAY VARIANT

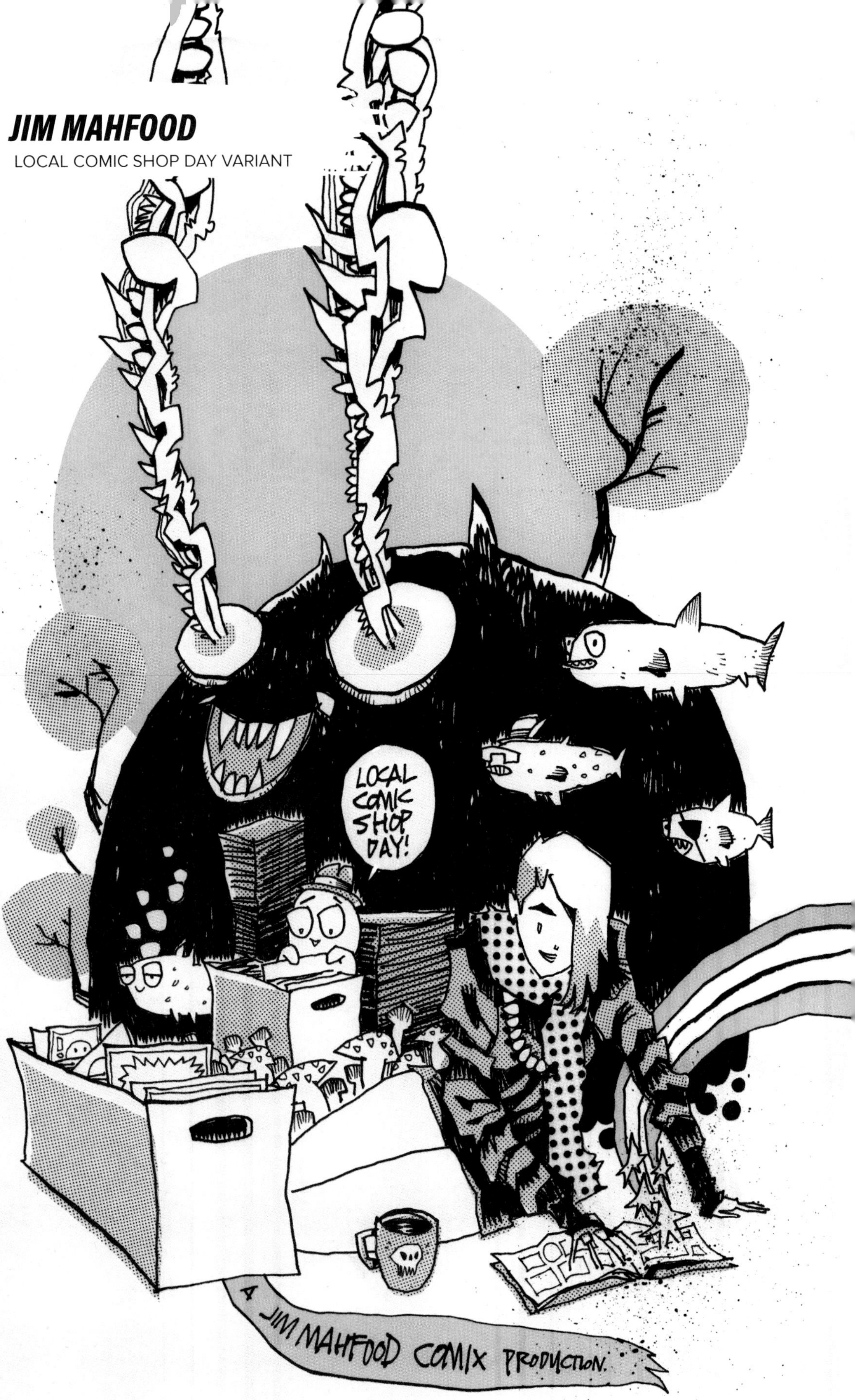
LOCAL COMIC SHOP DAY!
A JIM MAHFOOD COMIX PRODUCTION.

PEACH MOMOKO

RETAILER EXCLUSIVE VARIANT: 1 IN 25

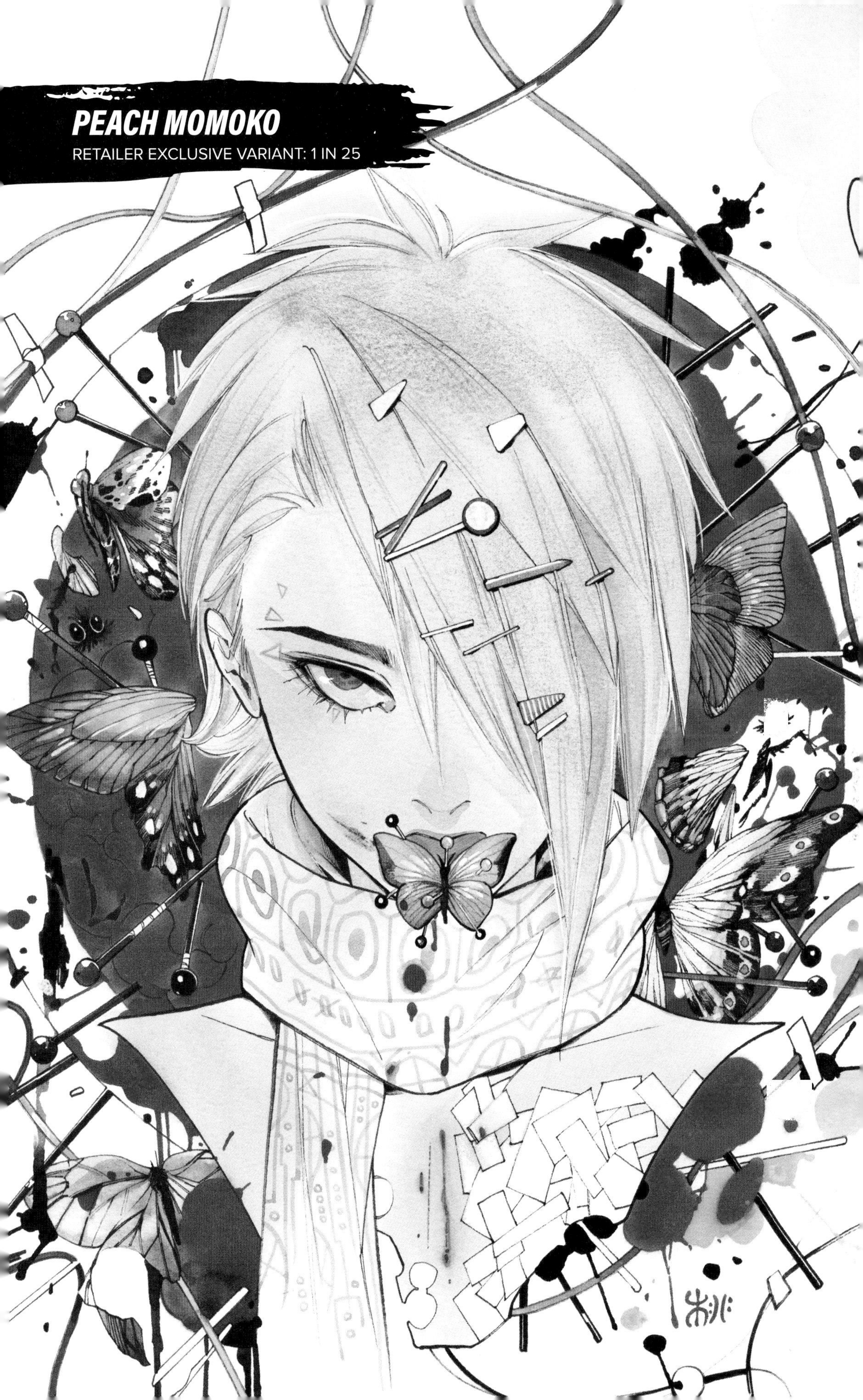

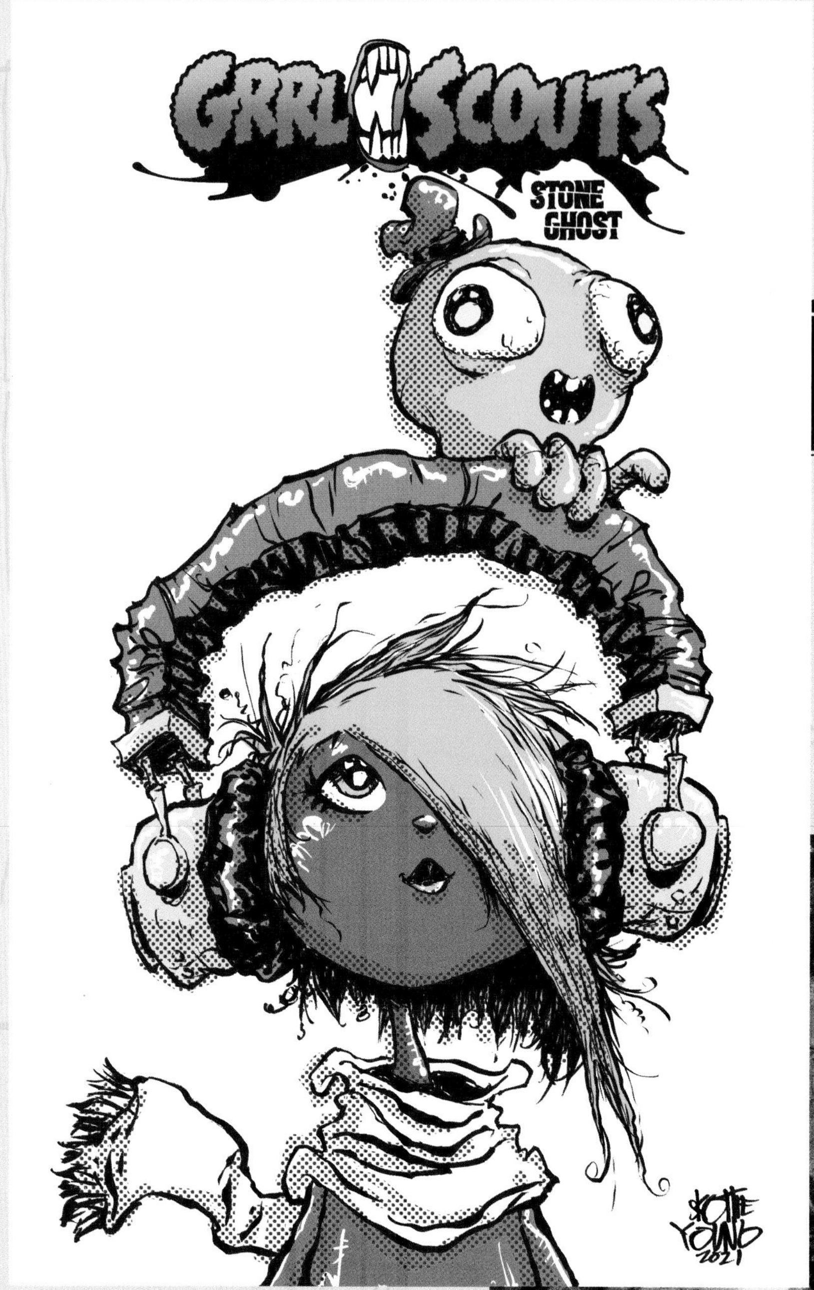
GRRL SCOUTS
STONE GHOST
SKOTTIE YOUNG 2021

SKOTTIE YOUNG
STUPID FRESH MESS
EXCLUSIVE VARIANT

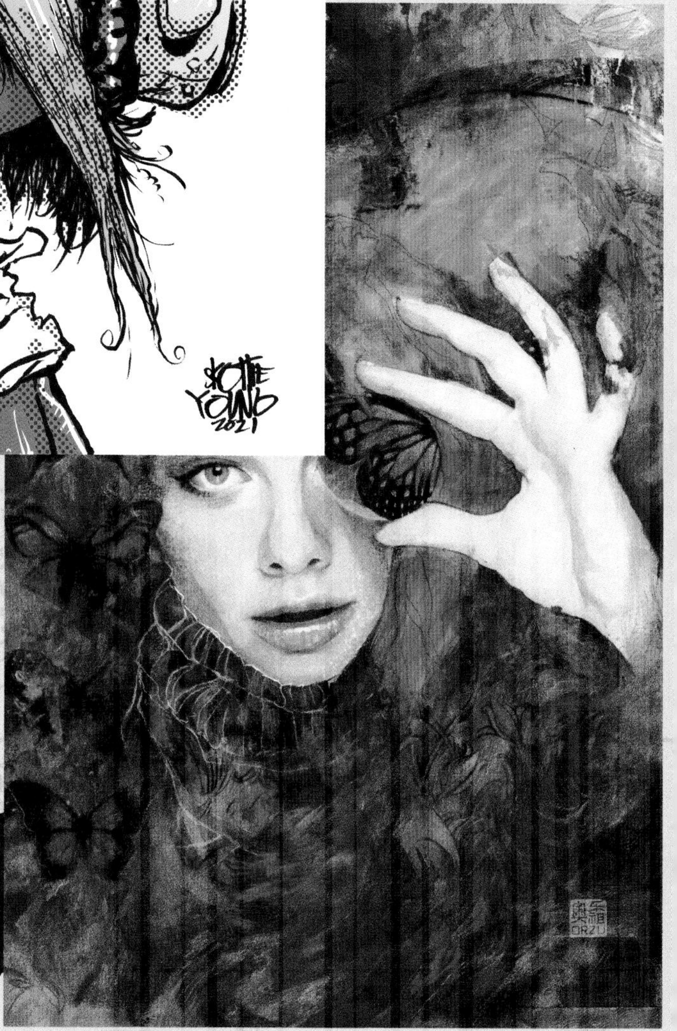
ORZU

ZU ORZU
THE COMIC CORNER STORE
EXCLUSIVE VARIANT

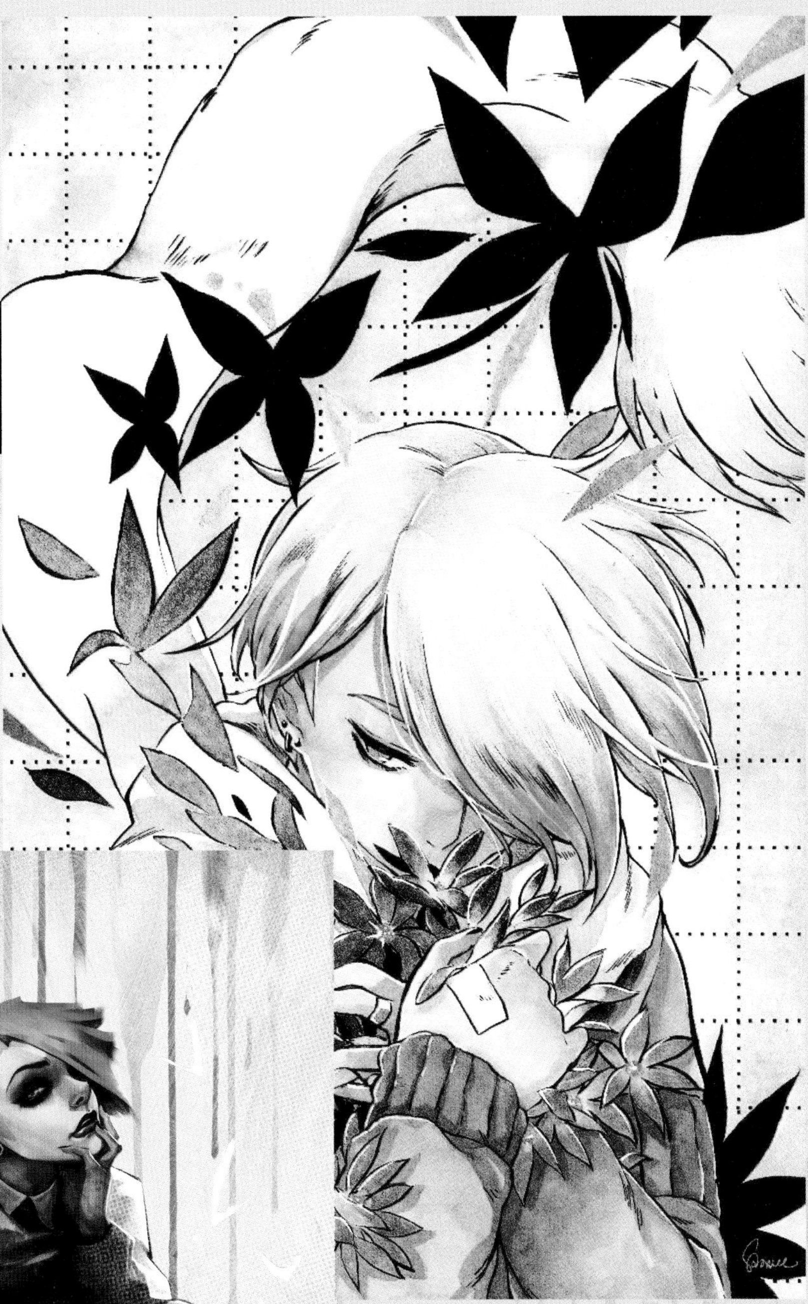

SAOWEE

COMIC GRAIL VAULT
EXCLUSIVE VARIANT

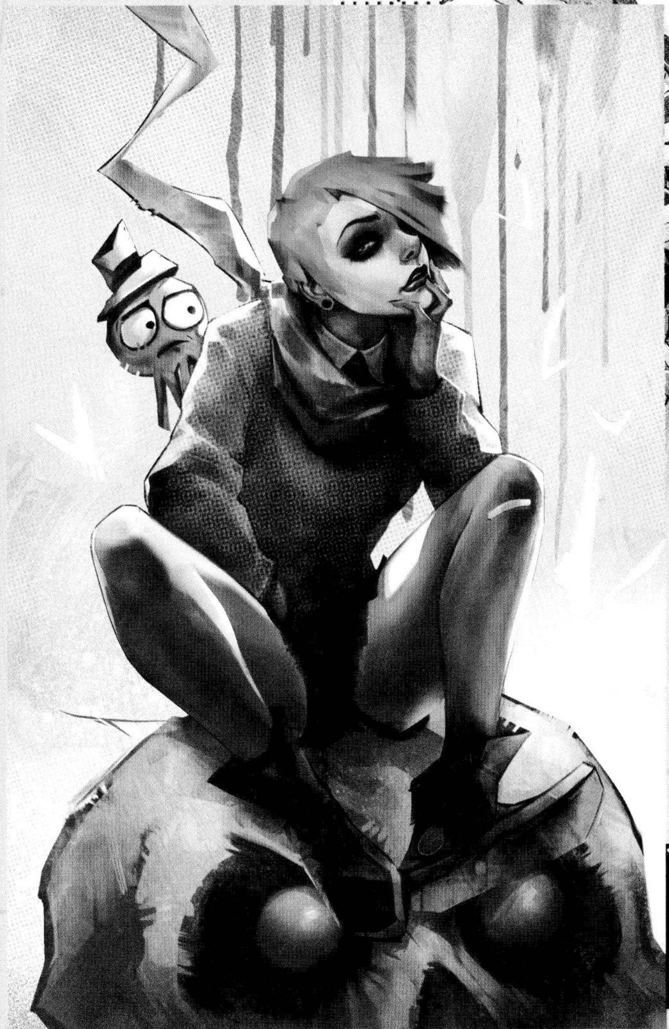

IVAN TAO

RABBIT COMICS STORE
EXCLUSIVE VARIANT

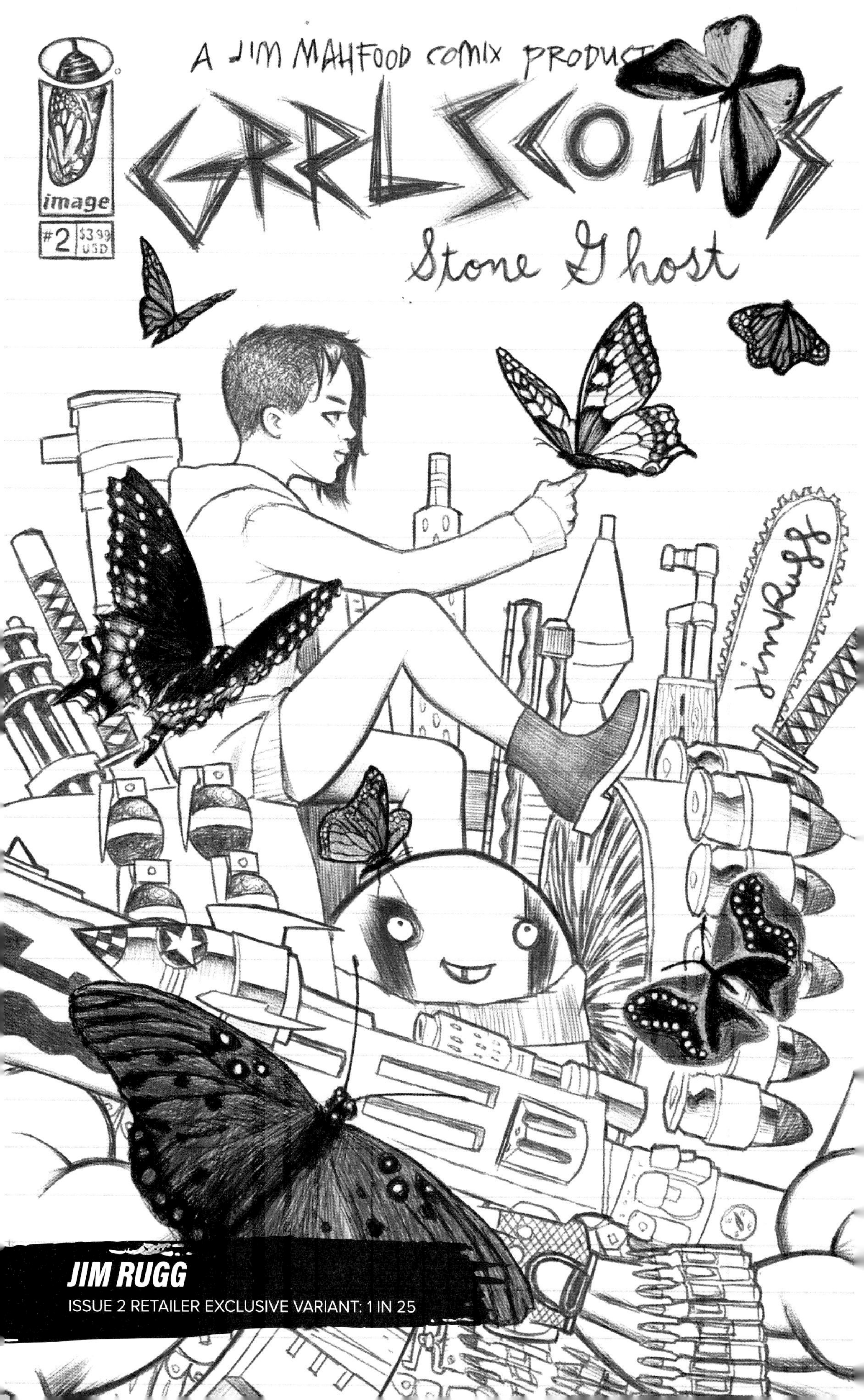
A JIM MAHFOOD COMIX PRODUCT
image
#2 $3.99 USD
GRRL SCOUTS
Stone Ghost
jim Rugg
JIM RUGG
ISSUE 2 RETAILER EXCLUSIVE VARIANT: 1 IN 25

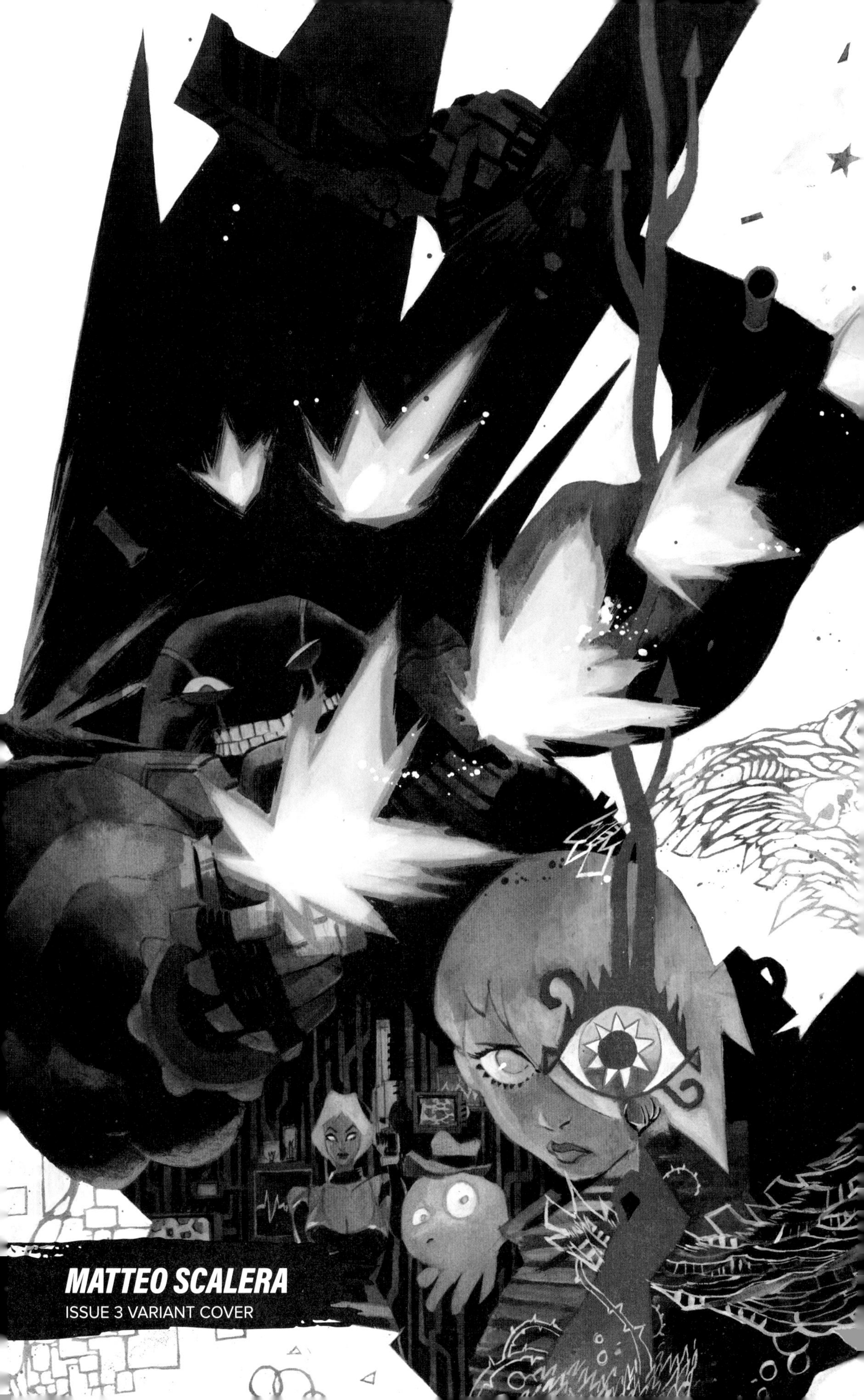

MATTEO SCALERA

ISSUE 3 VARIANT COVER

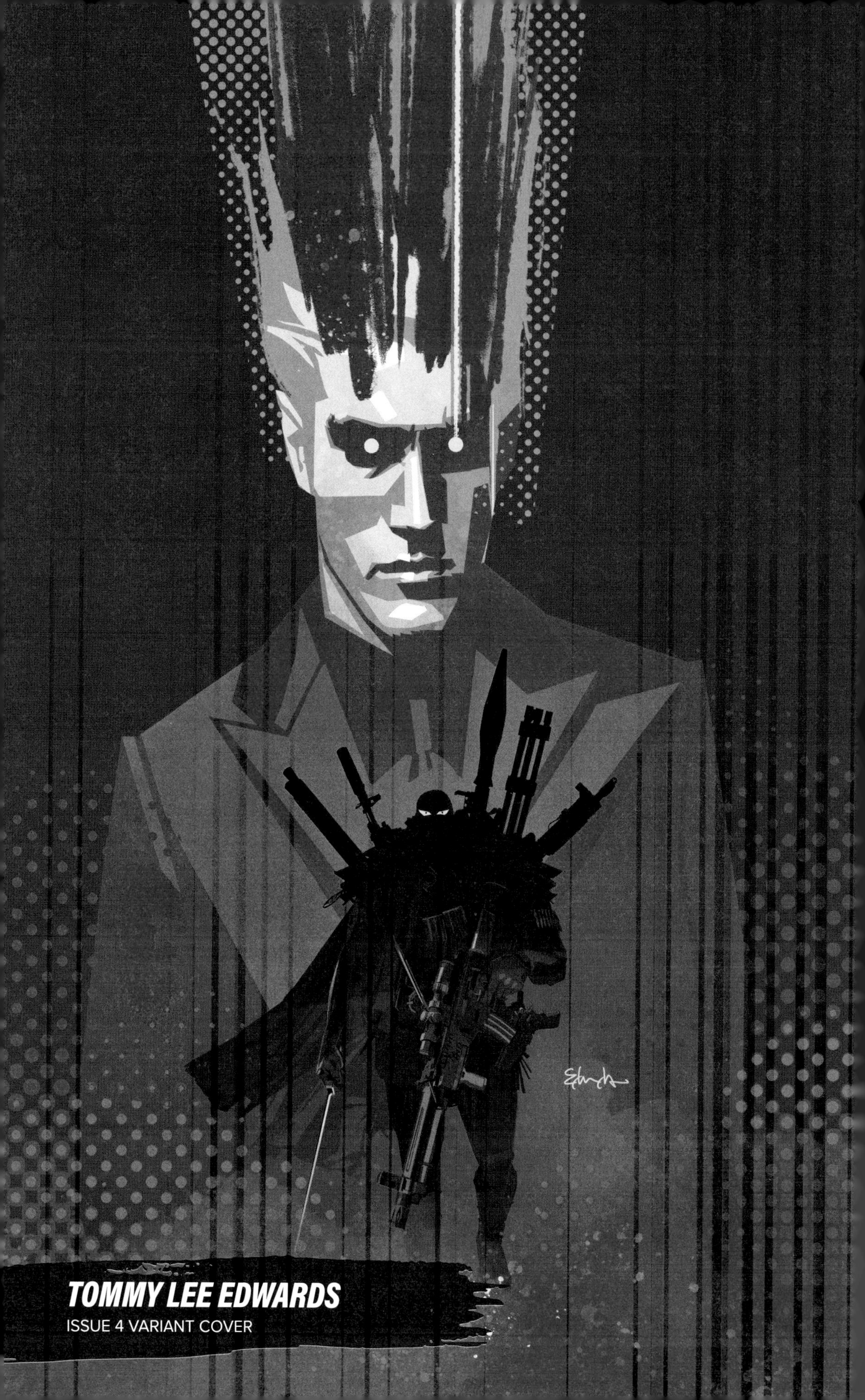

TOMMY LEE EDWARDS

ISSUE 4 VARIANT COVER

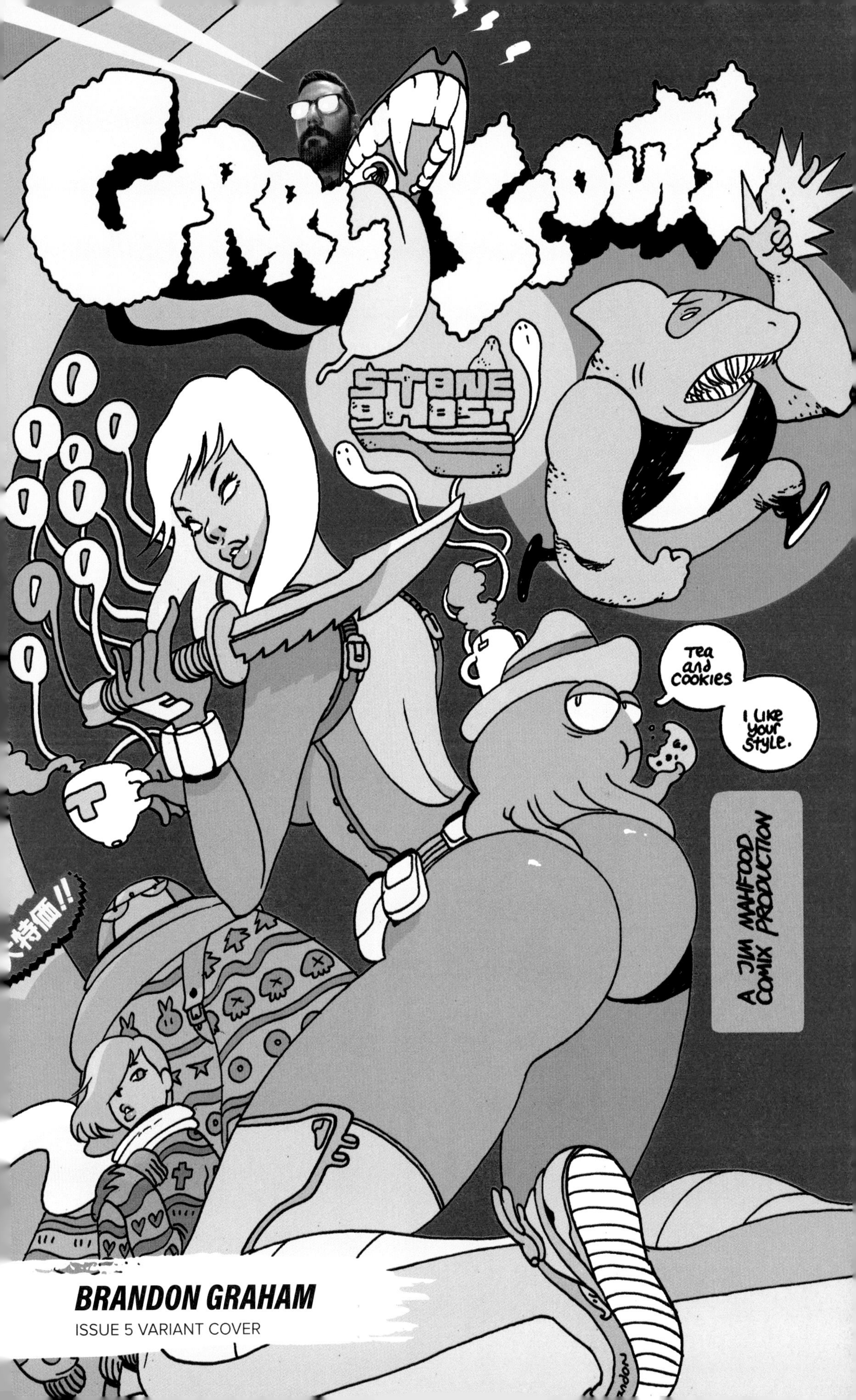

STONE GHOST
Tea and Cookies
I like your style.
A JIM MAHFOOD COMIX PRODUCTION
特価!!

BRANDON GRAHAM

ISSUE 5 VARIANT COVER

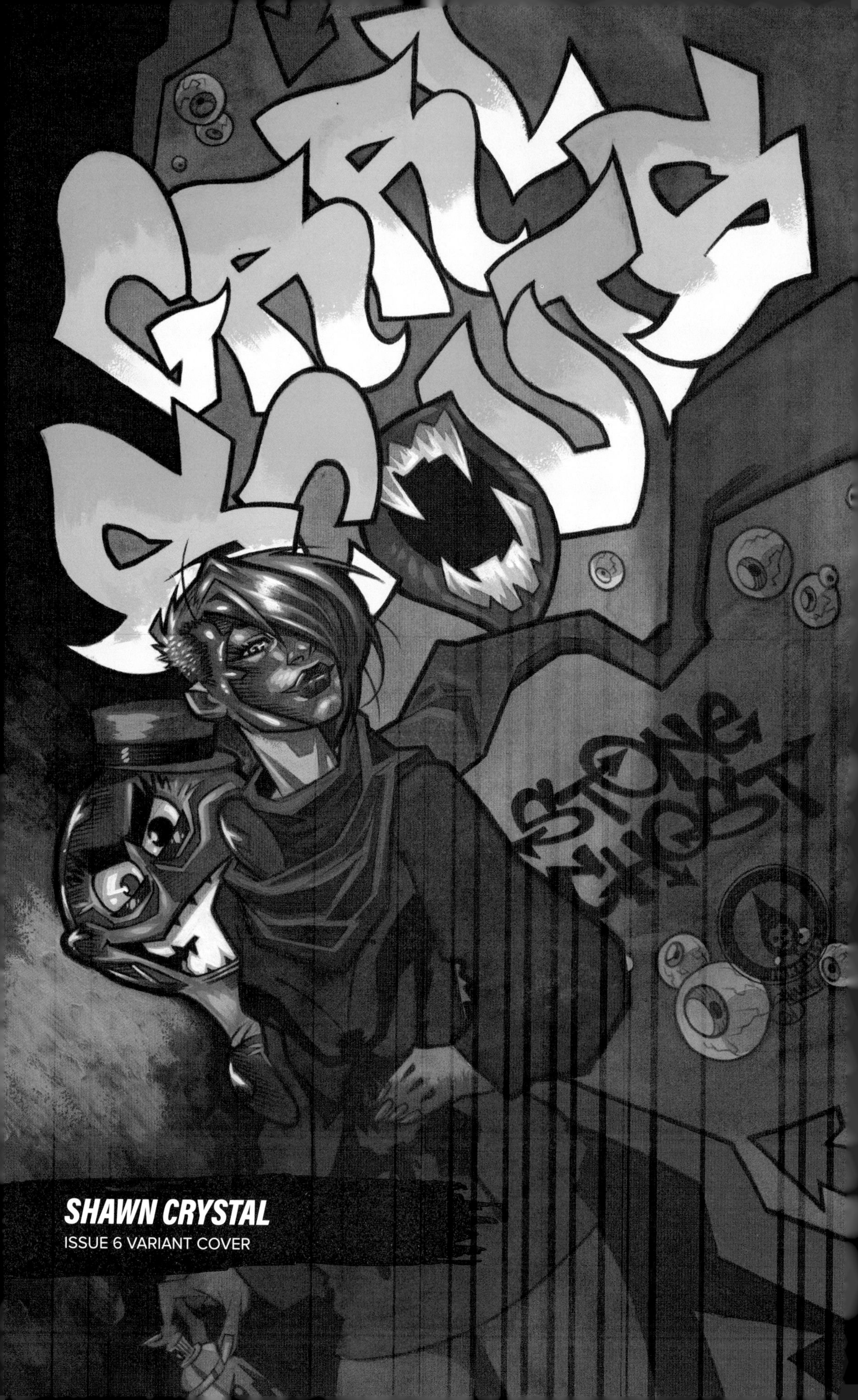

SHAWN CRYSTAL
ISSUE 6 VARIANT COVER

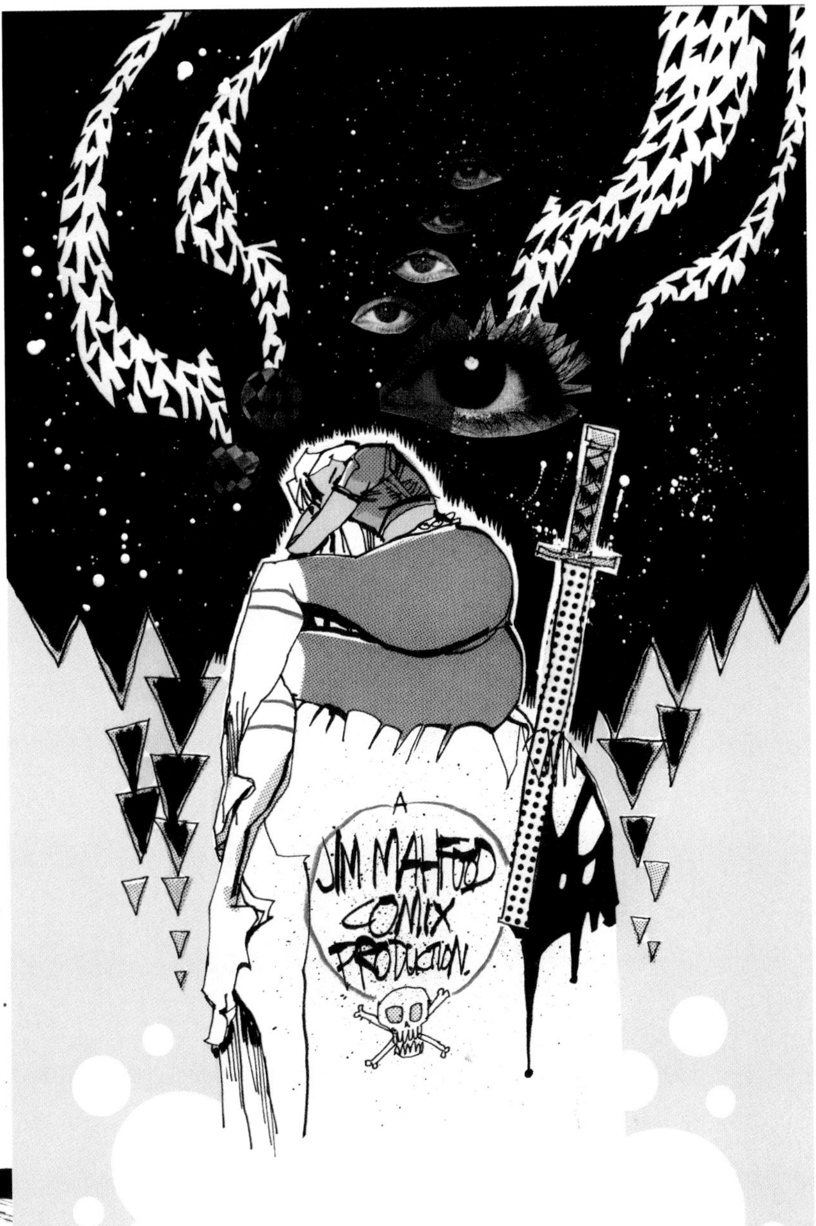
A
JIM MAHFOOD
COMIX
PRODUCTION.

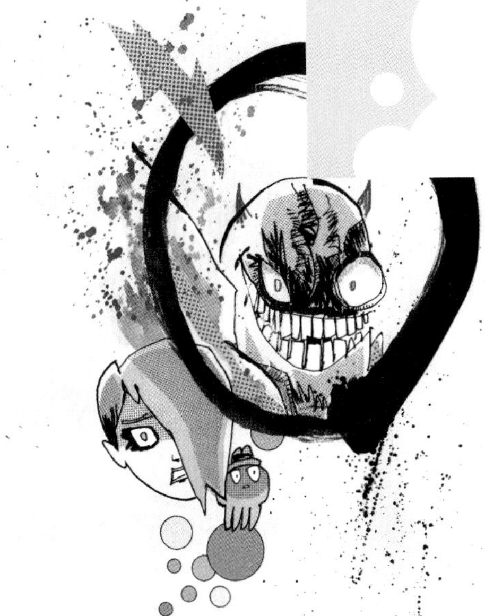

JIM MAHFOOD

UNUSED COVERS
FOR ISSUES 2 AND 5

SKETCHBOOK
AND BEHIND THE SCENES...

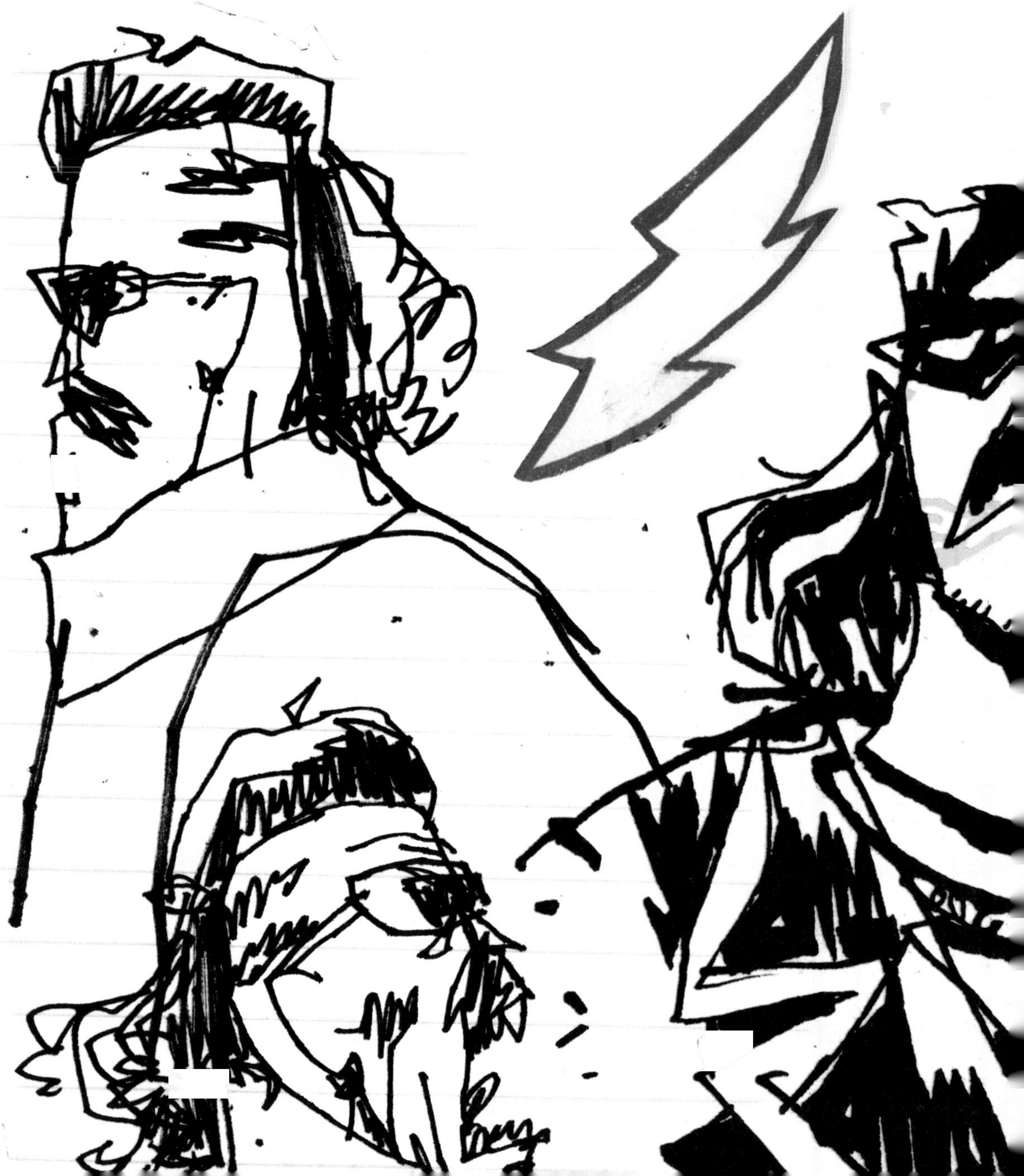

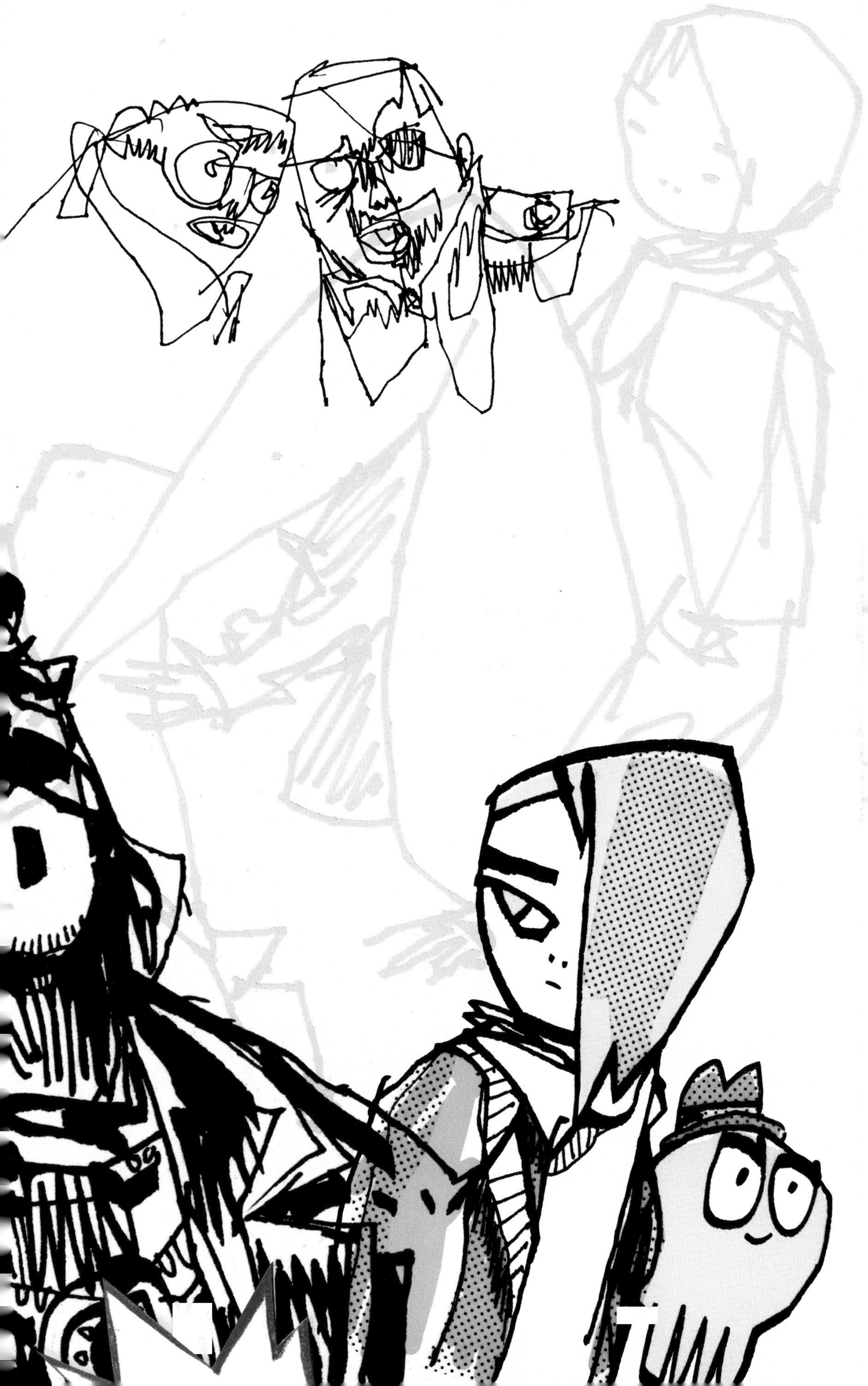

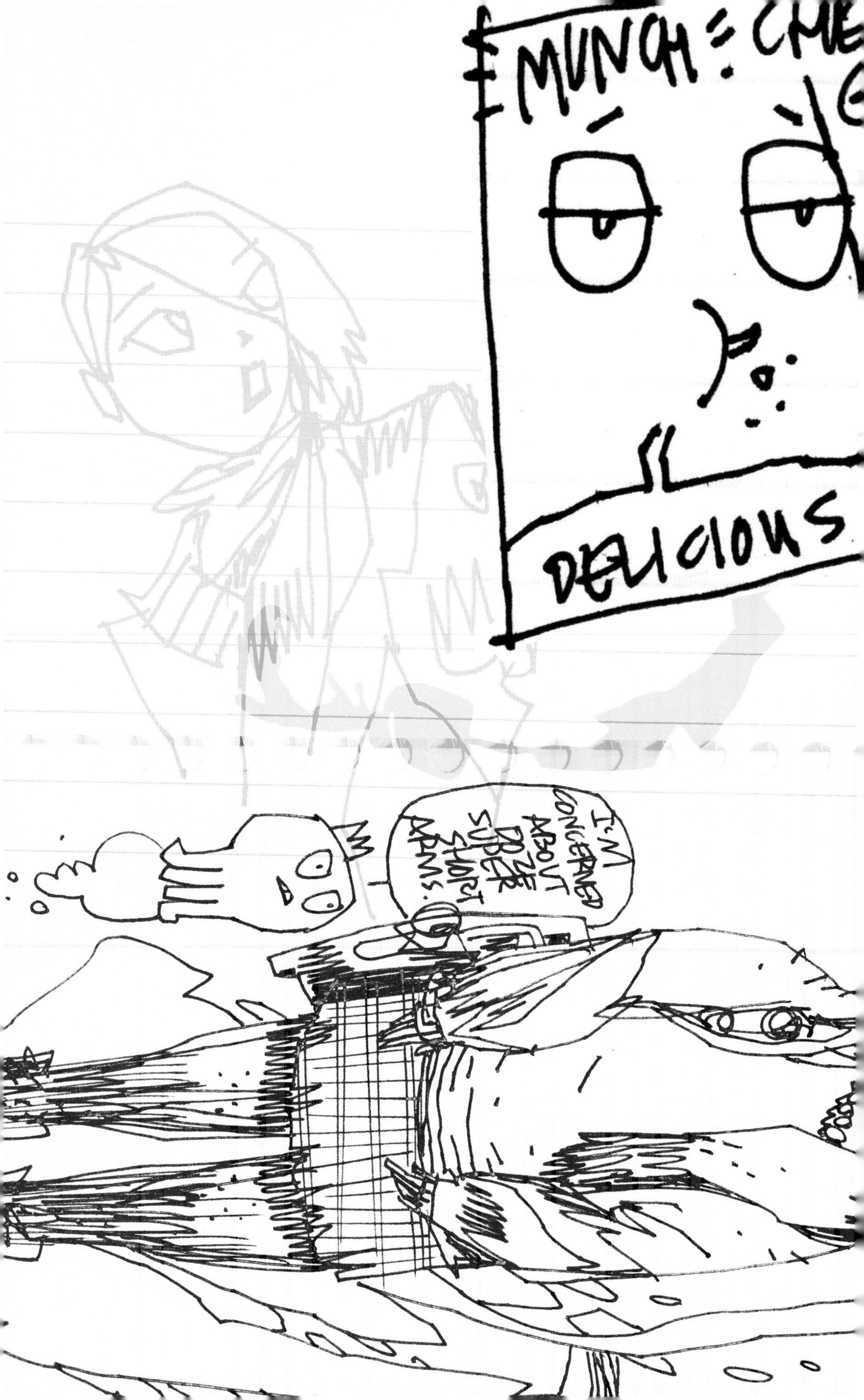
MUNCH = CHE
DELICIOUS
I'M CONCERNED ABOUT DOZE SUPER SHORT ARMS.

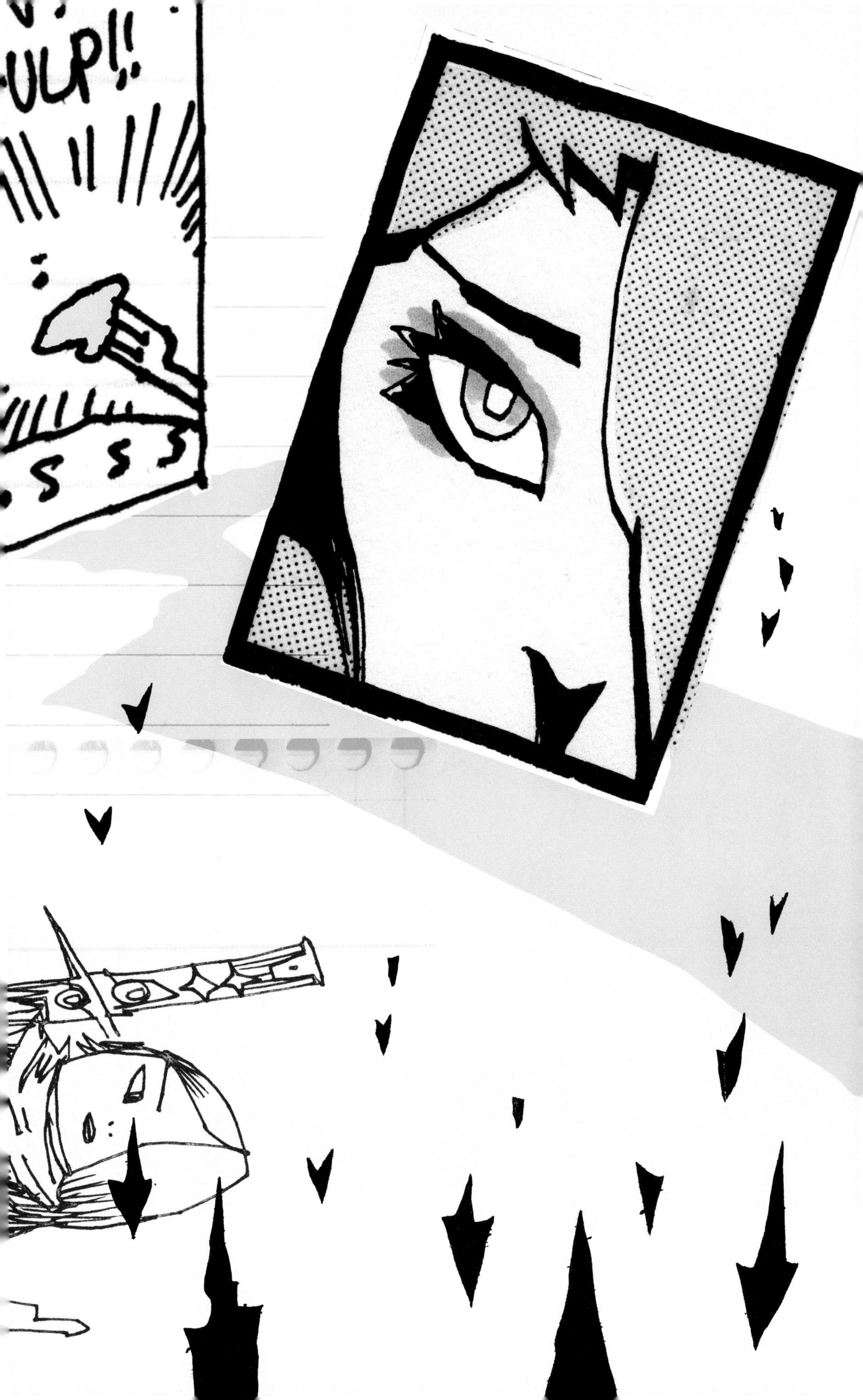
ULP!!

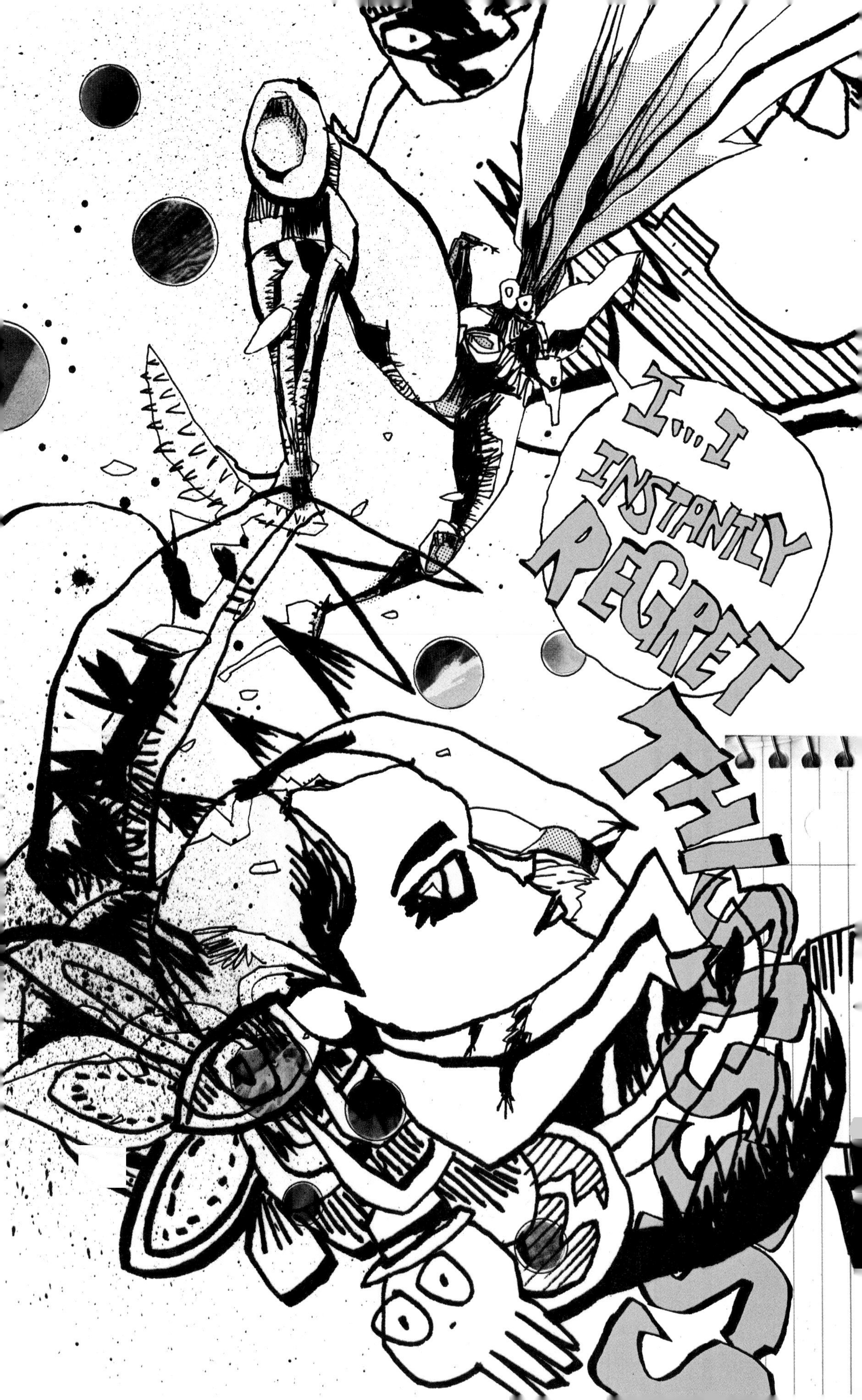
I...I INSTANTLY REGRET THIS

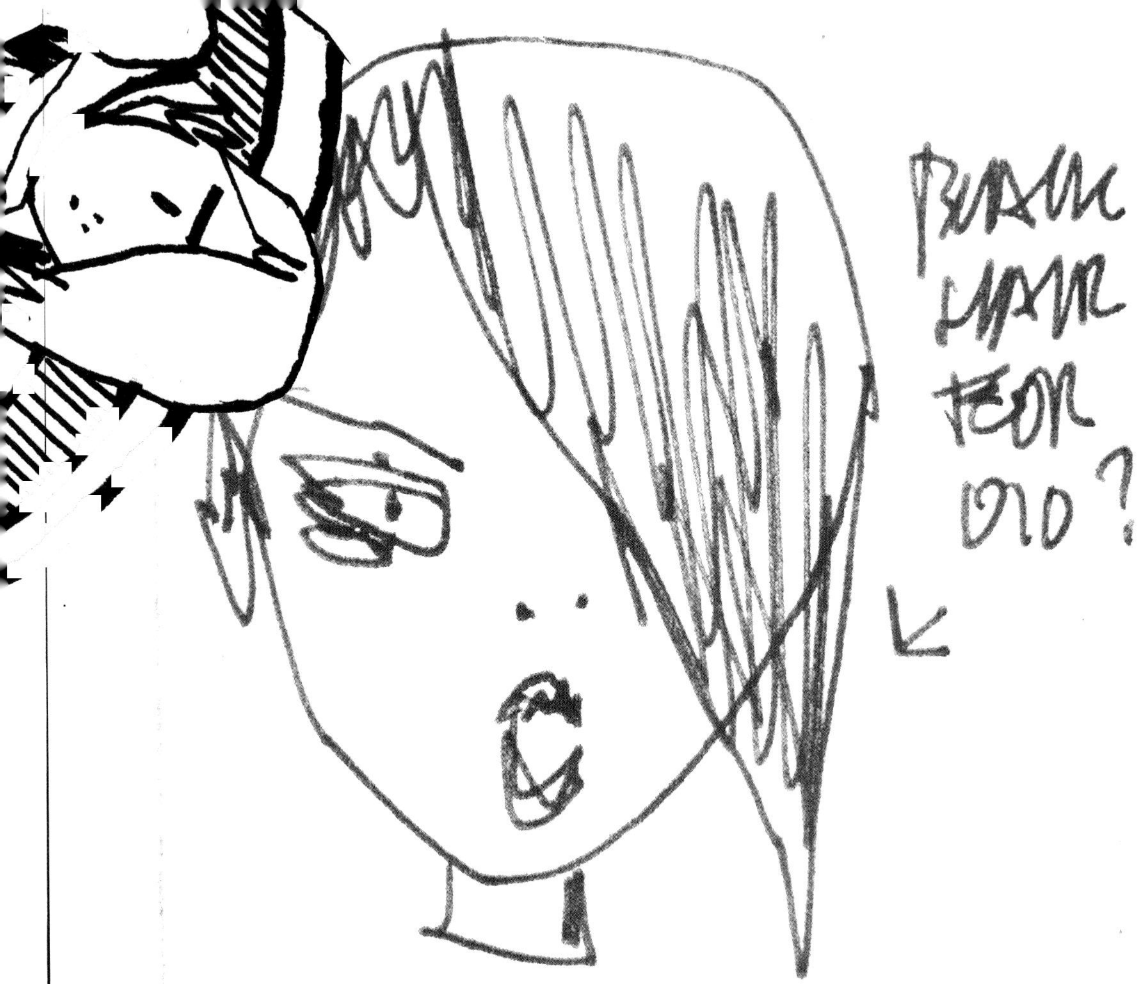
BLACK HAIR FOR DIO?

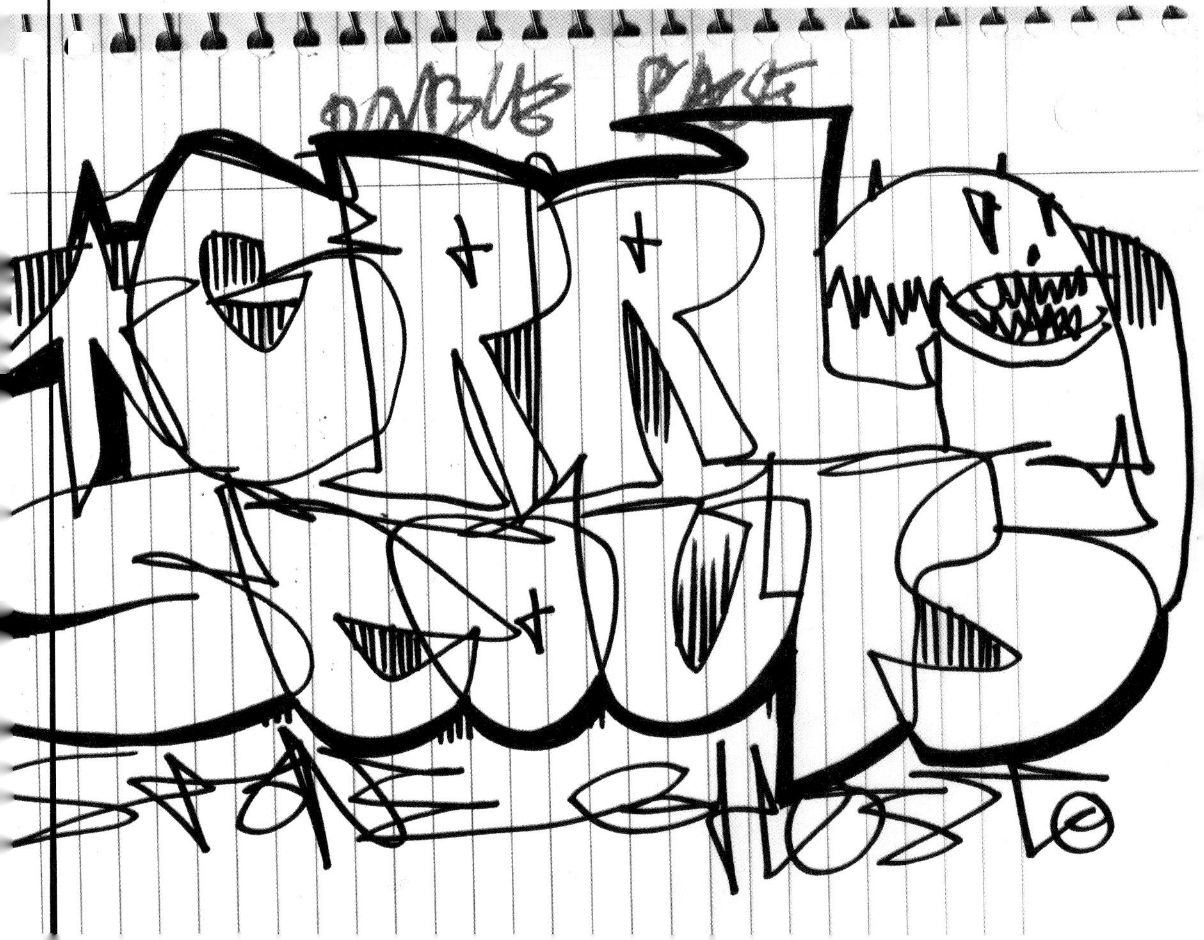
DOUBLE PAGE

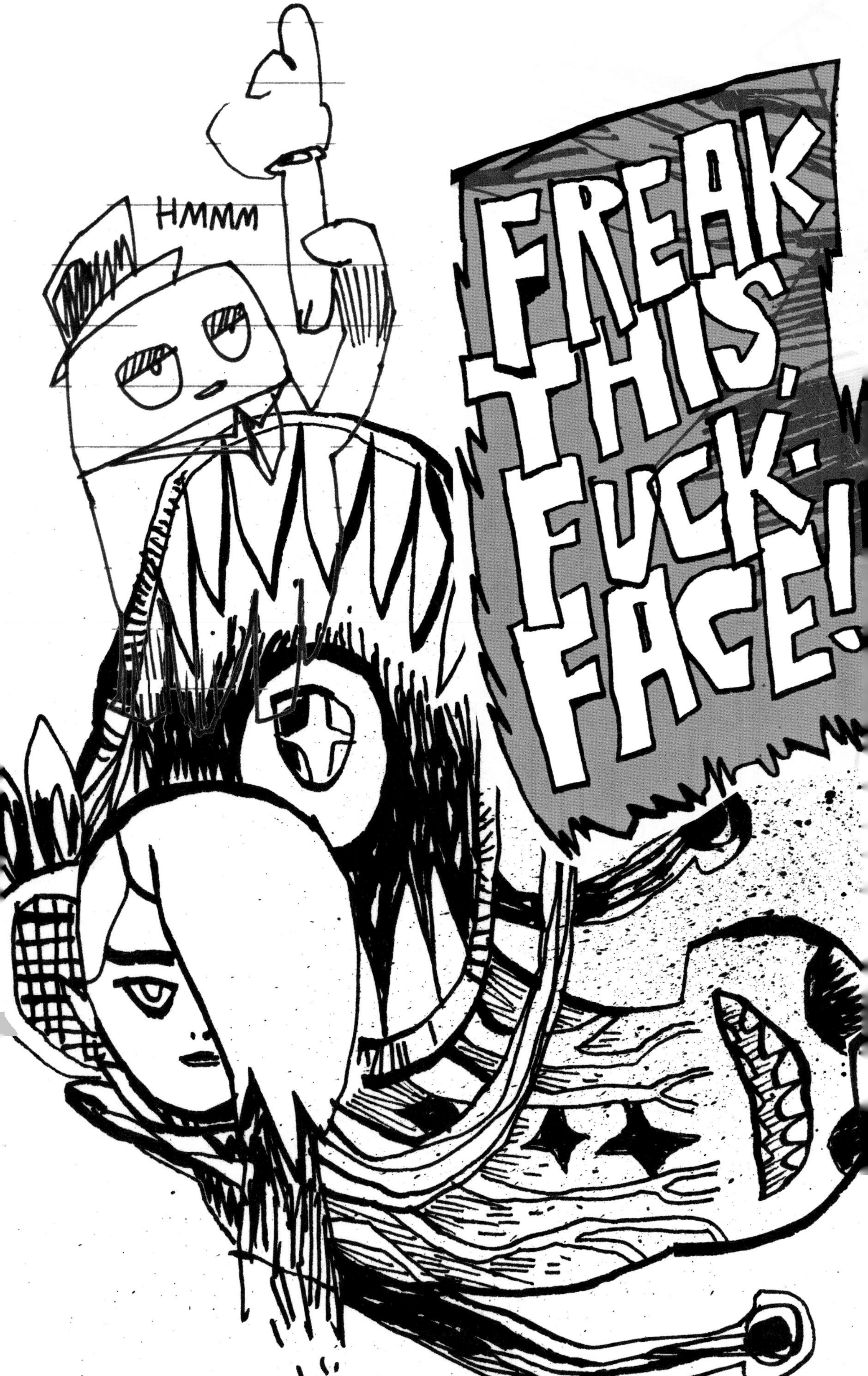
HMMM
FREAK THIS, FUCK-FACE!

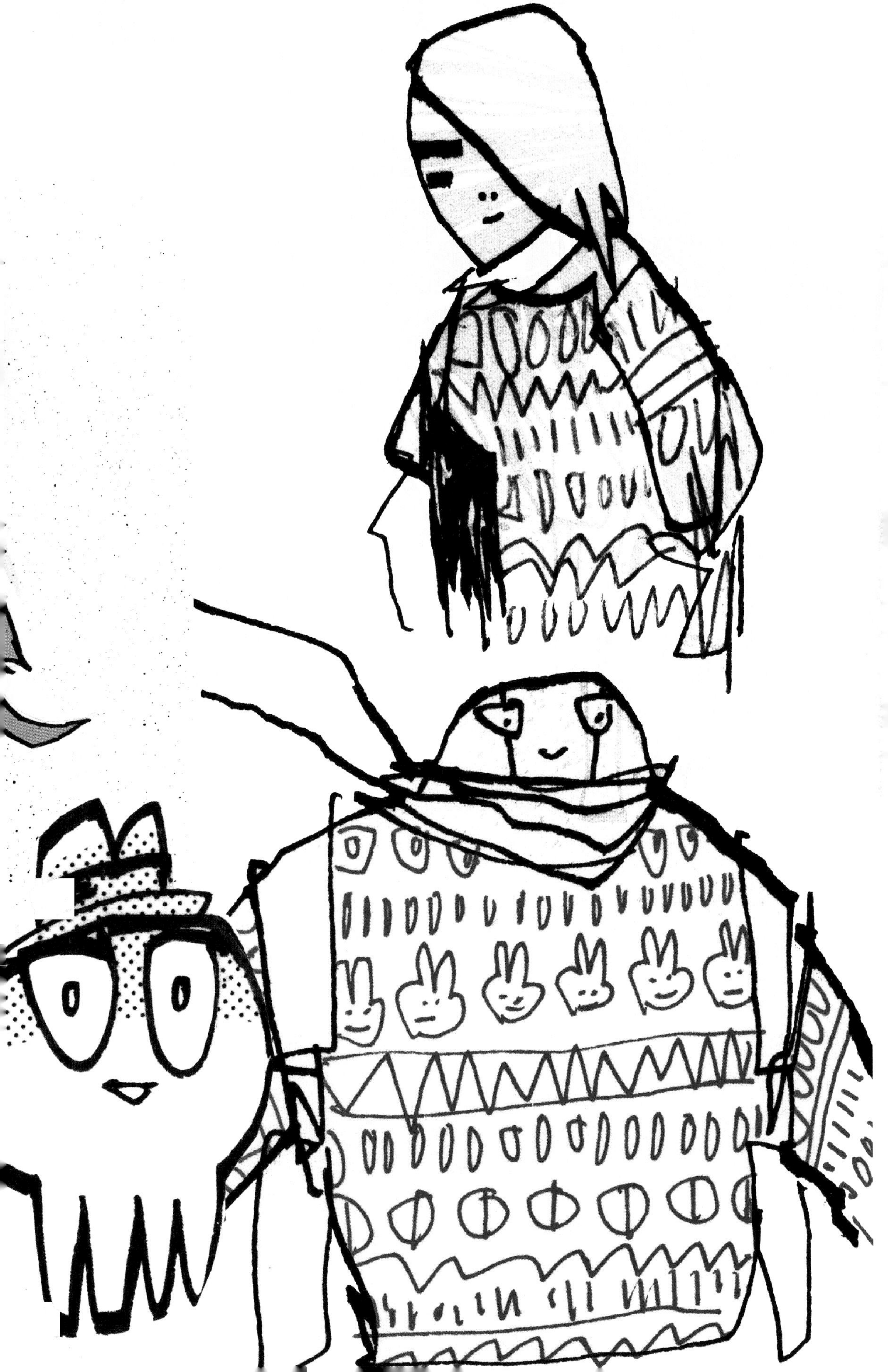

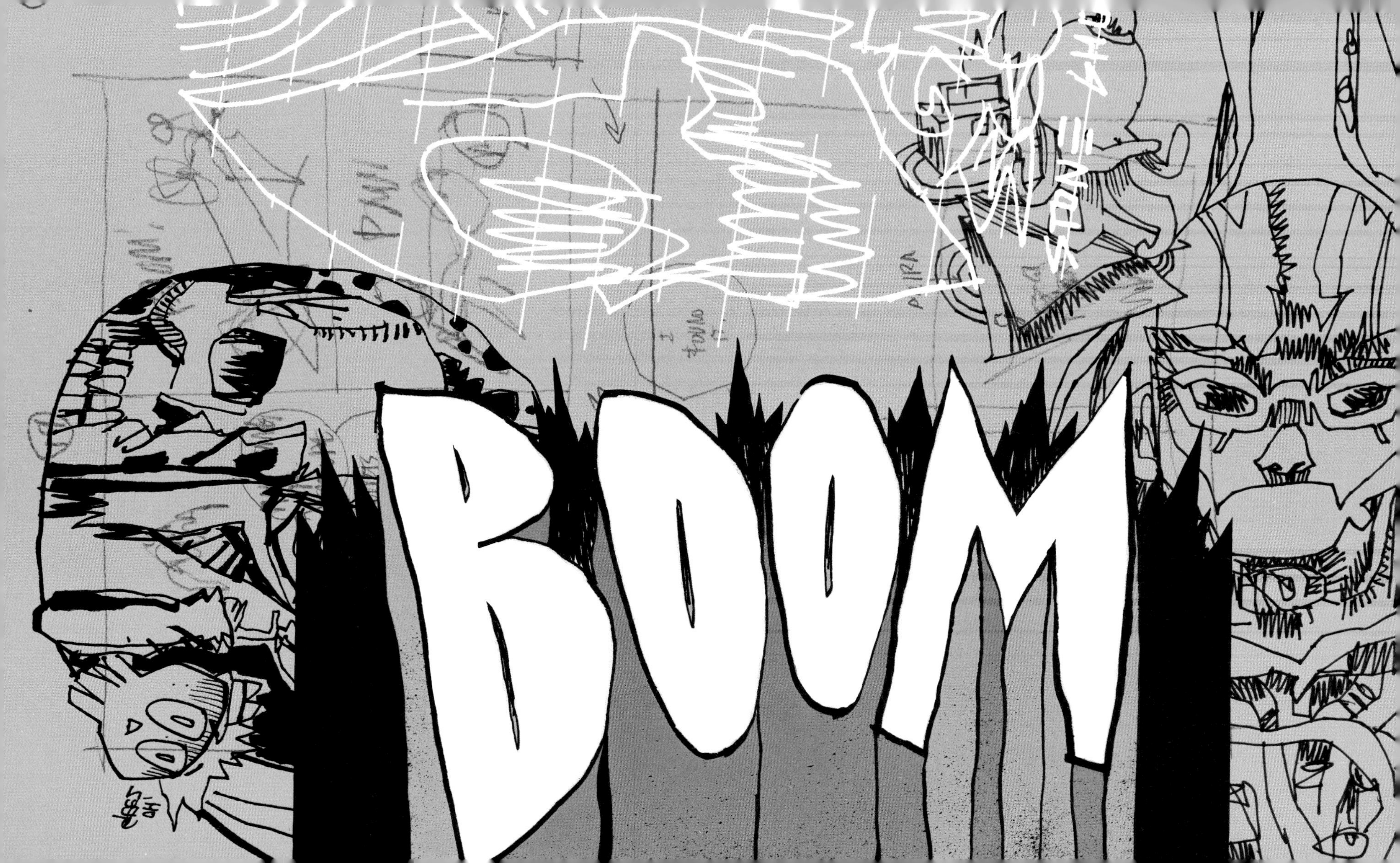
BOOM

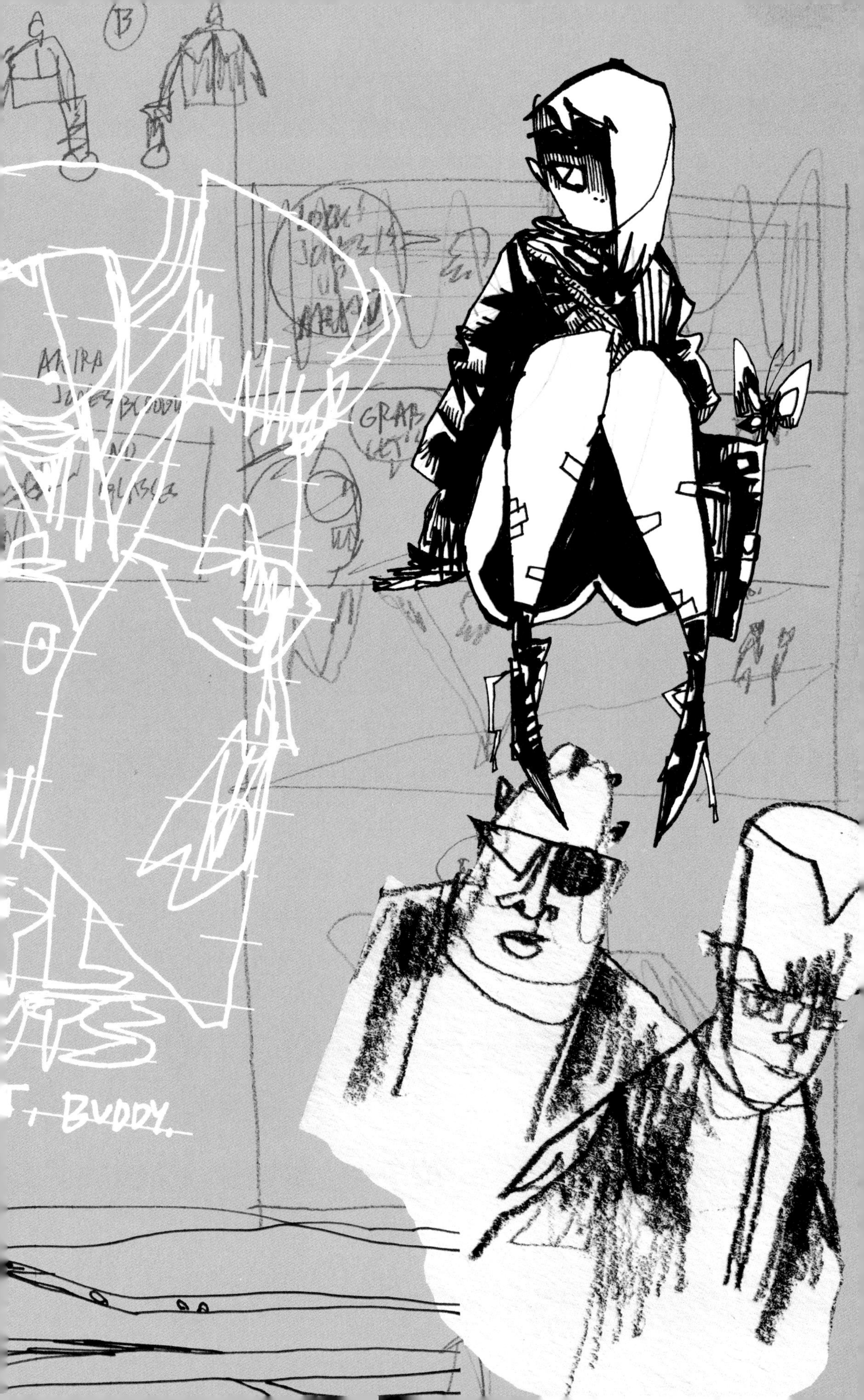
GRAB
BUDDY.

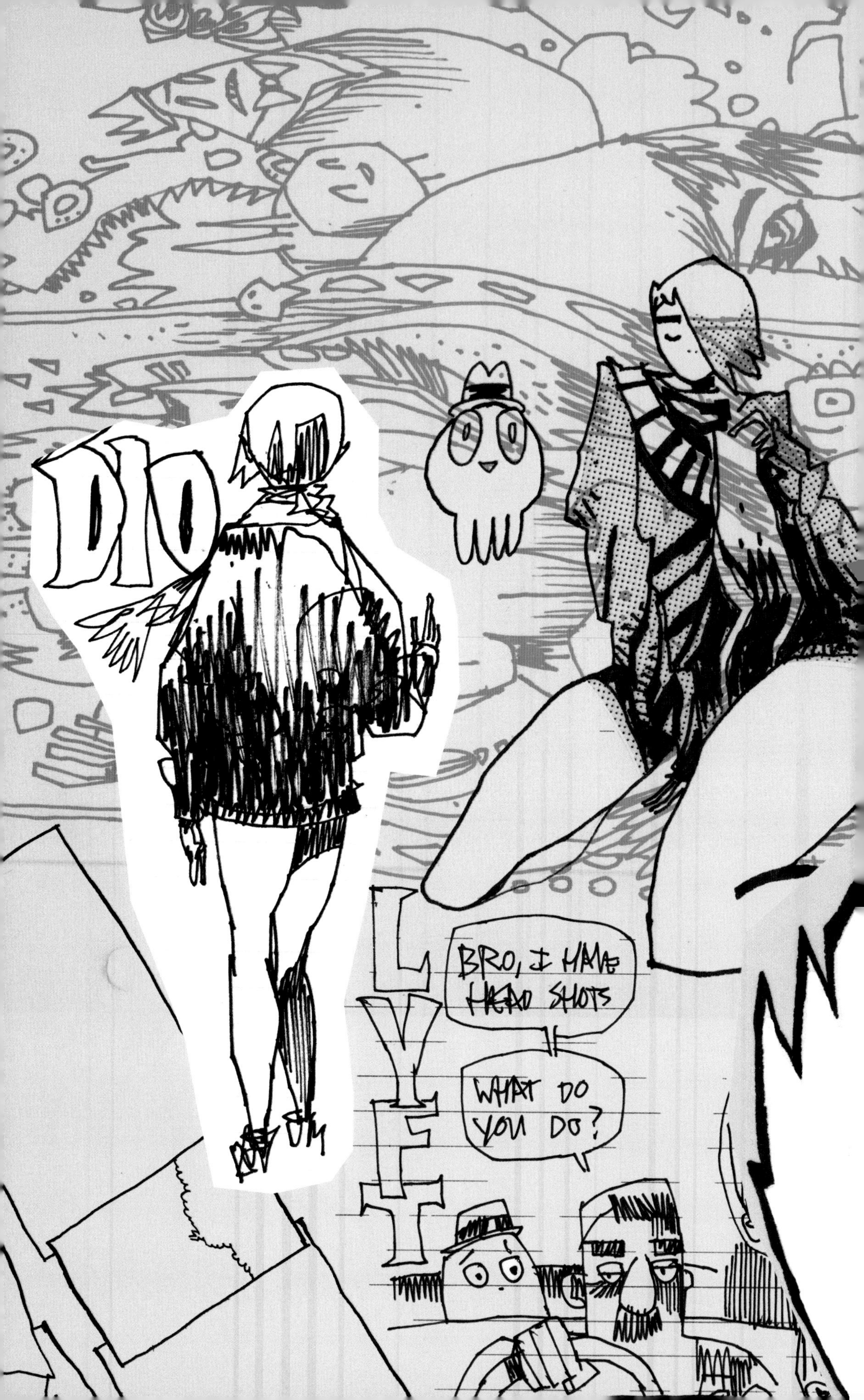
DIO
LYFE
BRO, I HAVE HEAD SHOTS
WHAT DO YOU DO?

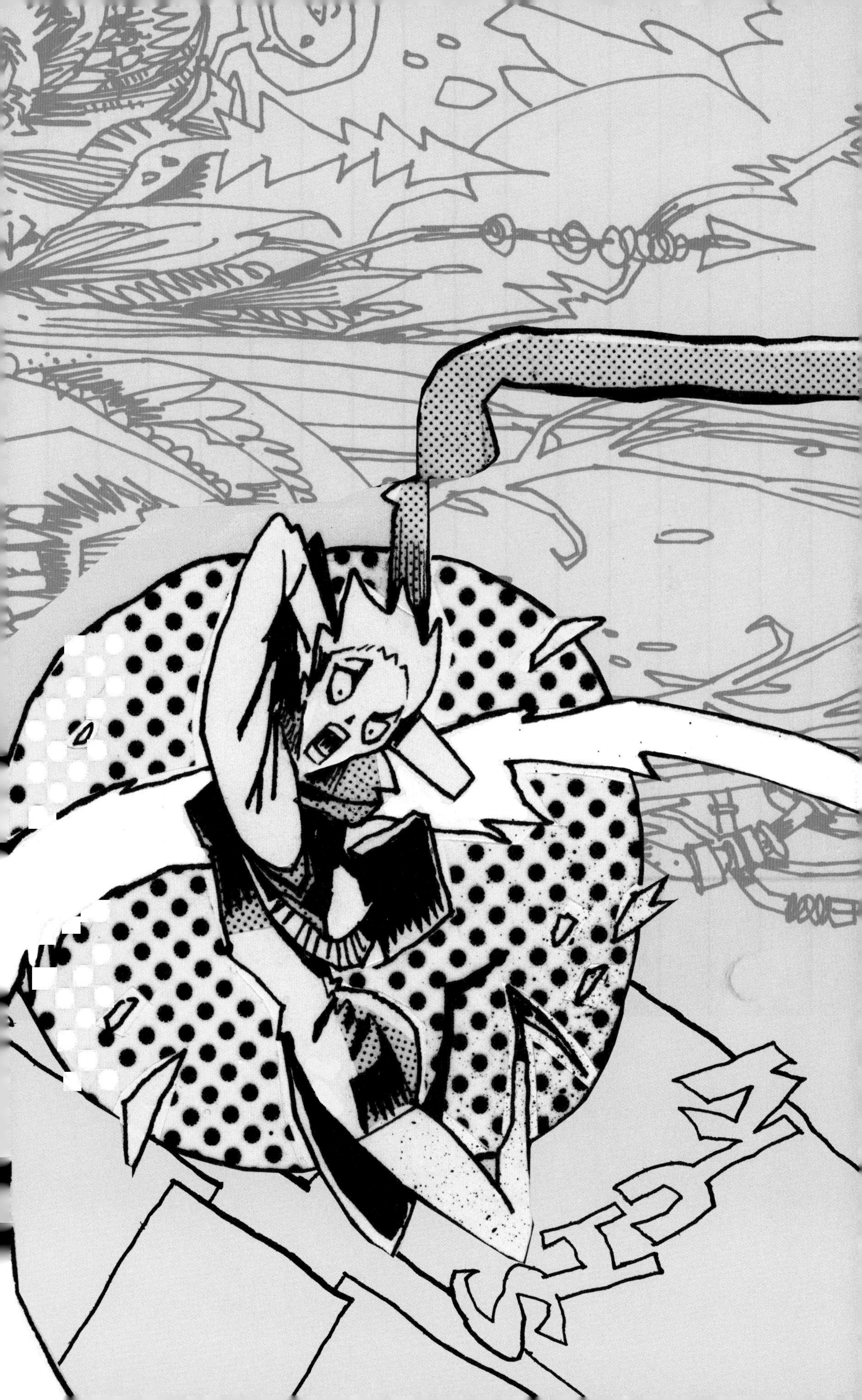

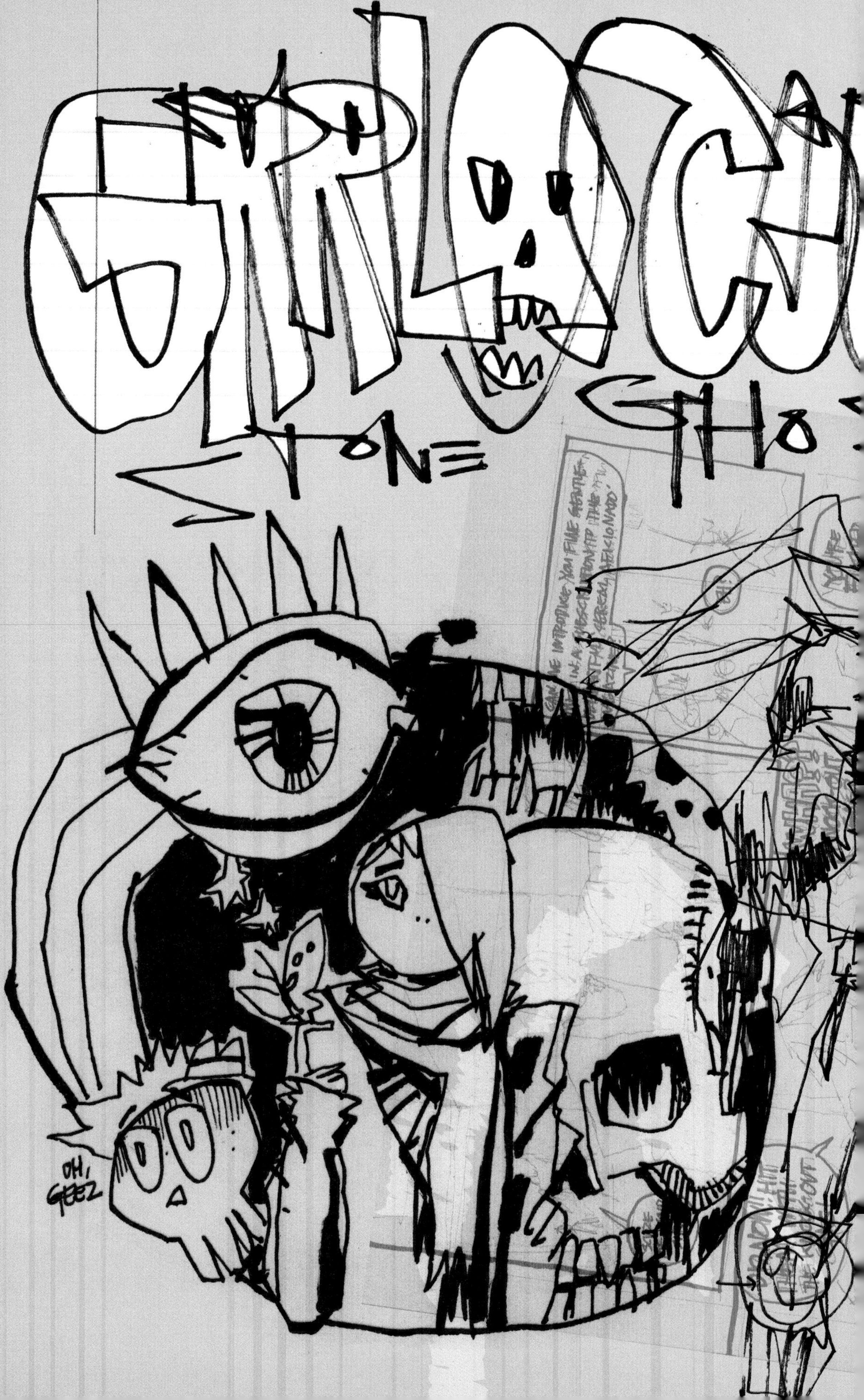
OH, GEEZ

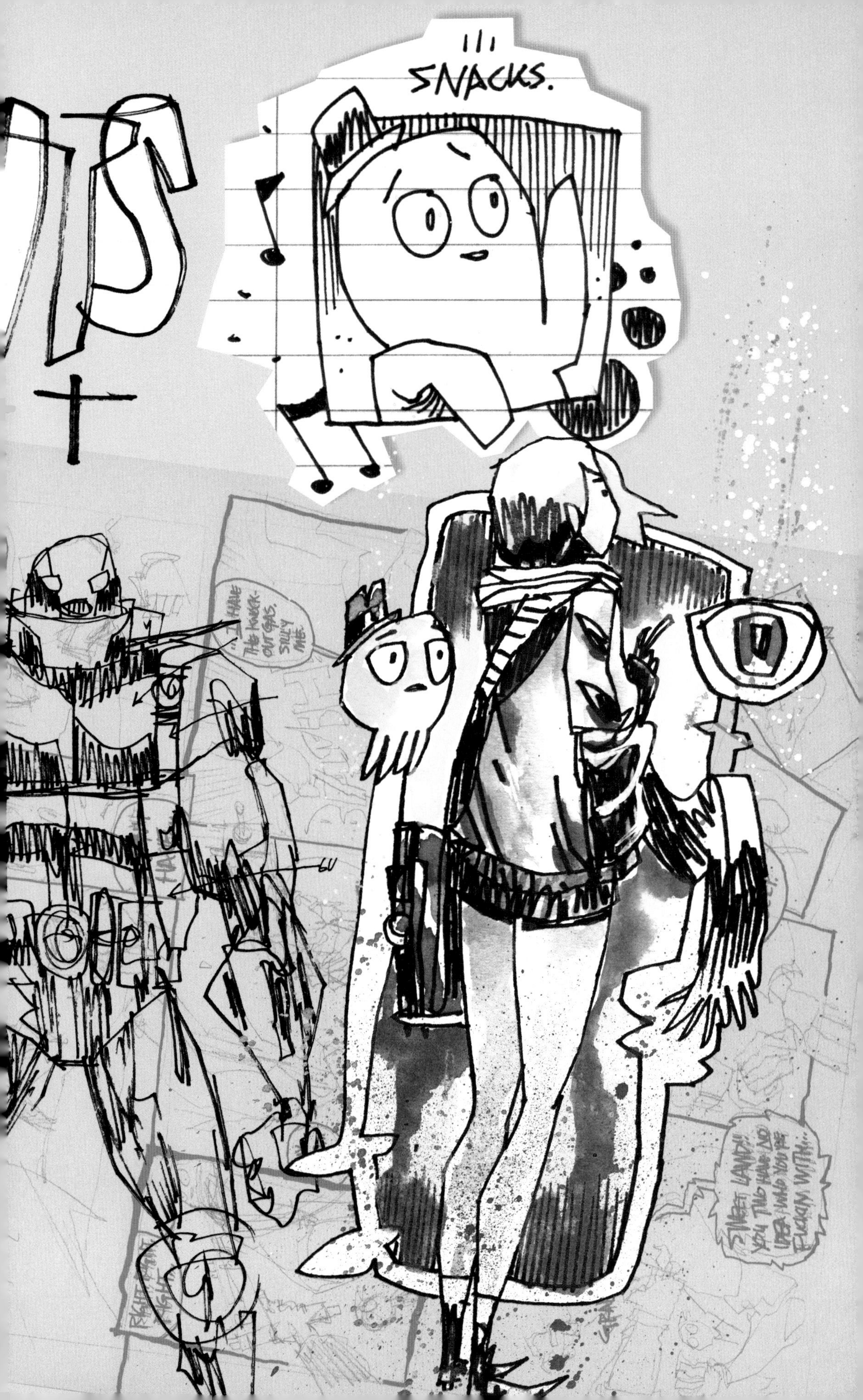
SNACKS.
...I HAVE THE KNOCK-OUT GAS. SILLY ME.
SWEET LAWD!! YOU TWO HAVE NO IDEA WHO YOU'RE FUCKIN WITH...

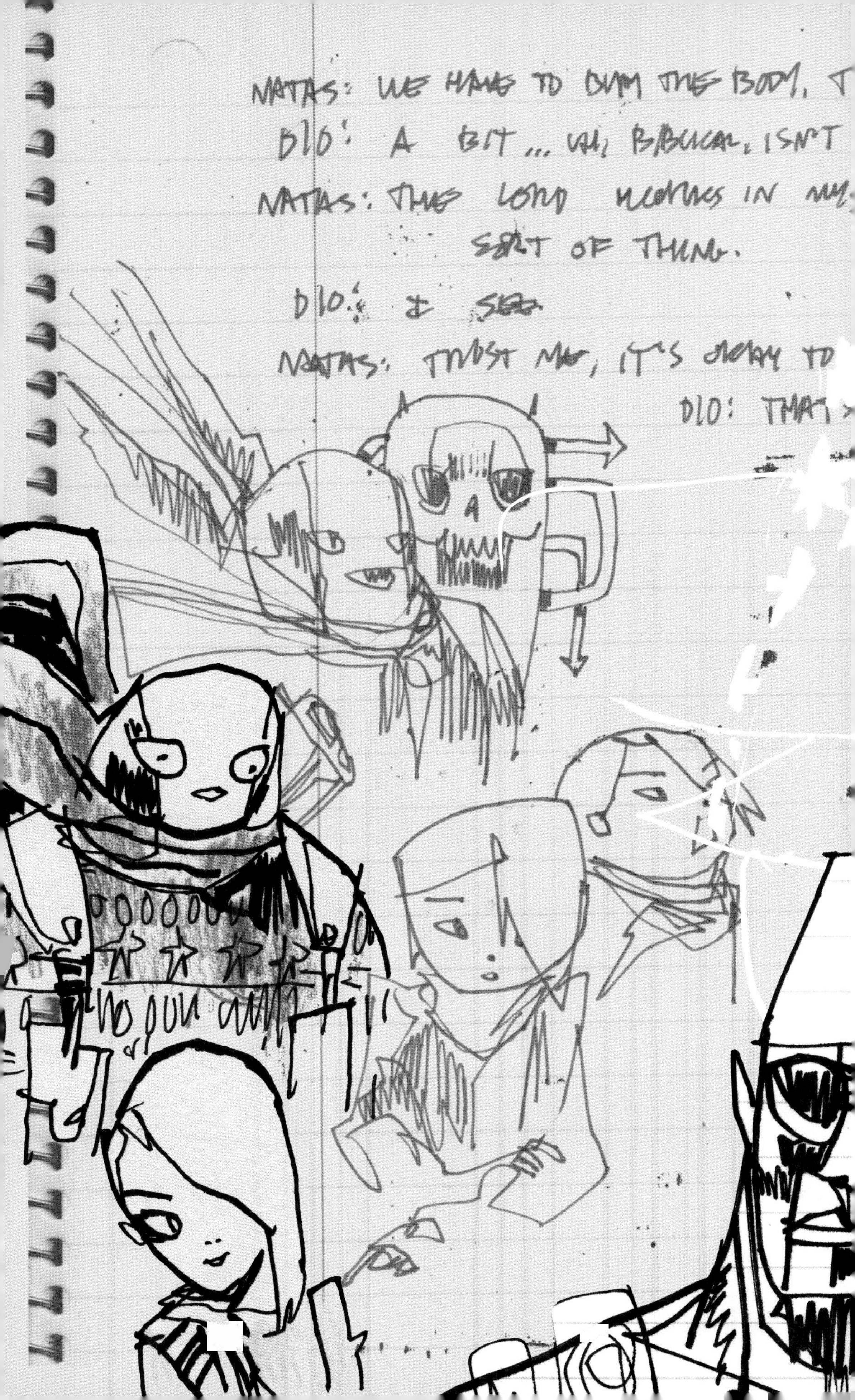
NATAS: WE HAVE TO BURN THE BODY. T
DIO: A BIT... UH, BIBLICAL, ISN'T
NATAS: THE LORD WORKS IN MY
SORT OF THING.
DIO: I SEE.
NATAS: TRUST ME, IT'S OKAY TO
DIO: THAT'S

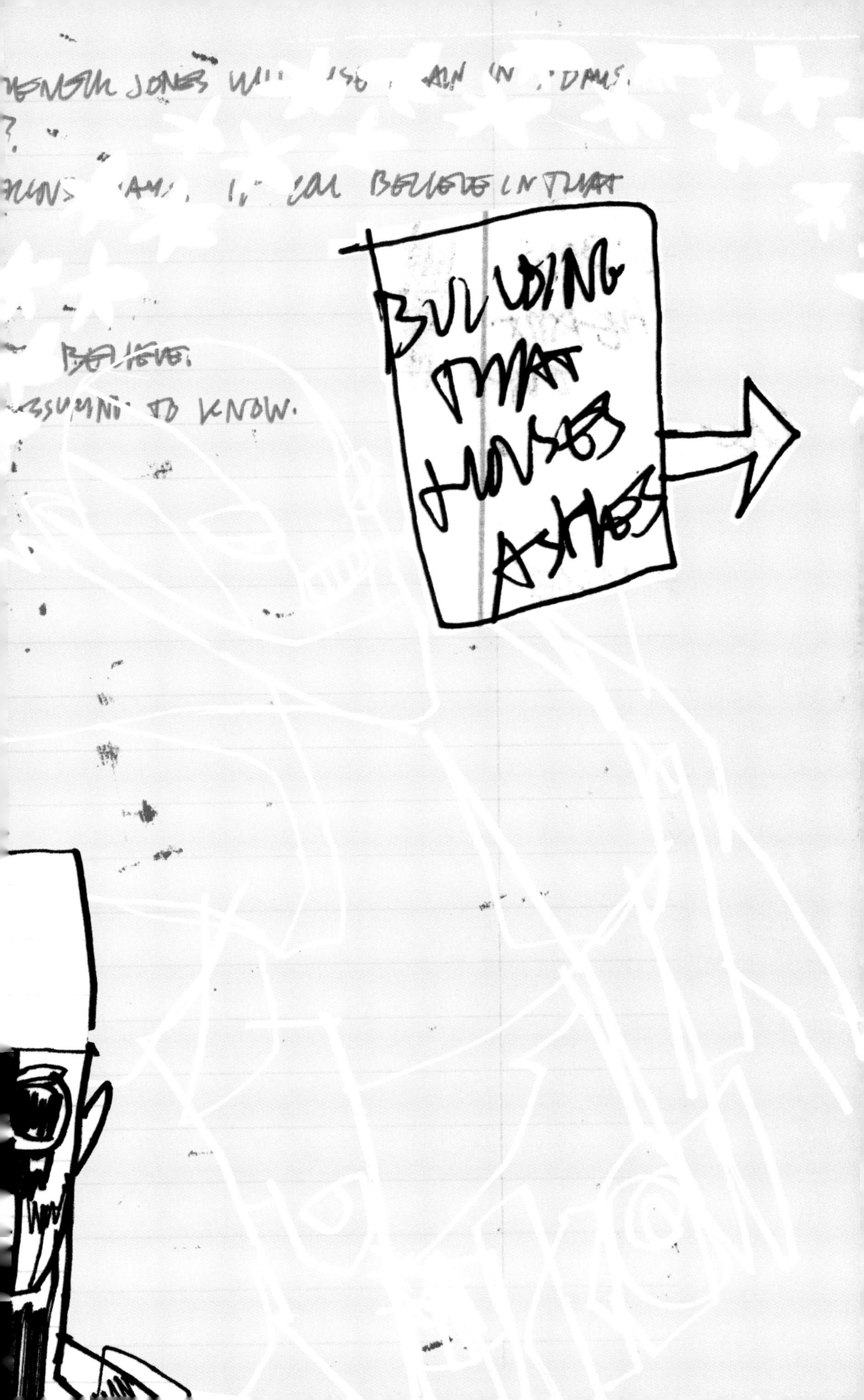
BELIEVE.
TO KNOW.
BUILDING THAT HOUSES ASHES

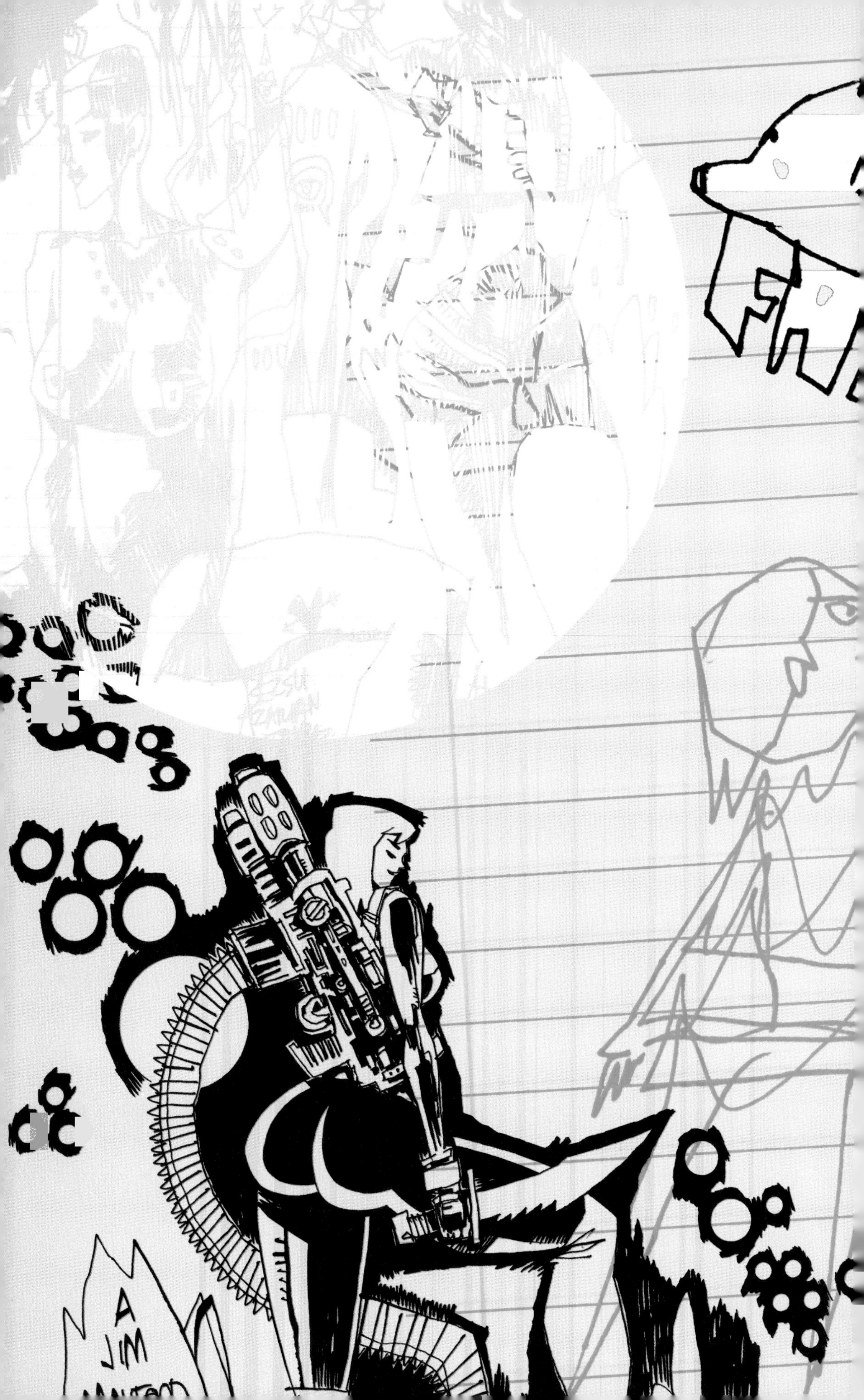
A JIM

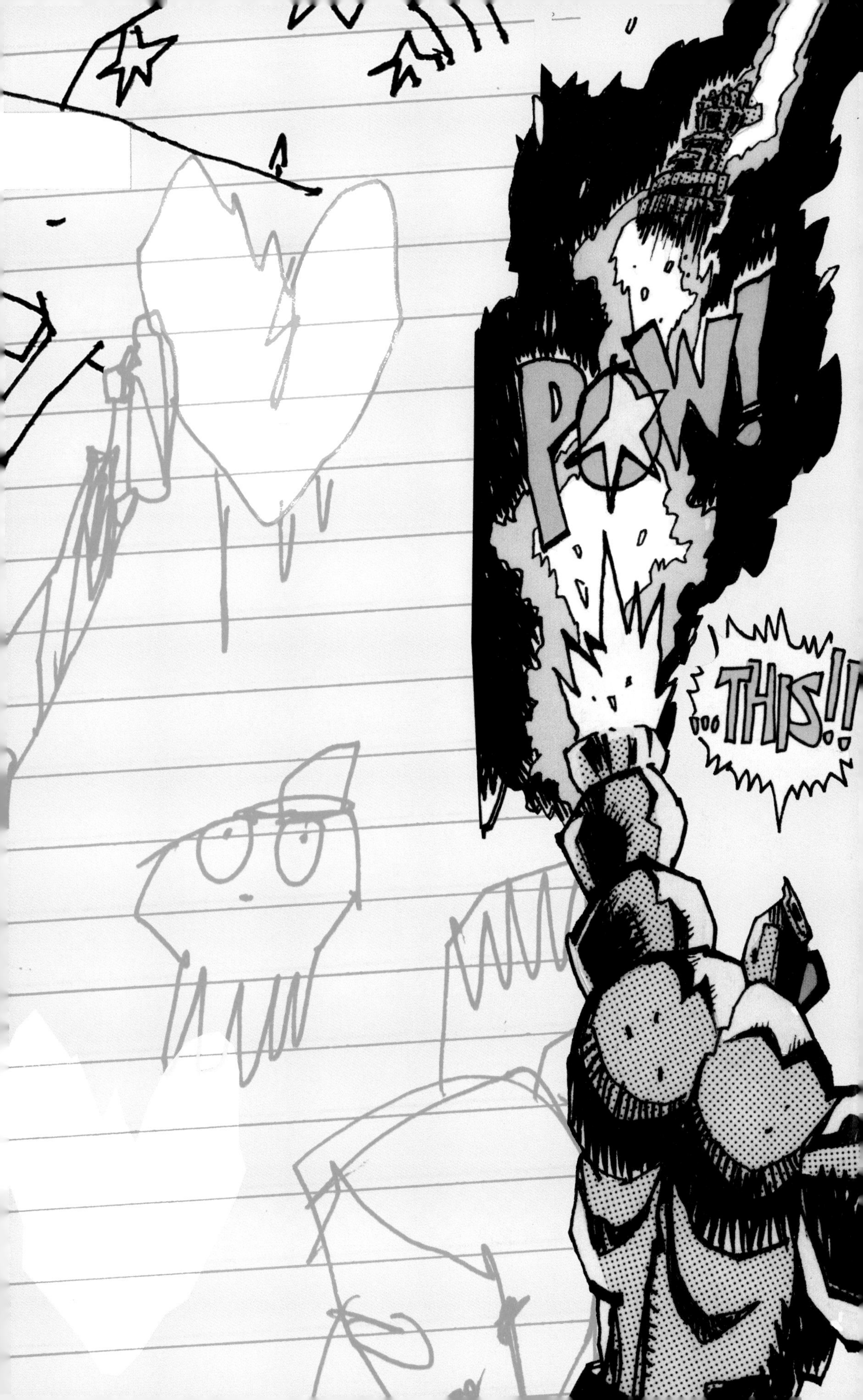
POW!
...THIS!!

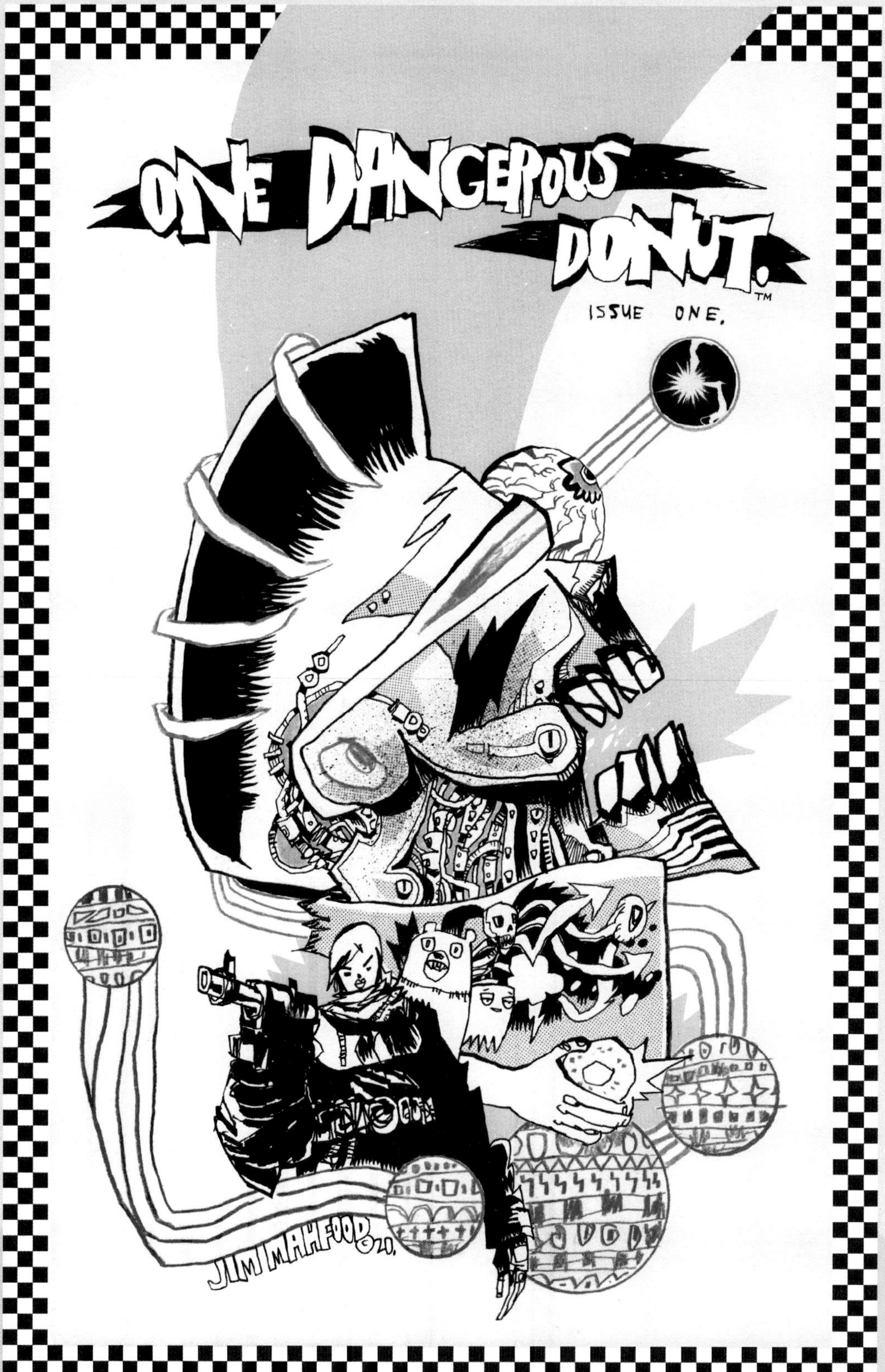
ONE DANGEROUS DONUT.
TM
ISSUE ONE.
JIM MAHFOOD ©20.

Jim Mahfood aka Food One is the Frank Zappa of the comics industry and illustration world. He began his career at age 15 working as an inker at Artline Studios in St Louis. In 1993 he moved to Kansas City and formed 40oz Comics with fellow funkateer Mike Huddleston. Mahfood self-published the first *Girl Scouts* (original spelling) comic book in 1995. Highlights of his career since then include the *Generation X Underground Special* for Marvel, illustrating Kevin Smith's *Clerks* comics, set design and mural work for *The Sarah Silverman Program*, the 2007-08 ad campaign art for *Colt 45* malt liquor, his creator-owned comic book titles *One Page Filler Man, Kick Drum Comix, Carl The Cat That Makes Peanut Butter Sandwiches, Los Angeles Ink Stains, Girl Scouts Vol. 1, Vol. 2: Work Sucks,* and *Vol 3: Magic Socks.* Other published works include *Everybody Loves Tank Girl, 21st Century Tank Girl, Tank Girl: All-Stars, MarijuanaMan* (with Ziggy Marley), *Miami Vice: Remix, The Visual Funk Art Book, Sadistic Magician, The Pop-Up Funk Book* (with Poposition Press), and *One Dangerous Donut.* Other notable works outside the field of publishing include the animated *D.I.S.C.O. Destroyer* shorts for MTV's Liquid Television (on YouTube), the *Girl Scouts Live Action Pilot* (with director Mike Diva, also on YouTube), an animated commercial for *Asics* shoes produced by Starburns, numerous loading screens for the incredibly popular *Fortnite* video game, and character design work for the Oscar-winning feature film *Spider-Man: Into The Spider-Verse.* Jim's infamous music podcast *Skull Funk Radio* is available for free on Spotify or at skullfunkradio.fireside.fm

jimmahfood.com

@jimmahfood